THE HOLY LAND IN THE MIDDLE AGES
Six Travelers' Accounts

THE HOLY LAND IN THE MIDDLE AGES
Six Travelers' Accounts

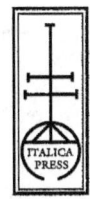

ITALICA PRESS
New York 2017

Copyright © 2017 by Italica Press

Italica Press Historical Travel Series

ITALICA PRESS, INC.
595 Main Street
New York, New York 10044
inquiries@italicapress.com

All rights reserved. No part of this publication may be reproduced, stored in a retrieval system, or transmitted, in any form or by any means, electronic, mechanical, photocopying, recording, or otherwise, without prior permission of Italica Press. It may not be used in a course-pack or any other collection without prior permission of Italica Press.

Library of Congress Cataloging-in-Publication Data
Title: The Holy Land in the Middle Ages : six travelers' accounts.
Description: New York, New York : Italica Press, 2015. | Series: Italica Press historical travel series | Includes bibliographical references and index.
Identifiers: LCCN 2016047243 (print) | LCCN 2016052660 (ebook) | ISBN 9781599103129 (hardcover : alk. paper) | ISBN 9781599103136 (pbk. : alk. paper) | ISBN 9781599103099 (diskette) | ISBN 9781599103105 (Kindle/Mobi)
| ISBN 9781599103112 (epub)
Subjects: LCSH: Palestine--History--To 1500. | Palestine--Description and travel. | Pilgrims and pilgrimages--Palestine.
Classification: LCC DS117 .H65 2015 (print) | LCC DS117 (ebook) | DDC 956.94/031--dc23
LC record available at https://lccn.loc.gov/2016047243

Cover illustration: Map of the Holy Land, from Abraham Ortelius, *Theatrum Orbis Terrarum* (Antwerp: Officina Plantiniana, 1595).

For a Complete List of Titles in Historical Travel
Please visit our Website at:
http://www.italicapress.com/index004.html

Contents

Illustrations	viii
Preface	xi
The Pilgrimage of the Holy Paula and the Letter of Paula and Eustochium	1
Introduction	1
The Pilgrimage of the Holy Paula by St. Jerome	7
The Letter of Paula and Eustochium to Marcella about the Holy Places	21
The Description of Syria and Palestine by Mukaddasi	27
Introduction	27
The District of Palestine by Mukaddasi	37
Diary of a Journey through Syria and Palestine by Nâsir-i-Khusrau	55
Introduction	55
Preface	62
Diary of a Journey through Syria & Palestine by Nâsir-i-Khusrau	63
Guide to the Holy Land by Theoderich of Würzburg	127
Preface to the First Edition	127
Preface	135
Introduction	137
Prologue	152
Guide to the Holy Land by Theoderich of Würzburg	153
The Itinerary of Benjamin of Tudela	217
Introduction	217
Excerpt from the Itinerary of Benjamin of Tudela	227
Gazetteer	241
Bibliography	313
Reference Works	313
Primary Sources	313
Secondary Works	316
Maps and Views of the Holy Land	321
Detail of Map of the Holy Land, c.1140.	322
Sallust-Type Map, c.1200.	324

The Holy Land

View of the Holy Land by Abraham and Jehuda Cresques, 1375.   325
View of the Holy Land (left panel)
  by Bernhard von Breydenbach, 1486.   326
View of the Holy Land (center panel) by Bernhard von
  Breydenbach, 1486.   328
View of the Holy Land (right panel)
  by Bernhard von Breydenbach, 1486.   330
World Map with Jerusalem at the Center, 1581.   332
Map of the Holy Land by Marino Sanudo, 1611.   334

Maps and Views of Jerusalem   337

Madaba Map of Jerusalem, c.570.   338
Plan of Jerusalem, c.1200.   340
Plan of Jerusalem, c.1200.   341
Map of Jerusalem by Nicolas of Lyra, c.1270–1349.   342
View of Jerusalem by Nicolas, of Lyra, c.1270–1349.   344
View of Jerusalem, c.1455.   345
View of Jerusalem by Conrad Grünenberg, 1487.   346
View of Jerusalem by Hartmann Schedel, 1493.   348
Destruction of Jerusalem by Hartmann Schedel, 1493.   350
Imaginary View of Jerusalem by Sebastian Brant, 1515.   352
View of Jerusalem by Sebastian Muenster, 1550.   353
View of Jerusalem by Sebastian Muenster, 1550.   354
View of Jerusalem by Noe Bianchi, ante 1569.   356
Map of Jerusalem by Benedictus Arias Montanus, 1572.   357
Woodcut Map of Jerusalem, c.1580.   358
Map of Jerusalem by Electus Zwinner, 1661.   360

Plans of Important Buildings   363

Plan of Jerusalem.   364
Plan of *Solomon's Temple*.   365
Plan of the Church of the Holy Sepulcher.   366
Plan of the Dome of the Rock.   367
Plan of El Aksâ Mosque, c.985.   368
Plan of El Aksâ Mosque, 1888.   369
Plan of the Temple Mount.   370
Plan of the Cave of the Patriarchs.   372

Index   373

Illustrations

Frontispiece. Caravan to Cathay. Atlas Catalan, 1375. Abraham and Jehuda Cresques. Bibliothèque nationale de France, Esp. 30.	ii
T-O World Map. From Isidore of Seville, *Etymologiarum*..., 1472.	x
Achon: Crusader sea wall, c.1920–33.	241
Achon: St. Jean d'Acre April 24th 1839 by David Roberts.	242
Achon: The Crusader Castle, c.1920–33.	242
Ajalon: Valley of Ajalon and Beth Horon, c.1900–20.	243
Al Madînah: Courtyard (southeast corner) of the holy mosque with the Garden of Fâtima.	243
Aleppo: View of from the castle, c.1900–20.	244
Ammân: View from acropolis hill, showing Roman theater [Solomon's Circus], c.1920–33.	245
View of Ascalon.	247
Bethel, c.1900–20.	248
Bethlehem by David Roberts, April 6th 1839.	248
Bethlehem, the Manger, between c.1890 and c.1900.	249
Bethlehem: Shrine of the Nativity Bethlehem, April 6th 1839 by David Roberts.	250
Bethlehem: Tomb of David by P. Bergheim, between 1860 and 1880.	250
Bethphage, between 1898 and 1914.	251
Bethsames (Beth Shemesh), May 1931.	252
Bethsaida, approximately 1900 to 1920.	252
Bethsan, between 1900 and 1920.	253
Ain Gedeirat, possibly Cadesbarne, between 1920 and 1933.	254
Caesarea: Ruins of ancient sea-front, c.1920 to 1933.	254
Cana, between 1989 and 1946.	255
Capernaum: Ruins of the synagogue. (Tel Hum), between 1898 and 1943.	256
Cariathiarim: Crusader church, north aisle, Oct. 10, 1941.	256
Cariathiarim: Excavations at Tell Beit Mirsim (Kirjath-Sepher) 1926.	257
Dead Sea: looking towards Moab by David Roberts, April 4th 1839.	258
Fountain of Elisha, approximately 1900 to 1920.	259

The Holy Land

Gibeleth, approximately 1900 to 1920.	260
Haifâ: View from top of Carmel approximately 1920 to 1933.	261
Hebron, between 1950 and 1977. Matson Photo service.	262
Jaffa by David Roberts, March 26th 1839.	263
Idumaea: Sunrise over Mountains of Edom from Dead Sea, c.1910.	263
Mosque el-Aksâ, approximately 1934 to 1939.	264
Bethany by David Roberts, April 1st 1839.	265
Tomb of Lazarus, between 1898 and 1914.	266
Jerusalem: Dome of the Ascension, between 1898 and 1946.	268
Dome of the Chain: Interior, 1940–46.	269
Gate Dâûd: David's Gate, date unknown.	270
Gate of David's Oratory: Jaffa Gate by P. Bergheim, between 1860 and 1880.	271
Damascus Gate.	273
Golden Gate by David Roberts, published 1842.	274
Gethsemane and Mount of Olive, 1933 or 1934.	275
Gethsemane, Church of St. Mary, Tomb of the Virgin, by P. Bergheim, between 1860 and 1880.	276
Jerusalem: Holy Sepulcher Church, Crusader's Façade, photo between 1898 and 1946.	277
Jerusalem: Holy Sepulcher Church, Holy Sepulcher Chapel, between 1989 and 1914.	280
Jerusalem: Holy Sepulcher Church, Chapel of St. Helena, published February 8, 1944.	281
Jerusalem: Chapel of Calvary in Church of the Holy Sepulcher, March 1942. Top, Greek, Left, Latin.	282
Jerusalem: Chapel of the Invention of the Cross in Church of the Holy Sepulcher, between 1898 and 1914.	283
Jerusalem: Mount of Olives and Gethsemane, general view, between c.1890 and c.1900.	285
Jerusalem: Church of the Ascension on the Mount of Olives by Francis Frith, 1862?	286
Fountain of Siloam in the Valley of Jehosophat by David Roberts, published 1842	287
Church of St. Anne, approximately 1900 to 1920.	289
Jerusalem: Stone of Unction, between 1934 and 1939.	290
Jerusalem: The Dome of the Rock, south façade, ablution basin through the cypress trees, between 1898 and 1946.	291

ILLUSTRATIONS

Jerusalem: The Dome of the Rock, north façade from arched street, between 1898 and 1946.	292
Jerusalem: Tomb of Absalom, photo by P. Bergheim, between 1860 and 1980.	293
Jerusalem: Tower of David with Citadel in background between 1898 and 1946 (above); Via Dolorosa, between 1898 and 1914 (below left).	294
Jordan River, between 1920 and 1933.	295
Jerusalem: Valleys of Jehoshaphat and Hinnom with Kedron Brook, between c.1900 and 1920.	295
Sea of Kinnereth, c.1925 to 1946.	297
Brook of Kedumin (Kishon River), between 1900 and 1920.	297
Christian Church of St George at Lud ancient Lydda by David Roberts, March 29 1839.	298
Mecca: Bird's-eye view of uncrowded Kaaba, c.1910.	299
Mambre Excavations, between 1950 and 1977.	299
Mount Ebal & Mount Gerizim, with Nâblus in foreground, between 1898 and 1946.	300
Mount Tabor from the Plain of Esdraelon by David Roberts, April 19th 1839.	302
Nâblus, between 1898 and 1946.	303
Nazareth by David Roberts, April 28th 1839.	303
Paneas, the ancient Caesarea Philippi by Francis Frith, 1862?	304
View from Quarantana of the Jordan Valley, approximately 1900 to 1920.	305
Ramleh, between c.1890 and c.1900.	306
Samaria: Church of St. John, interior, approximately 1900–1920.	307
Sarepta by David Roberts, April 27th 1839.	308
Sepphoris: Roman remains, approximately 1920 to 1933.	309
Tiberias: view, between 1934 and 1939.	311
Tomb of Rachel, on the road near Bethlehem, between 1898 and 1946.	311
Ancient Tyre from the Isthmus by David Roberts, April 27th 1839.	312

*

T-O World Map showing the three continents separated by the "T" of the waters. The Holy Land is at the center of the world's "O." From Isidore of Seville, Etymologiarum libri xx. *Augsburg: Günther Zainer, 1472.*

Preface

In a region often caricatured by the images and rhetoric of crusade and jihad, it is important to realize that through most of its medieval history the Holy Land was host to countless curious and devout travelers of all three faiths. They sailed to the same ports, walked and rode the same roads, lodged in the same cities and towns and visited and revered the same secular and sacred sites.

To recall this fact and to celebrate the Metropolitan Museum of Art's new exhibition, "Jerusalem, 1000–1400: Every People under Heaven," we have reissued *The Holy Land in the Middle Ages* in a new print edition. The following book offers important texts documenting these centuries of peaceful co-existence written by medieval Christian, Muslim and Jewish travelers to the Holy Land.

There has been a revival of "crusade studies" in recent years, sometimes marked by contentious claims of "clash of civilizations," the deeply violent nature of the religions of the book and the ineluctable structures of colonialism and militarism. But the following accounts offer a different narrative: of devotion that goes beyond religious labels, of a mixture of peoples and faiths that left room for curiosity and for a practical tolerance of the other. As the following pages reveal, the narrators of these works were less interested in issues of religious contention, territorial domination or cultural hegemony and more in the history, legends, art and architecture, the sounds, smells and tastes, the peoples, products and goods, and in the topography and sacred geography of the Holy Land.

These texts include:
* St. Jerome, *The Pilgrimage of Holy Paula*, c.382 CE
* Paula & Eustochium, *Letter to Marcella on the Holy Places*, 386
* Mukaddasi of Jerusalem, *Description of Palestine*, 985

The Holy Land

* Nâsir-i-Khusrau, *Diary of a Journey through Syria and Palestine*, 1047
* Theoderich of Würzburg, *Guide to the Holy Land*, c.1172
* Benjamin of Tudela, Description of the Holy Land, from his *Itinerary*, c.1173.

Along with these texts we also present visual evidence: nearly one hundred black & white and color photos, historical drawings and prints, seven building plans, a gallery of nine city views of Jerusalem from the sixth to the sixteenth century, and a gallery of eight maps of the Holy Land from c.1200 to 1630.

We have also included a concise, updated bibliography, offering reference works, primary sources and important secondary works. A lengthy and comprehensive index offers details of places, people and activities, with variant readings from the different editions and cross- and parallel-references.

Although there have been countless recent studies on every aspect of the medieval Holy Land, ranging from the crusade and jihad, to colonialism and trade, to art, architecture, music, food, daily life, material culture and religious belief and life, few new editions of the basic sources have appeared over the past thirty years since Italica Press began publishing its series on pilgrimage and medieval travel. The texts presented here — largely from the Palestine Pilgrims Text Society — remain the best available English translations of these works. We have therefore reissued them with their original prefaces and introductions. In only one case, Theoderich's *Guide to the Holy Land*, have we updated notes and bibliography to Ronald G. Musto's original general introduction, first published in 1986.

We hope that this collection will serve its readers well to both sample the variety and types of accounts available in the Middle Ages and to illustrate the cultural, mental and geographical worlds in which they were written.

New York City
November 2016

The Pilgrimage of the Holy Paula and the Letter of Paula and Eustochium

INTRODUCTION

The asceticism advocated with so much eloquence, by Ambrose at Milan and Jerome at Rome during the last quarter of the fourth century captivated the minds of Christians of all ranks. In Rome itself, where society was at the time under the influence of strong religious excitement, the opinions of Jerome were adopted with enthusiasm. Partly from love of novelty, partly from the striking contrast between the austere life of an ascetic and the dissolute manners of the age, asceticism became the fashion. Many ladies of noble birth, renouncing the pleasures of society, devoted their lives to religious observances and their wealth to good works; while others wandered off to lead a life of seclusion in lands that had once been hallowed by the presence of Christ or performed long weary pilgrimages to places that had been the scene of some memorable event in sacred history.

Among those who had been deeply moved by the preaching of Jerome were two ladies who afterwards became his most fervent disciples: Paula, a Roman matron of ancient lineage, great wealth, and high social rank; and Eustochium, her daughter, who, if we may believe her spiritual guide, was the first Roman maiden to take upon herself vows of virginity. During the synod held at Rome, under Pope Damasus, Paula entertained as her guest Epiphanius, the venerable bishop of Salamis, in Cyprus, and frequently received at her house Paulinus, bishop of Antioch. The presence of these holy men appears to have turned Paula's thoughts towards the East; at any rate, it

1

was during their visit that she, a weak, fragile woman, who had hitherto lived a life of luxurious ease and been daintily borne from house to house by her eunuchs, determined to face the dangers and hardships of a journey to St. Paul and Anthony in the desert. When spring arrived, and the bishops returned to their churches, Paula distributed her wealth to her family,[1] and, taking with her only Eustochium, accompanied them on their voyage. Why she changed her mind and finally settled at Bethlehem, we are not told; but the change was perhaps not unconnected with the return of Jerome to Palestine on the death of Damasus. Paula, after living twenty years in Bethlehem, died there, at the age of fifty-six, in 404 CE, and as she left Rome in the spring of 382 CE, her pilgrimage must have lasted about two years.[2]

It seems probable from the frequent use of the first person that Paula was accompanied by Jerome during a certain portion of her pilgrimage[3]; and we may perhaps infer, from its first occurrence in connection with Joppa, that she met him at that place, or possibly at Caesarea Palaestina, on his return to Palestine.

The geographical value of the work is slight, but it supplies us with many interesting particulars of the places

---

1. The expression *"cuncta largita est"* in chapter II, is not to be taken too literally, for we afterwards find St. Paula subscribing towards the expenses of the brethren in Cyprus (III); distributing alms at Jerusalem (VIII); assisting the monks at Nitria (XVIII); and building cells and monasteries, and founding inns in Palestine (XIX). Perhaps the meaning is that Paula realized her property and made suitable provision for her children before leaving Rome on her pilgrimage.

2. Paula is a saint of the Latin Church, her day being January 26. A description of her life and parentage will be found in *Smith's Dictionary of Christian Biography*, art. "Paula."

3. This was the opinion of Erasmus and is the view still held by the Latin Church.

Introduction to Paula & Eustochium

that a pilgrim of high social rank considered necessary to visit in the last quarter of the fourth century. Perhaps the most important notice is that of the tomb of Helena, queen of the Adiabeni, which is now the "Tombs of the Kings," to the north of Jerusalem.

From Rome Paula went down to the harbor, possibly Ostia, and thence, after bidding farewell to her children and relations, sailed for Cyprus. She stopped at Pontia (Ponza), Methone (Modon), Rhodes, and perhaps at Patara, in Lycia; and after reaching Cyprus, passed some time in visiting the numerous monasteries on the island.

From Cyprus she crossed to Seleucia, near the mouth of the Orontes, and then proceeded to Antioch, whence, after a short stay, she traveled, in the depth of winter, through Coele Syria to Berytus, and onwards by the usual coast road to Ptolemais. Here Paula appears to have left the coast, and to have followed the road across the plain of Esdraelon, "the plains of Megiddo" to Legio (Lejjûn), and thence to have crossed the hills to Caesarea Palaestina. She next visited Antipatris; Lydda, near which were Arimathea (Rantieh) and Nob (Beit Nûba); and Joppa. From this last place she returned to Emmaus — Nicopolis; and thence traveled by the Roman road through the Upper and Nether Bethorons to Gabaa (Gibeah of Benjamin); here she rested a short time before continuing her journey to Jerusalem by the great north road, which passes close to the tomb of Helena (Tombs of the Kings) and enters the city by the Damascus Gate.

At Jerusalem the proconsul, who was a friend of Paula's family, ordered the Praetorium to be prepared for her reception: but, in true pilgrim spirit, she declined the proffered hospitality and preferred to live in a "lowly cell" during her stay in the Holy City. The only holy places and relics mentioned in the narrative are the Cross, the Tomb, the stone that was rolled away from the mouth of the Sepulcher, the church on Mount Sion, the column of the flagellation in the portico of the church, and the place where the Holy Ghost descended on the disciples. It may perhaps be inferred, from the allusion to the gates "fallen into cinders and ashes," that, at the time of Paula's visit, the old wall on Sion was still a heap of ruins and had not been rebuilt.

From Jerusalem Paula proceeded, by Rachel's tomb, to Bethlehem, where she visited the "Grotto of the Savior" and was shown the inn, the stable, and the manger; she then went to the spot where the shepherds were keeping watch by night and afterwards passed by Philip's fountain at Beit Sûr; Escol, and the oak of Abraham, to Hebron. On her return journey to Jerusalem she visited Caphar Barucha, whence she saw in the distance the country of Sodom and Gomorrah, Zoar, and Engaddi, and Thecua (Tekoa).

Paula next traveled by Bethany and Adomim to Jericho, whence, after visiting Galgala and the fountain of Elisha, she went to the Jordan, to the spot where our Lord was baptized. From the Jordan she ascended to Bethel, and then passing through Shiloh, Shechem, and Samaria, came to Nazareth, whence she made an excursion to Cana and Capharnaum. On her return she climbed Mount Tabor, and here there is a break in the narrative of the journey, which is taken up again at Sochot (Shuweikeh). Paula probably returned to Jerusalem by the north road, and thence proceeded to Sochot by the Gaza road; and Jerome, possibly, did not think it necessary to describe a second time well-known towns, such as Samaria, Shechem, Bethel, and Bethlehem, which he had already noticed.

From Sochot Paula went to Samson's fountain, near Eleutheropolis, and the tomb of Micah at Morasthim; and then traveled by Maresa, Lachis, and the desert, to the Pelusiac branch of the Nile; she next passed through

Introduction to Paula & Eustochium

the land of Gessen (Goshen), and over the plains of Tanis on her way to Alexandria, whence she visited Nitria. After a short stay with the monks and ascetics of Nitria, she was seized with a longing to return to the holy places in Palestine, and taking ship at Pelusium, crossed the sea to Majuma, probably the Majuma of Gaza. From this port she went to Bethlehem, and there, for the next three years, she was busily occupied in building cells, monasteries, and inns for pilgrims.

Paula's tact and patience, and her great capacity for management, are praised by St. Jerome, who also states that she was a good linguist, and had learned Hebrew that she might sing the Psalms in the original. During her residence at Bethlehem she spent all her fortune in charity and in the erection of buildings for charitable purposes; and before her death she became involved in debt. When she died, the whole Church gathered together to bear her to her last resting-place in the "Grotto of the Nativity."

The letter of Paula and Eustochium to Marcella appears to have been written during the first six years of the residence at Bethlehem. It invites Marcella in glowing terms to join them in the Holy Land; contrasts the quiet seclusion of Bethlehem with the bustle and crowd of Jerusalem; and brings vividly before us the "enthusiastic delight with which these Roman ladies regarded every place and association in the Holy Land."

The letter indicates what route was considered desirable for pilgrims to follow and the holy places that they should see at the close of the fourth century. The tour from Jerusalem over Olivet to the Jordan, and thence to Bethlehem and Hebron, is usual at the present day. From the south the pilgrim is apparently taken over the maritime plain to Samaria, and thence, after visiting Nazareth and the Sea of Galilee, is brought back by Shiloh and Bethel to Bethlehem. The notice of the Holy Places is not quite so full as that in the *Pilgrimage of St. Paula*; but allusion is made to the "Tomb of David," which, though noticed by the Bordeaux Pilgrim, is not mentioned in the description of Paula's Journey.

Marcella, to whom the letter is addressed, was a wealthy Roman lady of illustrious family. She had been much impressed by the teaching of Athanasius, when he was an exile in Rome, and in CE 374 had been confirmed in her ascetic tendencies by the Egyptian monk Peter. She is said to have been the first lady in Rome to make the monastic profession; and after the arrival of Jerome her palace became "a kind of convent, dedicated to the study of the Scriptures, and to psalmody and prayer." Daily meetings were held, at which Jerome expounded the Scriptures to a circle of noble ladies, amongst whom Paula and Eustochium were prominent for their zeal and desire for knowledge. Marcella[4] resisted the efforts of her friends to draw her away from her charitable labors amongst the poor at Rome; and after a long life, devoted to good works, she died from the effect of injuries received during the sack of Rome by Alaric.

The known MSS of the *Perigrinatio Sanctae Paulae* belong to the eleventh century; and a list of these, as well as of the principal printed editions, is given in the preface to the *Itinera Hierosolymitana et Descriptiones Terrae Sanctae*, vol. i., p. xvi., published by the Société de Orient Latin.

C.W. Wilson

---

4. For further details of the life of Marcella, see Smith's *Dictionary of Christian Biography*, art. "Marcella."

The Pilgrimage of the Holy Paula
by St. Jerome

382 CE

Translated by Aubrey Stewart

I

When imperial letters brought the bishops of the East and West together to Rome on account of certain disputes of the churches, Paula beheld those admirable men and high-priests of Christ, Paulinus, the bishop of the city of Antioch, and Epiphanius, bishop of Salamis in Cyprus which is now called Constantia; of whom she had Epiphanius as her guest, while, though Paulinus lived in another house, she made him as it were her own by her kindness. Excited by their virtues, she at times thought of leaving her native land. Forgetful of her house, of her children, of her family, of her property, of everything connected with the world, she desired to proceed alone, if one may so speak, and unaccompanied into the desert of Paul and Anthony.

II

When at length the winter was spent, and the sea was open, the bishops returned to their churches, and she herself longed and prayed to sail with them. Why make my tale longer? She went down to the harbor, accompanied by her brother, her relatives, her connections, and, more than these, by her children, who strove to surpass the affection of the kindest of mothers. Soon the sails were swelling in the breeze, and the ship, guided by the oars, gained the open sea. Little Lexotius piteously stretched forth his

The Holy Land

hands from the shore. Rufina, a grown-up girl, by her tears silently besought her mother to stay until she was married. Yet she herself, without a tear, turned her eyes heavenwards, overcoming her love for her children by her love for God. She forgot that she was a mother, that she might prove herself the hand-maiden of Christ. Her frame was wrung with anguish, and her limbs seemed as though they were torn asunder as she struggled with her grief; and she was all the more to be admired because she had such strong affection to subdue. The sufferings of those who fall into the hands of the enemy and undergo the hardships of captivity are not more cruel than the sufferings of parents separated from their children. Yet, unnatural as is this separation, she, in the fullness of her faith, endured it; nay, her mind looked forward to it with rapture; and despising the love of her children through her greater love towards God, she contented herself with the companionship of Eustochium alone, the partner of her resolve and of her journey. Meanwhile the ship was ploughing the sea; and while all those on board looked back towards the shore, she kept her eyes turned away, that she might not see those whom she could not see without misery. I protest, none ever so loved her children, for before setting out she gave them all her property, disinheriting herself on earth that she might find an inheritance in heaven.

III

Being carried to the island of Pontia, which once was ennobled by the exile thither, under the Emperor Domitian, of that most noble of women, Flavia Domitilla, for her profession of the name of Christian, and seeing the cells in which she had endured her long martyrdom, taking the wings of faith, she longed to see Jerusalem and the holy places. The winds were sluggish, and all speed was slow. Between Scylla and Charybdis, entrusting herself to

the Adriatic Sea, she came as if over a pond to Methone, and there having a little refreshed her fragile form:
"Placed on the shore her dripping limbs awhile,
Then on, by Malea and Cythera's isle;
She passes next between the Cyclades,
And threads her passage through those narrow seas."
At length, after Rhodes and Lycia, she saw Cyprus, where she fell at the feet of the holy and venerable Epiphanius, and was kept there by him for ten days, not, as he meant, for rest, but for the service of God, as was proved by the facts. For, visiting all the monasteries of that country, as far as she was able she left behind her assistance for the expenses of the brethren, whom love of the holy man had collected thither from all the world.

IV

Thence by a short voyage she crossed the channel to Seleucia, whence she ascended to Antioch. After being detained there a short time by the kindness of the holy confessor Paulinus, with the burning ardor of faith the noble dame, who before used to be carried by the hands of eunuchs, set out in the midst of winter, sitting upon an ass. I pass over the journey through Coele Syria and Phoenicia, for I have not determined to write her itinerary (*hodoeporicon*); I shall name those places only which are contained in the Sacred Volumes. Leaving Berytus, a Roman colony, and the ancient city of Sidon; on the shore of Sarepta, she entered the Tower of Helias, in which she adored the Lord and Savior; she then passed over the sands of Tyre, in which Paul impressed his knees [Acts 21:5], to Acco, which is now called Ptolemais, and crossing the plains of Megiddo, witnesses of the death of Josiah, she entered the land of the Philistines.

V

Having in turn admired the ruins of Dor, once a very powerful city; and Strato's tower, named Caesarea in honor of Caesar Augustus, by Herod, king of Judaea, in which she beheld the house of Cornelius, [which is] a church of Christ, and the houses of Philip, and the chamber of the four virgin prophetesses, she next visited Antipatris, a small half-ruined town, which Herod named after his father; and Lydda, which is turned into Diospolis, renowned for the resurrection and restoration to health of Dorcas and Aeneas: and not far from thence, Arimathea, the town of Joseph who buried the Lord; and Nobe, once a city of priests, now a tomb of the slain; and Joppa, the harbor of the fugitive Jonah, and which, to allude to the fables of the poets, witnessed Andromeda chained to the rock: then, retracing her steps, [she came] to Nicopolis which was formerly called Emmaus, in which the Lord, made known in the breaking of bread, consecrated the house of Cleophas as a church.

VI

And setting out from thence, she ascended to Upper and Lower Bethoron, cities founded by Solomon, but afterwards destroyed by various storms of war, beholding on her right Ajalon and Gabaon, where Jesus the son of Nave [*Septuagint* form of Joshua, the son of Nun], fighting against five kings, gave orders to the sun and moon, and where he condemned the Gabaonites, because of the frauds and wiles by which they had obtained the treaty, to be drawers of water and hewers of wood [Josh. 9:22–27]. In Gabaa, a city destroyed even to the ground, she stayed for a short time—remembering its sin, and the concubine cut into pieces, and the three hundred men of the tribe of Benjamin reserved for the sake of the Apostle Paul [Phil. 3:5]. Why do

Pilgrimage of the Holy Paula by St. Jerome

I delay long? Leaving on the left the tomb (mausoleum) of Helena, the queen of the Adiabeni, who in time of famine helped the people with a gift of corn, she entered Jerusalem, the city of three names — Jebus, Salem, Jerusalem— which by Aelius, afterwards Hadrian, was raised from its ruins and ashes into Aelia. When the proconsul of Palestine, who knew her family very well, sent apparitors before her, and ordered the Praetorium to be prepared for her, she chose a lowly cell, and visited all places with such fervor and zeal, that had she not been in a hurry to see the remainder, she would not have been able to be torn away from the first. Prostrate before the cross, she adored it as though she saw the Lord hanging upon it; entering the sepulcher of the resurrection, she kissed the stone which the angel moved from the door of the tomb, and with faithful mouth kissed "the very place of the body" on which the Lord had lain, as one who thirsts drinks long-desired waters. What tears, what groans, what sorrow she displayed, all Jerusalem is witness, and the Lord Himself whom she called upon.

VII

Leaving that place she ascended Sion, which signifies "citadel," or "watch-tower." David once took this city by storm, and rebuilt it. Wherefore about the captured city is written, "Woe to thee, city of Ariel" [Is. 24:1] — that is, "lion of God, and one most strong" — "which David took by storm"; and about that which was built, "Her foundations are upon the holy hills. The Lord loveth the gates of Sion more than all the dwellings of Jacob" [Ps. 87:1, 2]. Not those gates which we behold at this day, fallen into cinders and ashes, but the gates against which the infernal one prevaileth not, and through which the multitude of believers enter into Christ. There was shown a column supporting the portico of a church, stained with the blood of the Lord, to which He is said to have been bound and scourged. The place was shown where the Holy Spirit descended upon the souls of over one hundred and twenty believers, that the prophecy of Joel [2:28] might be fulfilled.

VIII

Thence, having from her small means distributed money among the poor and her fellow-servants [of Christ], she proceeded to Bethlehem, and, on the right side of the road, stood beside the tomb of Rachel, where she bore Benjamin, not as she called him, when dying, "Benoni," that is, "the son of my sorrow," but, as his father prophesied in the Spirit, "the son of my right hand" [Gen. 35:18]. From thence she reached Bethlehem, and, entering the Grotto of the Savior, when she saw the holy inn of the Virgin and the stable in which "the ox knew his owner, and the ass his master's crib" [Is. 1:3], that it might be fulfilled which is written in the same prophet, "Blessed are ye that sow beside all waters, that send forth thither the feet of the ox and the ass" [Is. 32:20], she [Paula] declared in my hearing, that, by the eyes of faith, she could see the Infant Lord, wrapped in swaddling-clothes, wailing in the manger, the Magi adoring, the star shining above, the Virgin mother, the careful nursing, the shepherds coming by night that they might see the Word which had been made, and might even then declare the beginning of the Evangelist John, "In the beginning was the Word, and the Word was made flesh"; the little children massacred, Herod raging, Joseph and Mary fleeing into Egypt. With mingled joy and tears she said: "Hail, Bethlehem, house of bread, in which was born that Bread which came down from Heaven. Hail, Ephratah, richest and most fruitful region, whose produce is God; of which Michaeus prophesied: 'And thou, Bethlehem Ephratah, though thou be little among the thousands of Judah, yet out of thee shall He come forth unto me that is to be ruler in Israel; whose goings forth have been from of old, from everlasting. Therefore will He give them up, until the time that she which travaileth hath brought forth: then the remnant of His brethren shall return unto the children of Israel" [Mich. 5:2]. For in thee is born a Prince who was begotten before the morning star, whose birth from His Father is beyond all time. And in thee the root of the family of David remained until a Virgin bore a Son, and the remainder of the people that believed in Christ were turned to the children of Israel, and preached freely. 'It was necessary that the word of God should first have been spoken to you: but seeing ye put it from you, and judge yourselves unworthy of everlasting life, lo, we turn to the Gentiles' [Acts 13:46] For God said, 'I am not sent but unto the lost sheep of the house of Israel' [Matt. 15:24]. And at that time the words of Jacob concerning Him were brought to pass: 'The scepter shall not depart from Judah, nor a lawgiver from between his feet, until Shiloh come; and unto Him shall the gathering of the people be' [Gen. 49:10]. Well did David swear, well did he make vows, saying, 'Surely I will not come into the tabernacle of my house, nor go up into my bed; I will not give sleep to mine eyes, or slumber to mine eyelids, until I find out a place for the Lord, an habitation for the mighty God of Jacob' [Ps. 132:3–5]. And at once he set forth what he desired, and, with prophetic eyes, saw that He should come whom we believe to have already come. 'Behold, we heard of Him in Ephratah, and found Him in the fields of the wood' [Ps. 132:6, 7]. Indeed "Zo," the Hebrew word, as I have learned from your teaching, does not mean Mary, the Mother of the Lord, that is, her; but Himself, that is, Him. Wherefore he speaks boldly, 'We will go into His tabernacle; we will worship in the place where His feet have trod.' And I, a miserable sinner, have been judged worthy to kiss the manger in which the Lord wailed as an infant, to pray in the grotto in which the Virgin Mother bore a Child, the Lord. This is my rest, because the Lord is my country; here I will dwell, because the Savior has chosen it. 'I have prepared a lamp for my Christ. My soul shall live to Him, and my seed shall serve Him'" [cf. Ps. 132:14, 17].

IX

Not far from thence she descended to the Tower Ader, that is, "of the flock," near which Jacob fed his flocks, and the shepherds watching by night were worthy to hear, "Glory to God in the highest, and upon earth peace to men of goodwill" [Luke 2:14]. While they kept sheep, they found the Lamb of God of pure and most clean fleece, which, while all the earth was dry, was filled with dew from heaven, and whose blood bore the sins of the world, and, when sprinkled upon the door-posts, drove away the destroyer of Egypt.

X

At once, with hurried steps, she began to proceed along the ancient road which leads to Gaza, the "power," or the "treasure," of God, and to reflect silently within herself how the Ethiopian eunuch, typifying the nations of the Gentiles, changed his skin, and, while he searched the Old Testament, found the fountain of the Gospel. From thence she turned to the right hand through Bethsur, and thence came to Escol, which means "cluster of grapes." From hence, as a testimony of a very fertile land, and as a type of Him who saith, "I have trodden the winepress alone, and of the people there was none with Me" [Is. 63:3], the spies carried off a bunch of grapes of wonderful size.

XI

At no long distance from hence she entered the Cells of Sara, seeing the birthplace of Isaac and the traces of the oak of Abraham, under which he saw the day of Christ [cf. Gen. 18], and rejoiced. Rising from thence she went up to Hebron. This is Cariatharbe [Judg. 1:10], that is, "the town of the four men," Abraham, Isaac, Jacob, and Adam the Great, who, the Hebrews say, is buried there, according to the Book of Jesus, the son of Nave, although most people think that the fourth was Caleb [Josh. 15:15], whose tomb, made of brick, is shown. Having seen these, she cared not to go to Cariathsepher, that is, "the village of letters," because, despising the perishing letter, she had found the life-giving Spirit. Rather did she admire the upper and nether springs which Othoniel, the son of Kenez the son of Jephone [Othniel, the son of Kenaz, the son of Jephunneh (Josh. 15:16–19)], took for the southern land and parched possession, and by their leading made the dry fields of the Old Testament well watered, that he might find the redemption of former sins in the waters of baptism.

XII

On the next day, when the sun was risen, she stood on the brow of Caphar Barucha, that is, "the town of blessing," to which place Abraham followed the Lord. From hence looking down upon the wide desert, and what was once the country of Sodom and Gomorrah, of Adama and Seboim, she beheld the garden of balsam and the vineyards of Engaddi; and Segor, the three-year-old heifer [Is. 15:5], which was formerly called Bala, and is in the Syrian tongue "Zoar," that is, "little one." She remembered the cave of Lot, and bursting into tears, warned the maidens, her companions, to avoid wine, wherein is excess; his descendants are the Moabites and the Ammonites. For a long time she stayed in the south, at the place where the bride found the bridegroom lying, and where Joseph made merry with his brethren.

XIII

Shall I return to Jerusalem by Thecua, the birthplace of Amos; shall I behold the brilliant light [or cross] of the Mount of Olives, from which the Savior ascended to His Father, on which every year a red heifer was burned whole as an offering to the Lord, and whose ashes atoned for the sins of the people of Israel, in which, according to Ezechiel [10:18, 19], cherubim proceeding from the Temple founded the Church of the Lord? Afterwards, entering the tomb of Lazarus, she saw the house of Mary and Martha, and Bethphage, the town of the jawbones of the priests, and the place where the playful colt of the Gentiles received the reins of God, and strewn with the clothes of the Apostles, furnished a soft back for a seat.

XIV

By a straight journey she proceeded to Jericho, reflecting on that man in the Gospel who was wounded; and when the priests and Levites, in the harshness of their minds, passed by, [reflecting] on the kindness of the Samaritan, that is, of the shepherd who put the half-dead man upon his own beast, and brought him to the fold of the Church; and the place Adomim, which is translated "of blood," because much blood was shed there in the frequent inroads of robbers; and the sycamore tree of Zacchaeus, that is, the good works of penitence, by which he trod under foot his long bloody and wicked sins of rapine, and from a height of virtues beheld the exalted Lord; and beside the way the place of the blind men, who by receiving their sight, typified the sacraments of both peoples who believed in the Lord. Entering Jericho, she saw the city of which Hiel laid the foundation in Abiram, his first-born, and whose gates he set up in Segub, the youngest of his children. She beheld the camp of Galgala, and the hill of the foreskins, and the mystery of the second circumcision; and the twelve stones, which, brought thither from the bed of the Jordan, confirmed the foundation of the twelve Apostles; and the old fountain of the law, bitter and barren, which Helisarus flavored, by his wisdom, and turned into sweetness and fruitfulness. Scarcely was the night past before she, with fervent zeal, came to the Jordan, stood on the bank of the river, and, as the sun rose, remembered the Sun of righteousness; how the priests stood on dry ground in the middle of the bed of the Jordan; and how, at the bidding of Helias and Helisseus, the river, the waters standing on either side, afforded a passage; and how, by His baptism, the Lord cleansed the waters which had been defiled by the Flood and stained by His death.

XV

It would be long, if I would speak of the Valley of Achor, that is, of tumult and disturbance, in which she reproved theft and avarice; and of Bethel, the House of God, in which Jacob, naked and poor, slept upon the bare ground, and placing under his head a stone, which in Zacharias [3:9] is said to have seven eyes, and in Isaiah [28:16] is called the stone of the corner, saw a ladder reaching to heaven above which the Lord leaned, offering His hand to those who climbed, and casting down from above those who were negligent. She also, from the opposite side, revered the tombs on Mount Ephraim, of Jesus the son of Nave, and of Eleazar, the son of Aron the priest, one of whom is buried in Thamnathsare, on the north side of Mount Gaash, the other in Gabaa of his son Phinees; and she sufficiently wondered that the divider of possessions had chosen the mountainous rough parts for himself.

XVI

Why should I speak of Silo, in which the destroyed altar is shown even at the present day, and where the tribe of Benjamin pre-enacted the rape of the Sabine women by Romulus? She passed through Sichem, not, as most travelers spell it, Sichar, which now is named Neapolis, and entered the church built upon the side of Mount Gerizim, round about Jacob's Well; at the mouth of which the Lord sat, thirsty and hungry, and was filled by the faith of the woman of Samaria, who having had five husbands, the books of Moses, and the sixth, the error of Dositheus, which she boasted that she possessed, found the true Messiah and the true Savior. Turning away from thence she saw the sepulchers of the twelve patriarchs, and Sebaste, that is, Samaria, to which, in honor of Augustus, Herod gave the name of Augusta in its Greek form. There lie Heliseus and Abdias the prophets, and he, than whom there was not a greater among those born of women, John the Baptist. Here she trembled at many wonders; for she beheld demons roaring with various torments, and, before the sepulchers of the saints, men who howled like wolves, barked with the voices of dogs, roared with those of lions, hissed like serpents, bellowed like bulls, while others turned round their heads and touched the ground behind their backs with the crown of their heads, and women hung by their feet with their clothes flowing over their faces. She pitied them all; and having shed tears for each, begged the mercy of Christ [for them]. Weak as she was, she on foot ascended the mountain, in which, in two caves, during the time of persecution and famine, Abdias [Obadiah] the prophet fed a hundred prophets with bread and water.

XVII

Thence, by a swift journey, she proceeded to Nazareth, the nurse of the Lord; Cana and Capharnaum, the witnesses of His miracles; the lake of Tiberias, consecrated by the voyage of the Lord; and the wilderness, in which many thousands of people were satisfied with a few loaves, and, from the remnants of those who had eaten, twelve baskets [typifying the tribes of Israel] were filled. She climbed Mount Tabor, upon which the Lord was transfigured. She saw at a distance the mountains, Hermon and Hermoniim, and the very wide plains of Galilee, upon which Sisara and all his army were overthrown before the conquering Barach; the brook Cison, which divided the midst of the plain; and opposite was shown the town of Naim, in which the son of the widow was raised to life.

XVIII

Time rather than matter would fail me if I wished to detail all the places to which the devout Paula wandered with incredible faith. I will pass over to Egypt; and at Sochot, and the Fountain of Samson which he brought forth from the grinding tooth of the jawbone, I will rest for a while and lave my parched mouth, that refreshed I may behold Morasthim, once the sepulcher of the prophet Michaea, and now a church. I will leave on one side Chorraei and Gethaei, Maresa, Idumaea, and Lachis. Over softest sands, which draw down the steps of those who cross them, and over the wide waste of the desert, I will come to Sior, the river of Egypt, which is translated "the muddy," and will pass through the five cities of Egypt which speak the Canaanitish tongue [cf. Is. 19:18], and the land of Gessen and the plains of Tanis, in which God wrought wonders; and the city of No, which afterwards was called Alexandria; and Nitria, the town of the Lord, in which the filth of many is daily washed away by the pure nitre of virtues. When she saw this, she was met by the holy and venerable Bishop Isidorus the Confessor, and by innumerable crowds of monks, many of whom were exalted to the rank of priests and deacons; and she rejoiced to the glory of God, but confessed herself unworthy of so much honor. Why need I mention the names of Macarius, of Arsenius, of Serapion, and those of the other pillars of Christ? Whose cell did she not enter? — at whose feet did she not prostrate herself? Through each of the holy men she believed herself to see Christ; and whatever she bestowed upon them she rejoiced that she bestowed upon the Lord. Her zeal was wonderful—her courage scarcely credible for a woman. Forgetful of her sex and of the weakness of her frame, she desired to dwell with her maidens among so many thousands of monks. And perhaps, as all invited her, she would have obtained her desire, had not a greater longing for the holy places drawn her back.

XIX

On account of the ardent warmth [of her faith], proceeding by sea from Pelusium to Majuma, she returned with so great swiftness that you would think her a bird. And not long afterwards, intending to dwell for ever in holy Bethlehem, she remained for three years in a narrow lodging while she was building cells and monasteries and founded inns for different kinds of pilgrims by the side of the road upon which Mary and Joseph found no resting place.

Up to this point be her journey described, which she performed accompanied by many virgins and by her daughter.

*

The Letter of Paula and Eustochium to Marcella about the Holy Places

386 CE

Translated by Aubrey Stewart

I

If, after the Passion of Our Lord, this place is accursed, as the wicked say that it is, what did St. Paul mean by hastening [Acts 20:16] to Jerusalem, that he might keep the day of Pentecost there? Why did he address those who would have held him back, saying: "What do you, weeping and breaking my heart? For I am ready not to be bound only, but also to die at Jerusalem, for the name of the Lord Jesus" [Acts 21:13]. What did all those other holy and illustrious men mean, whose alms and oblations, after the preaching of Christ, were sent to the brethren who were at Jerusalem? It would be a long task to mention, year by year, from the Ascension of our Lord to the present day, how many bishops, how many martyrs, how many men eloquent in ecclesiastical learning, have come to Jerusalem, thinking themselves to be lacking in religion and in learning, and not to have received, as the saying is, a full handful of virtues, unless they had adored Christ in those very places from which the Gospel first shone forth from the Cross. Indeed, if even a distinguished orator [Cicero, *De Div. in Caecil.* 12.7] thought somebody worthy of blame because he had learned Greek not at Athens but at Lilybaeum, and had learned Latin, not at Rome, but in Sicily, because of course each province has something peculiar to itself, which another cannot possess in the same degree; why should we suppose that anyone can reach the highest pitch of devotion without the help of our Athens? Yet we do not say this because we deny that the kingdom of God is within us, or that there are holy men in other regions also, but because what we especially assert is this, that those who are the foremost men of the whole earth all alike flock hither together.

II

To these places we have come, not as persons of importance, but as strangers, that we might see in them the foremost men of all nations. Indeed, the company of monks and nuns is a flower and a jewel of great price among the ornaments of the Church. Whoever may be the first men in Gaul hasten hither. The Briton, separated from our world [Virgil, *Ecl.* 1.67], if he has made any progress in religion, leaves the setting sun and seeks a place known to him only by fame and the narrative of the Scriptures. Why need we mention the Armenians, the Persians, the nations of India and Ethiopia, and the neighboring country of Egypt, abounding in monks, Pontus and Cappadocia, Coele Syria, and Mesopotamia, and all the multitudes of the East, who, fulfilling the words of our Savior, "Wherever the carcass is, thither will the eagles be gathered together" [Matt. 24:28], flock into these places and display to us examples of diverse excellence?

III

Their speech differs, but their religion is one. There are almost as many choirs of psalm-singers as there are different nations. Among all this will be found what is, perhaps, the greatest virtue among Christians — no arrogance, no overweening pride in their chastity; all of them vie with one another in humility. Whoever is last is reckoned as first. In their dress there is no distinction, no ostentation. The order in which they walk in procession neither implies disgrace nor confers honor. Fasts also fill no one with pride, abstinence is not commended, nor is modest repletion condemned. Every man stands or falls by the judgment of his own Lord; no one judges another, lest he should be judged by the Lord. And here the practice of backbiting, so common in most countries, finds absolutely no place. Far from hence is luxury and self-indulgence.

IV

There are so many places of prayer in the city itself, that one day cannot suffice for visiting them all. However, to come to the village of Christ [Bethlehem] and the inn of Mary (for everyone praises most that which he possesses), by what words, with what voice, can we describe to you the grotto of the Savior? That manger, too, wherein the babe wailed, is better honored by silence than by imperfect speech. Where are spacious porticos? Where are gilded ceilings? Where are houses decorated by the sufferings and labors of condemned wretches? Where are halls built by the wealth of private men on the scale of palaces, that the vile carcass of man may move among more costly surroundings and view his own roof rather than the heavens, as if anything could be more beauteous than creation [*mundus*]? Behold, in this little nook of the earth the Founder of the heavens was born; here He was wrapped in swaddling clothes, beheld by the shepherds, shown by the star, adored by the wise men. This place, I conceive, is holier than the Tarpeian Rock, which by its having been frequently struck by lightning shows that it is displeasing to God.

V

Read the Revelation of John, and consider what he says of the scarlet woman, and the blasphemies written upon her brow, of the seven hills, of the many waters, and of the fall of Babylon. "Come out of her," said the Lord, "come out of her, my people, that you be not partakers of her sins, and that you receive not of her plagues" [Rev. 18:4]. And turning back to Jeremiah, listen to a like Scripture. "Flee out of the midst of Babylon, and deliver every man his soul. For Babylon the great is fallen, is fallen, and is become a habitation of devils and a hold of every unclean spirit" [Jer. 51:6, Rev. 18:2]. There is the Holy Church, there are the triumphs of the apostles and martyrs, there is the true confession of Christ, the faith preached by the Apostle, and despised by the Gentiles, there the name of "Christian" is daily exalted; but worldliness, authority, the life of a great city, meetings and exchanges of salutations, praise and blame of one another, listening to others or talking to them, or even against one's will beholding so great a congregation of people, is foreign to the ideal set before monks and their quiet seclusion; for if we see those who visit us we lose our quiet, and if we do not see them we are accused of pride. Sometimes, also, that we may return the calls of our visitors, we proceed to the doors of proud houses, and amid the sneering remarks of the servants enter their gilded portals.

VI

But in the village of Christ, as we said before, all is rusticity, and except for psalms, silence. Wherever you turn yourself, the ploughman, holding the plough-handle, sings Alleluia; the perspiring reaper diverts himself with psalms, and the vine-dresser sings some of the songs of David while he trims the vine with his curved knife. These are the ballads of this country, these are the love-songs, as they are commonly called; these are whistled by the shepherds and are the implements of the husbandman. Indeed, we do not think of what we are doing or of how we look, but see only that for which we are longing.

VII

Oh, when will that time come when a breathless messenger shall bring us the news that our Marcella has reached the shore of Palestine, and all the choirs of monks, all the troops of nuns shall shout applause? We already are eager to start, and though no vehicle is expected, yet we wish to run to meet it. We shall clasp your hands, we shall behold your face, and shall scarcely be able to leave your long-wished-for embrace. When will that day come, when we shall be able to enter the grotto of our Savior? to weep with our sister, and with our mother, in the Sepulcher of the Lord? Afterwards, to kiss the wood of the Cross, and on the Mount of Olives, together with our ascending Lord, to lift up our hearts and fulfill our vows? to see Lazarus come forth bound with grave clothes, and to see the waters of Jordan, made more pure by the baptism of the Lord? And thence to go to the folds of the shepherds, and pray in the tomb of David? To behold Amos the prophet even now lamenting on his rock with his shepherd's bugle-horn? To hasten to the tabernacles or tombs of Abraham, Isaac, and Jacob, and their three noble wives? To behold the fountain wherein the eunuch was baptized by Philip? To go to Samaria and adore with equal fervor the ashes of John the Baptist, of Elisha, and of Abdia? To enter the caves, wherein, in time of persecution and famine, troops of prophets were fed.

VIII

We shall go to Nazareth, and, according to the interpretation of its name, shall behold the flower of Galilee. Not far from thence will be seen Cana, wherein the waters were turned into wine. We shall go on to Itabyrium [Mount Tabor], and shall see the tabernacles of the Savior, not, as Peter would have built them, with Moses and Elias, but with the Father and the Holy Spirit. Thence we shall come to the Sea of Gennesareth, and shall see the five and four thousand men in the desert fed with five and seven loaves. Before us will appear the city of Naim, at whose gates the widow's son was raised from the dead. We shall see, too, Hermoniim [Ps. 42:6] and the Brook of Endor [Ps. 83:9, 10] whereat Sisera was overcome. We shall also see Capharnaum, that familiar witness of the miracles of our Lord, and likewise the whole of Galilee. And then, accompanied by Christ, when we have returned to our grotto, after passing Silo and Bethel, and the other places in which the banners of the Church have been raised, as though to celebrate the victories of the Lord, we will sing constantly, we will often weep, we will pray without ceasing, and, wounded by the dart of our Savior, we will repeat together, "I have found Him whom my soul sought for; I will hold Him fast and will not let Him go" [Song. (Cant) 3:4].

*

The Description of Syria and Palestine by Mukaddasî

INTRODUCTION

Shams ad Dîn — "the Sun of Religion" — Abu 'Abd Allah Muhammad, the son of Ahmad, the son of Abu Bakr the architect, commonly known as Mukaddasî — the Hierosolomite — was born at Jerusalem in the year of the Flight 336 (CE 946). For his personal history, we have to rely entirely on what can be put together from such incidental references to his adventurous career as occur in the pages of his book, for no biography of him is to be found in the volumes of Ibn Khallikan, nor has any notice of his life been met with in the voluminous compilations of the historiographers or the contemporary annalists. Mukaddasî makes no special mention of his father, Ahmad, but his grandfather, Abu Bakr, appears to have acquired fame throughout Syria as an architect, for besides numerous minor works, his grandson gives an interesting account of his labors at the port of Acre, which he undertook to reconstruct and fortify at the command of Ibn Tûlûn, the then-ruler of Egypt, in whose dominions Syria was included. The family name of Mukaddasî was Al Bashârî, and we gather that his paternal ancestors had been settled in the neighborhood of Jerusalem ever since the early days of the Muslim conquest. His mother's family had originally belonged to the town of Biyâr, in the province of Jurjân, in Persia, not far from the frontier of Khurasân; and from thence his maternal grandfather, Abu-t Tayib ash Shawâ, had migrated during the troublesome days which witnessed the rise of the Khurramite sect, and accompanied by eighteen of his kinsmen had come to settle in Jerusalem. Abu-t Tayib would appear to have been a man of considerable wealth, and a kindred taste in literary and artistic matters, leading him to form a close friendship with Abu Bakr, the architect, the alliance between the families was cemented by the marriage of their children. Muhammad al Mukaddasî, the child of this marriage, inherited a strong predilection for architectural subjects from both his grandfathers; and the natural bent being fostered by his education, such notices of the various buildings as he met with during his travels, and described in his book, are the more valuable, by reason of the careful and almost scientific detail of his description, and the just use of the appropriate technical terms.

Mukaddasî, as appears from his book, had the advantage of an excellent education. He was no mean proficient in the theological and juridical sciences of the day, and besides this was sufficiently versed in mercantile affairs to turn his voyages to profit. He takes occasion himself to remark that his talents, both as theologian and merchant, had frequently served him in good stead during his journeys, and further had made him friends among all classes. In 356 AH (967 CE), when he had attained the age of twenty, he visited for the first time Mecca, and performed the rites of the pilgrimage. It was only when he had attained his fortieth year, however, and after long journeys and much study, that he ventured to set himself to the composition of his book. "For years past," he writes in his preface, "I have devoted myself to this science of geography, which, alas! of others is now so neglected; and though it may be in but a perfunctory manner, I have constantly studied the art thereof, having it in mind to write a description of all the countries of Islâm." After briefly indicating the points which he deems most worthy of discussion in a compendium of geography, he proceeds to give an account of his labors, which are, perhaps, best described in his own words, though in translating them we have somewhat condensed the form.

Introduction to Description by Mukaddasi

"Now for the purpose of writing this book I have spent my substance in journeyings, and have worn myself out in mercantile voyagings. And I have begun to write it only now after sojourning long time in many lands, visiting all the countries of Islâm, everywhere frequenting the society of the learned, serving in the service of princes, attending the courts of the judges, listening to the lectures of the jurisprudists, and so attaining to all the knowledge that I could, in both letters and the scriptures. For a time I studied the traditions, and then passing through the schools of the Ascetics and Sûfi philosophers, lived among the Rhetoricians, and the Rhapsodists. In every country I made myself a home, trading among the people whereby to gain a livelihood, eating with all manner of men, learning all things of each one, walking a-foot on my journeys that I might measure the distances, searching out the boundaries of the provinces, acquiring by practice the dialects of each nation, noting the complexion of the race in every clime, and becoming initiated into the secrets of their religious sects. And thus in every land have I inquired and made myself acquainted with its divisions and zones, its climate, its waters, its natural wealth, and its physical peculiarities." All this preparatory work Mukaddasî carried out systematically during a full score of years, and hence it is not surprising that he ended by writing a book totally unlike any that had yet appeared. Others, such as Ibn Haukal Istakhri and Ibn Khurdadbih had written road-books, describing the various countries of Islâm, and detailing their chief towns and their rivers and mountains; "but I," boasts Mukaddasî, "have not plagiarized from their writings — and he who has read their works will acknowledge this. Also, though my book be amenable to criticism, yet since all that I have written is of my very own experience, herein must it differ from all previous works.... In each case I have clearly stated such scenes as I have witnessed with my own eyes, and have given the authority where I describe from the reports of others; also do I make no excuse for mentioning such celebrated personages as I have met with in my travels." Mukaddasî's preface ends by stating that he completed his work in the year of the Flight 375 (CE 985), "in the chief town of Fârs, which same is in the dominion of the Commander of the Faithful, Abu Bakr 'Abd al Karîm At Tâi' Billah; while over the Lands of the West rules Abu Mansûr Nizâr Al 'Aziz Billah, Commander of the Faithful."

These two rival Commanders of the Faithful were At Tâi', the twenty-fourth khalif of the House of 'Abbâs, who was reigning at Baghdad, and Al 'Azîz, the fifth of the Fatimite khalifs of Egypt, the father of the celebrated mad Khalif Hâkim, whose apotheosis is a chief tenet of the religion of the Druzes. As contemporary with Mukaddasî, we may call to mind that, in CE 985, far away from Syria, here in the west, in England, the Saxon Ethelred the Unready was making his last feeble struggle against the Danes, alternately bribing with *Danegelt*, and treacherously ordering massacres, both courses inevitably leading to the coming of Canute. Across the Channel Hugh Capet, count of Paris and Orleans, was, in 987, proclaimed king of France, at Noyon; while fifteen years before this date the great Emperor Otto had died, and ten years had yet to run before Hungary was to become Christian under King Stephen. More than a century, counting from the days when our author was penning his description of Palestine, had to elapse before the pilgrimage of Hermit Peter to Jerusalem (CE 1093) and the decrees of the Council of Clermont would start the chivalry of the West on their long Crusade against the powers of Islâm; and on this point it is curious to note how little, according to Mukaddasî's account, the Christian pilgrims had, during his age, to suffer for the sake of their religion at the hands of the rulers of Syria. Christians and Jews, he says, had the upper hand then in Jerusalem. But these were the days before the mad Khalif Hâkim had set his soldiers to destroy the Church of the Resurrection at Jerusalem (CE 1010), and there was then no tax imposed on the pilgrim as the price of his admission into the Holy City. From the time of Omar, who had made the treaty with the Patriarch Sophronius, down to the period of Hâkim's furious onslaught — for over three centuries and a half — the pilgrims from the West had, with small hindrance, been able to visit all the sacred sites of Palestine; and over and above their spiritual advantages, they found in their pilgrimage no mean source of worldly gain, for there was great profit arising from mercantile dealings with the Saracens. As Mukaddasî quaintly puts it, "the Holy Land is truly a mine of profit both for this world and the next."

In the times to which we are alluding — that is, towards the close of the ninth century of our era — there were three khalifs, each styling himself the Commander of the Faithful, and peaceably reigning, if not actually ruling, in parts of the now disunited empire of Islâm. Far in the West, at Cordova, reigned Hishâm II, tenth khalif of the Spanish Omeyyads; and though in his days the Muhammadan power in Andalusia was already on the wane, the great schools of Seville and Cordova were already rising to become the centers whence radiated such learning as could pierce the gloom of the Middle Ages. In Egypt, as before noted, ruled the fifth Fatimite khalif Al 'Aziz, father of the mad Hâkim, who succeeded in AH 382 (CE 992). The Fatimites based their claim to the Commanding of the Faithful on their alleged descent from the Imâm Husain, the son of the Khalif 'Ali, and Fâtimah, daughter of the Prophet. They were powerful sovereigns, and at one time governed, from their metropolis at Cairo, the greater part of northern Africa, with Syria, and the Hijjâz, including the two Holy Cities of Mecca and Medînah. During the 270 years that their dynasty held power, the Fatimites were the great rivals of the Abbaside khalifs; and half a century after the date of our author, in AH 447 (CE 1055), their generals were pillaging Baghdad itself, forcing the Khalif Al Kâim to flee for his life to Ana, while, during forty weeks the public prayers were read in the name of the Fatimite khalif in the mosques of the Abbaside capital on the Tigris.

During the days of Mukaddasî, however, it was At Tâi', of the House of Abbâs, who was the khalif, in name, at Baghdad. During the earlier years of his reign all the power of the state had been centered in the hands of the great Buyide prince, whose province was Persia, 'Adud ad Daulah. After the latter's death, however, in AH 372 (CE 982), his sons and successors began to quarrel over the spoil; and although — during half a century yet of bloodshed and turmoil — the Buyides were supreme in Baghdad, being the viceroys of the khalif, who had now made formal renunciation of his temporal dominion, their star was already on the wane before the rising power of the Seljûk Turks, who were now becoming inheritors of the rule of the Samanide Amirs in all the fertile lands of Central Asia. Upper Mesopotamia and the northern parts of Syria were, in Mukaddasî's days, in the hands of the Hamdânî princes, who dwelt at Mosul and Aleppo; and far away in Afghanistan, as yet unknown to fame, Mahmûd, of Ghaznah, was a boy-commander in his father's armies, already preparing himself for the conquest of India.

Such, in briefest outline, was the condition of things political at the time when Mukaddasî wrote his work. Of the writing of the book itself some account has already been given. The chapter which is here translated will afford a fair specimen of the general style of our author; and since he was, herein, describing his native land, he wrote with ample knowledge of the subject, and hence with greater fullness than in the other sections of his work. Of the whole book, the present chapter occupies barely a tenth part;[1] for besides a long preface on personal matters, and a detailed exposition of the contents of his work, with remarks on "Orientation" and the "Dimensions of Countries," our author treats in separate chapters, of the Arabian Peninsula, and then, in turn, of each of the countries of the East, from Mesopotamia to Turkistân and Sind, following which come Egypt and the countries of the West as far as Spain, which last, however, he had not himself visited.

As regards style, Mukaddasî's book, in the original, is pleasant to read, from the vigorous, idiomatic language in which it is written. In the preface he states that in the description of each country he intends to make use of such expressions as are current in the vernacular dialect; and he writes his introduction, he says, in the idiom of his own dear land of Syria. It is not surprising, therefore, to discover that many of his words are lacking in our Arabic dictionaries; and the text, even with the learned Dutch editor's notes and glossary, is not always easy to translate. Our author's descriptions are, however, clear and succinct, and his diction is, as a rule, simple and straightforward. If at times he wastes, as we should think, valuable space in an endeavor to make a display of his casuistical adroitness, somewhat may be excused him for the fashion of his age, when all great wits employed their ingenuity in the puerilities of dialectic; and as regards Mukaddasî's quibbling, it may be affirmed that he is not more futile in his subtleties than are many of the great schoolmen who followed in the succeeding centuries.

1. This edition presents an even more abbreviated version covering only those parts pertaining to the district of Palestine.

The translation here given was my work during the winter of the year 1884, when I was living at Haifâ, in Palestine. The text I had before me is that so admirably edited by De Goeje, in his *Bibliotheca Geographorum Arabicorum* (Leiden, 1877). Since my return to England I have seen the translation of the major portion of this same chapter of Mukaddasî's book published in German by J. Gildemeister in the *Zeitschrift des Deutschen Palaestina-Vereins* 7 (1884). The German professor, however, has not given the chapter entire, he has made not a few slips (as, for instance, when he states that our author was born in AH 366, and wrote his book in 375), and when he finds some difficulty in following Mukaddasî's descriptions (e.g., in the case of the Damascus Mosque), he often, to our mind, somewhat hastily concludes that the text is corrupt.

Also, Dr. Gildemeister makes little attempt at identifying places mentioned, with such names as are found on the modern maps; he does not state clearly whether a place is, or is not, to be found, and too often assumes in his readers a knowledge of Arabic which is hardly justifiable in a translation. It is, however, only just that I should acknowledge that from the references in many of his notes I have been set on the right track for acquiring the desired information.

...The system adopted in the transliteration of the Arabic names is that now in common use, well-known names, however, are often retained in the spelling sanctioned by usage. In my translation I have kept as closely as was possible to the text. Any considerable additions, required to render the meaning clear, are enclosed in brackets; but I have not thought it necessary to mark all cases where I have replaced the ever-recurring relative pronoun of the Arabic by its antecedent noun or sentence, in order to make the English clear and more idiomatic. The *Memoirs of the Survey of Western Palestine* have been constantly at my elbow, and to their pages I would refer the reader for the description of the sites as they exist at the present day.

In conclusion it is a pleasure to me to have an opportunity of expressing my thanks to Sir C. Wilson for valuable suggestions and emendations, that have enabled me to correct not a few of the notes which are added for the elucidation of the text. In most cases I have, by his permission, merely incorporated among my own notes the information which he was good enough to place at my disposal....

— Guy Le Strange

The District of Palestine by Mukaddasî

c.985 CE

Translated by Guy Le Strange

The District of Filastîn (Palestine). Its capital is Ar-Ramlah. Among its cities are: Bait-al-Makdis (Jerusalem), Bait Jibrîl, Ghazzah (Gaza), Maimâs, 'Askalân [Ascalon], Yâfah [Caipha], Arsûf, Kaisariyyah (Caesarea), Nâbulus [Shechem], Arîhâ [Jericho], 'Ammân.

I. Ar-Ramlah

Ar-Ramlah [Ramleh] is the capital of Palestine. It is a fine city and well built; its water is good and plentiful; its fruits are abundant. It combines manifold advantages, situated as it is in the midst of beautiful villages and lordly towns, near to holy places and pleasant hamlets. Commerce here is prosperous, and means of livelihood easy. There is no finer mosque in Islâm than the one in this city; its bread is of the best and the whitest; its lands are well favored above all others, and its fruits are of the most luscious. The capital stands among fruitful fields, walled towns, and serviceable hospices. It possesses magnificent hostelries and pleasant baths, dainty food and various condiments, spacious houses, fine mosques and broad roads. As a capital it possesses many advantages. It is situated on the plain and is yet near both to the mountains and the sea. It has both fig trees and palms; its fields need no irrigation, and are by nature fruitful and rich. Its disadvantages, on the other hand, are, that in winter the place is a slough of mud, while in summer it is a powder-box of sand, where no water flows, neither is anything green, nor is the soil humid, nor is there snow. Fleas here abound. The wells are deep and salt, and the rain-water is hoarded in closed cisterns; hence the poor go thirsty, and strangers seek in vain. So too the seats before the baths are filled with expectant bathers, while the servants are grinding at the water-wheels. The city occupies the area of a square mile; its houses are built of finely-quarried stones. The best known among its gates are the Gate of the Soldier's Well [Darb Bîr al 'Askar], the Gate of the 'Annabah Mosque, the Gate of Jerusalem, the Gate of Bîla'ah [?], the Lydda Gate [Darb Ludd], the Jaffa Gate [Darb Yâfâ], the Egypt Gate [Darb Misr], and the Dâjûn Gate. Close to Ar-Ramlah is the town of Dâjûn, with its mosque. It is inhabited mostly by Samaritans. The chief mosque of Ar-Ramlah is in the market, and it is even more beautiful and graceful than that of Damascus. It is called Al Abyad [the White Mosque].

In all Islâm there is found no finer Mihrâb than the one here, and its pulpit is the most exquisite that is to be seen after that of Jerusalem; also it possesses a beautiful minaret, built by the Khalif Hishâm ibn 'Abd al Malik. I have heard my uncle relate that when the khalif was about to build the minaret it was reported to him that the Christians possessed columns of marble, then lying buried beneath the sand, which they had prepared for the church of Bâli'ah; thereupon the Khalif Hishâm informed the Christians that either they must show him where the columns lay, or that he would demolish their church at Lydda, in order to employ its columns for the building of his mosque. So the Christians pointed out where they had buried their columns and they are very thick and tall and beautiful. The covered portion of the mosque is flagged with marble, and the court with other stone, all carefully laid together. The gates of the covered part are made of cypress wood and cedar, carved in the inner parts, and very beautiful in appearance.

II. Jerusalem

Jerusalem, Bait-al-Makdis [the Holy City], also known as Îliyâ and Al Balât. Among provincial towns none is larger than Jerusalem, and many capitals are in fact smaller, as, for instance, Istakhr and Kâ-in and Al Firmâ. Neither the cold nor the heat is excessive here, and snow falls but rarely. The Kâdi Abu'l Kâsim, son of the kâdi of the Two Holy Cities, inquired of me once concerning the climate of Jerusalem. I answered, "It is betwixt and between — neither very hot nor very cold." Said he in reply, "Just as is that of Paradise." The buildings of the Holy City are of stone, and you will find nowhere finer or more solid constructions. In no place will you meet with a people more chaste. Provisions are most excellent here, the markets are clean, the mosque is of the largest, and nowhere are holy places more numerous. The grapes are enormous, and there are no quinces to equal those of the Holy City. In Jerusalem are all manner of learned men and doctors, and for this reason the hearts of men of intelligence yearn towards her. All the year round, never are her streets empty of strangers. Now one day at Busrah I was seated in the assembly of the Chief Kâdi Abu Yahya ibn Bahrâm, and the conversation turned on the city of Cairo. Then one said, speaking to me, "And can any city be more illustrious?" I replied, "Why, yes, my own native town!" Said he, "But is any pleasanter than Cairo?" I answered, "Yes again, my native town." It was said, "Ah, but Cairo is the more excellent, and the more beautiful, and the more productive of good things, and the more spacious." Still, to each and all I replied, "Not so! it is my native town." Then the company were astonished, and they said to me, "Thou art a man of erudition, but thou dost advance now more than can be accorded to thee, in our belief. Verily thou art even as the man who owned the she-camel, and colloquied with Al Hajjâj! But the Arab brought up his camel in proof. Now do thou do likewise, and we will deem thee a man of wit." So I answered them and spake: "Now, as to my saying that Jerusalem is the most illustrious of cities, why is she not one that unites the advantages of this world to those of the next? He who is of the sons of this world and yet is ardent in the matters of the next, may with advantage seek her markets; while he who would be of the men of the next world, though his soul clings to the good things of this, he, too, may find these here! And as to Jerusalem being the pleasantest of places in the way of climate, why the cold there does not injure, and the heat is not noxious. And as to her being the finest city, why, has any seen elsewhere buildings finer, or cleaner, or a mosque that is more beautiful? And as for the Holy City being the most productive of all places in good things, why Allah — may He be exalted — has gathered together here all the fruits of the lowlands, and of the plains, and of the hill country, even all those of the most opposite kinds; such as the orange and the almond, the date and the nut, the fig and the banana, besides milk in plenty, and honey and sugar. And as to the excellence of the City! Why, is not this to be the plain of marshalling on the Day of Judgment, where the gathering together and the appointment will take place? Verily. Makkah [Mecca] and Al Madînah [Medînah] have their superiority by reason of the Ka'abah and the Prophet—the blessing of Allah be upon him and his family — but verily, on the Day of Judgment, they will both come to Jerusalem, and the excellences of them all will there be united. And as to Jerusalem being the most spacious of cities; why, since all created things are to assemble there, what place on the earth can be more extensive than this!"

And the company were pleased with my words, agreeing to the truth of them.

Still Jerusalem has some disadvantages. Thus, it is reported as found written in the Torah, that "Jerusalem is as a golden basin filled with scorpions." Then you will not find baths more filthy than those of the Holy City; nor in any town are provisions dearer. Learned men are few, and the Christians numerous, and the same are unmannerly in the public places. In the hostelries taxes are heavy on all that is sold, for there are guards at every gate, and no one is able to sell aught whereby to obtain a profit, except he be satisfied with but little gain. In this city the oppressed have no succour; the meek are molested, and the rich envied. Jurisconsults remain unvisited, and erudite men have no renown; also the schools are unattended, for there are no lectures. Everywhere the Christians and the Jews have the upper hand; and the mosque is void of either congregation or assembly of learned men.

Jerusalem is smaller than Makkah, and larger than Al Madînah. Over the city is a castle [Al Kal'ah], one side of which is against the hill-side, while the other is defended by a ditch. Jerusalem has eight iron gates:

Bâb Sihyûn (of Sion),
Bâb at Tîh (of the Desert of the Wanderings),
Bâb al Balât (of the Palace, or Court),
Bâb Jubb Armiyâ (of Jeremiah's Grotto),
Bâb Silwân (of Siloam),
Bâb Arîhâ (of Jericho),
Bâb al 'Amûd (of the Columns),
Bâb Mihrâb Dâûd (of David's Oratory).

There is water in Jerusalem in plenty. Thus, it is a common saying, that "There is no place in Jerusalem but where you may get water and hear the Call to Prayer; and few are the houses that have not cisterns one or more." Within the city are three great tanks, namely, the Birkat Bani Isrâîl, the Birkat Sulaimân, and the Birkat 'Iyâd. In the vicinity of each of these are baths, and to them lead the water channels from the streets. In the haram area there are twenty underground cisterns of vast size, and there are few quarters of the city that have not public cisterns, though the contents of these last is only the rain water that drains into them from the streets. At a certain valley, about a stage from the city, they have gathered together the waters and made there two pools [Solomon's Pools], into which the torrents of the winter rains flow. From these two reservoirs there are channels bringing the water to the city, which are opened during the spring in order to fill the cisterns in the haram area and also those in other places.

The Masjid al Aksâ [Aksâ Mosque] lies at the southeastern corner of the Holy City. The stones of its foundations (of the outer wall), which were laid by David, are ten ells, or a little less in length. They are chiselled, finely faced, and jointed, and of hardest material. On these the Khalif 'Abd al Malik subsequently built [c.690 CE], using smaller but well-shaped stones, and battlements are added above. This mosque is even more beautiful than that of Damascus, for during the building of it they had for a rival and as a comparison the great church [Church of the Holy Sepulcher] belonging to the Christians at Jerusalem, and they built this to be even more magnificent than that other. But in the days of the Abbasides occurred the earthquakes which threw down most of the main building; all, in fact, except that portion round the Mihrâb. Now when the khalif [Khalif Al Mahdi] of that day obtained news of this, he enquired and learned that the sum at that time in the treasury would in no wise suffice to restore the mosque. So he wrote to the governors of the provinces and to other commanders, that each should undertake the building of a colonnade. The order was carried out, and the edifice rose firmer and more substantial than ever it had been in former times. The more ancient portion remained, even like a beauty spot, in the midst of the new; and it extends as far as the limit of the marble columns, for, beyond, where the columns are of concrete, the later part commences. The main building of the mosque has twenty-six doors. The door opposite to the Mihrâb is called Bâb an Nahâs al A'tham [the Great Brazen Gate]; it is plated with gilded brass and is so heavy that only a man strong of shoulder and of arm can turn it on its hinges. To the right hand of the Great Gate are seven large doors, the mid-most one of which is covered with gilt plates; and after the same manner there are seven doors to the left. And further, on the eastern side are eleven doors, unornamented. Over the first-mentioned doors, fifteen in number, is a colonnade supported on marble pillars, lately erected by 'Abd Allah ibn Tâhir. In the court of the mosque, on the right-hand side, are colonnades supported by marble pillars and pilasters; and on the further side are halls, vaulted in stone. The center part of the main building of the mosque is covered by a mighty roof, high-pitched and gable-wise, behind which rises a magnificent dome. The ceiling everywhere, with the exception of that of the halls on the further side of the court, is formed of lead in sheets, but in these halls the ceilings are faced with mosaics studded in.

The Court [of the Haram Area] is paved in all parts; in its center rises a platform, like that in the mosque at Al Madînah, to which, from all four sides, ascend broad flights of steps. On this platform stand four domes. Of these, the Dome of the Chain, the Dome of the Ascension, and the Dome of the Prophet, are of small size, and their domes are covered with sheet lead and are supported on marble pillars, being without walls. In the center of the platform is the Dome of the Rock, which rises above an octagonal building having four gates, one opposite to each of the flights of steps leading up from the court. These four are, the Kiblah [Southern] Gate, the Gate of Isrâfîl [to the east], the Gate As Sûr [of the Trumpet, to the north],

THE HOLY LAND

and Bâb an Nisâ [the Women's Gate], which last opens towards the west. All these are adorned with gold, and closing each of them is a beautiful door of cedar-wood finely worked in pattern. These last were sent by command of the mother of the Khalif Al Muktadir Billah. At each of the gates is a balustrade of marble and cedar-wood, with brass-work without; and in the railing, likewise, are gates, but these are unornamented. Within the building are three concentric colonnades, with columns of the most beautiful marble, polished, that can be seen, and above is a low vaulting. Within these again is the central hall over The Rock; the hall is circular, not octagonal, and is surrounded by columns of polished marble supporting round arches. Built above these, and rising high into the air, is the drum in which are large openings; and over the drum is the Dome. The Dome, from the floor up to the pinnacle, which rises into the air, is in height a hundred ells, and from afar off, you may perceive on the summit of the Dome, its beautiful pinnacle, the size of which is a fathom and a span. The Dome, externally, is completely covered with brass plates, gilt, while the building itself, its floor and its walls, and the drum, both within and without, are ornamented with marble and mosaics, after the manner that we have already described when speaking of the mosque of Damascus. The cupola of the Dome is built in three sections: the inner is of ornamental plates; next come iron beams interlaced, set in free so that the wind may not cause it to shift; and the third casing is of wood, on which are fixed the outer plates. Up through the middle of the cupola goes a passage way, by which a workman may ascend to the pinnacle for aught that may be wanting, or in order to repair the structure. At the dawn, when the light of the sun first strikes on the cupola and the drum catches the rays, then is this edifice a marvellous sight to behold, and one such that in all Islâm I have never seen its equal; neither have I heard tell of aught built in pagan times that could rival in grace this Dome of the Rock.

The mosque [Aksâ] is entered through thirteen openings closed by a score of gates. These are, the Bâb Hittah [Koran 2.55], the two Gates of the Prophet, the Gates of the Mihrâb Maryam, the two Gates Ar Rahmah, the Gate of the Birkat [or Pool of] Bani Israîl, the Gates Al Asbât, the Hâshimite Gates, the Gate of Al Walîd, the Gate of Ibrahîm [Abraham], the Gate of Umm Khâlid and the Gate Dâûd [of David].

Of the holy places within [the Haram area] are the Mihrâb Maryam (the Oratory of Mary), Zakariyyah (of Zachariah), Ya'kûb (of Jacob), and Al Khidr (of Elias or St. George), the Station of the Prophet and of Jibraîl (Gabriel), the Place of the Ant, and of the Fire, and of the Ka'abah, and also of the Bridge As Sirât, which shall divide heaven and hell.

On the north side [of the court of the Aksâ Mosque?] there are no colonnades. The main building of the mosque does net extend to the eastern wall of the area, the constructions here, as it is said, never having been completed. Of the reason for this, they give two accounts. The one is that the Khalif Omar commanded the people to erect a building "in the Western part of the area, as a place of prayer for Muslims"; so they left this space [which is on the eastern side] unoccupied, in order not to go counter to his injunction. The other reason given is that it was not found possible to extend the main building of the mosque as far as the southeast angle of the area wall, lest the Mihrâb [the niche facing Mecca], in the center place at the end of the mosque should not have been opposite The Rock under the Dome, and such a case was repugnant to them. But Allah alone knows the truth.

The dimensions of the sanctuary area are, length 1,000 ells — of the royal Hâshimite ells — and width, 700. In the ceilings of its various edifices there are 4,000 wooden beams, supported on 700 marble columns; and the roofs are overlaid with 45,000 sheets of lead. The measurement of the Rock itself is, 33 ells by 27, and the cavern that lies beneath will hold 69 persons. Its endowment provides monthly for 100 kists of olive oil, and in the year they use 800,000 ells of matting. The mosque is served by special attendants; their service was instituted by the Khalif 'Abd al Malik, the men being chosen from among the royal fifth of the captives taken in war, and hence they are called Al Akhmâs (the Quintans). None besides these are employed in the service, and they take their watch in turn beside the Rock.

III. Sulwân

Sulwân [Siloe] is a place on the outskirts of the city. Below the village is the 'Ain Sulwân [Pool of Siloe], of fairly good water, which irrigates the large gardens which were given in bequest [Wakf] by the Khalif 'Othmân ibn 'Affân for the poor of the city. Lower down than this, again, is Bîr Ayyûb. It is said that on the Night of 'Arafât the water of the holy well Zamzam, at Makkah, comes underground to the water of the pool. The people hold a festival here on that evening.

IV. Wâdî Jahannam

Wâdî Jahannam runs from the angle of the sanctuary area to its furthest point, all along the east side. In this valley are gardens and vineyards, churches, caverns and chapels, tombs, and other remarkable spots, also cultivated fields. In its midst stands the church which covers the Sepulcher of Mary, and above, overlooking the valley, are many tombs, among which are those of Shaddâd ibn Aus ibn Thâbit and 'Ubâdah ibn as Sâmit.

V. Jabal Zaitâ

Jabal Zaitâ [Mount of Olives] overlooks the Great Mosque from the eastern side of the Valley [of Kedron]. On its summit is a mosque built in memory of 'Omar, who sojourned here some days when he came to receive the capitulation of the Holy City. There is also here a church built on the spot whence Christ ascended into heaven; and further, nearby is the place called As Sâhirah, which, as I have been informed on the authority of Ibn 'Abbâs, will be the scene of the Resurrection. The ground is white, and blood has never been spilt here.

VI. Bait Lahm

Bait Lahm [Bethlehem] is a village about a league away, in the direction of Hebron. Jesus was born here; and there grew up here the palm tree [Koran 19.29], for although in this district palms are never found, this one grew by a miracle. There is also a church [Basilica of the Nativity], the equal of which does not exist anywhere in the country round.

VII. Habrâ

Habrâ [Hebron], the village of Abraham the friend of God. Within it is a strong fortress, which, it is said, is of the building of the Jinns, being of great squared stones. In the middle of this place rises the dome built, since the times of Islâm, of stone, which covers the Sepulcher of Abraham. The Tomb of Isaac lies forward, within the main building of the mosque, while that of Jacob is in the further part. Near by each one of the prophets lies his wife. The garden round has become the mosque-court, and built about it are rest-houses for the pilgrims, which thus adjoin the sanctuary. Thither also has been conducted a small water-channel. All the country round Hebron, for the distance of half a stage, is filled with villages, and vineyards, and grounds bearing grapes and apples, and it is even as though it were all but a single orchard of vines and fruit trees. The district goes by the name of Jabal Nusrah. Its equal for beauty does not exist elsewhere, nor can any fruits be finer. A great part of them are sent away to Egypt and into all the country round. At times, here, apples of good quality will sell at a thousand for the dirham; and the weight of a single apple, occasionally, will attain to the equivalent of a hundred dirhams. In the sanctuary at Hebron is a public guest-house, with a kitchener, a baker, and servants appointed thereto. These present a dish of lentils and olive oil to every poor person who arrives, and it is even set before the rich if perchance they desire to partake of it. Most men erroneously imagine that this dole is of the original guest-house of Abraham, but in truth the funds come from the bequests of Tamim ad Dârî and others. It so being, in my opinion it were, perhaps, better to abstain from receiving these alms (lest the money have been unlawfully obtained). Also there was once an amîr of Khurasân — may Allah have confirmed his dominion — who assigned to this charity 1,000 dirhams yearly; and further, Al 'Âdil, the Shâr, the ruler of Ghurjistân, gave great bequests to this house. At the present day, in all Islâm, I know of no charity or almsgiving that is better regulated than is this one; for those who travel and are hungry may eat here of good food, and thus is the custom of Abraham continued, for he, during his lifetime, rejoiced in the giving of hospitality, and, after his death, Allah — may He be exalted — has allowed of the custom becoming perpetuated; and thus I myself, in my experiences, have been partaker of the hospitality of the Friend of God.

A league distant from Hebron is a small mountain, which overlooks the Lake of Sughar [the Dead Sea] and the site of the Cities of Lot. Here stands a mosque built by Abu Bakr as Sabahî, called Al Masjid Al Yakîn. In this mosque is seen the Bedstead of Abraham, which is now sunk about an ell into the earth. It is related that when Abraham first saw from here, afar off, the Cities of Lot, he stood as one rooted, saying, "Verily I now bear witness, for the word of the Lord is The Truth" [*Al Yakîn*].

The territory of the Holy City is counted as all the country that lies round within a radius of forty miles, including Jerusalem with its dependent villages. For twelve miles the frontier follows the shore [of the Dead Sea] over against Sughar and Maâb; then for five miles it lies through the desert, and into the districts towards the south, even to the country that lies beyond Al Kusaifah and the land that is over against it. On the north the frontier reaches to the limits of Nâblus. This, then, is the Land which Allah — may He be exalted — has called "Blessed" [Koran 21.71]; it is a country where, on the hills are trees, and in the plains, fields that need neither irrigation nor the watering of rivers, even as the Two Men [Caleb and Joshua] reported to Moses the son of 'Amrân, saying, "We came on a land flowing with milk and honey." I myself at times in Jerusalem have seen cheese sell at a sixth of a dirham for the ratl, and sugar at a dirham the ratl; and for that same sum you could obtain either a ratl and a half of olive oil or four ratls of raisins.

VIII. Bait Jibrîl

Bait Jibrîl is a city partly in the hill country, partly in the plain. Its territory has the name of Ad Dârdûm, and there are here marble quarries. The district sends its produce to the capital, which is thus the emporium for the neighbouring country. It is a land of riches and plenty, possessing fine domains. The population, however, is now on the decrease, and impotence has possession of many of its men.

IX. Ghazzah

Ghazzah (Gaza) — A large town lying on the high road into Egypt, on the border of the desert. The city stands not far from the sea. There is here a beautiful mosque; also will be seen the monument of the Khalif Omar; further, this city was the birth place of [the great Traditionist] Ash-Shâfi'î, and possesses the tomb of Hâshim ibn 'Abd Manâf [the great grandfather of the Prophet].

X. Mîmâs

Mîmâs lies on the sea. It is a small fortified town and belongs to Ghazzah.

XI. 'Askalân

'Askalân [Ascalon] is on the sea. A fine city and strongly garrisoned. Fruit is here in plenty, especially that of the sycamore tree, of which all are free to eat. The great mosque stands in the market of the clothes-merchants, and is paved throughout with marble. The city is spacious, opulent, healthy, and well fortified. The silkworms of this place are renowned, its wares are excellent, and life there is pleasant. Also its markets are thronged, and its garrison alert. Only its harbor is unsafe, its waters brackish, and the sandfly called "dalam" is most hurtful.

XII. Yâfah

Yâfah [Caipha], lying on the sea, is but a small town, although the emporium of Palestine and the port of Ar-Ramlah. It is protected by an impregnable fortress, with iron gates; and the sea gates also are of iron. The mosque is pleasant to the eye, and overlooks the sea. The harbor is excellent.

XIII. Arsûf

Arsûf is smaller than Yâfah, but is strongly fortified and populous. There is here a beautiful pulpit, made in the first instance for the mosque of Ar-Ramlah, but, which being found too small, was given to Arsûf.

XIV. Kaisâriyyah

Kaisâriyyah [Caesarea of Palestine]. On the coast of the Greek [or Mediterranean] Sea: there is no city more beautiful, nor any better filled with good things: plenty has its well-spring here, and useful products are on every hand. Its lands are excellent, and its fruits delicious; the town also is famous for its buffalo milk and its white bread. To guard the city there is an impregnable fortress, and without lies the well-populated suburb which the fort protects. The drinking-water of the inhabitants is drawn from wells and cisterns. Its Great Mosque is very beautiful.

XV. Nâbulus

Nâbulus [Neapolis, Sichem] lies among the mountains. It abounds in olive trees, and they even name it the "Little Damascus." The town, situated in the valley, is shut in on either hand by the two mountains [Ebal and Gerizim]. Its marketplace extends from gate to gate, and a second goes to the center of the town. The Great Mosque is in its midst and is very finely paved. The city has through it a stream of running water; its houses are built of stone, and some remarkable mills are to be seen here.

XVI. Arîhâ

Arîhâ (Jericho) — This is the City of the Giants, and therein is the gate of which Allah spake unto the children of Israel [Koran 5.25]. There grows in these parts much indigo and many palms, and the city possesses villages in the Ghaur [of the Jordan], whose fields are watered from the springs. The heat in Jericho is excessive. Snakes and scorpions are numerous, also fleas abound. The serpents called Tariyâkiyyah come from hence, from the flesh of which, used therein, depends the excellence of the Tariyâk [Theriack or Antidote] of Jerusalem. The people are brown-skinned and swarthy. On the other hand, the water of Jericho is held to be the lightest [and best] in all Islâm; bananas are plentiful, also dates and flowers of fragrant odor.

XVII. 'Ammân

'Ammân, lying on the border of the desert, has round it many villages and cornfields. The Balkâ district, of which it is the capital, is rich in grain and flocks; also many streams, the waters of which work the mills. In the city, near the marketplace, stands a fine mosque, the court of which is ornamented with mosaic. We have heard said that it resembles that of Makkah. The Castle of Goliath is on the hill overhanging the city, and therein is the Tomb of Uriah, over which is built a mosque. Here, likewise, is the Circus of Solomon. Living here is cheap, and fruit is plentiful. On the other hand, the people of the place are illiterate, and the roads thither wretched. But the city is even as a harbor of the desert, and a place of refuge for the bedawîn Arab.

XVIII. Ar Rakîm

In the village of Ar Rakîm, which lies about a league distant from 'Ammân and on the border of the desert, is a cavern with two entrances — one large, one small — and they say that he who enters by the larger is unable to leave by the smaller unless he have with him a guide. In the cave are three tombs, concerning which Abu-l Fadl Muhammad ibn Mansûr related to me the following Tradition of the Prophet; and his authority was Abu Bakr ibn Sa'îd, who held it of Al Fadl ibn Hammâd, the same having the authority of Ibn Abi Maryâm, who related it as coming from Ismâ'îl ibn Ibrahîm ibn 'Ukbah, who held it of Nâfi', who said that 'Abd Allah, the son of the Khalif Omar, was wont to relate the story, he himself having heard it from the mouth of the Prophet — the grace of Allah be upon him and His peace! Thus he spoke: "While three men once were walking together heavy rain overtook them and drove them into a cavern of the mountain. And on a sudden there fell, from the mountain above, a rock that blocked up the mouth of the cave, and behold they were shut in. Then one of them called to the others, saying, 'Now, mind ye of such good deeds as ye have done, and call on Allah thereby, beseeching Him, so that for the sake thereof perchance He may cleave this rock before us.' Then one of them cried aloud, saying, 'Allah! of a truth have not I my two parents who are old and feeble, besides my children, of whom I am the sole protector? And when I return to them, I do milk the kine, and give first of the milk to my two parents, even before giving of it to my children. Now on a certain day, after the morning was long past, and I came not to them until it was night, I found my parents slumbering. Then I milked the kine, as was my wont, and I brought of the milk and came and stood near by unto them, but feared awaking them from their sleep; and further, I dared not give of it to the children before the setting of it before them, although the children, in truth, were in distress for want thereof. And thus I remained waiting till the breaking of the dawn. Now, since Thou knowest well how

I did this thing from fear of Thy face, so therefore now cause this rock to cleave before us, that through the same we may perceive the sky.' Then Allah caused a cleft to split in the rock, and through it they perceived the sky. Then the second one cried aloud, and said, 'Allah! was there not the daughter of my uncle, whom I loved passionately, as only man can love? And when I sought to possess her, she would refuse herself to me saying that I should bring her a hundred pieces of gold. Then I made effort and collected those hundred pieces, bringing them to her. But even as I was entering to possess her, she cried aloud, and said, 'O servant of Allah, fear Him! and force me not, except in lawfulness.' So I went from her. And now, verily, as Thou knowest that I did even this from the fear of Thy face, so therefore cleave unto us again a portion of this rock.' And Allah did cleave thereof a further cleft. Then the last man cried aloud, and said, 'Allah! did I not hire a serving man for the customary portion of rice. And when his task was accomplished, he said to me, 'Now give to me my due.' And I gave to him his due; but he would not receive it, and despised it. Then I ceased not to use the same for sowing till, of profit, I became possessed of cattle and of a neat-herd slave. And after long time he came to me and said, 'Fear Allah! and oppress me not; but give to me my due.' And I, answering him, said, 'Go thou, then, to these cattle and their herdsmen and receive them.' Said he again, 'Fear Allah! and mock me not.' And I answered him, 'Verily I mock thee not, and do thou take these cattle and their herdsmen.' And at last he, taking them, went his way. And now, since Thou knowest how I did this thing in fear of Thy face, do Thou cause what of this rock remaineth to be cleft before us.' Then Allah caused the whole of it to become cleft before them."

*

Diary of a Journey through Syria and Palestine by Nâsir-i-Khusrau

INTRODUCTION

Abu Mu'in Nâsir, the son of Khusrau, was born at a village in the neighbourhood of Balkh in the year 1003 CE (394 AH), and claimed to be descended, in the eighth degree, from Imâm Ali ar Rizâ, whose tomb, at the present day is shown in the Shrine at Mash-had.

During the earlier years of his life, Nâsir-i-Khusrau, it would appear, travelled through the northern provinces of India, and visited Multân, possibly in the service of Sultan Mahmûd of Ghaznah, or of his son, Mas'ûd; for he alludes in one of his works to having attended the court of these princes. For a number of years, however, subsequent to these early travels, Nâsir-i-Khusrau stayed at home, and occupied a post of some importance in the administration of Ja'afar, or Jughri Beg — elder brother of the celebrated Tughrul Beg, founder of the Saljûkî dynasty — who was then governor of Khurasân.

From his own confession, Nâsir-i-Khusrau had all his life been somewhat addicted to the pleasures of the wine-cup. One night, however, as he was travelling on a tour of inspection, connected with the affairs of his office, in the provinces lying between Balkh and Marv, there appeared to him in his sleep the vision of a holy personage, who admonished him to repent of his iniquities while there was yet time; and, at his question, indicated the pilgrimage to Mecca as the path most likely to conduce to his spiritual regeneration. This was in the year 1045 CE (437 AH), when Nâsir was aged forty-two. The vision made such an impression on his mind that he started immediately for Marv, made known his desire to set out on the pilgrimage, and after giving in his accounts, obtained his dismissal from the beg's service. A few months later, in the spring of 1046, Nâsir — accompanied by his brother, and attended by a young Indian slave — set out from Marv on his pilgrimage to the Holy Cities.

In the middle of the eleventh century CE, the power of the Fatimite khalifs at Cairo was at its height. Mustansir billah was master of all the land of Egypt, as well as westward along the north African coast, and in Sicily; while his lieutenants governed not only the Hijjâz, with the two Holy Cities of Mecca and Medînah, but also the greater part of Syria and Palestine, with the third Holy City of Jerusalem.

At Baghdad the Abbaside khalif ruled, but the government was entirely in the hands of the Buyide princes, whose authority was recognised throughout Mesopotamia and southern Persia. In Khurasân and the East, the Saljûk power was on the rise. Tughrul Beg had already defeated the sultan of Ghuznî, and was now turning his arms against the Bani Marwân, and other princes who held semi-independent states in the north-western provinces of Persia, and in Upper Mesopotamia.

Such, then, in brief outline, was the condition of things political when our pilgrim set out on his journey west. From Marv, going by the highroad through Sarakhs, he reached Nishâpûr, at that time the seat of Tughrul Beg's government, and after a short stay set forth again, this time in company with the sultan's secretary, who had business in the western provinces of the Saljûk Empire. They passed through Kumis to Damghân, and thence skirting the southern spurs of the great mountain-chain of the Elburz, and with the desert lying on the left hand, came to Ray (Rhages), the ruins of which may yet be seen a few miles south of the modern Tehran. From Ray the route lay still along the mountain skirts to Kasvîn, and thence crossing to Shemirân, the capital of the Tarim province, they went on to the great city of Tabrîz, in Azerbaijân, the ancient Media. Toward the end of September, after spending some three weeks in the capital of Azerbaijân, Nâsir set out again, and, travelling along the southern shore of the Van Lake, reached Bitlis, in Armenia, having experienced some trouble in the mountain passes on account of the heavy falls of snow that had recently occurred. From Bitlis they journeyed on, passing through the pine forests that clothe the mountain-slopes in these parts, and by the last days of November reached Miyâfarikîn, the chief town of the province of Diyâr Bakr. Nine leagues from Miyâfarikîn lay the fortress of Amid, by which our pilgrim went, and thence took the caravan route across the fertile plains of Mesopotamia to Harrân, the chief town of Diyâr Modhar, which was reached in the last days of December, 1046. A day's journey from Harrân brought him to Sarûj, and two days later, in the first days of January, 1047 CE, he crossed the Euphrates to enter the province of Syria.

The account Nâsir-i-Khusrau gives of his travels through Syria and Palestine is translated in full in the following pages. He remained four months in Syria and Palestine, and in the first days of May left Jerusalem for Mecca to be present at the 'Arafât ceremonies. Two months later, however, by the end of the first week of July, he was back again in Jerusalem, and shortly after set out by the land route for Egypt, arriving there in the first week of August, 1047. Nâsir-i-Khusrau's description of Egypt under the Fatimite Khalif Al Mustansir, forms one of the most interesting sections of his work, but space forbids our entering into details. He stayed in Egypt eight months on his first visit, and in the middle of April, 1048, set out from Cairo at the season of the pilgrimage, and going down the Red Sea by boat, landed at Al Jâr, whence, after four days' march, he reached Medînah. Being pressed for time,

The Holy Land

he only halted here a couple of days, and then took the road south to Mecca, where he accomplished the pilgrim rites, and returned with least possible delay to Egypt, since the whole of the Hijjâz was at this time suffering from the scourge of pestilence and famine. Two years later, in April, 1050, he finally left Egypt on his return journey to Persia, and, going up the Nile to Asiût, took the road to Aidhab, where he stayed for three months before crossing the Red Sea to Jiddah. This time he journeyed so leisurely that it was only in September that he once more reached Mecca. His description of this city is detailed and most interesting, and he took part a second time in the pilgrim rites, sojourning there till May, 1051, when he set out across the great desert of Arabia for Lahsa, on the Persian Gulf. He was, however, detained during four months at Falaj, in Yamâmah, and thence, passing hurriedly through Lahsa, went on to Basrah, which was reached in December, 1051. Here Nâsir-i-Khusrau remained a couple of months to repose after the fatigues of his desert journey, and in the latter days of February, 1052, took ship for Mahrubân, off the coast of Fârs. Our pilgrim's route, from the coast up to Isfahân, lay through Errajân and the mountain passes of Western Fârs. Setting out from Maccabeus, in the last days of June, Nâsir-i-Khusrau, despite the heat and the lack of water, took the desert route by Nain, Tabûs, Tûn, and Kain, reaching Sarakhs by the 1st of October, and Marv on the 15th of the same month.

Without stopping more than a couple of days at Marv, Nâsir-i-Khusrau, accompanied by the brother who, it would appear, had kept with him during all the seven long years of his pilgrimage, set out hurriedly for Balkh, for he had heard that his third brother, Khâjih 'Abd ul Jalîl, of whom he had had no news during all these years, was now living there in the service of Jughri Beg, the amîr of Khurasân.

Introduction to Diary by Nâsir-i-Khusrau

"It was Saturday, the 26th day of Jumâdi al Akhir, of the year 444 (that is, the 23rd of October, 1052 CE), that we three brothers found ourselves once again united, and rejoiced in the sight each of the other. Oft had we abandoned all hope, and from manifold dangers experienced had despaired of life. But now we gave thanks to God — be He praised and glorified! — for all that He had brought to pass; and that same day we all once again entered Balkh together."

So ends the account of Nâsir-i-Khusrau's pilgrimage. But little is really known of his subsequent history, and we need not here enter into the discussion of whether or no the erotic and pantheistic poetry that was current under his name was actually written by him, or by some different person bearing somewhat the same name.

The manuscripts used by me for this translation are two, both in the British Museum. Add. 18,418 is a small and beautifully written MS. in a neat Shikastah handwriting, which, however, is not very easy to read on account of the lack of the diacritical points. This MS. was copied in CE 1691 (Ramadan, AH 1102). Or. 1991, the other MS., is only a very meagre epitome of the foregoing, taken from a copy in the library of Nawwâb Ziyâ ad Dîn Khân, of Dehli; it has proved, however, useful for discovering the true reading of some of the proper names. The Persian text of the whole work, with a French translation, was published some years ago by the learned Orientalist, M. Charles Schefer.[1] I make no apology for having used his text (printed from one or two other MSS.) for the emendation of that afforded

---

1. *Sefer Nameh: Relation du Voyage de Nassiri Khosrau*, publié, traduit et annoté par Ch. Schefer, Membre de l'Institut, etc. Paris, 1881. An English translation of our pilgrim's description of Jerusalem was published in vol. vi., N.S., p. 142, of the J. R. A S. For archaeological purposes, however, this translation is almost useless.

by the British Museum copies. The English translation now published is my own, and differs in many important points from his French version. In translating into a Western tongue the description of buildings and places given us by a mediaeval and oriental pilgrim, a knowledge of the language merely does not suffice, and the translator has need, if possible, to be intimately acquainted with the buildings and places described, in order, from his personal recollections, now and again to add (in brackets) the few words of explanation needful to make the ancient description comprehensible. Further, I have thought it well to add such notes as were sufficient to identify the various proper names, and call attention to matters of more particular importance.

A few words may be said, in conclusion, regarding the measures and weights used by the pilgrim in his Diary. The day's march he estimates at so many *Farsakhs*, which is the Greek *Parasang*, and is a distance varying between three and four miles (according to the road and the country), being what a caravan horse will walk in the hour. I have translated *Farsakh* by "league," and as the day's march is always reckoned by hours, this term is sufficiently exact for practical purposes. In his measurements of buildings our Pilgrim makes use of two units of length: namely, *Gez* and *Arsh*. The latter is the equivalent of the Arabic *Dhira'*, the cubit; while the *Gez* is generally reckoned to be longer than the cubit, and is given in the dictionaries as roughly equivalent to the English "yard." A careful comparison of the many passages in which our pilgrim has used these terms has, however, shown me that with him they are synonymous terms, corresponding to a measure of somewhat under two English feet.[2] I have been careful in my translation to

2.   See p. 88, n. 49; p. 102, n. 79; p. 104 n 83.

keep to the word "cubit" for the Persian *Arsh*, while *Gez* is always rendered by our etymologically synonymous word "ell." The only measure of weight used is the *Mann*, which is equivalent to about 3 1/2 lb. avoirdupois, and one hundred of them go to the *Kharwar* or ass-load. The coin in which the pilgrim notes the price of various articles he comes across is the Maghribî, or Fatimite gold Dînâr, struck in Egypt, and current in all the western Muslim lands; its value may be roughly estimated at ten shillings.

In conclusion, I would express my grateful thanks to Col. Sir C. Wilson for the many valuable suggestions he has sent me, with permission to use them in the notes to the present pilgrim. In Appendix C will be found a long note by him on the identification of the Gates of the Haram Area, in conformity with which I have written the notes to my translation.

— Guy Le Strange

Preface

The following book is a modernized version of Guy Le Strange's 1885 edition of Nâsir-i-Khusrau *Diary of a Journey through Syria and Palestine*, published in volume 4 of the Palestine Pilgrims' Text Society series. The present edition follows Le Strange's faithfully with a few modifications and additions.

Diary of a Journey through Syria & Palestine by Nâsir-i-Khusrau

1047 CE

Translated by Guy Le Strange

1. Saturday,[1] the 2nd of Rajab of the year 438 (January 2, 1047 CE), we reached Sarûj, and on the second day, having crossed the Euphrates, came to Manbij. This is the first of the towns of Syria. It was now the month Bahman (January) of the ancient (Persians),[2] and the weather in these lands was extremely pleasant. There are no buildings outside the town of Manbij. Thence we journeyed to the city of Aleppo (Halab). From Miyâfârikîn to Aleppo is a

---

1. According to Dr. Wüstenfeld's Tables, this day fell on a Friday.

2. As a Muslim, our author dates his journal according to the Year of the Flight (with the Arabic months), which is lunar, and, therefore, fails to correspond with the seasons. The ancient Persian year of the Era of Yazdagird was, however, in use among his countrymen. It was solar, consisted of 12 months, of 30 days each (with 5 days intercalary), and began on the 21st of March of each year (Nauruz — New Year's Day), when the sun enters Aries.
The Persian months are :
    1. Farwardîn (corresponding generally with April, but beginning on the 21st of March).
    2. Ardîbihisht (May).
    3. Khûrdâd (June).
    4. Tîr (July).
    5. Murdâd (August).
    6. Shahrîwâr (September).
    7. Mihr (October).
    8. Âbân (November).
    9. Azur (December).
    10. Dai (January).
    11. Bahman (February).
    12. Isfandârmuz (March).
The Era of Yazdagird is dated from the first year of the reign of that king (CE 632), the last of the Sassanians.

hundred leagues (farsakh).

2. Aleppo appears a fine city. It has great walls, whose height I estimate at twenty-five cubits (ârsh); also a strong castle, entirely built on the rock, which I consider to be as large as the castle at Balkh. All the houses and buildings of Aleppo stand close next to one another. This city is the place where they levy the customs (on merchandise passing) between the lands of Syria and Asia Minor, and Diyâr Bakr and Egypt and 'Irâk, and merchants and traders come there from all these lands to Aleppo. The city has four gates, namely, Bâb al Yahûd (the Jews' Gate), Bâb Allah (the Gate of Allah), Bâb al Jinân (the Gate of Paradise), and Bâb Antâkiyah (the Gate of Antioch). The weight used in the bazaars here is the Dhâhirî Ratl (or pound),[3] which contains 480 dirhams weight.

3. Leaving Aleppo, and going south, after twenty leagues you reach Hamâ (Hamath), and then Hims (Emessa), and after that Damascus, which lies fifty leagues from Aleppo. From Aleppo to Antioch is twelve leagues, and to the city of Tarabulus (Tripoli) is a similar distance; and they say that to Kustantiniyyah (Constantinople) is two hundred leagues. We left the city of Aleppo on the 11th of Rajab (January 11), and, after marching three leagues, came to a village called, in particular, Kinnasrîn[4]; and the next

---

3. The Dhâhirî Ratl (from the Greek λιθρα) is the pound weight instituted by the Fatimite Khalif Dhâhir li Izâzi Din Allah, who reigned from 1020 to 1035 CE. Counting the dirham at 47½ English grains, this gives 22,800 grains, or about 3¼ pounds.

4. This is the reading of the Elliot Epitome and the B.M. MS Kinnasrîn was also the name of the whole district. For *Khâssah Kinnasrin*, "Kinnasrîn in particular," M. Schefer's text reads *Jund Kinnasrîn*, i.e., "the province of Kinnasrîn"; but *Jund Kinnasrîn* cannot be the name of the *town*; and the reading of our MS is certainly to be preferred.

day, after six leagues more, reached Sarmin, a town that is without walls.

4. Six leagues further we came to Ma'arrah an Nu'man,[5] which has a stone wall and is a populous town. At the city gate I saw a column of stone on which something was inscribed in a writing other than Arabic. Someone I asked concerning it said it was a talisman against scorpions, and because of it no scorpion could ever come into or remain in the town; and even if one were to be brought in and then set free, it would flee and not remain in the place. The height of this column, according to my estimation, might be ten cubits. The bazaars of Ma'arrah an Nu'man I saw full of traffic. The Friday Mosque is built on a height, in the midst of the town, so that from whatever side you would enter the mosque, you go up by thirteen steps. The arable land belonging to the town is all on the hillside and is of considerable extent.[6] There are here also fig-trees and olives and pistachios and almonds and grapes in plenty. The water for the city is from the rains and also from wells.

There was living here (at this date) a certain person called Abu 'l 'Alâ Ma'arrî, who, though blind, was the chief man of the city. He possessed great wealth and slaves and numerous attendants; it was as though all the inhabitants of the city were of his people. As for himself, he had adopted the way of the ascetics, being clothed in a rug (*gilîmi*), sitting quiet in his house, and taking for his daily bread half a *Mann* (or about one and a half pounds) of barley bread and beyond this eating nothing more. As I

5. So called after Nu'man ibn Bashîr, a Companion of the Prophet, to distinguish it from the other Ma'arrahs.

6. Thus in the B.M. MS M. Schefer's text reads "Their arable land grows wheat." (*Gandum-ast* instead of *Kûh-ast*.) But the above is more likely to be the correct reading, since wheat is in no way peculiar to Ma'arrah, and the town does stand on a height surrounded by hills. (See Baedeker, *Syria and Palestine*, 1876, p. 559.)

heard, the gate of his house is always open, and his lieutenants and servants regulate the affairs of the city, but in all matters refer to him for orders. He refuses his goods to no man, while he remains fasting by day and constant in prayer by night; for he is occupied in no worldly affairs (of his own). This person, too, has attained such renown as a poet and writer that the learned of Syria, Maghrib and Irâk, all agree that in these days no one is his equal, nor can be. He has written a book under the name of *Al Fusûl wa-l Ghâyat* (The Divisions and Conclusions), wherein enigmatical words are employed with such wonderful and eloquent conceits and similitudes that one can understand only a very small part of it, and only when one has perused the work under the author's direction. (So enigmatical and wonderful is this book) that they even malign him by claiming that he has attempted therein to rival the Koran itself. There are continually with him some two hundred people who come from all parts of the world to attend his lectures on poetry and diction; and I heard that he has himself written over 100,000 couplets. A certain person asked him why, since God — may He be praised and magnified! — had endowed him with all this wealth and goods, was it that he gave all to other men and used none for himself. The answer was, "No more than what I must eat, can I take." When I passed through Ma'arrah this Abu 'l 'Ala was still living.[7]

5. Rajab, the 15th of the year 438 (January 15th, 1047), we came from Ma'arrah an Nu'mân to Kafar Tâb[8]; and

---

7. Abu 'l 'Alâ was born in CE 973, and died in 1057. His biography is given in Ibn Khallilîân's *Biographical Dictionary* (translated by De Slane, vol. i., p. 94): and Dr. Rieu, of the British Museum, has published his life and works under the title of *De Abul Alae Poetae Arabici Vita et Carminibus*, etc., Bonnae, 1843.

8. The name is plainly written in the B.M. MS The Elliot Epitome has *Kûmât,* and M. Schefer's text *Kuwaimât,* which he rightly conjectured to be a clerical error for the above-mentioned town.

then on to the city of Hamâ (Hamath), which is a well-populated city on the bank of the river 'Âsi (Orontes). This stream is called the 'Asi (meaning, "the Rebel"), because it flows towards the Greek territory; that is to say, it is a rebel to go from the lands of Islâm to the lands of the Infidel. They have set up numerous waterwheels on its banks.

6. From Hamâ onwards there are two roads: one towards the sea-coast, lying through the western parts of Syria; and one directly south, going to Damascus. We went by the coast-road, and in the mountains saw a spring which, they say, flows with water once a year, when the middle day of the (lunar) month of Sha'abân is past. It continues running for three days, after not a single drop of water more flows until the next year.[9] A great many people visit this place in pilgrimage seeking propitiation whereby to approach God— may He be praised and glorified! — and they have constructed a building and a water-tank here. When we had passed by this place, we came to a plain[10] that was covered everywhere with narcissus flowers in bloom, so that the whole plain appeared white, and we had to ride on from their very profusion, coming at last to a town called 'Arkah. After we had passed 'Arkah two leagues, we came to the shore of the sea, and making our way southward along the coast, after five leagues we reached the city of Tripoli (Tarabulus).

7. From Aleppo to Tripoli is forty leagues, and because of the way we marched, we reached the latter

9. This is the source of the Sabbatical River of antiquity, visited by Titus (Josephus' *Wars*, 7.5.i). It is at the present day called Fawwârah ad Dair, "The Fountain of the Convent," i.e. of Mar Jirjis (St. George), alluded to by our author in the lines following. Josephus asserts that the spring ceases to flow on Saturdays. The Muslims of the present day say Fridays.

10. The Bukai'ah, called in Crusading chronicles La Boquie of Krak des Chevaliers, Kal'at al Husn (and not to be confounded with the Bik'a plain of Coelo-Syria).

THE HOLY LAND

city on Saturday, the 5th of Sha'abân (February 6th). The whole neighborhood of the town is occupied by fields and gardens and trees. Sugar-cane[11] grows here luxuriously, and likewise orange and citron trees[12]; also the banana, the lemon, and the date. They were, at the time of our arrival, extracting the juice of the sugar-cane. The town of Tripoli is so situated that three sides are on the sea, and when the waves beat, sea-water is thrown against the city walls. The fourth side, which faces land, is protected by a mighty ditch, lying east of the wall, in which an iron gate, solidly built, opens. The walls are all of hewn stone, and the battlements and embrasures are similar. Along the battlements are placed balistae

11. The cultivation of the sugar-cane in the West spread from Khuzistân in Persia, and throughout the Middle Ages Shuster (the ancient Susa) was renowned for its manufacture on a large scale. The art of sugar-refining was very extensively practised by the Arabs, and under their rule the growth and manufacture of the cane spread far and wide, from India to Morocco, and was introduced to Europe through the Muslim dominions in Spain and Sicily.

12. The careful researches of Gallesio have proved that India was the country from which the orange spread to Western Asia and eventually to Europe. From remote antiquity the orange was cultivated in Hindustan, and before the close of the ninth century the bitter variety seems to have been well known to the Arabs, who had introduced it into the countries of south-western Asia. The Arab historian, Mas'ûdi, who wrote in the year 943 CE (332 AH), has the following account of the introduction of orange and citron trees. The translation is from vol. ii., p. 438, of M. B. de Meynard's text, published by the Société Asiatique: "The orange-tree *(Shajar an nâranj)* and the tree bearing the round citron *(al utruj al mudawwar)* were brought from India, since the year 300 AH (912 CE), and were first planted in 'Omân. Thence they were carried via Al Basrah into 'Irâk and Syria, whereby they have become very numerous in the houses of the people of Tarsûs and other of the Syrian frontier towns: also in Antioch and in all the Syrian coast towns, with those of Palestine and Egypt, where, but a short time ago, they were unknown. The fruits, however, have lost their original perfume and flavor, as also the fine color they have in India, and this is because of the change from their own peculiar soil, and the climate and the water."

('arrâdah), for they fear the Greeks, who are given to attacking the place in their ships. The city measures a thousand cubits long and wide. Its hostelries are four and five stories high, and there are even some that are six. The private houses and bazaars are well built and so clean that one might take each to be a palace for its splendor. Every kind of meat and fruit and edible thing that ever I saw in all the land of Persia, is available here, and a hundred degrees better in quality. In the midst of the town is the great Friday Mosque, well kept and finely adorned and solidly constructed. In the mosque court is a large dome built over a marble tank in the middle of which is set a brass fountain. In the bazaar, too, they have made a watering-place, where there are five spouts with abundant water for the people to take from; and the overflow, going along the ground, runs into the sea. They say there are twenty thousand men in this city, and the place possesses many adjacent territories and villages. They make here very good paper,[13] like that of Samarkand, only of better quality.

The city of Tripoli belongs to the (Fatimite) sultan of Egypt. The origin, as I was told, is that when, a certain time ago, an army of the infidels from Byzantium came against the city, the Muslims from Egypt came and fought the infidels and put them to flight. The sultan of Egypt has remitted his right to the land-tax *(kharâj)* in the city. There is always a body of the sultan's troops in garrison here with a commander set over them to keep the city safe from the enemy. The city, too, is a place of customs, where all ships that come from the coasts

---

13. This is the *Charta Damascena,* or *bombycina,* of the Middle Ages — *cotton*-paper, which the Arabs had first learnt to make after taking Samarkand in CE 704. Although as early as the tenth century (CE) *bombycinum* was used at Rome, cotton-paper did not come into general use in Europe much before the middle of the thirteenth century, and *linen*-paper was first made in the fourteenth century.

of the Greeks and the Franks, and from Andalusia and the Western lands (called *Maghrib*) have to pay a tithe to the sultan. These sums are employed for the rations of the garrison. The sultan also has his own ships here, which sail to Byzantium and Sicily and the West to carry merchandise. The people of Tripoli are all of the Shî'ah sect. The Shî'ahs in all countries have built for themselves fine mosques. There are in this place houses like Ribâts (which are caravanserais, or watch-stations), only that no one dwells there on guard, and they call them *Mash-hads* (or places of martyrdom). There are no houses outside the city of Tripoli, except two or three of the Mash-hads that are above described.

8. And after this, leaving the city of Tripoli, we journeyed along the seashore, our faces towards the south; and after a league or so I saw a fortress called Kalamûn,[14] within which there is a spring of water. From here we came on to the town of Tarâbarzan,[15] which lies five leagues distant from Tripoli. Once we passed there, we went on to the town of Jubail. This last is a city built in the form of a triangle, one angle lying out to sea and surrounding it are high, well-built walls. All round the town are date-palms and other trees of a warm region. I met a boy there who had in his hand two roses, one red, one white, and both already full-blown, though it was still but the 5th day of the month

14. The B.M. MS has *Bû Kalamûm*.

15. This name, which is very clearly written in identically the same way in all the MSS, is possibly, as M. Schefer suggests, a mistaken reading in the author's note-book for Batrûn (the classical Botrys), which, for position, would agree with the distances given. I should, however, be disposed (considering now all the MSS give Tarâbarzan), perhaps, to consider the name in the MSS as a corruption of Theouprosopon, the Greek name for the promontory (N. of Batrûn), now known as Râs ash Shakkah. Theouprosopon, written in Arabic characters (Tûbarsabûn), might more easily become Tarâbarzan than this last be a corrupt reading for Batrûn, which was a perfectly well-known town.

Isfandârmuz (or March) of the ancient Persians, being in the Persian era (of Yazdagird) the year 415.

9. From Jubail we came on to Bairût. Here I saw an arch of stone so great that the roadway went right through it; and the height of the arch I estimated at fifty ells *(Gez)*.[16] The side walls of the arch are built of white stone, and each block must be over a thousand Manns (or about a ton and a half) in weight. The main building is of unburnt brick, built up a score of ells high. Along the top of the same are set marble columns, each eight[17] ells tall, and so thick that with difficulty could two men with their arms stretched embrace the circumference. Above these columns they have built arcades, both to right and to left, all of stones exactly fitted and constructed without mortar or cement. The great center arch rises up between and towers above the arcades by a height of fifty cubits. The blocks of stone that are used in the construction of these arches, according to my estimate, were each eight cubits high and four cubits across, and by conjecture each must weigh some seven thousand Manns (or about ten tons). Every one of these stones is beautifully fashioned and sculptured after a manner that is rarely accomplished, even in (soft) wood.

Except for this arch no other (ancient) building remains. I inquired in the neighborhood what might have been its purpose, to which the people answered that — as they had heard — this was the Gate of Pharaoh's garden; also that it was extremely ancient. All the plain around this spot is covered with marble columns with their capitals and shafts. These were all of marble and

---

16. This must have been the remains of one of the baths or theatres with which Herod Agrippa embellished Berytus; or, possibly, of the celebrated College.

17. The B.M. MS may read "twenty Gez," but this is doubtless a clerical error.

chiselled, round, square, hexagonal or octagonal; and all in such extremely hard stone that an iron tool can make no impression on it. Now, in all the country round there is apparently no mountain or quarry from which this stone can have been brought. There is also another kind of stone that has an appearance of being artificial,[18] and, like the first stone, this too is not workable with iron. In various parts of Syria there may be seen some five hundred thousand columns or capitals and shafts of columns that no one now knows who made them, or can say for what purpose they were hewn, or from where they were brought.

10. From Bairût we came on to the city of Sidon (Saidâ), also on the seashore. They cultivate here much sugar-cane. The city has a well-built wall of stone and four gates. There is a fine Friday Mosque, very agreeably situated, the whole interior of which is spread with matting in colored designs. The bazaars are so splendidly adorned that, as I first saw them, I imagined the city to be decorated for the arrival of the sultan or in honor of some good news. When I inquired, however, and they said it was customary for their city to be always thus beautifully adorned. The gardens and orchards of the town are such that one might say each was a pleasure garden laid out at the fancy of some king. Kiosks are set therein, and the greater number of the trees are of those that bear fruit.

11. Five leagues from Sidon we came to Tyre (Sûr), a town that rises on the shore of the sea. They have built the city on a rock (that is in the sea), after such a manner that the town-wall, for one hundred yards only, is upon the dry land, and the remainder rises up from out the very

---

18. Referring doubtless to basalt or granite, of which ancient columns are frequently found.

water. The walls are built of hewn stone, their joints being set in bitumen in order to keep the water out. I estimated the area of the town to be a thousand (cubits)[19] square, and its caravanserais are built of five and six stories set one above the other. There are numerous fountains of water; bazaars are very clean; also great is the quantity of wealth exposed. This city of Tyre is, in fact, renowned for wealth and power among all the maritime cities of Syria. The population for the most part are of the Shi'ah sect, but the kâdî (or judge) of the place is a Sunni. He is known as the son of Abu 'Akil and is a good man, also very wealthy. They have erected a Mash-had (a shrine, or place of martyrdom) at the city gate, where one may see great quantities of carpets and hangings and lamps and lanterns of gold and silver. The town itself stands on an eminence. Water is brought thereto from the mountain; and leading up to the town-gate they have built arches (for the aqueduct), along which the water comes into the city. In these mountains is a valley[20] over against this city and running eastward, through which, after eighteen leagues, you come to the city of Damascus.

12. After leaving Tyre, we travelled seven leagues, and came to the township of Acre ('Akkah), which, in official documents, is named Madînat 'Akkah. The city stands on an eminence, the ground sloping, but in part level, for all along this coast they only build towns where there is an elevation, being in terror of an encroachment of the waves of the sea. The Friday Mosque at Acre is in the centre of the town and rises taller than all the other edifices. All its columns are of marble. To the right hand,

---

19. *Arsh* is, I suppose, to be understood. None of the MSS give the measure employed.

20. This must be the valley of the Battâf, along which ran the road from Acre to Damascus.

outside the mosque, and towards the Kiblah (south), is the tomb of the Prophet Sâlih[21] — peace be upon him!

The court of the mosque is partly paved with stone, and the other part is sown with green herbs, for they say it was here that Adam — peace be upon him! — first practised husbandry. I made a measurement of the city: its length is two thousand ells, and its breadth five hundred ells. Its walls are extremely strong, and to the west and south is the sea. On the southern side is what is called the Mînâ (or Port). Now, most of the towns upon this coast have a mînâ, which is constructed for the harbouring of ships. It resembles, so to speak, a stable, the back of which is towards the town with the side-walls stretching out into the sea. Seaward, for a space of about fifty ells, there is no wall, but only chains stretching from one wall's end to the other. When they wish to let a ship come into the Mînâ, they slack the chains until they have sunk beneath the surface of the water sufficiently to let the ship pass over them (into the harbor); then they tighten up the chain again so as to prevent any strange vessel coming in to make an attempt against the ships.[22] Outside the eastern gate and on the left-hand is a spring, to which you descend by twenty-six steps before reaching the water. This they call the 'Ain al Bakar (the Ox Spring), relating how it was Adam — peace be upon him! — who discovered this spring and gave his oxen water there, whence its name of "the Ox Spring."

---

21. According to the Koran (7.71), Sâlih was the prophet sent to convert the tribe of Thamûd. He is variously identified with the Peleg of Gen. 11:16 or the Schelah of 11:13.

22. For a description of the Port of Acre and the method of its construction, see print edition of Mukaddasi, pp. 29–31.

13. When you leave this township of Acre and go eastwards, you come to a mountain region,[23] where there are various places of martyrdom of the prophets — peace be upon them! — and this region lies beside the road to Ramlah. It had always been my intention to visit these holy sepulchres and seek to obtain thereby a blessing before God — may He be exalted and glorified! — and since the people of Acre told me that there were in those parts along the roads disorderly men, who set upon anyone whom they saw to be a stranger in order to rob him of everything that he had, I deposited the money I had with me in the mosque of Acre before setting out from that city by the eastern gate on Saturday[24] the 23rd of Sha'abân, of the year 438 (22nd February, 1047). The first day I went and visited the tomb of 'Akkah,[25] who is the founder of the city of Acre ('Akkah), a very pious and great person. Now, I had no guide with me who knew the road, and I became somewhat bewildered, when suddenly by the mercy of God — may He be exalted and glorified! — on that first day I met a Persian of the province of Azerbaijân, who, already once before having made the visitation to these blessed sepulchres, had now come into those parts a second time with a like intention. In thankfulness for the favor that God — may He be exalted and glorified! — had thus vouchsafed to me, I made a prayer of two prostrations *(rik'ahs)*, beseeching Him in my orisons that He would grant to me grace to fulfil all the pious intentions that I had formed.

23. The mountainous region of Lower Galilee.

24. A Sunday, according to the Tables.

25. M. Schefer's text reads *'Akk*; the two MSS of the B.M. give the name as above.

So proceeding, we came to a village named Birwah,[26] and I made my visitation of the tombs, which are seen there, of 'Ish (Esau) and Sham'ûn (Simeon) — peace be on them both! From Birwah we went on to Dâmûn,[27] where there is a small cavern. Here I also made visitation, for they say it is the sepulchre of Dhu'l Kifl[28] — peace be on him! Thence we passed to another village, called A'bilîn,[29] where there is the tomb of Hûd — peace be upon him! — which I visited. Within the enclosure here is a mulberry tree[30]; and there is likewise the tomb of the prophet 'Uzair[31] — peace be upon him! — which I visited. And from there, going in a southerly[32] direction, we came to a village called Hadhîrah, and opening to the west of this village is a valley. In this valley is a spring of clear water gushing out from a rock, and over against the spring and upon the rock they have built a mosque. In this mosque are two chambers built of stone, with the ceiling likewise of stone. The door is so small that a man can enter only with difficulty. Within there are two tombs placed close side by side, one of which is that of Shu'aib

26. The B.M. MS reads "Barzan" in error.

27. The B.M. MS reads in error *Dâmî* for Dâmûn, which last is found in M. Schefer's text.

28. The prophet, Dhu'l Kifl, according to Muslim tradition, was the son of the patriarch Job.

29. This name in the B.M. MSS is corrupted to Akhir 'Anân.

30. *Khartûl*. M. Schefer reads *Kharnûb* — the carob or St. John's Bread.

31. Ezra or Esdras. Koran 9.30: "Moreover, the Jews say, "Uzair is the Son of God.'" According to Muslim tradition, Ezra was raised to life after he had been a hundred years dead and dictated to the scribes (from memory) the whole Jewish law, which had been lost during the Captivity.

32. The direction is, I think, mistaken, and we should read "eastward."

(Jethro)[33] — peace be upon him! — and the other that of his daughter, who was the wife of Musa (Moses) — on him, too, be peace! The people of the village are assiduous in keeping the mosque and the tombs swept clean and in setting the lamps and other such matters. From this place we went on to a village called Irbil, on the south side of which rises a mountain. On the mountain is an enclosure, which same contains four graves — those of the sons of Ya'kûb (Jacob) — peace be upon him! — who were brothers of Yûsûf (Joseph)[34] — upon him, too, be peace! And going onward I came to a hill and below the hill a cavern in which was the tomb of the mother of Moses — peace be upon him! — and I made my visitation there also.

14. Leaving this place, we came down a valley, at the further end of which were visible the lake and the city of Tabariyyah (Tiberias), upon the shore of the same. The length of the lake (of Tiberias) I would estimate at six leagues, and its breadth may be three. The water of the lake is sweet and of good flavour. The town lies on the western shore. The waters from the hot springs nearby and the drainage water from the houses all flow into the lake, and yet the population of the city and of the places along the shores of the lake nonetheless all drink from these waters. I heard that once upon a time a certain governor of the city gave orders that they should prevent the refuse of the city and the sewerage from draining into the lake. But (after his orders were carried out) the water of the lake itself became fetid, so as to be no longer

33. See Koran 7.83. The tomb of Shu'aib (Jethro) is now shown on the Mountain of Hattîn, so celebrated in tradition as the Mount of the Beatitudes and also in history as the battle-field where the Crusaders were defeated by Saladin.

34. Yakût, in his "Geographical Dictionary" (Text, 1.184), mentions these tombs, and states them to be those of Dan, Issachar, Zebulon, and Gad.

fit for drinking. And when he ordered that the sewers should again be allowed to drain there, the lake water became once more sweet as before. The city has a strong wall, which beginning at the borders of the lake goes all round the town, but on the water side there is no wall. There are numberless buildings erected in the very water, for the bed of the lake in this part is rock, and they have built pleasure-houses that are supported on columns of marble rising up out of the water. The lake is very full of fish. The Friday Mosque is in the midst of the town. At the gate of the mosque is a spring, over which they have built a hot-bath, and the water of this spring is so hot that until it has been mixed with cold water you cannot bear to have it poured over you. They say this hot-bath was built by Solomon, the son of David — peace be upon them both! — and I myself did visit it. There is, too, on the western side of the town of Tiberias a mosque known as the Jasmine Mosque (Masjid-i-Yâsmin). It is a fine building, and in the middle part rises a great platform *(dukkân),* where they have their Mihrâbs (or prayer niches). All round those they have set jasmine shrubs from which the mosque derives its name. In the colonnade, on the eastern side, is the tomb of Yûsha'ibn Nûn (Joshua, the son of Nun), and underneath the great platform mentioned above are the tombs of the Seventy Prophets — peace be upon them! — whom the children of Israel slew. South of Tiberias lies the Dead Sea or Lake of Lût (Lot). The waters of this last lake are salt, although the (fresh) waters of the Lake of Tiberias flow down into it. The cities of Lot were along its borders, but no trace of them remains. A certain person related to me that in the salt waters of this lake there is a black substance that collects together from the foam and is like the form of a bull's (carcass floating). This stuff (which is asphalt) resembles stone, but is not so hard. The people of the country gather it and break it in pieces, sending it to all the cities and countries round. When the lower part of a tree is covered with some of this (asphalt), no worm will ever do the tree a harm. In all these parts they preserve the roots of the trees by this means and thus guard against the damage to the gardens that would arise from worms and things that creep below the soil. The truth, however, of all this rests on the credibility of the word of him who related it to me. They say, too, that the druggists also will buy it, for they hold that a worm, which they call the "Nuktah," attacks their drugs, and that this (asphalt) preserves them from that. In the town of Tiberias they make prayer-mats of reeds, which sell in the place itself for five Maghribî Dînârs (or over £2) a piece. On the west of the city rises a mountain, upon which a castle[35] has been built in hewn stone, and there is there an inscription in Hebrew characters stating that at the time it was cut the Pleiades stood at the head of the zodiacal sign of the Ram. The tomb of Abu Hurairah[36] (the Prophet's companion) lies outside

---

35. These must be the ruins of Herod's Castle, now called "Kasr Bint al Malik" (the Palace of the King's Daughter), lately visited and described by Herr Schumacher in the P.E.F. *Quart. State,* of April, 1887.

36. The celebrated Abu Hurairah, one of the Prophet's companions, died in AH 57 (CE 677), at 'Akik. His body was taken into Madînah and buried in the well-known cemetery of Al Baki' — so say the Arab historians. (Cf. Ibn Khallikan's *Biographical Dictionary,* translated by De Slane, 1:570.) In confirmation of our pilgrim's account that his tomb was in old times shown at a village near Tiberias is "a stone of 'Ajlûn marble," measuring 2 feet 7 inches by 2 feet, lately discovered in this neighborhood by Herr Schumacher. It bears on its face an Arabic inscription to the following effect (see *Quart. State.,* P.E.F., April, 1887, p. 89): "In the name of Allah, the Compassionate, the Merciful, say: He is one God — God the Everlasting! He begetteth not, and He is not begotten, and there is none like unto Him (Koran 112). This is the Tomb of Abu Hurairah, the companion of Allah's apostle; upon whom be Allah's peace and

the city, towards the south, but no one can go and visit it, for the people who live here are of the Shi'ah sect, and as soon as anyone comes to make the visitation, the boys begin a tumult and raise a disturbance about him that ends in stone-throwing, from which some injury results. This was why I did not make my visitation to this place; but turning aside I proceeded on to a village that is called Kafar Kannah. To the south of this village is a hill on the top of which they have built a fine monastery. It has a strong gate, and the tomb of the Prophet Yûnis (Jonas)[37] — peace be upon him! — is within. Nearby the gate of the monastery is a well, and its water is sweet and good. When I had made my visitation at this place, I came on thence to Acre, which is four leagues distant, and remained in that city for a day.

15. And afterwards, leaving Acre, we went on to a village called Haifâ, the road all the way lying over the sands, the sand here being of the kind that the goldsmiths of Persia use in their business and know under the name of "Mekkah sand." This village of Haifâ lies on the seashore, and there are here palm gardens and trees in numbers. There are in this town shipbuilders, who build very large craft. The seagoing ships of this place are known by the name of "Judî." Leaving Haifâ, we proceeded on to a village called Kanîsah

---

His blessing." In the place where this stone was discovered Herr Schumacher noted traces "of an ancient mosque"; unfortunately, however, he does not state anything concerning the appearance and age of the characters used in this interesting epitaph. Yâkût, writing about the year CE 1225, in his great *Geographical Dictionary*, at the end of the article on *Tiberias* (Text 2:512), likewise notes that "on the slope of the hill of Tabariyyah is a tomb which they say is the tomb of Abu Hurairah — Allah accept him! — though his tomb is also (found) at Al Bakî' and at Al 'Akîk (at Madînah)." In his article on (Jabneh or Jabneel) *Yubnâ* (op. cit., 4:1007), Yâkût, however, again notes that in this town also is a tomb said by some to be that of Abu Hurairah.

37. The name of the prophet is omitted in both the B.M. MSS.

[Kunaisah], and beyond this the road leaves the seashore and enters the hills, going east through a stony desert place, which is known as Wâdî Tamasih (or the Valley of Crocodiles). After passing two leagues, however, the road turns back and goes once more along the beach, and in these parts I saw great quantities of the bones of marine monsters set in the earth and clay and become, so to speak, petrified by the action of the waves that beat over them. Passing these, we arrived at the city named Kaisariyyah (Caesarea), which lies seven leagues distant from Acre.

16. Caesarea is a fine city with running waters and palm gardens and orange and citron trees. Its walls are strong, and it has an iron gate. There are fountains that gush out within the city and also a beautiful Friday Mosque, situated so that you may sit in its court and enjoy the view of all that is passing on the sea. There is preserved here a vase made of marble that is like Chinese porcelain, and it is large enough to contain a hundred Manns weight of water (or about thirty-four gallons).

17. On Saturday, the last day of the month of Sha'abân (29th February), we set forth again, travelling over the sand that is the kind mentioned before as "Mekkah sand." After a while we came to a place where I saw many fig trees and olives, for here the road lies all through a country of hills and valleys. After traveling thus for several leagues, we reached a city called Kafar Sâbâ, also Kafar Sallâm.[38] From this city on to Ramlah is just three leagues, and all along the way are trees of the kinds above described.

18. Sunday, the day of the new moon of the month of Ramadan (the 1st of March), we came to Ramlah. From Caesarea to Ramlah is eight leagues. Ramlah is a great city with strong walls of great height and thickness

---

38. Our pilgrim is, of course, mistaken in writing of Kafar Sâbâ and Kafar Sallâm as one and the same place (the MSS all read as in the text).

built of mortared stone and with iron gates opening in. From the town to the seacoast is a distance of three leagues. The inhabitants get their water from the rainfall, and in each house is a tank for storing the rain in order that there is always a supply. In the middle of the Friday Mosque is also a large tank, and from it, when it is filled with water, anyone who wishes may take. The area of the mosque measures two hundred paces *(Gâm)* by three hundred. Over one of its porches *(suffah)* is an inscription stating that on the 15th of Muharram of the year 425 (10th of December, 1033 CE), there came an earthquake[39] of great violence, which threw down a large number of buildings, but that no single person sustained an injury. In the city of Ramlah there is marble in plenty, and most of the buildings and private houses are of this material; and, further, the surface thereof they do most beautiful sculpture and ornament. They cut the marble here with a toothless saw, which is worked with Mekkah sand. They saw the marble in the length, as is the case with wood, to form the columns — not in the cross — also they cut it into slabs. The marbles that I saw here were of all colors, some variegated, some green, red, black and white. There is, too, at Ramlah, a particular kind of fig, and no better exists anywhere, and this they export to all the countries round. This city of Ramlah, throughout Syria and the West, is known under the name of Filastîn.[40]

19. On the 3rd of Ramadan (3rd March) we left Ramlah, and travelled to a village, called Latrûn(?)[41], and

---

39. This earthquake is mentioned by the Arab annalists, who state that a third of Ramlah was thrown down, the mosque in particular being left a mere heap of ruins.

40. Major Fuller begins his translation (*J.R.A.S.*, 6 NS:142) at this point.

41. In M. Schefer's text and the B.M. MSS this name is written Khâtûn, a mistake, doubtless, as the French savant remarks, for

from there on to another village, called Kariat-al-'Anab. By the wayside I noticed, in quantities, plants of rue *(Sadâb)*, which grows here of its own accord on these hills and in the desert places. In the village of Kariat-al-'Anab there is a fine spring of sweet water gushing out from under a stone, and they have placed all around troughs with small buildings contiguous (for the shelter of travellers).

20. From this village we proceeded onward, the road leading upward, and I had imagined that we should come to a mountain, and then going down on the further side that we should arrive at the Holy City. But after we had continued our upward road some way, a great plain opened out in front of us, part of which was stony, and part of it with good soil. And here, as it were, on the summit of the mountain, lay before our view Bait al Mukaddas (the Holy City). From Tripoli, which is by the seashore, to the Holy City is fifty-six leagues, and from Balkh to the Holy City, eight hundred and seventy-six leagues. It was the 5th of Ramadan, of the year 438 (5th March, 1047 CE), that I thus came to the Holy City, and the full space of a solar year had elapsed since I set out from home, having all that time never ceased to travel onward, for in no place had I yet sojourned to enjoy repose. Now, the men of Syria and of the neighboring parts call the Holy City (Bait al Mukaddas) by the name of Kuds (the Holy); and the people of these provinces, if they are unable to make the pilgrimage (to Mekkah), will go up at the appointed season to Jerusalem and there perform their rites and on the feast day slay the sacrifice, as it is customary to do (at Mekkah on the same day). There are years when as many as twenty thousand people will be present at Jerusalem during the first days of the (pilgrimage) month of Dhu-1 Hijjah, for they bring their children also with them in order to celebrate their circumcision.

Latrûn, which is *Castrum boni Latronis,* the village of the penitent thief according to the Crusading chronicles.

THE HOLY LAND

From all the countries of the Greeks, too, and from other lands, the Christians and the Jews come up to Jerusalem in great numbers in order to make their visitation to the Church (of the Resurrection) and the Synagogue that is there; and this great Church (of the Resurrection) at Jerusalem we shall describe further on in its proper place.

The country and villages round the Holy City are situated upon the hillsides; the land is well cultivated, and they grow corn, olives and figs. There are also many kinds of trees here. In all the country around there is no (spring) water for irrigation, and yet the produce is very abundant, and the prices are moderate. Many of the chief men harvest as much as 50,000 Manns weight (or about 16,800 gallons) of olive oil. It is kept in tanks and in pits, and they export it to other countries. It is said that drought never visits the soil of Syria. I heard from a certain person, on whose word I can rely, that the Prophet — peace be upon him, and the benediction of Allah! — was seen in a dream by a saintly man, who addressed him, saying, "O Prophet of God, give me assurance forever of my daily bread"; and the Prophet — peace be upon him! — replied: "Verily it shall be warranted unto thee, even by the bread and oil of Syria."

21. I now purpose to make a description of the Holy City. Jerusalem is a city set on a hill, and there is no water there except what falls in rain. The villages around have springs of water, but the Holy City has no springs. The city is enclosed by strong walls of mortared stone, and there are iron gates. Round about the city there are no trees, for it is all built on the rock. Jerusalem is a very great city, and, at the time of my visit, there were in it twenty thousand men. It has high, well-built and clean bazaars. All the streets are paved with slabs of stone, and wheresoever there was a hill or a height, they have cut it down and made it level so that as soon as the rain falls the whole place is washed clean. There are in the city numerous artificers, and each craft

has a separate bazaar. The mosque lies at the (south) east quarter of the city, whereby the eastern city wall forms also the wall of the mosque (court). When you have passed out of the mosque, there lies before you a great level plain, called the Sâhirah,[42] which, it is said, will be the place of the Resurrection, where all mankind shall be gathered together. For this reason men from all parts of the world come here to make their sojourn in the Holy City till death overtakes them, in order that when the day fixed by God — be He praised and exalted! — shall arrive, they may be ready and present at the appointed place.

O God! in that day do Thou vouchsafe to Thy servants both Thy pardon and Thy protection! Amen. O Lord of both worlds!

22. At the border of this plain (of the Sâhirah) there is a great cemetery, where there are many places of pious renown, where men come to pray and offer up petitions in their need. May God — be He praised and glorified! — vouchsafe unto them their desires. Grant unto us also, O God, our needs, and forgive our sins and our trespasses, and have mercy upon us, O most Merciful of the merciful!

Lying between the mosque and this plain of the Sâhirah is a great and steep valley, and down in this valley, which is like a fosse, are many edifices built after the fashion of ancient days. I saw here a dome cut out in the stone, and it is set upon the summit of a building. Nothing can be more curious than it is, and one asks how it came to be placed in its present position. In the mouths of the common people it goes by the appellation of Pharaoh's House.[43] The valley of which we are speaking is the Wâdî Jahannam.[44] I inquired

42. The B.M. Epitome is the only MS that spells this name right. Other MSS have *Sâmirah*.

43. The building alluded to is the so-called Tomb of Absalom.

44. This Valley of Gehenna is not the Jewish valley of that name, but the Valley of Kedron or Jehoshaphat.

how this name came to be applied to the place, and they told me that in the times of the Khalif Omar — may Allah receive him in grace! — the camp (of the Muslims, who had come up to besiege Jerusalem) was pitched here on the plain called Sâhirah, and that when Omar looked down and saw this valley, he exclaimed, "Verily this is the Valley of Jahannum." The common people state that when you stand at the brink of the valley you may hear the cries of those in Hell, which come up from below. I myself went there to listen, but heard nothing.

23. Going south of the city for half a league and down the gorge, you come to a fountain of water gushing from the rock. They call this the 'Ain Sulwân (the Spring of Siloam). There are all around the spring numerous buildings, and the water flows from there on down to a village, where there are many houses and gardens. It is said that when anyone washes from head to foot in this water he obtains relief from his pains and will even recover from chronic maladies. There are at this spring many buildings richly endowed for charitable purposes; and the Holy City itself possesses an excellent Bîmâristân (or hospital), which is provided for by considerable sums that were given for this purpose. Great numbers of (sick) people are served here with potions and lotions, for there are physicians who receive a fixed stipend and attend at the Bîmâristân.[45]

24. The Friday Mosque (which is the Aksâ) lies on the east side of the city, and (as before noticed) one of the walls of the mosque Area is on the Wâdî Jahannam. When you examine this wall, which is on the Wâdî, from the outside of the mosque, you may see that for the space of a hundred cubits it is built up of huge stones, set without mortar or cement. Inside the mosque Area it is

---

45. The MS of the Epitome breaks off here, leaving out the remainder of the description of Jerusalem.

level all along the summit of this wall. The (Aksâ) mosque occupies the position it does because of the stone of the Sakhrah. This stone of the Sakhrah is what God — be He exalted and glorified! — commanded Moses to institute as the Kiblah (or direction to be faced at prayer). After this command had come down, and Moses had instituted it as the Kiblah, he himself lived but a brief time, for his life was suddenly cut short. Then came the days of Solomon — upon him be peace! — who, seeing that the rock (of the Sakhrah) was the Kiblah point, built a mosque around the rock, whereby the rock stood in the middle of the mosque, which became the oratory of the people. So it remained down to the days of our Prophet Muhammad, the Chosen One — upon him be blessings and peace! — who likewise at first recognized this to be the Kiblah, turning towards it at his prayers; but God— be He exalted and glorified! — afterwards commanded him to institute, as the Kiblah, the House of the Ka'abah (at Mekkah).[46] The description of the rock will be given below in its proper place. Now, it was my desire to obtain the measurements of the (Haram Area around the) mosque, and I said to myself, first I will come exactly to know the place in all its aspects and see the whole of it, and afterwards will I take the measurements. But after passing some time in the Noble Sanctuary and examining it, I came on an inscription upon a stone of an arch in the north wall (of the Haram Area), not far from the Dome of Jacob (Kubbat Ya'kûb)[47] — on whom be peace! In this inscription the length of the Haram Area was set down at seven hundred and four cubits *(arsh)*,

46. In the early days of the Hijrah, when the Prophet had fled to Medinah and for a time had thoughts of abandoning Mekkah and its Ka'abah, he directed his followers to pray facing in the direction of Jerusalem. It was only in Rajab, AH 2, that the Ka'abah was definitely instituted as the Muslim Kiblah.

47. The small building to the south of the present Bâb al 'Atm (plan, C).

and the breadth at four hundred and fifty-five cubits, of the royal measure.[48] The royal ell *(gez-i-malik)* is the same as that which is known in Khurasân as the Gez-i-Shâigân (the King's Ell) and is equivalent to one and a half of the (common) cubits *(ârsh)* or a fraction less.[49] The area of the Noble Sanctuary is paved with stone, the joints being set in lead.

25. (As we have said before) the Haram Area lies in the eastern part of the city, and through the bazaar of this (quarter) you enter the Area by a great and beautiful *(Dargâh* or) gateway, that measures thirty ells in height, by twenty across. This gateway has two wings, in which open halls, and the walls of both gateway and halls are adorned with colored enamels (Mînâ), set in plaster, cut into patterns, so beautiful that the eye becomes dazzled in contemplating them. Over the gateway is an inscription, which is set in the enamels, giving the titles of the Sultan (who is the Fatimite khalif) of Egypt, and when the sun's

48. The identical slab with the inscription mentioned by the pilgrim was discovered by M. Clermont-Ganneau, in 1874, in the north wall of the Area, a little west of the Bâb al 'Atm. Part of the inscription, however, had become damaged. It runs as follows: "In the name of Allah, the Compassionate, the Merciful; the length of the Masjid is seven hundred and four and…ty ells, and its breadth is four hundred and five and fifty ells, the ell being the ell of.…" According to M. Ganneau's view, the space for the Arabic word representing the tens in the enumeration of the length will only allow of the number having been originally "eighty" or "thirty." M. Schefer (on the authority of M. Alric, Chancelier du Consulat de France à Jerusalem) states that the inscription may still be clearly read — "length 750 ells, breadth 455 ells, of the royal ell." All the MSS of our pilgrim agree in the numbers — 704 and 455 — for the length and breadth. The author of the *Muthir al Ghirâm,* who saw the inscription in CE 1351 (and whose text is copied by both Suyûti and Mujir ad Dîn), gives the figures as 784 and 455. For further notices of this inscription see a paper in the *Journal of the Royal Asiatic Society,* April, 1887, p. 270.

49. In this passage *gez* (ell) and *arsh* (cubit) are used as synonymous terms.

rays fall on this it shines so that the sight is bewildered at its splendor. There is also a great dome that crowns this gateway, which is built of squared stones.[50] Closing the gateway are two carefully constructed doors. These are faced with Damascene brass-work, which you would take to be gold, for they are gilt, and ornamented with figured designs. Each of these doors is fifteen ells in height, by eight ells across. The gateway we have just described is called the Bâb Dâûd (the Gate of David; plan, I)[51] — peace be upon him! After passing this gateway (and entering the Haram Area), you have on the right two great colonnades *(riwâk)*,[52] each of which has twenty-nine marble pillars, whose capitals and bases are of colored marbles, and the joints are set in lead. Above the pillars rise arches, that are constructed of masonry, without mortar or cement, and each arch is constructed of no more than five or six blocks of stone. These colonnades lead down to near the Maksûrah (or main building of the Aksâ Mosque).[53] On your left hand (as you enter the Gate of David), and towards the north, there is likewise a long colonnade with sixty-four arches, supported by marble pillars. In this part of the wall there is also a gate called Bâb as Sakar (the Gate of Hell).[54]

50. M. Schefer's text here and in several other places gives *Munhadim* ("destroyed") for *Muhandam* ("squared by the rule"), as the word is correctly written in the margin of the B.M. MSS.

51. This is the gate that is now called *Bâb as Silsilah,* the Gate of the Chain.

52. These colonnades go along the western wall of the Haram Area.

53. The main building of the Aksâ Mosque is often referred to by our pilgrim as the "Maksurâh," which more properly is the name given to the railed oratory for the sultan which the mosque contains.

54. *Bâb as Sakar,* the Gate of Hell, is probably the present Bâb an Nâdhir (plan, E).

The greater length of the Haram Area extends from north to south, but if the space occupied by the Maksârah (or Aksâ Mosque) is deducted, the shape of the court is square with the Kiblah point lying towards the south.

26. In the north part (of the Haram Area) is a double gateway, the gates of which are side by side, each seven ells across by twelve high. This gateway is called the Bâb al Asbât (the Gate of the Tribes). When you have passed this gateway, there is still another great gateway in the breadth of the Haram Area (which is the north wall) in the portion running eastward.[55] There are here three gates side by side, of a like size to the Bâb al Asbât, and they are each fashioned in iron and adorned with brass, than which nothing can be finer. These (three) gates they call the Bâb al Abwâb (the Gate of Gates), for the reason that, whereas elsewhere the gateways are only double, there is here a triple gateway. Running along the north part of the Haram Area and between the two gateways just mentioned is a colonnade with arches that rest on solid pillars, and adjacent to it is a dome that is supported by tall columns and adorned with lamps and lanterns. This is called Kubbat Ya'kûb (the Dome of Jacob)[56] — peace be upon him! — for at this spot was his place of prayer. And further, along the breadth (or northern wall) of the Haram Area is a colonnade, in the wall of which is a gate that leads to two cloisters *(daryûzah)* belonging to the Sûfîs who have their place of prayer here and have built a fine Mihrâb

---

55. From our pilgrim's description (and the texts of all the MSS agree in this passage), the gateway he calls "the Gate of the Tribes," would be now known as Bâb Hittah (plan, B); while the present Gate of the Tribes at the NW angle (plan, A) is named by him "the Gate of Gates." See Appendix C.

56. This building still exists close to the south of the Bâb al 'Atm (plan, C), which last must be the gate mentioned by our pilgrim as leading to the cloisters of the Sufis.

(or oratory). There are always in residence a number of Sûfîs, who make this (oratory) the place of their daily devotions, except on Friday, when they go into the Noble Sanctuary in order to attend the service of prayer. At the north (west?) angle *(rukn)* of the Haram Area is a fine colonnade, with a large and beautiful dome. On this dome there is an inscription stating that this was the oratory (Mihrâb) of Zakariyyâ,[57] the prophet — peace be upon him! — for they say that he used to continue ceaselessly in prayer at this spot. In the eastern wall of the Haram Area there is a great gateway [the Golden Gate, (plan, N and O)] skillfully built of squared stones, so that one might almost say the whole was carved out of a single block. Its height is fifty ells, and its width thirty, and it is sculptured and ornamented throughout. There are ten beautiful doors *(dar)* in this gateway (set so close) that between any two of them there is not the space of a foot. These doors are all most skillfully wrought in iron and Damascene brass-work set in with bolts and rings. They say this gateway was constructed by Solomon, the son of David — peace be upon him! — to please his father. When you enter this gateway facing east, there are on your right-hand two great doors. One of them is called Bâb ar Rahmah (the Gate of Mercy), and the other Bâb at Taubah (the Gate of Repentance); and they say of this last that it is the gate where God — be He exalted and glorified! — accepted the repentance of David — upon whom be peace! Near this gateway is a beautiful mosque.[58] In former times it was only a

---

57. Zachariah's Mihrâb is at present shown at a niche in the eastern wall of the Aksâ Mosque (plan, l). It is impossible to identify the place mentioned in the text with any building standing.

58. This I understand to refer to a building occupying the position of what is now known as Kursî Sulaimân, the Throne of Solomon (plan, V).

hall *(dahlîz)*, but they turned the hall into a mosque. It is spread with all manner of beautiful carpets, and there are servants especially appointed to it. This spot is greatly frequented by the people, who go to pray there and seek communion with God — be He exalted and glorified! — for this is the place where David — peace be upon him! — was vouchsafed repentance, other men may hope to be turned likewise from their sinfulness. They relate that David — peace be upon him! — as he crossed the threshold to enter this building, had, through divine revelation, the joyful news that God — glory and praise be to Him! — accepted of his repentance; and thereupon David halted at this spot and worshipped. And I, Nâsir, also stationed myself to pray here and besought of God — be He praised and glorified! — to give me grace to serve Him and repent of my sins.

May God — be He exalted and glorified! — grant grace to all His servants whom He hath received in favor; and for the sake of Muhammad and his family, the Pure Ones, vouchsafe to all repentance of their sins!

27. Adjacent to the east wall, and when you have reached the south (eastern) angle (of the Haram Area) — the Kiblah point lying before you, south, but somewhat aside — there is an underground mosque, to which you descend by many steps.[59] It is situated immediately to the north of the (south) wall of the Haram Area, covering a space measuring twenty ells by fifteen, and it has a roof of stone, supported on marble columns. Here was the Cradle of Jesus. The cradle is of stone and large enough for a man to make his prayer prostrations in it. I myself

---

59. These substructures at the SE angle of the Noble Sanctuary are on the foundations of what appears to have been an old corner tower and lie adjacent to what were known to the Crusaders under the name of Solomon's Stables. At the present day they are still shown as the "Cradle of Jesus" (plan, p).

said my prayers there. The cradle is fixed into the ground so that it cannot be moved. This cradle is where Jesus was laid during his childhood and where He held converse with the people. The cradle itself, in this mosque, has been made the Mihrâb (or oratory); and there is likewise, on the east side of this mosque, the Mihrâb Maryam (or Oratory of Mary); and another Mihrâb, which is that of Zakariyyiâ (Zachariah) — peace be upon him! Above these Mihrâbs are written the verses revealed in the Koran that relate respectively to Zachariah and to Mary. They say that Jesus — peace be upon Him! — was born in the place where this mosque stands. On the shaft of one of the columns there is impressed a mark as though a person had gripped the stone with two fingers; and they say that Mary, when taken in the pangs of labor, seized the stone with one hand. This mosque is known by the title of Mahd 'Isâ (the Cradle of Jesus) — peace be upon Him! — and they have suspended a great number of lamps there of silver and of brass that are lighted every night.

28. After passing the entrance to this mosque, near the (southeast) angle of the east wall (of the Haram Area), you come to a great and beautiful mosque, which is other than that called the Cradle of Jesus and is of many times its size. This is called the Masjid al Aksâ (or the Further Mosque), and it is that to which Allah— be He exalted and glorified!— brought His chosen (Apostle) in the night journey from Mekkah, and from here caused him to ascend up into Heaven, as it is referred to in the words of the Koran, "I declare the glory of Him who transported His servant by night from the Masjid al Haram (the Sacred Temple at Mekkah) to the Masjid al Aksâ (the temple that is more remote at Jerusalem]."[60] On this spot they have built with utmost skill a mosque. Its floor is spread with

---

60. Koran 17.1.

beautiful carpets, and special servants are appointed for its service, to serve there continually.

29. From the (southeast) angle and along the south wall (of the Haram Area) for the space of two hundred ells, there is no building, and this is (part of) the court (of the Haram Area). The main building (of the Aksâ Mosque)[61] is very large and contains the Maksûrah (or space railed off for the officials), which is built against the south wall (of the Haram Area). The length of the western side of the main building (of the Aksâ) measures four hundred and twenty cubits, and the width of it is one hundred and fifty cubits.[62] The Aksâ Mosque has two hundred and eighty marble columns supporting arches that are fashioned of stone, and both the shafts and the capitals of the columns are sculptured. All joints are riveted with lead, so that nothing can be more firm. Between the columns measures six ells, and the mosque is everywhere flagged with colored marble with the joints likewise riveted in lead. The Maksûrah is facing the center of the south wall (of the Mosque and Haram Area) and is of such a size as

---

61. The Persian word, Pûshish, "covered part," corresponds with the Arabic term, *Mughatta*, which has the same signification. The covered part of a mosque is the main building over the great Mihrâb and the pulpit, in front of which public worship is performed, and is so-called to distinguish this part from the mosque court with its minor chapels and colonnades, all of which, however, are considered to form a necessary part of the mosque (Masjid) and to be included under the general term.

62. These are the figures in the B.M. MS, which are also those of M. Schefer's translation. His text, however, runs as follows, and differs both from his translation and the text of the B.M. MS: "The main building of the (Aksâ) mosque is very large. Its length is four hundred and *eight* cubits, and the Maksûrah lies to the right hand against the south wall. The western side of the main building measures four hundred and fifty cubits in the width." The figures, however, in both versions are much in excess of the true measurements. (See Appendix A.)

to contain sixteen columns. Above rises a mighty dome[63] that is ornamented with enamel work after the fashion seen in other parts of the Noble Sanctuary. In this place there is spread Maghribî matting, and there are lamps and lanterns, each suspended by its separate chain.

The great Mihrâb (or prayer niche towards Mekkah) is adorned with enamel work,[64] and on either side the Mihrâb are two columns of marble of the color of red carnelian. The whole of the low wall round the Maksûrah is built of colored marble. To the right (of the Great Mihrâb) is the Mihrâb of (the Khalif) Mu'âwiyah, and to the left is the Mihrâb of (the Khalif) Omar — may Allah grant him acceptance! The roof of the (Aksâ) Mosque is constructed of beautifully sculptured wood. Outside the doors and walls of the Maksârah and in the parts lying towards the court (of the Haram Area) are fifteen gateways *(dargâh)*, each of which is closed by a finely wrought door measuring ten ells in height by six ells in the breadth. Ten of these doorways open in the (east) wall (of the mosque), which is four hundred and twenty cubits in length, and there are five in the width (or north wall) of the mosque, that measures one hundred and fifty cubits.[65] Among these gates there is one of brass, most finely wrought and beautiful, so that one would say it was of gold set in with

---

63. In 425 AH (1033), the dome of the Aksâ Mosque was seriously damaged by a shock of earthquake. It was restored next year by order of the Fatimite khalif of Egypt, Ad Dhâhir, the work, according to the extant inscription in the Dome, having been terminated in the month Dhû l Ka'adah, 426 AH (September 1035), that is, less than eleven years prior to our pilgrim's visit.

64. The present Mihrâb only dates from the time of Saladin, who restored the whole of the Aksâ Mosque after retaking the Holy City from the Crusaders.

65. The fifteen gates are mentioned by Mukaddasi, who, however, states that these were *all* on the north side of the mosque, adding that eleven others opened on the east side. (See Appendix A.)

fired-silver (niello?) and chased.[66] The name of the Khalif Al Mamûn is upon it,[67] and they relate that Al Mamûn sent it from Baghdâd. When all these gates of the mosque are set open the interior of the building is light, as though it were a court open to the sky. When there is wind and rain they close these gates, and then the light comes from the windows.

Along all the four sides of the main building (of the Aksâ Mosque) are chests *(sandûk)* that belong each to one of the various cities of Syria and 'Irâk, and near these the Mujâwirân (or pilgrims who are residing for a time in the Holy City) take their seat, even as is done in the Haram Mosque at Mekkah — may Allah, be He glorified! ennoble the same.

Beyond the main building (of the Aksâ), along the great (south) wall (of the Haram Area) mentioned above, rises a colonnade of forty-two arches, the columns being all of colored marble. This colonnade joins the one that is along the west (wall of the Area).[68] Inside the main building (of the Aksâ) there is a tank in the ground which, when the cover is set on, lies level with the floor, and its use is for the rain water, which, as it comes down, drains there. In the south wall (of the Haram Area) is a gate leading to the places for the ablution, where there is running water.[69]

66. This is "the Great Brazen Gate," mentioned by Mukaddasi.

67. M. Schefer is, I believe, incorrect when he states in a note to his translation (p. 81, note 2), that this inscription of Al Mamûn is extant. It is certainly not reproduced by M. de Vogüé in his work on *Le Temple de Jerusalem* (p. 85), which is the reference given by M. Schefer, and I can find no mention of it elsewhere.

68. See above. This is in the place afterwards occupied by the hall erected by the Knights Templars for their armory and which at the present opens from the Aksâ Mosque and is called Baka'at al Baidha, or Aksâ al Kadîmah (plan, U).

69. This gate did not appear to exist in 1888. The Bâb al Mutawadda (the Gate of the Place of Ablution) then opened on

When a person has need to make the ablution (before prayer), he goes down to this place and accomplishes what is prescribed; for had the place (of ablution) been set outside the walls, by reason of the great size of the Haram Area, no one could have returned in time, before the appointed hour for prayer had gone by.

30. The roofs of all the buildings in the Haram Area are covered with lead. Below ground-level are numerous tanks and water-cisterns hewn out of the rock, for the Noble Sanctuary rests everywhere on a foundation of live rock. There are so many of these cisterns that, however much rain falls, no water flows away to waste, but is all caught in the tanks, from which the people come to draw it. They have constructed leaden conduits for carrying the water down, and the rock cisterns lie below these, with covered passages inside leading down, through which the conduits pass to the tanks, whereby any loss of water is saved, and impurities are kept out. At a distance of three leagues from the Holy City I saw a great water-tank, into which pour all the streams that flow down from the hills.[70] From there they have brought an aqueduct that comes out into the Noble Sanctuary. Of all the parts of the Holy City this is where water is most plentiful. But in every house, also, there is a cistern for collecting the rain water, for other than this water there is none, and each must store the rain that falls upon his roof. The water used in the hot

---

the west side of the Haram Area (plan, H) and had nothing to do with the one mentioned here, which Le Strange takes to have been in the souterains of the Aksâ. The Ablution-place was just within the northern entrance to the Double Passage close to the Well of the Leaf. There were still the remains of water-pipes here and of chambers. Ibn Batûtah, in CE 1326, states that, "in the south wall (of the Haram Area) is a single gate, that by which the Imâm enters." (Edition by B. de Meynard, 1:121). (See also below.)

70. Solomon's Pools in Wâdî Urtas.

baths and other places is solely from the storage of the rains.

The tanks that are below the Haram Area never need to be repaired, for they are cut in the live rock. Any place where there may have been originally a fissure or a leakage, has been so solidly built up that the tanks never fall out of order. It is said that these cisterns were constructed by Solomon — peace be upon him! Their roofing is like that of a baker's oven *(tannûr)*. Each opening is covered with a stone, as at a well-mouth, in order that nothing may fall down there. The water of the Holy City is sweeter than the water of any other place and purer; and even when no rain falls for two or three days the conduits still run with water, for though the sky is clear and there is no trace (of cloud), the dew causes drops to fall.[71]

31. As I have written above, the Holy City stands on the summit of a hill, and its site is not on level ground. The place, however, where the Noble Sanctuary stands is flat and level; but outside the Area the enclosing wall varies in height in different places, because where the fall is abrupt, the Haram wall is the highest, for the foundation of the wall lies at the bottom of the declivity; and where the ground mounts, the wall, on the other hand, has been built less high.

Wherever, in the city itself and in the suburbs, the level is below that in the Haram Area, they have made gateways, like tunnels *(nakab),* cut through, that lead up into the court (of the Noble Sanctuary). One of these is called Bâb an Nabî (or the Gate of the Prophet) — peace and blessing be upon him! — which opens towards the Kiblah point, that is towards the south.[72]

---

71. Mukaddasi (print ed., p. 84) remarks on the plentiful dew-fall in Palestine and says that "every night when the south wind blows, the gutters of the Aksâ Mosque are set running."

72. From its orientation south, this gate cannot be the present

DIARY OF JOURNEY BY NÂSIR-I-KHUSRAU

(The passage-way of this gate) is ten ells broad, and the height varies by reason of the steps; in one place it is five ells high, and in others the roof of the passage-way is twenty ells above you. Over this passage-way has been erected the main building of the (Aksâ) Mosque, for the masonry is so solidly laid that they have been able to raise the enormous building that is seen here without any damage arising to what is below. They have made use of stones of such a size that the mind cannot conceive how by human power they were carried up and set in place. It is said, however, that the building was accomplished by Solomon, the son of David — peace be upon him! The Prophet — peace and blessing be upon him! — on the night of his Ascent into Heaven *(Mi'râj)*, passed into the Noble Sanctuary through this passage-way, for the gateway opens on the road from Mekkah. Near it, in the wall, is seen the imprint on the stone of a great shield. It is said to be that of Hamzah ibn 'Abd al Mutallib, the Prophet's uncle — peace be upon him! — who once seated himself here with his shield on his back, and leaning against the wall, left its mark there. This gateway of the Haram leading into the tunnelled passage-way is closed by a double-leafed door, and the wall of the Haram Area outside it is a height of near upon fifty ells. The reason for the piercing of this gateway was to enable the inhabitants of the suburb lying obliquely beyond to enter the Haram Area at their pleasure without having to pass through other quarters of the city. To the right of this gateway in the wall there

---

Gate of the Prophet, otherwise called Bâb al Maghâribah, or of the Moghrebins, which opens west, at the south extremity of the west wall (plan, K). Nâsir's Gate of the Prophet most probably opened at the place in the south wall originally occupied by either the Double Gate or the Triple Gate, both of which were closed in the nineteenth century. (See Appendix C.)

is a block of stone eleven[73] cubits high and four cubits across, and this is larger than any other of the stones of the wall, although there are many others that measure four and five ells across set in the masonry at a height of thirty and forty ells.

32. In the width of the Haram Area there is a gate opening towards the east called Bâb al 'Ain[74] (or the Gate of the Spring). Passing out from it you descend a declivity to the Spring of Silwân (Siloam). There is also another gate (the passage-way which) is excavated in the ground, and it is called Bâb al Hittah (the Gate of Remission).[75] They say that this is the gate by which God — be He exalted and glorified! — commanded the Children of Israel to enter the Noble Sanctuary, according to His word — be He exalted! — (in the Koran 2.55): "Enter ye the gate with prostrations, and say (Hittah), 'Remission!' and We will pardon you your sins and give an increase to the doers of good."

33. There is still another gate (to the Haram Area), and it is called Bâb as Sakînah (the Gate of the Shechînah, or Divine Presence),[76] and in the hall *(dahlîz)* adjacent to it is a mosque that has many Mihrâbs (or prayer niches). The door at the entrance is barred, so that no one can pass

---

73. M. Schefer's text reads "fifteen." Referring apparently to the stones in the Great Course.

74. The width *(pahnâ)* would seem to imply the south wall of the area, and in this case the walled-up Single Gate is probably the one referred to. But if the Bâb al 'Ain was in the east wall it must then be identified with the gate sometimes called Bâb al Janâiz (the Gate of the Funerals), long since walled up (plan, P).

75. The present Bâb an Nabî (plan, K).

76. The Gate of the Shechînah (according to Suyûti) stood close beside the Bâb as Silsilah, the Gate of the Chain (plan, I), and both gate-ways opened apparently into the same street. The present Bâb as Salâm.

through. They say that the Ark of the Shechînah, which God — be He exalted and glorified! — has alluded to in the Koran, was once placed here, but was borne away by angels. The whole number of gates, both upper and lower, in the Noble Sanctuary of the Holy City, is nine, and we have here above described them.[77]

34. In the middle of the court of the Haram Area is the platform (*dukkàn*; plan), and set in the midst of it is the Sakhrah (or Rock; plan, b), which before the revelation of Islâm was the Kiblah (or point turned to in prayer). The platform was constructed because the Rock, being high, could not be brought within the compass of the main building (of the Aksâ Mosque). Therefore the foundations of this platform were laid, measuring three hundred and thirty cubits by three hundred,[78] and the height was twelve ells. The surface of the same is level and beautifully paved with slabs of marble with similar walls, all the joints being riveted with lead. Along the edge of its four sides are parapets of marble blocks that fence it round, so that, except by the openings left for that purpose, you cannot come in. From up on the platform you command a view over the roofs of the (Aksâ) Mosque. There is an underground tank in the midst of the platform, where all the rain-water that falls on the platform itself is collected by means of conduits; and the water of this tank is sweeter

---

77. Ten gates in all have been mentioned, viz.: 1. Al Hittah; 2. An Nabî; 3. Al 'Ain; 4. Ar Rahmah and At Taubah; 5. Bâb al Abwâb; 6. Al Asbât; 7. To Sûfî Cloisters; 8. As Sakar; 9. Dâûd; 10. As Sakînah. (See further Appendix C.)

78. The dimensions of the width (300 cubits) are omitted in the B.M. MS, and are inserted from M. Schefer's text. The platform at the present day measures roughly: north side, 530 feet; south side, 435 feet; east side, 550 feet; west side, 560 feet. Three hundred and thirty cubits for the length north to south gives 660 feet, and three hundred cubits (?) for the breadth east and west gives 600 feet, which, if exact, would show that in our pilgrim's days the platform was larger than it was in the late nineteenth century.

and purer than the water of any of the other tanks in the Haram Area.

35. On the platform rise four domes. The largest of them is the Kubbat as Sakhrah (the Dome of the Rock), and this Rock was the old Kiblah. This dome is situated so that it stands in the middle of the platform, which itself occupies the middle of the Haram Area. The edifice is built in the form of a regular octagon, and each of its eight sides measures three-and-thirty cubits.[79] There are four gates facing the four cardinal points, namely, east, west, north, and south; and between each of these is one of the oblique sides of the octagon. The walls are everywhere constructed of squared stones and are twenty cubits (in height). The Rock itself measures a hundred ells round. It has no regular form, being neither square nor circular but is shapeless, like a boulder from the mountains. Beyond the four sides of the Rock rise four piers of masonry that equal in height the walls of the (octagonal) building, and between every two piers, on the four sides, stand a pair of marble pillars, which are like the height of the piers. Resting on these twelve piers and pillars is the structure of the dome, under which lies the Rock; and the circumference of the dome is one hundred and twenty cubits.[80] Between the walls of the (octagonal) building and the circle of piers and pillars — and by the term "pier" *(sutûn)* I understand a support that is built up, and is square; while the term "pillar" *(ustuwânah)* denotes a support that is cut from a single block of stone,

---

79. Each of the sides of the octagonal building measures rather over sixty-six feet, giving roughly two feet for the size of the cubit.

80. From the very exact plans in M. de Vogüé's *Jerusalem*, the full diameter of the drum of the Dome is twenty-three metres or seventy-five and a half feet. This gives a circumference of two hundred and thirty-seven feet, which agrees very well with the hundred and twenty cubits (two hundred and forty feet) of the text.

and is round — between this inner circle of supports, then, and the outer walls of the edifice, are built eight[81] other piers of squared stones, and between every two of them are placed, equidistant, three columns in colored marble. Thus, while in the inner circle between every two piers there are two columns, there are here (in the outer circle) between every two piers, three columns.[82] On the capital of each pier are set four volutes *(shâkh)*, from each of which springs an arch; and on the capital of each column are set two volutes; so that at every column is the spring of two arches, while at every pier is the spring of four.

The great Dome, which rises above the twelve piers standing round the Rock, can be seen from the distance of a league away, rising like the summit of a mountain. From the base of the Dome to its pinnacle measures thirty cubits, and this rises above the (octagonal) walls that are twenty ells high — for the Dome is supported on the pillars that are similar in height to the outer walls — and the whole building rises on a platform that itself is twelve ells high, so that from the level of the Court of the Noble Sanctuary to the summit of the

---

81. The B.M. MS and M. Schefer's text both give "six" as the number of piers in the outer circle, but this neither corresponds with what follows some lines below (where the total number of the piers in outer and inner circles is stated to be twelve, *i.e.,* four plus eight), nor with the actual condition of the Dome of the Rock, which apparently never had more than four piers in the inner, and eight in the outer circle.

82. Thus in all MSS, but possibly our pilgrim has made a mistake. To agree with the present arrangement of piers and columns he should have said: "Between each of the four piers of the inner circle are three columns, and between each of the eight outer piers are two columns," *i.e.* (4 + 8) twelve piers, and (4 x 3 plus 8 x 2) twenty-eight columns. See however, Al 'Ya'kûbî's description (circa 874 CE), as given in the *Quart. State.* for April, 1887 (p. 95), who says there are twelve piers and thirty columns.

Dome measures a total of sixty-two ells.[83] The roofing and the ceiling of this edifice are in woodwork that is set above the piers and the pillars and the walls after a fashion not to be seen elsewhere. The Rock itself rises out of the floor to the height of a man, and a balustrade of marble goes around it in order that no one can lay his hand on it. The Rock inclines on the side that is towards the Kiblah (or south), and it appears as though a person walked heavily on the stone when it was soft like clay, whereby the imprint of his toes had remained there. There are on the rock seven such footprints, and I heard it stated that Abraham — peace be upon him! — was once here with Isaac — upon him be peace! — when he was a boy, and that he walked over this place, and that the footprints were his.

In the house of the Dome of the Rock men are always congregated, pilgrims and worshippers. The place is laid with fine carpets of silk and other materials. In the middle of the Dome and over the Rock, there hangs from a silver chain a silver lamp, and there are in other parts of the building great numbers of silver lamps on each of which is inscribed its weight. These lamps are all the gift of the (Fatimite khalif, who is) sultan of Egypt, and according to the calculation I made, there must be here silver utensils of various kinds weighing a thousand Manns (or about a ton and a half). I saw there a huge wax taper that was seven cubits high and three spans *(shibr)* in diameter. It was (white) like the camphor of

---

83. I note this as the principal passage for proving that Nâsir-i-Khusrau uses the terms *gez* (ell) and *arsh* (cubit) synonymously. On a previous page he has said that the platform is twelve *arsh* high; here he says it measures twelve *gez*, and this added to twenty *gez* (walls) and to thirty *arsh* (dome) makes sixty-two *gez*. The height of the Dome of the Rock, measuring from floor to the summit of the Dome, is roughly one hundred and twelve feet. Our pilgrim estimates it (deducting the height of the platform) at fifty ells or cubits, *i.e.*, one hundred feet.

Zibâj,[84] and (the wax) was mixed with ambergris. They told me that the sultan of Egypt sent hither every year a great number of tapers, and among the rest, the large one just described, on which the name of the sultan was written in golden letters.

The Noble Sanctuary is the third of the Houses of God — be He exalted and glorified! — and the doctors of religion concur in saying that a single prayer offered up here in this Holy City is granted the effect of twenty-five thousand prayers said elsewhere; just as in Medinah, the City of the Prophet — peace and benediction be upon him! — every single prayer may count for fifty thousand, while each that is said in Mekkah, the Venerable — God, be He exalted, ennoble the City! — will pass for a hundred thousand. And God — be He exalted and glorified! — give grace to all His servants, that they may one day acquit themselves of such prayers!

As I have said before, all the roof and the exterior parts of the Dome of the Rock are covered with lead, and at each of the four sides of the edifice is set a great gate with double folding-doors of sâj-wood (or teak). These doors are always kept closed. Besides the Dome of the Rock there is (on the platform) the dome called Kubbat as Silsilah (or the Dome of the Chain; plan, c). The chain is that which David — peace be upon him! — hung up, and it was so that none who lied could grasp it, the unjust and the wicked man could not lay a hand on it, which is a certified fact and well known to the learned. This Dome is supported on eight marble columns and six stone piers,[85] and on all sides it is open, except on

---

84. Zibâj or Zâbij — according to the author of the *Marâsid al Ittilâ* — is the name of the country in the further parts of India, on the frontiers of China, i.e., Cochin China..

85. The present Dome of the Chain had six columns in the inner circle supporting the cupola and eleven columns in the outer circle (counting the two built in on either side the prayer niche).

the side towards the Kiblah point, which is built up and forms a beautiful Mihrâb.

36. And again, on the platform, is another Dome, that surmounts four marble columns. This, too, on the Kiblah side, is walled in, forming a fine Mihrâb. It is called Kubbat Jibraîl (the Dome of Gabriel; plan, e); and there are no carpets spread here, for its floor is formed by the live rock that has been made smooth here. They say that on the night of the Mi'râj (the ascent into heaven), the steed Burâk was tied up at this spot until the Prophet — peace and benediction be upon him! — was ready to mount. Lastly, there is yet another dome, lying twenty cubits distant from the Dome of Gabriel, and it is called Kubbat ar Rasûl (or the Dome of the Prophet; plan, d) — peace and benediction be upon him![86] This dome, likewise, is set upon four marble piers.

37. They say that, on the night of his ascent into heaven, the Prophet — peace and benediction be upon him! — prayed first in the Dome of the Rock, laying his hand upon the Rock. And as he came forth, the Rock, to do him honor, rose up, but the Prophet — peace and benediction be upon him! — laid his hand thereon to keep it in its place, and there firmly fixed it. But, by reason of this uprising, even to the present day, it is here partly detached (from the ground below). The Prophet — the peace of Allah be upon him, and His benediction! — went on from there and came to the dome that is now named after him, and there he mounted (the steed) Burâk; and for this reason is the dome venerated. Underneath the Rock is a large cavern, where they continually burn tapers, and they say that when the Rock moved in order to rise up (in honor of the Prophet), this space below was left void,

---

86. Le Strange claims that it was also known as the Kubbat al Mi'râj, the Dome of the Ascension, although Mikkadâsi lists these as two separate structures.

and that the Rock became fixed, and so it has remained, even as may now be seen.

38. Now, regarding the stairways that lead up on to the platform of the court of the Noble Sanctuary, these are six in number, each with its own name.

On the side (south) towards the Kiblah, there are two flights of steps that go up onto the platform. As you stand by the middle of the retaining wall of the platform (on the south), there is one flight to the right hand and another to the left. That on the right is called Makâm an Nabî (the Prophet's Station) — peace be upon him! — and that lying on the left is called Makâm Ghûri (or the Station of Ghûri). The stairway of the Prophet's Station is so called for that on the night of his ascent the Prophet — upon him be peace and blessing! — went up to the platform by it, going from it to the Dome of the Rock. And the road hither from the Hijjâz comes by this stair. At the present day this stairway is twenty cubits broad, and each step is a rectangular block of carefully chiselled stone in one piece, or sometimes in two. The steps are laid in such a fashion that it would be possible to ride on horseback up onto the platform thereby. At the top of this stairway are four piers *(sutûn)* of marble, green like the emerald, only that the marble is variegated with numberless colored spots; and these pillars are ten cubits in height and so thick that it would take two men to encompass them. Above the capitals of these four pillars rise three arches, one opposite the gate, and one on either side, and (the masonry) crowning the arches is flat-topped and rectangular with battlements *(kangurah)* and a cornice *(shurfah)* set therein. These pillars and the arches are ornamented in gold and enamel work, and none could be finer.

The balustrade *(dâr-âfrîn)* round the (edge of the) platform is of green marble variegated with spots, so that one would say it was a meadow covered with flowers in bloom.

The stairway of Makâm Ghûri consists of a triple flight, and the three lead up together onto the platform, one in the middle and two on either side, so that by three ways people can go up. At the summit of each of the three flights are columns supporting arches with a cornice. Each step is skillfully cut of squared stone, as noted above, and each may consist of two or three blocks in the length. Over the arcade above is set a beautiful inscription in gold, stating that it was constructed by command of the Amîr Laith ad Daulah Nûshtakîn Ghûrî, and they told me that this Laith ad Daulah had been a servant of the sultan of Egypt and had these steps and gangways built.[87]

On the western side of the platform there are, likewise, two flights of steps leading up and constructed with the same skill as those I have just described. On the east side there is but one flight. It is built like the foregoing with columns and an arch with battlements above, and it is named Makâm Sharkî (or the Eastern Station). On the northern side (of the platform) there is also a single stairway, but it is higher and broader than are any of the others. As with those, there are here columns and arches built (at the top of the flight), and it goes by the name of Makâm Shâmî (that is, the Syrian or Northern Station). According to the estimate I made, these six flights of steps must have had expended upon them one hundred thousand dinars (or £50,000).

---

87. Anûshtakîn Amîr al Juyûsh (Generalissimo), originally a Turk slave from Khoten, was governor of Syria, under the Fatimite Khalif Ad Dhâhir, from 419 AH (1028 CE) to 433 (1041). It would appear that this stairway was destroyed during the Frank occupation, or later, for in the nineteenth century there is no triple flight of steps leading up on this side of the platform. There are, however, two separate stairways, as of old, but each is of a single flight (see plan).

39. In the court of the Haram Area, but not upon the platform, is a building resembling a small mosque. It lies towards the north side[88] and is a walled enclosure *(hadhîrah)* built of squared stones with walls of over a man's height. It is called the Mihrâb Dâûd (or David's Oratory). Near this enclosure is a rock, standing up about as high as a man, and the summit of it, which is uneven, is rather smaller than would suffice for spreading out a (prayer) rug *(zîlû)*. This place, they say, was the Throne of Solomon (Kursî Sulaimân), and they relate that Solomon — peace be upon him! — sat on it while occupied with building the Noble Sanctuary.

40. Such, then, are the sights that I saw in the Noble Sanctuary of the Holy City and noted down in the diary that I wrote; and, lastly, among other wonders that I saw in the Sanctuary of the Holy City was the Tree of the Houris.[89]

41. Now, it was my intention to go down from the Holy City and make my visitation (at Hebron to the tomb of) Abraham, the Friend of the Merciful — peace and benediction be upon him! — and on Wednesday, the first day of the month of Dhû-l Ka'adah, of the year of the Flight 438 (29th April, 1047 CE), I set out. From the Holy City to Hebron is six leagues, and the road runs towards the south. Along the way are many villages with gardens and cultivated fields. Trees that

---

88. This Mihrâb Dâûd, which is said to be in the northern portion of the Haram Area and near the Kursî Sulaimân (plan, V), can hardly be the place named "the Oratory of David," which is a niche in the great south wall of the Area (plan, g). It is probably the Kubbat Sulaimân of Mujîr ad Dîn, near the Bâb al 'Atm and lying south-west of that gate.

89. According to Muslim tradition, the Houris appeared to Muhammed under some trees not far from the Platform of the Rock when he came here on the night when he went up to heaven on the steed Burâk.

need little water — for example, the vine and the fig, the olive and the sumach — grow here abundantly and of their own accord. A couple of leagues from the Holy City is a place where there are four villages, and there is a spring of water with numerous gardens and orchards and it is called Farâdîs (or the Paradises) on account of the beauty of the spot.[90] At the distance of a league from the Holy City is a place belonging to the Christians, which they hold in greatest veneration, and there are always numerous pilgrims of their people who come here to perform their visitation. The place is called Bait al Lahm (Bethlehem). The Christians hold a festival here, and many will come for it all the way from Rûm (or the Greek Empire). The day I myself left the Holy City I passed the night at Bethlehem.

The people of Syria, and the inhabitants of the Holy City, call the Sanctuary (or Mash-had at Hebron) Khalîl (that is, "the Friend" of Allah, Abraham) — His blessing be upon him! — and they never make use of the real name of the village, which name is Matlûn. This Sanctuary has belonging to it very many villages that provide revenues for pious purposes. At one of these villages is a spring, where water flows out from under a stone, but in no great abundance, and it is conducted by a channel cut in the ground to a place outside the town (of Hebron), where they have constructed a covered tank for collecting the water, so that none may go to waste; and so that the people of the town and the pilgrims may be able to supply their wants. The sanctuary (Mash-had) stands on the southern

---

90. These must be in the valley of Urtâs, which runs down to Jabal Faradîs — the ancient Herodium and vulgarly called Frank Mountain. In the name *Urtâs*— where are the so-called "Pools of Solomon" — M. Schefer would see a corruption of the Latin *Hortus,* with the same meaning as Firdûs (Plural, Furâdîs), which is the original Persian word for a paradise or park.

border of the town and extends towards the southeast. The sanctuary is enclosed by four walls built of squared masonry and in its upper part (the area) measures eighty cubits long by forty cubits across.[91] The height of the (exterior) walls is twenty cubits, and at their summit the width of the walls is two cubits. The Mihrâb (or niche) and the Maksûrah (or enclosed space for Friday prayers) stand in the width of the building (at the south end).[92] In the Maksûrah are many fine Mihrâbs. There are two tombs occupying the Maksûrah, laid so that their heads lie towards the Kiblah (point, south). Both these tombs are covered by cenotaphs built of squared stones as high as a man. That on the right hand (to the west; plan, A) is the grave of Isaac, son of Abraham; and that on the left (or to the east; plan, B) is the grave of his wife (Rebecca) — peace be upon them! Between the two graves may measure the space of about ten cubits. In this part of the sanctuary the floor and the walls are adorned with precious carpets and Maghribî matting that is more costly even than brocade *(dîbâ)*. I saw here a piece of matting serving as a prayer-rug, which they told me the Amîr al Juyûsh (or captain-general) in the service of the sultan of Egypt, had sent here, and they said that at Cairo (Misr) this prayer-rug had been bought for thirty gold Maghribî dinars (or about £15). Now, the same quantity of Rûmî (or Greek) brocade would not have cost so much, and the equal of this mat I never saw anywhere else.

42. Leaving the Maksûrah, you find in the court of the sanctuary two buildings. Facing the Kiblah (point, south), the one lying on the right (or to the west) contains the tomb of Abraham (plan, C), the Friend of Allah — His blessing

91. Our pilgrim's measurement is considerably under the real size.

92. The present building, known as the church, is of the time of the crusades. The building Nâsir saw has disappeared.

be upon him! This building is of such a size that inside it is another building which you cannot enter, but which has in it four windows through which the pilgrims, who stand about it, may look and view the tomb that is within. The walls and the floor of this chamber are covered with brocade, and the cenotaph is made of stone, measuring three ells (in length) with many silver lamps and lanterns hung above it. The other edifice, lying on the left as you face the Kiblah (or on the eastern side), has within it the Tomb of Sarah (plan, D), the wife of Abraham — peace be upon him! Between the two edifices is the passageway that leads to both, and this is like a hall *(dahlîz)*, and here numerous lamps and lanterns are also suspended. After passing by these two edifices, you come to two other sepulchral chambers lying close to one another, that to the right (or on the west side) containing the tomb of the Prophet Jacob (plan, E) — peace be upon him! — and that to the left (or east side) the tomb of his wife (Leah; plan, F). Beyond this again are other buildings, where Abraham — the blessing of Allah be upon him! — was wont to dispense his hospitality, but within the sanctuary there are only these six tombs. Outside the four walls (of the sanctuary) the ground slopes away, and here on the (west) side (plan, G)[93] is the Sepulchre of Joseph, the son of Jacob — peace be upon them both! — over whose gravestone they have built a beautiful dome.

On this side, where the ground is level — that is, beyond the Sepulchre of Joseph and the sanctuary — lies a great cemetery, whither they bring the dead from many parts to be buried. On the flat roof of the Maksûrah, in the (Hebron) Sanctuary, they have built cells for the reception of the pilgrims who come hither; and their revenues for this charity are considerable, being derived from villages and houses in the Holy City. They grow at Hebron for

93. See Appendix B.

the most part barley, wheat being rare; but olives are in abundance. The pilgrims, and voyagers, and other guests (of the sanctuary) are given bread and olives. There are very many mills here worked by oxen and mules that all day long grind the flour; and, further, there are slave-girls who, during the whole day, are baking bread. The loaves they make here are each a Mann in weight (or about three pounds), and to every person who arrives they give daily a loaf of bread and a dish of lentils cooked in olive-oil, also some raisins. This practice has been in usage from the days of [Abraham] the Friend of the Merciful — peace be upon him! — down to the present hour; and there are some days when as many as five hundred pilgrims arrive, to each of whom this hospitality is offered.

It is said that in early times the sanctuary (at Hebron) had no door into it, and so no one could come nearer to (the tombs) than the outer porch *(îwân)*, whence, from outside, they performed their visitation. When, however, the (Fatimite Khalif) Mahdi came to the throne of Egypt,[94] he gave orders that a door should be opened (into the sanctuary), and he provided utensils and carpets and rugs, besides having many (convenient) edifices built. The entrance door of the sanctuary is in the middle of the northern wall[95] and is four ells high from the ground. On either side of it are stone steps, one stairway for going up, and one for coming down, and the gateway is closed by a small iron door.

94. 'Ubaid Allah al Mahdi, the founder of the Fatimite dynasty, who, in the year 306 AH (918 CE), was for some time master of Egypt.

95. The only doorway that pierced the Haram walls at the time is at about the center of the eastern wall (plan). As, however, the Kiblah point is really southeast — though our pilgrim always speaks of it as south — the long wall of the Haram on the left hand (facing the Kiblah) is in truth the northeast wall, and a door in it might be said to face north, for northeast.

43. From Hebron I came back to the Holy City and then set out on foot with a company of people who intended to make the journey to the Hijjâz. Our guide was a certain man, Abu Bakr Hamadânî by name, who was of a pleasant countenance and sturdy, and he walked afoot. We started from the Holy City on the 15th of Dhlû-1 Ka'adah, in the year 438 (14th May, 1047 CE); and, after three days, reached a place called Ar'ar,[96] where there is running water and trees. Thence we came on to a further stage,[97] called Wâdî-l Kurâ, from where after ten days' journey we reached Mekkah. No (pilgrim) caravan had arrived there that year from any quarter, and provisions were scarce, for everybody was in fear of the (bedawîn) Arabs. At Mekkah we alighted in the street of the perfume-sellers, which is by the Gate of the Prophet — peace be upon him! — and on Monday were present at 'Arafât. When I had come back from the ceremony, I remained but two days longer at Mekkah; and then took the road towards Syria, returning to (Jerusalem) the Holy City, which I entered again on the 5th of Muharram, of the Lunar year (of the Flight) 439 (2nd July, 1047). I shall not now give a description of Mekkah and the pilgrimage there, but shall reserve all mention thereof till I come to speak of my subsequent visit.

44. In the Holy City (of Jerusalem), the Christians possess a church which they call Bai'at-al-Kumâmah (which is the Church of the Resurrection [Holy

---

96. So in all the MSS, including the Epitome, which begins again at this point. M. Schefer's translation gives "Izra," but he adds in a note that the reading of the name is uncertain. Ar'ar or Ar'air is probably Aroer, on the Arnon (Wâdî Môjib). Wâdî-l Kurâ lies on the limit of the territory of Medînah.

97. The B.M. MS breaks off here, and, leaving out a page, continues with the words translated on p. 116, n. 98. My translation is from M. Schefer's text.

Sepulcher]), and they hold it in great veneration. Every year great multitudes of people from Rûm (the Greek Empire) come here to perform their visitation, and the emperor of Byzantium himself even comes here, but privily, so that no one should recognise him. In the days when (the Fatimite Khalif) Al Hâkim-bi-amr-Allah was ruler of Egypt, the Greek Caesar had come after this manner to Jerusalem. Al Hâkim having news of it, sent for one of his cup-bearers and said to him, "There is a man of so and such a countenance and condition whom you will find seated in the mosque (Jâmi') of the Holy City; go, therefore, and approach him, and say that Hâkim has sent you to him, lest he should think that I, Hâkim, did not know of his coming, but tell him to be of good cheer for I have no evil intention against him."

Hâkim at one time ordered the Church (of the Resurrection) to be plundered, which was so done, and it was left in ruins. For some time it remained thus; but afterwards the Caesar of Byzantium sent ambassadors with presents and promises of service and concluded a treaty in which he stipulated for permission to defray the expenses of rebuilding the church, and this was ultimately accomplished.

At the present day the church is a most spacious building and is capable of containing eight thousand people. The edifice is built with the utmost skill of colored marbles, with ornamentation and sculptures. Inside, the church is everywhere adorned with Byzantine brocade worked in gold with pictures. And they have portrayed Jesus — peace be upon Him! — who at times is shown riding upon an ass. There are also pictures representing other Prophets, as, for instance, Abraham and Ishmael and Isaac and Jacob with his sons — peace be upon them all! These pictures they have overlaid with a varnish of the oil of Sandaracha (*Sandarûs* or red juniper), and for the face of each portrait they have made a plate of thin glass, which is set thereon and is perfectly

THE HOLY LAND

transparent. This dispenses with the need for a curtain, and prevents any dust or dirt from settling on the painting, for the glass is cleaned daily by the servants (of the church). Besides this (Church of the Resurrection) there are many others (in Jerusalem), all very skillfully built, but to describe them all would lead into too great length. In the Church (of the Resurrection) there is a picture divided into two parts representing heaven and hell. One part shows the people of paradise in Paradise, while the other shows the people of hell in Hell, with all that there is therein; and assuredly there is nowhere else in the world a picture such as this. There are seated in this church great numbers of priests and monks[98] who read the Evangel [Gospel] and say prayers. Both by day and by night they are occupied after this manner.

45. Now, it was my intention to have left the Holy City, and gone by sea to Egypt — before returning from there to Mekkah — but the wind was so contrary as to make a sea-voyage impossible. I set out, therefore, by the land-road, and after passing Ramlah came to the city called 'Askalân (Ascalon). The bazaar and the mosque are both fine; and I saw here an arch, which they told me was ancient and had been part of a mosque. The arch was built of such mighty stones that, should any desire to throw it down, he would spend much money before he could accomplish it. On the road beyond Ascalon I saw many villages and towns, to note each of which would be wearisome; so I omit the mention of the places I passed before coming to the town called Tînah, which is a harbour with many ships; and from Tînah I took passage in a ship going to Tinnîs (in Egypt).

*

98. See p. 114, n. 97.

APPENDIX A

Mukaddasii, who wrote his description of Jerusalem in 985 CE, describes the Aksâ Mosque of his day as having fifteen doorways opening to the north, and eleven opening to the east (above, p. 43). The plan of the Aksâ Mosque must then have been very different from what it now is, and Professor Hayter Lewis's restoration (reproduced here from his paper in the *Pal. Expl. Fund Quart. Stat*, for January, 1887) shows what the plan of the building must have originally been.

In CE 1033 (AH 425) the great earthquake occurred[1] which, half a century after Mukaddasi's time, threw down a great part of the edifice.

From Nâsir-i-Khusrau's description, dating from CE 1047 (438 AH), or thirteen years after this earthquake, it would appear that the Aksâ, when rebuilt, had been greatly curtailed in the width (east and west), while the length remained much the same. The plan of the mosque visited by Nâsir-i-Khusrau, with five gateways to the north and ten to the east, could not have been very different from that of the building as it at present exists.[2] It must, however, be confessed that the dimensions recorded by Nâsir-i-Khusrau — east wall (length) 420 cubits, or about 840 feet, and north wall (width) 150 cubits, or about 300 feet[3] — are greatly in excess of those of the present edifice, since the Masjid al Aksâ of today measures only about 260 feet in the length, north to south, with 190 feet in the width (of the seven aisles, side by side) east to west. Nâsir's measurement of the length would indeed make the porch of the Aksâ stand beyond (north of and covering) the Dome of the Rock. The figures given, therefore, must

1. See above, p. 94, note 61.
2. See plan.
3. These figures are twice repeated (see above p. 94 and p. 95).

be corrupt, and for cubits 420 and 150, I imagine we ought to read, cubits 120 and 100; which would roughly agree with the present measurements. This alteration, however, is entirely arbitrary, and I have left the figures to stand in the translation as found in the MSS. The figures of M. Schefer's Text,[4] 408 cubits by 450, are even more ridiculously in excess than those of the B.M. MSS. Nâsir's measurement of the open space between the southeast corner of Haram Area and the east wall of the Aksâ, "two hundred ells,"[5] is, on the other hand, exact, for the actual measurement is as near as may be 400 feet.

※

4. See above p. 94, n 62.
5. See p. 93 above.

APPENDIX B.

The following account of the "Invention" of the Tomb of Joseph is found in the *Description of Jerusalem and of Hebron* written by Mujîr ad Diîn, in the year 1496 CE. I have translated it from the Arabic text printed at Cairo in AH 1283 (1866)[1]:

"The Tomb of Joseph is in the plot of ground lying outside Solomon's enclosure (the Haram). It stands opposite the Tomb of Jacob, and is near that of his forefathers Abraham and Isaac. Now, Ibrahim ibn Ahmad al Khalanjî states that he was requested by one of (the Khalif) Al Muktadir's[2] women — Al 'Ajûz by name — who was sojourning at the Holy City, to proceed to the place where, according to the tradition, Joseph was buried, and having discovered the sepulchre, to erect over it a building. So Al Khalanjî set forth with workmen, and they found the place where, according to tradition, Joseph was buried, namely, outside the Enclosure (of Solomon), and opposite the Tomb of Jacob; and they bought the field from its owner and began to lay it bare. In the very place indicated by the tradition they came on a huge rock; and this, by order of Al Khalanjî, was broken into. They tore off a portion, "and," says Al Khalanjî, "I being with the workmen in the trench, when they raised up the fragment, lo! below it lay (the body of) Joseph — peace be upon him! — beautiful and glorious to look on, as he is always represented to have been. Now, first there arose from the place an odor of musk; following it, however, came a strong wind; so I caused the workmen to set down into its place again the fragment of rock to be as it had been before.

1. P. 64 *et seq.*
2. Reigned 295–320 AH (908–32 CE).

"And afterwards they built over this place the Dome which can be seen there to this day, in proof that the tradition is a true one, and that the Patriarch is buried beneath. This Dome stands without the walls of Solomon's Enclosure, and to the west of it, being within the Madrasah, called after Al Malik an Nâsir Hasan[3]; which at the present day is called Al Kala'ah (the Castle). You enter it through the gate of the mosque which opens towards the market, and leading to the Eunuch's Spring ('Ain at Tawâshî). It is a place much frequented (by pilgrims, who are shown) here the grave (of Joseph). One of the Guardians of Hebron, Shahâb ad Dîn Ahmad al Yaghmûrî[4] by name, pierced a gateway in the western wall of (the Haram, which is) Solomon's Enclosure, and this opens opposite to the Tomb of our Lord Joseph. He also set a monument *(ishârah)* over this lower tomb to mark the same and to be similar to monuments that are over the other graves that lie in the Mosque (or Haram) of Abraham. This was done during the reign of Sultân Barkûk."[5]

See plan.

*

[3]. One of the Mamlûk sultans of Egypt. He was assassinated in 762 AH (1361 CE).

[4]. Governor of Jerusalem and Hebron in 796 AH (1394 CE).

[5]. The Mamlûk Sultan of Egypt, who reigned 784–801 AH (1382–99 CE).

Appendix C

The Gates of the Haram Area

By Col. Sir C. W. Wilson, K.C.B., K.C.M.G., F.R.S., R.E.

In the note on the Gates of the Haram Area, which I contributed to Mr. Guy le Strange's translation of Mukaddasi, I was misled by the statements of Mujîr ad Dîn and modern tradition, which follows that author. A comparison of the descriptions of Mukaddasi (985 CE), and Nâsir-i-Khusrau (1047 CE) with each other, and with the description of Mujîr ad Dîn (1496 CE) and existing remains, enables me to correct in great measure the errors in my former note, to identify many of the gates with some degree of certainty and to show that a change took place in the Arab nomenclature of the gates between the eleventh and fifteenth centuries; possibly when Jerusalem was captured by Salâh-ad-Dîn.

Nâsir describes the Bâb an Nabî (Gate of the Prophet),[1] beneath the Mosque al Aksâ, in such terms as to leave no doubt of its identification with the double gateway and passage leading upwards from it beneath the Mosque to the Haram Area. He also mentions another gate, Bâb al Hittah (Gate of Remission),[2] as being excavated in the ground; and the only known gate of the Haram of this character is the closed Gate of Muhammad, or of the Prophet, beneath the Bâb al Maghâribah [plan, K]. If now we turn to Mukaddasi's list of gates, we find that he commences with Bâb Hittah, that his second gate is the two Gates of the Prophet, and that he

1. See above.
2. See above.

ends with the Gate Dâûd, which is, without dispute, the Bâb as Silsilah (the Gate of the Chain, [plan, I]) of the present day. The inference I draw from this is that Mukaddasi named the gates in order, commencing with the Bâb Hittah, and ending with the Bab Dâûd, and not, as I supposed in my former note, at haphazard.

In attempting to identify the gates with those which now exist, it is necessary to bear in mind that the Haram Area, with its buildings and the approaches to it, have been much altered at various periods, as, for instance, during the Latin kingdom; after the recapture of the city by the Saracens; and when the walls were rebuilt by Sultan Sulaiman in the sixteenth century.

Following Mukaddasi's list, we have:

1. Bâb al Hittah (Gate of Remission). The Bâb al Hittah of Nâsir, which was excavated in the ground. This is the present closed gate, Bâb al Burâk, or Bâb an Nabî Muhammad, beneath the modern Bâb al Maghâribah [plan, K], It is called Bâb an Nabî by Mujîr ad Dîn, who places the Bâb al Hittah in the north wall of the Haram.

2. The two Gates of the Prophet (Mukaddasi) ; the Gate of the Prophet in the south wall and beneath the Mosque al Aksâ, of Nâsir. The present double gate, the Arab name of which is the Gate of the Old Aksâ, as given by Mujîr ad Dîn.

3. The Gates of the Mihrâb Maryâm [Mukaddasi]. These gates must have been close to the Mihrâb Maryâm,[3] in the southeast corner of the Haram, from which they take their name. They apparently correspond to the Bâb al 'Ain, of Nâsir,[4] and are represented either by the closed Single Gate, in the south wall, or by the Triple Gate.

4. The two Gates Ar Rahmah (Mukaddasi). The Bâb ar Rahmah and Bâb at Taubah, of Nâsir, so called by Mujîr

3. See Mukaddasi above.

4. See above.

ad Dîn (plan, N and O). The double gateway known as the Golden Gate.

5. The Gate of the Birkat Banî Israîl [Mukaddasi]. The eastern gate in the north wall is called by Nâsir the Bâb al Abwâb (Gate of Gates). It is now called, as in Mujîr ad Dîn, the Bâb al Asbât (Gate of the Tribes) [plan, A], and opens to the road over the dam at the east end of the Birkat Israîl.

6. The Gates al Asbât, of the Tribes [Mukaddasi]. It corresponds to the Bâb al Asbât of Nâsir,[5] which was in the north wall to the west of the Gate of Gates. It is now called Bâb al Hittah (Gate of Remission) [plan, B], and was known by this same name to Mujîr ad Dîn, who gives with reference to it the legend applied by Nâsir to Gate No. 1.

7. The Hâshimite Gates [Mukaddasi]. These appear to be the gate leading to two cloisters *(daryûzah)*, belonging to the Sûfîs, said by Nâsir[6] to have been in the north wall, to the west of the Bâb al Asbât. It is apparently the modern Bâb al 'Atm [plan, C], which is called by Mujîr ad Dîn, Bâb ad Dawâtir (or Dawâdariyyah), from a school of the same name, and said by him to be the gate by which Omar entered on the day of conquest.

8. The Gate of Al Walîd [Mukaddasi] is possibly the Bâb al Ghawânimah, in the northwest corner of the Haram Area [plan, D]; it is given the latter name by Mujîr ad Dîn, who says it was formerly called the Gate of Ibrahîm.

9. The Gate of Ibrahîm [Mukaddasi] is perhaps the same as the Bâb as Sakar (Gate of Hell), which is the only gate that Nâsir mentions in the west wall, to the north of the Bâb Dâûd.[7] It is apparently the modern Bâb an Nâdhir (the Gate of the Inspector) [plan, E], which, according to Mujîr ad Dîn, was formerly called the Gate of Michael,

---

5. Above, p. 90.
6. Above, p. 90.
7. Above, p. 89, n 54.

and was an ancient gateway. The street 'Akabat at Takiyah, which runs westward from the Bâb an Nâdhir, is supposed to follow the line of an ancient street, which supports the view that this gateway is on the site of a much older one.

10. The Gate of Umm Khâlid [Mukaddasi]. Either the modern Bâb al Hadîd (the Iron Gate) [plan, F], or the Bâb al Kattanin (Gate of the Cotton Merchants) [plan, G], which, according to Mujîr ad Dîn, was in his time near the Gate of the Bath.

11. The Gate Dâûd [Mukaddasi] is the same as the Bâb Dâûd (Gate of David) of Nâsir. It is now the Bâb as Silsilah (Gate of the Chain) [plan, I], and the adjoining Bâb as Salâm (Gate of Peace) is the Bâb as Sakînah of Nâsir.[8] Mujîr ad Dîn mentions this double gate under the names Bâb as Sakînah, and Bâb as Silsilah, and says that the latter was formerly called the Bâb Dâûd.

One gate mentioned by Mujîr ad Dîn, the Gate of Burâk, appears to have been completely destroyed when the walls were rebuilt by Sultan Sulaimân in the sixteenth century. He says that the east gate of the Dome of the Rock, called the Gate of Israfîl, led to the steps of Burâk, which were opposite the Dome of the Chain; and that opposite the steps was the Gate of Burâk [plan, P], so-called because the Prophet entered by it on his night journey. It was named also the Gate of Funerals, because they went out by it. This is the Gate of Jehoshaphat of the Crusaders, but it does not appear to have been in existence when Mukaddasi and Nâsir wrote their descriptions. The table on the next page shows concisely the proposed identifications.

8. Above, p. 100.

Diary of Journey by Nâsir-i-Khusrau

Mukaddasî, 985 CE	Nâsir-i-Khusrau, 1047 CE	Mujîr ad Dîn, 1496 CE	1888 CE
1. Bâb al Hittah	Bâb al Hittah	Bâb al Nabî	Bâb al Nabî, below Bâb al Maghâribah (Plan, K)
2. Bâb an Nâbi	Bâb an Nâbi	Gate of the Old Askâ	Gate of the Old Askâ (Double Gate)
3. Gates of the Mihrâb Maryâm	Bâb al 'Ain (?) (Gate of the Spring.		Single Gate (?) or Triple Gate (?)
4. Gates ar Rahmah	Bâb ar Ramah, and Bâb at Taubah	Bâb ar Ramah, and Bâb at Taubah	Bâb ar Ramah, and Bâb at Taubah (Golden Gate). plan, N znd O
5. Gate of the Birkat Bani Isrâîl	Bâb al Abwâb	Bâb al Asbât	Bâb al Asbât (plan, A)
6. Bâb al Asbât	Bâb al Asbât	Bâb al Hittah	Bâb al Hittah plan, B
7. Hâshimite Gates	Gate to the Sûfî's Cloister	Bâb al Dawâtir	Bâb al 'Atm (plan, C)
8. Gate of al Walîd		Bâb al Ghawânimah	Bâb al Ghawânimah (plan D)
9. Gate of Ibrahîum	Bâb as Sakar (?)	Bâb an Nâdhir	Bâb an Nâdhir (plan, E)
10. Gate of Umm Khâlid		Bâb al Hadîd or Bâb al Kattânîn	Bâb al Hadîd (plan, F) or Bâb al Kattânîn (plan, C)
11. Bâb Dâud	Bâb Dâûd, Bâb as Sakînah	Bâb as Silsilah, Bâb as Sakînah	Bâb as Silsilah, (plan I) Bâb as Salâm

Guide to the Holy Land by Theoderich of Würzburg

PREFACE TO THE FIRST EDITION

Nothing certain seems to be known of Theoderich except his name.[1] It is probable that he is the Dietrich mentioned in John of Würzburg's "Introductory Epistle," but there is no certain proof of this, nor have we any means of identifying him with "Theodericus, Praepositus de Werdea," or "Theodericus, Praepositus de Onolsbach," whom we find mentioned in the records of Würzburg at the end of the twelfth century. Probably, as is stated in the Preface to John of Würzburg,[2] he was that Theoderich who became bishop of Würzburg in 1223. He was, we know, a German and, almost certainly, a Rhine-lander; for he tells us how on Palm Sunday he and his companions buried their fellow-pilgrim named Adolf of Cologne in the Potter's Field near Jerusalem, while the comparison of the Church of the Holy Sepulchre at Jerusalem with the church at Aix-la-Chapelle proves that he was familiar with that country.

Theoderich and John of Würzburg in many parts of their narratives, especially when describing what they did not personally behold, agree very closely, using in some instances the same words. They may have copied one another, but it seems more probable that both of them, or at any rate John of Würzburg, as also Eugesippus Fretillus and other writers, copied this part from a brief geographical and historical account of the Holy Land

1. Stewart bases much of his preface on that of Tobler's Latin edition.

2. John of Wurzburg, *Description of the Holy Land*, trans. Aubrey Stewart (London: Palestine Pilgrims' Text Society, 1896; reprint ed., New York: AMS, 1971), pp. ix–x.

and its neighbourhood which was then much in men's hands, and which will here for the sake of shortness be called "the old compendium." A certain amount of light is given us by the expressed intention of John of Würzburg to write only about Jerusalem and its neighbourhood — "the holy places within and without the walls being those which alone we mean to describe...whereas we have no intention of giving any account of those which are in the neighbouring province, knowing that enough has been already said about them by other writers." It is worthy of remark that Thietmar[3] does the exact opposite of this, although there was much to be said about Jerusalem, because that city had already been thoroughly described by many writers. Indeed, John of Würzburg does not carry out his intention, since he gives a circumstantial account of the holy places of Galilee also, whereby he excites the suspicion that in so doing he merely acted as a copyist, since one would not willingly suppose that the account of the more distant regions was added to that of the topography of Jerusalem and its neighbourhood by another hand.

Theoderich starts with the distinct declaration that his description rests partly upon what he himself saw, and partly upon trustworthy accounts received from others[4]; but even when he is dealing with these "trustworthy accounts" or with the "old compendium," he proceeds far more self-reliantly than John. Moreover, his narrative, besides being fuller, contains many vivid touches which are wanting in the other. The people shouting their "Dex aide" and "Holy Sepulchre" while awaiting the descent of the holy fire on Easter Day "not without tears;" the stacking up of the pilgrims' crosses on the top of the rock of Calvary, and the bonfire made of them on Easter Eve; the ignorant pilgrims who piled up

3. See Laurent, xxvi.
4. Prologue, chaps. 25 and 51.

Preface to Guide by Theoderich of Würzburg

heaps of stones in the valley of Hinnom and expected to sit upon them in the Day of Judgment; the account of how terribly he and his companions were alarmed at the Saracens — "un peuple criard," Kinglake calls the Arabs in "Eothen," quoting Lamartine — who were beginning to plough up a field by the side of the road to Shechem, and yelling horribly, "as is their wont when they are setting about any piece of work;" the description of what he saw with his own eyes *(vidimus)* of the wealth and charity of the Hospitallers, and of the power of the Templars; the Norman-French names of "Belmont," "Fontenoid," and "Montjoye," which sound so strangely in the country of the Bible; the throng of ships in the dangerous harbour of Acre, with his own "buss" amongst them; and the view from the Mountain of Temptation over the wide darkling plain, covered with numberless pilgrims, each bearing a torch, and watched, no doubt, by the "infidels" on the Arabian hills beyond Jordan — all these are invaluable helps towards forming a picture of the Holy Land in the time of the Frankish kings.

A distinction must be made between what Theoderich saw and what he only describes by hearsay; the former is clear, complete, and full of new facts, while the latter is brief, and, as a rule, confusedly written. He appears to have landed at Acre (Ptolemais), journeyed thence to Jerusalem, visited Jericho and the Jordan, and returned by the same road, although he may have personally visited Nazareth by way of Tiberias and Mount Tabor. His account of the Sea of Gennesareth is hopelessly confused, probably through copyists' errors. However, he not only describes clearly all that he saw, but describes it so naively and intelligently as to win the reader's esteem.

Our Saviour lies nearer his heart than anyone else. He speaks of His Mother with due respect, but shows no trace of the mariolatry of later ages. He is superior to many travellers of the present day in that he directs no sarcasm against men of other faiths[5]; and one can hardly expect to find in him the modern historical and critical spirit. The book contains so few of the pious reflections behind which men often conceal their ignorance of the affairs of this life, that one could wish for more and fuller expressions of the writer's personal feelings. Such as there are, are upright and honourable, and are spoken from the heart. Although the writer, as we learn from Chapter XXIX, was a priest, he never obtrudes his priestly dignity upon us; indeed, it seems almost strange that he never alludes to having read prayers, or even having performed his devotions at any of the holy places. At the period at which he wrote, spiritual things were held in honour as a matter of course, so that it appeared unnecessary for him to make any effort to excite the feelings of his readers or hearers.

There can be no doubt that the pilgrimage of Theoderich took place in the time of the Crusaders, before their expulsion from Jerusalem in 1187. A number of particulars prove that he sojourned in the city while it was still under the rule of the Frankish kings. All we have left to do is to fix the exact year. In Chapter XXX, we read that Emaded-Din Zenghi, called Sanginus or Sanguineus,[6] beheaded six monks in a monastery on the banks of the Jordan. This apparently took place in 1138, when the Turks crossed the Jordan, and made a plundering raid through the districts of Jericho and Tekoa. Eight years after this "razzia" Zenghi was murdered. In Chapter XII we find the name of the patriarch Fulcher, who held the patriarchate from 1146 to 1157.

---

5. With the exception of the Jews, against whom he levels many of the charges common in the anti-Semitic literature of the day. See Introduction, p. 139 below.

6. See Edward Gibbon, *The History of the Decline and Fall of the Roman Empire* (London: Methuen, 1912; reprint ed. New York: AMS, 1974), chap. 59.

Preface to Guide by Theoderich of Würzburg

In the Temple of the Lord, Theoderich,[7] besides the date 1101, read that it was finished in the sixty-third year after the taking of Jerusalem, which brings us to the year 1164. In Chapter XLV we find it mentioned that Paneas was taken by the Muslims in the year 1171. The description of the tombs of the kings in Chapter XII brings us down to Amaury or Amalric, who died on the 11th of June, 1173.

Thus it appears that 1173 is the latest date mentioned: the next thing to be considered is whether the tombs were rightly pointed out to him, which is no very easy matter. Theoderich came from the Chapel of St. Helena into the great Church of the Holy Sepulchre, and proceeded into the south transept, with the altar close by to the southward. Here he mentions five[8] tombs on the south side in front of the door, whereof the first, being that of the brother of the reigning king of Jerusalem (Baldwin III), was abutting on the choir of the canons, which is called at the present day the Catholicon of the Greek Church. In case the words "the tomb of the brother of the king of Jerusalem, named Baldwin," should not be sufficiently clear, the explanation, I think, is given by the sentence: "The fourth tomb is that of the father of the present king, that is, of Amalric." According to chronological order the tombs are as follows:

First Godfrey's, which stands third as you go from the tomb of Baldwin III towards the choir, next to Baldwin II's.

Secondly, Baldwin I's, the second in the row.

Thirdly, that of Baldwin II (du Bourg), the father of Queen Milicent, and of Judith, the abbess of St. Lazarus of Bethany, the fifth in the row.

---

7. Chap. 15.

8. Stewart provides a lengthy Appendix closely examining the historical evidence for the tombs and the list of Latin kings that follows below. This Appendix has been omitted in the present edition.

Fourthly, Fulke's, the father of Baldwin III, and of Amalric, the fourth in the row.

And fifthly, that of Baldwin III, the first in the row.

Now, no one can deny that Theoderich made his pilgrimage to the Holy Land during the life-time of King Amalric, who reigned from 1162 to 1173. It is very important to observe that the tomb of Baldwin III was pointed out as that of the brother of the king, because the actually reigning king was assumed to be well known, and, therefore, one easily sees why his tomb does not occur in the list, because he was still alive. We have already, therefore, mention of the year 1171, and we must not go beyond the year 1173, in which Amalric died, so that the pilgrimage of Theoderich must have taken place between the year 1171 and 1173.

Other less definite considerations point to the same date. Theoderich says of the Chapel of the Holy Sepulchre,[9] that on account of the partial fading of the colours he was quite unable to read the inscriptions on the arches; which is a proof that he made his visitation late, yet not at the very latest time, since we do not hear of the chapel being divided into two parts,[10] and Phocas dwells especially upon the fact that the Emperor Manuel Comnenus, who reigned from 1143 to 1180, entirely covered the sepulchre with gilding. It is very likely that Theoderich saw the Chapel of the Sepulchre during the time of its restoration, since, although he could not read the faded inscriptions, he tells us that he read the antiphonal hymn *Christus resurgens* in golden letters, whereas John of Würzburg

---

9. See chap. 5.

10. See John Phocas, *The Pilgrimage of Johannes Phocas* (London: Palestine Pilgrims' Text Society, 1896; reprint ed., New York: AMS, 1971), p. 19; and Innominatus, IV, in *Anonymous Pilgrims*, trans. Aubery Stewart, (London: Palestine Pilgrims' Text Society, 1894; reprint ed., New York: AMS, 1971), chapt. 15.

describes it as in silver letters. Theoderich saw the gilded turret above the chapel with its dome and cross when the gilding was bright and fresh, John merely speaks of a cupola covered with silver; which proves, what we have already gathered from the "Introductory Epistle" of the latter, that he was the precursor of Theoderich.[11] From Theoderich we also learn that the Templars were engaged in building a new church on Mount Moriah, about which he uses the same expression as John of Würzburg, who says: "Cum extructione novae ecclesiae nondum tamen consummatae."[12] Moreover, the theory that John was the earlier pilgrim is supported by the latter's remark that at Shechem "a church is now being built" over Jacob's Well, whereas Theoderich speaks of it as being already built. It does not, however, seem to accord with this evidence that Theoderich speaks of the church of the Pater Noster, or of our Saviour, as "being now building," whereas John speaks of it as already built. At any rate, we may gather from this that the two pilgrimages left but a short interval between them. Lastly, we may remark that Theoderich mentions a new cistern on the way from Jerusalem to Bethlehem, in his description of the valley of Hinnom, which, without doubt, was the Lacus Germani, the Birket es-Sultan of the present day, of which we find no other mention previous to 1176. On the other hand, we know that the well of Job (Bir Eyûb), at the confluence of Hinnom and Cedron, was first discovered by Germanus in 1184, and could not, therefore, be alluded to by Theoderich.

From internal evidence we learn that Theoderich's pilgrimage took place in the spring of the year, at the *passagium vernale*, in March, or Easter, not the *passagium aestivale*, in August, on St. John's Day. Theoderich saw ripe

11. See chap. 5.

12. Although the construction of the new church was not yet completed.

barley in the plain of Jericho on the Monday after Palm Sunday, and on the Wednesday in Easter week he was at Acre on his way home.

The references in the notes are to the English translations of the pilgrims.[13]

— Aubrey Stewart

13. This is a reference to the publications of the Palestine Pilgrims' Text Society (Committee of the Palestine Exploration Fund), which published annotated English translations of the medieval guides to the Holy Land during the last decade of the 19th century. Stewart's translation of Theoderich, as well as several other works translated and edited by him, appeared in this series.

Preface

The following book is a modernized version of Aubrey Stewart's 1897 edition of Theoderich's Description of the Holy Land, a translation of the *Libellus de locis sanctis* published in volume 5 of the Palestine Pilgrims' Text Society series. The present edition follows Stewart's faithfully with a few modifications and additions. These include the modernization of certain Victorian usages in the text, including archaisms like "beginneth," modernizaton of capitalization and spelling, and the reorganization of some of Stewart's large text blocks into smaller paragraphs. There was, happily, need for very few of these changes, and Stewart's text shares the PPTS virtue of highly readable English translations created in an era when English prose had reached classic form.

To aid the reader in following and referring to the text this edition has retained the original chapter numbers and order but has also split the text into three parts for easier reference. These are:

I. The description of Jerusalem proper (1–18)
II. The description of the area around Jerusalem, including the Mount of Olives, Bethany, and Bethphage (19–27)
III. The rest of the Holy Land (28–51).

The annotations to this edition are intended to supplement Stewart's own with the findings of modern studies on the geography, topography, and archeology of the Holy Land and with appropriate historical information where necessary. Many of Stewart's original citations, shortened in the expectation that they would be comprehensible to the readers of the Palestine Pilgrims' Series, have been expanded to conform with modern methods or, where superseded by modern findings, replaced altogether.

There is no intention to present any original research but to provide the reader with some of the best contemporary studies available. The bibliography both offers a supplement to the sources noted by Stewart and provides a solid introduction to the area of study for anyone who might want to pursue a topic further.

The illustrations accompanying the text are drawn from high or late medieval sources and are included to show some of the sites in the Holy Land and the geographical world of the Mediterranean in the Middle Ages. The maps of Jerusalem and the Holy Land that accompany the text are original to this edition.

INTRODUCTION

Theoderich's Guide to the Holy Land is one of the best known and most widely used of the medieval pilgrims' guides to Jerusalem and the Holy Land.[1] Written c.1172 by the German monk Theoderich, it is a complete guide to the city's sacred sites, history and legends and to places of interest in the Crusader State only fifteen years before the destruction of the kingdom by Saladin.

Since the first publication of Aubrey Stewart's edition of Theoderich's *Description of the Holy Places* in 1897, scholars have made great strides in understanding the world that Theoderich described. The fields of Crusade history, especially the discussion of the institutions, economy, social life and customs of the Latin Kingdom, of travel literature and the history of trade and navigation in the Middle Ages, and the study of popular spirituality — most especially of the cult of the saints and of pilgrimage — and the related movements of the Twelfth Century Renaissance have all shed significant light on the era of the Crusades. This introduction is intended to survey some of these findings and to highlight some of the elements of Theoderich's *Guide* not covered by Stewart's preface that would be of interest to a modern general reader.

THEODERICH

Little more is known about Theoderich's life and work than what Stewart offered, except for the suggestion that he was a monk of Hirsau, the autonomous abbey about 40 miles east of Strasbourg. Most recently this theory has been summarized by François Dolbeau[2] and rests on internal evidence and on

1. For the most recent research and bibliography see Barbara Drake Boehm and Melanie Holcomb, eds., *Jerusalem, 1000–1400: Every People under Heaven* (New York: Metropolitan Museum of Art, 2016).

2. "Théodericus, De locis sanctis: Un second manuscrit, provenant de Saint-Barbe de Cologne," *Analecta Bollandiana* 103.1–2 (1985): 113–14.

137

the new paleographical interpretation of an abbreviation of Theoderich's place of origin in the Latin text of his guide,³ from Herbipolensis, or "of Würzburg" to Hirsaugiensis, or "of Hirsau." The fact that the only other manuscript of the work, now in Minneapolis,⁴ derives from the monastery of St. Barbara in Cologne also points to the Rhine Valley origin of the work and its author.

Theoderich provided detailed descriptions of the architecture of the Holy Land, especially the Church of the Holy Sepulcher in Jerusalem. His comments on the uses and juxtaposition of architectural elements, his knowledge of building materials and housing styles, and his accurate comparison to buildings in Europe, leads one to gather that he was familiar with at least the vocabulary of architecture, and may himself have been an architect. Shortly after Theoderich's return to Wurzburg, the monks of Eichstätt to the south began construction on their own replica of the Holy Sepulcher, and Theoderich's first-hand research cannot be ruled out either as a source for their design or part of a more general fashion of imitation.⁵

Harry W. Hazard, ed., *The Art and Architecture of the Crusader States*. Vol. 4 in *A History of the Crusades*, Kenneth M. Setton, ed., 6 vols. (Madison, WI: University of Wisconsin Press, 1977), p. 412. On Hirsau see Pierre-Roger Gaussin, *Les Cohortes du Christ* (Rennes: Ouest France, 1985), 120–21.

3. In the edition of M.L. and W. Bulst, Theodericus, *Libellus de locis sanctis* (Heidelberg: Editiones Heidelbergensis, 1976), p. 4. Like that of T. Tobler, *Theoderici libellus de locis sanctis* (St. Gall and Paris, 1865), this new edition is based on the only manuscript then known, Vienna, Österreichische Nationalbibliothek MS 3529, folios 192–207, dating from the fifteenth century. The most recent edition of the work is that of Sabino de Sandoli, O.F.M., *Itinera hierosolymitana crucesignatorum (saec. xii-xiii)*, vol. 2 (Jerusalem: Franciscan Printing Press, 1980), which reproduces Tobler's Latin text along with a new Italian translation.

4. University Library, MS 13 +.1, folios 89–119. Discovered by Dolbeau.

5. For Eichstätt, see Diarmuid Ó. Riain, "An Irish Jerusalem in Franconia: The Abbey of the Holy Cross and Holy Sepulchre at Eichstätt," *Proceedings of the Royal Irish Academy. Section C: Archaeology, Celtic Studies, History, Linguistics, Literature* 112C (2012): 219–70.

At the same time we should note his almost complete disinterest in the political situation in the Latin Kingdom or in its neighbors. For someone so observant of materials and styles, this complete disregard for personalities and policies offers an interesting insight into the psychological world of a medieval pilgrim. For Theoderich, and his readers, it was the sacred geography of the pilgrim, not the political geography of the crusader, that really mattered.

In another area Theoderich also seems to have been a man of his time: the anti-Semitism that, if certainly not universal, was at least widespread both in his native Rhineland and in the Latin Kingdom during the Crusade period.[6] His repetition of several incidents in the New Testament in which the Jews are reported to have sought to harm Jesus or were actually blamed for his crucifixion are supplemented here by other tales. These include the story of the Jew who attempted to steal the Virgin Mary's veil from her tomb in chapter 23 and the story in chapter 50 of the Jews of Beirut who attempted to repeat the torments of Christ on his image. While much of Theoderich's prejudice may have traveled with his pilgrim's baggage, he may also have picked up these stories from his Latin guides at the sites he describes or from the written sources he used to supplement his own account.

THE TWELFTH-CENTURY RENAISSANCE

We should also understand Theoderich's *Guide* in the context of the cultural and intellectual movements of his age. Chief among these is the what has been termed

---

6. See Steven Runciman, *A History of the Crusades,* 3 vols. (New York: Harper & Row, 1964), 1: 134–41, 2: 295–96; Joshua Prawer, *The Crusaders' Kingdom* (New York: Praeger, 1972), pp. 57–59, 234-56; F.E. Peters, *Jerusalem* (Princeton, NJ: Princeton University Press, 1985), pp. 288–90, 327–29. For general background see Sara Lipton, *Dark Mirror: The Medieval Origins of Anti-Jewish Iconography* (New York: Metropolitan Books/Henry Holt and Company, 2014).

the Twelfth Century Renaissance,[7] the general revival of interest in ancient learning and piety that extended to all aspects of religious and intellectual life. This Renaissance saw proper models for the present age in the imitation of the pure sources of antiquity, whether Christian or pagan. Thus the century witnessed the revival of Aristotle for the methods and subjects of philosophical discussion, as well as the absorption of Greek science and geography, of Roman law and grammatical tracts, a revival of Latin poetry and history writing, and a renewed interest in the classics of Christian learning: the Greek and Latin Fathers of the early Church.

In religious life this Renaissance meant a great evangelical awakening, as itinerant preachers and new religious orders attempted to revive the spiritual life of Christendom through the literal imitation of the poverty, humility, and charity of the Gospels and of the early church. Thus groups like the Waldensians and the Franciscans at the end of the century and reformers as diverse as Arnold of Brescia and Bernard of Clairvaux set about to live the evangelical life of simple imitation. At the same time a series of "second" popes, such as Innocent II, Urban II and Anacletus II, took names that recalled the very first Roman popes of the early church and so pointed to these figures of Christian antiquity as concrete models of Christian leadership.

While the historical consciousness of the time certainly saw nothing like the critical approach of modern history writing and archeological study, the twelfth century did witness a new critical attitude to the study of the Bible.[8]

7. See Charles Homer Haskins, *The Renaissance of the Twelfth Century* (Cleveland and New York: Meridien, 1966); and Christopher Brooke, *The Twelfth Century Renaissance* (New York: Harcourt Brace Jovanovich, 1976); Alex J. Novikoff, *The Twelfth Century Renaissance: A Reader* (Toronto: University of Toronto Press, 2016);

8. The basic book remains Beryl Smalley, *The Study of the Bible in the Middle Ages* (Notre Dame, IN: University of Notre Dame Press, 1970).

INTRODUCTION TO GUIDE BY THEODERICH OF WÜRZBURG

The study of the sacred texts became the model for all forms of learning from the liberal arts to historical narrative and theological speculation; while the events of the New Testament and the sacred history and places of the Old Testament were studied with renewed interest for both scriptural exegesis and factual information and were well known to all educated people.

POPULAR SPIRITUALITY

This renewed interest in Christian antiquity coincided with, and no doubt reflected, the same impulses as the new popular spirituality of the time.[9] As never before in Christian history the people of the West now began to turn to Gospel imitation in larger and larger numbers. Two of the best known examples of this spirit were, paradoxically, the renewed interest in the cult of the saints and the related rise in the number and extent of pilgrimages to their shrines.

Believing that the relics of the saints and the centers of their cults possessed great spiritual and historical power that enabled the faithful to participate in the saint's closeness to God, medieval men and women began flocking to the shrines of the most renowned in record numbers. Thus pilgrimages to such venerated sites as St. James of Compostela in northern Spain, to the sites of the martyrdoms of Peter and Paul in Rome, and to the most sacred sites of Jerusalem and the Holy Land gave the pilgrim the ability to literally relive the life and sufferings of the saints and so repeat the sacred and heroic deeds of antiquity

---

9. For introductions see Rosalind and Christopher Brooke, *Popular Religion in the Middle Ages: Western Europe 1000-1300* (London: Thames & Hudson, 1984), especially pp. 14–30; and André Vauchez, *The Spirituality of the Medieval West: From the Eighth to the Twelfth Century* (Kalamazoo, MI: Cistercian Publications, 1993).

in the present time.¹⁰ The pilgrimage journey itself and the hardships that it involved also allowed pilgrims to expiate their own guilt for sins. The further off the pilgrimage site and the more difficult the journey, the better the imitation.

Thus the journey to Jerusalem held out the greatest prospect for grace as both the most difficult, perilous, and remote of pilgrimage sites; while the ability to literally and physically retrace the footsteps of Christ and the apostles consummated the meaning of religious reform in the twelfth century. In Jerusalem and the other sacred places of the Holy Land the pilgrim could reexperience the sufferings of their Savior and gain the benefits of his death in grace and forgiveness.

In addition to this act of penitence and grace, the journey to Jerusalem also held deep mystical and legendary meaning for medieval men and women, for the sacred city was believed to be the center of the world, the omphalos or navel, the sacred hub of the world's orb.¹¹ At the same time, it was the ideal of the sacred city — for Jerusalem was both the center of Christian history, the stage of Christ's redemptive sacrifice and resurrection, and the end of all history. It was, as the book of the Apocalypse assured its readers, the city of the final days, the heavenly city that would be granted by heaven to replace the kingdom of the world, whether of Rome or of Babylon.

Medieval people fully understood that this Heavenly Jerusalem¹² was a mystical goal that ended and transcended history. It was the last and best city, whose walls were jaspar,

---

10. See Labarge, Prescott, and Sumption in the bibliography.

11. See John Kirtland Wright, *The Geographical Lore in the Time of the Crusades* (New York: Dover, 1965), pp. 259-60; Naomi Reed Kline, *Maps of Medieval Thought: The Hereford Paradigm* (Woodbridge: Boydell & Brewer, 2001), esp. 191-218; and P.D.A. Harvey, *The Hereford World Map: Introduction* (Hereford: Hereford Cathedral, 2010).

12. The reference is from Apoc. 21:9-21.

Introduction to Guide by Theoderich of Würzburg

whose foundations were fixed with precious jewels, whose twelve gates were pearls, and whose streets were paved with gold. Yet for many the heavenly city, the goal of history, was confused with the earthly city, the center of the physical globe and the goal of earthly pilgrimage. Thought of the earthly Jerusalem could, and often did, strike deep chords of mystical and apocalyptic expectation, while with the eleventh and twelfth centuries many saw their pilgrimages to the city, whether armed or unarmed, as a fulfillment of the prophesies in the Apocalypse and hoped that reaching the physical city would bring the bliss of the elect promised by the vision of the heavenly city.[13]

The Route to Jerusalem

Pilgrimage may have been an act of apocalyptic spirituality, penitence for sin, and of evangelical imitation; yet it was also the opportunity to travel and to explore, whether this meant a week's excursion to a local shrine or the ultimate pilgrimage, the journey to Outremer, the land across the sea. As such the pilgrimage offers us many valuable and fascinating glimpses into the material life of the Middle Ages: of geographical knowledge and lore, and of medieval travel, its seasons, conditions, duration, forms of transport, food, booking arrangements, contracts and costs, dangers and pleasures.

By the late twelfth century the path of the pilgrim, well trodden since at least the fourth century,[14] had been deepened and widened by the Crusades.[15] Launched in 1095, the First

---

13. Apoc. 21:22–27, 22:1–5. See Jay Rubenstein, *Armies of Heaven: The First Crusade and the Quest for Apocalypse* (New York: Basic Books, 2011).

14. For a description of the routes see Runciman, 1: 121–94.

15. The Crusades have taken on a new interest and controversy in recent years with much new historiography of varying views. See Jonathan Riley-Smith, *The Crusades, Christianity, and Islâm* (New York: Columbia University Press, 2008).

The Holy Land

Crusade had conquered Jerusalem and surrounding Palestine as far south as Gaza and the Sinai and as far north as Tripoli in Lebanon and east as far as Edessa (Urfa) in modern Turkey. The expedition had followed well known pilgrimage routes. The land routes lead from southeastern Germany: Regensburg along the Danube and through the Balkans to Constantinople. Here it met the southern, Italian, route across the Adriatic from Brindisi or Bari to Dyrrhachium in modern Albania, which from there followed the ancient Via Egnatia across the Balkans to the Byzantine capital. The land route then led the pilgrim and crusader through Asia Minor: Nicea, south to Iconium, then along the coast via Tarsus or through the interior through Caesarea until the roads converged at the Cilician Gates and poured out into Syria at Antioch. At that point the land route left the Byzantine Empire for the Crusader states.

The pilgrim's other alternative was the sea route, no less dangerous due to the constant threat of piracy, but perhaps quicker in the proper season and at least unhindered by tolls, greedy princes or hostile tribes along the way. Many pilgrims thus made their way to the great Mediterranean ports: Genoa and Pisa or, if coming from central Europe, across the Alps to Venice. Marseille served intermittently for French pilgrims and Crusaders. From these shipping centers, bustling and prosperous city-states in the twelfth century, the pilgrim's company would sign up with a shipping company that dealt almost exclusively in the pilgrimage trade, carrying the faithful in large tours eastward and returning home from the Levant with high-profit cargos of spices, jewels, silks, ivory, sugar — and slaves — supplemented by returning pilgrims, lightened of at least their European sins and most of their travel funds.

Once in an Italian port,[16] Theoderich and his companions may have taken advantage of one of the

---

16. On shipping in the Mediterranean see Fernand Braudel, *The Mediterranean and the Mediterranean World in the Age of Philip*

many advertised specials offered by the pilgrim agencies: special fares, including accommodations and food on board, tours of the Holy Land, and return voyage. Accommodations there were provided by the many inns or pilgrim hospices. Most pilgrim sailings were set for the spring, the passagium vernale, some in the summer passage, the passagium aestivale. Most pilgrims then spent the spring or summer in Outremer and returned with the southerly wind no later than September or October. Few sailings were ever made in the winter, when the brutal north winds brought occasional snows and constant storms throughout the Mediterranean.

By the end of the Crusades, in the fourteenth century, pilgrim ships could carry as many as 1,000 passengers with crew and cargo. These ships included both huge galleys, lanteen rigged and equipped with oars, the favored form of Mediterranean transport into the nineteenth century, or the more sturdy and roomy "buss," the great round ships with some square rig on which Theoderich sailed, some of which measured over 100 feet long, 40 feet wide and weighed up to 1,000 tons. The average ship was about half this size.

Accommodations were less than luxurious.[17] All but the most wealthy pilgrims would consider themselves lucky if the travel mat that they carried tied to their backpack or stowed in their travel chests was laid in the same spot every night and provided enough room to stretch out.

II, 2 vols. (New York: Harper & Row, 1972), 1: 103–67, 246-67; Robert S. Lopez and Irving W. Raymond, eds., *Medieval Trade in the Mediterranean World* (New York: W.W. Norton, 1967), pp. 239–337. For pilgrims' shipping, accommodations, voyages, etc. see Prawer, pp. 195–204; Hazard, pp. 44–47. For new studies see Ruth, Gertwagen and Elizabeth Jeffreys, eds., *Shipping, Trade and Crusade in the Medieval Mediterranean: Studies in Honour of John Pryor* (Farnham, Surrey: Ashgate, 2012).

17. See Prawer, pp. 201-3; Hazard, pp. 46–50.

Most days were spent above decks, meals had to be simple due to the constant danger of fire from open hearths on board. Yet meals were provided, and these usually consisted of the pilgrim bread, biscotum, supplemented by sweet wine, some cheese and scanty vegetables, salted meat and whatever provisions the wise pilgrim — like the traveler on the Istanbul Express today — managed to gather together before embarking.

Cleanliness aboard ships was minimal, sleeping quarters were infested with lice, vermin and rats, fresh foods and water went bad after only a few weeks if not replenished. Considering the fact that most of the pilgrim's cabin companions had just come from a month or two on foot across Europe, and that some had already taken ascetic vows not to bathe or to clean their hair, all in all the journey really must have been an act of imitation of the early martyrs. Yet it was a special type of martyrdom that the traveler has always willingly embraced, that had its own mortifications as well as its own spiritual rewards. Landlocked Europeans experienced the sun and warmth of Mediterranean lands and saw, smelt, and felt the high seas for the first time in their lives. Pilgrims from small villages and towns visited lands of legend and enchantment: Italy and perhaps Sicily, St. Paul's Malta, the Morea and Achaia in Greece, Crete and Cyprus, not to mention the fabled cities of the Levant, and Jerusalem itself.

If all went well with wind, ship, and safety, usually in a ship convoy — the journey eastward could take as little as four weeks, with stops at coastal ports and islands all along the way, and as long as eight to ten weeks against contrary winds, or if layed up for repairs. Pilgrims traveling via Genoa and Pisa generally followed these cities' trade routes to Acre (Acco or Ptolomais), while Venetian ships made land at their fondaco or emporium in Tyre. Theoderich, then, probably made his journey up the Rhine valley to Bavaria and then

INTRODUCTION TO GUIDE BY THEODERICH OF WÜRZBURG

crossed the Alps and Lombardy before reaching either Genoa or Pisa. We assume this since he tells us that he departed from Acre (chapter 40, p. 202), and his narrative seems to indicate that this is where he also began his itinerary.

At Acre, the pilgrim port closest to Jerusalem, the pious traveler would pass through customs clearance and then choose a route[18]: either via Galilee, bearing north toward Lake Tiberias (Sea of Galilee) and then south through Samaria and Judaea to Jerusalem, or the pilgrim could take the southern, more direct, Seaside Road to the city. This seems to have been the way Theoderich's company passed, since the sites he describes in Part III roughly follow this itinerary: Acre, Mount Carmel, south down the coast passed Chateau Pelerin, Caesarea and Jaffa, Lydda, Ramleh, and from there inland through Beit Nûba and the Judaean Hills. He also vividly describes the Jezreel Valley south and east of Mount Carmel, and so must have also crossed this region at some time during his stay. Finally, approaching Jerusalem from the north, Theoderich would have reached the crest of Montjoye, the pilgrim's first joyous sight of the sacred city spread out below.

By 1172 Jerusalem probably had a population of about 30,000 out of a total population for the kingdom of nearly 250,000. Acre led the list with about 60,000 people. Tyre boasted about 40,000. Though large by northern European standards, these numbers were small by Mediterranean, especially Middle Eastern, norms. There were also about 20 cities with populations of around 5,000 spread across the Latin Kingdom. The Latin population, which tended to concentrate in the cities, has been estimated at about 100,000.[19]

---

18. On routes see Prawer, pp. 204–13; Hazard, pp. 50–68.

19. See Hans Eberhard Mayer, *The Crusades* (New York: Oxford University Press, 1972), pp. 153–54; Prawer, pp. 82–83.

In Part I Theoderich lays out all the standard sights in Jerusalem in excellent order and vivid description. He seems to have followed the western route through the city, the path that placed the Via Dolorosa, or the route of Christ's passion and death, from Mount Sion on the south, northeast to the Antonia fortress, and then west to Mount Calvary and the Holy Sepulcher.

Immediately outside the city Theoderich also followed the standard tour to Bethany and Bethphage to the east of the Kedron Valley and Mount of Olives. From there he seems to have joined one of the tours heading out to the Jordan Valley, including Mount Quarantana, the Jordan itself, and the reputed site of Christ's baptism. After stopping at the oasis of Jericho, he then probably returned via Jerusalem before heading to Bethlehem and Hebron in the Judaean Hills to the south.

His knowledge of regions further south and east — the Dead Sea, Transjordan, and Arabia — is mostly second-hand, a combination of hearsay, legend, and other accounts. But Theoderich does seem to have traveled to the southwest, to Gaza and Ascalon, standard stops on a pilgrim's tour. Returning again to Jerusalem, Theoderich then made a series of day or week trips, much like the modern tourist: to Emmaus, Ramatha [Ramathaim], Shiloh, certainly north to Nâblus (Neapolis), and Nazareth, and may even have traveled as far north as Tiberias on the Sea of Galilee.

It seems almost certain that he could not have traveled further north than that, since he describes the city of Banyas as being in Christian hands, when it was actually taken by Nur ed-Din a decade before. His descriptions of the sources of the Jordan in the underground river of Dan and the Jor probably confuses actual descriptions of marshes north of Lake Hulah with medieval legends about these two streams. His descriptions of most of Galilee, Idumaea, Syria,

INTRODUCTION TO GUIDE BY THEODERICH OF WÜRZBURG

Phoenicia, including Beirut and modern Lebanon, depend on biblical passages and legend.

Theoderich almost certainly visited Tyre, perhaps on his way back to the coast, and gives a vivid, if succinct, description of the city, its walls, double harbor, and great harbor chain. From there he seems to have traveled south along the coast back to Acre, from which he departed.[20]

GEOGRAPHICAL KNOWLEDGE

Many of the sites Theoderich describes in the Holy Land and specifically in Jerusalem are so accurately drawn that he has become a major source for medieval knowledge of the region, Jerusalem's topography, and the history of the art and archeology of the kingdom.[21] His work still offers valuable descriptions of fields full of ripe barley or roses, groves of palm or olive, orchards, various stone and soil types, of Muslims living in the Crusader state carrying on their customary agricultural routine with their own work routines and songs.[22]

Much of his description of the border lands of the Holy Land, however, are rather fanciful. We have already mentioned places, such as the sources of the Jordan, for which he relies on second-hand sources like the "old compendium," and regions where he could not have been both because the topography he describes is incorrect and the political situation out of date. Yet even here his *Guide* is a valuable resource for the light it sheds on the geographical lore of the Middle Ages and on the

20. Stewart notes that Theoderich departed on Wednesday of Easter Week. But whether of the same year is doubtful; the sights visited certainly cover a wide range and reflect prolonged stay and description.

21. See Hazard, pp. 10–11, 117-18; Peters, pp. 321–22, 326–27.

22. For medieval European views of Muslims see John V. Tolan, *Saracens: Islâm in the Medieval European Imagination* (New York: Columbia University Press, 2002); idem, *Sons of Ishmael: Muslims through European Eyes in the Middle Ages* (Gainesville: University Press of Florida, 2008).

age's sacred geography. Here we find Jerusalem as center of the world, a cosmological fact marked clearly in its stones and pavements; here too are rivers that run underground, the Dead Sea that once a year, on the anniversary of the destruction of Sodom and Gomorrah, throws up their stone and wood, and the pillar of salt that was once Lot's wife.

The Guide As Travel Literature

All in all, then, Theoderich's *Guide to the Holy Land* is an important monument in the history of travel literature, both in unique qualities of description and travel narrative and in its qualities common to the genre of pilgrims' guides.

The work derives from Christian geographies and itineraries derived from ancient sources and supplemented by the Bible. Examples include the guides to the Holy Land[23] by the Bordeaux Pilgrim in 333, St. Silvia's voyage in 385, St. Jerome's description of St. Paula's journey in the fifth century, Antoninus Martyr and Theodosius in the sixth century, Arculfus in the seventh, and Bernard the Wise c.870.

Pilgrim guides at the time of the Crusades[24] seem to have begun with that of Saewulf in 1102/3. Nearly contemporary with Theoderich are those of John of Würzburg, Rabbi Benjamin of Tudela, the Russian Abbot Daniel, and John Phocas, all referred to by Stewart in the preface and notes. Even by the early twelfth century, however, these guides had become standardized, often copied from two collections known as the "old" and "new compendium." While Theoderich does sometimes borrow from these, as in his descriptions of the Desert Elim and Sinai in chapter 31, he is one of the unique guides of the period, for his account depends almost entirely on his own observation. Where it

---

23. For these and other guides see the volumes in the Palestine Pilgrims' Text Society, 1–3.

24. See Wright, pp. 115–18.

does not, he usually informs the reader that he had relied on secondary sources.

One must really wait until the mid-thirteenth century to find works of similar importance and first-hand immediacy: the narratives of mission journeys to central Asia and China[25] by the Franciscans John of Plano Carpini and Benedict the Pole (1245–27), William of Rubruck (1253–54) and John of Monte Corvino (1289-91), and the most famous medieval travel book, the *Travels of Marco Polo* (1269–92). By the fourteenth century the obvious fabrications of Sir John Mandeville's travels to the Orient reflect the closing of the Levant to Europeans once again as the Crusade movement ground to a halt and word of foreign lands came only from the occasional pens of missionaries in the East, or not at all.

— Ronald G. Musto

---

25. See Christopher Dawson, ed., *Mission to Asia* (New York: Harper & Row, 1966); *The Travels of Sir John Mandeville* (New York: Dover, 1964); and Marco Polo, *The Travels* (New York: Penguin Books, 1967).

Prologue

Theoderich, the meanest of all monks and Christian men, addresses himself to all worshipers of the holy and indivisible Trinity, and more especially to the lovers of our most gracious Lord Jesus Christ.

So may they learn on earth below to share our Savior's pain,
That they with joy hereafter may deserve with him to reign.

We have been careful to note down, in writing on paper, everything relating to the holy places where our healer and Savior, when actually present in the flesh, accomplished the duties and mysteries connected with his blessed humanity and our salvation, which we have either ourselves seen with our own eyes or have learned from the truthful tales of others. This we have done in order that, according to the best of our ability, we may satisfy the desires of those who are unable to proceed there in person by describing those things that they cannot see with their own eyes or hear with their ears. Be it known to our readers that we have labored at this task to the intent that by reading this description or tale they may learn always to bear Christ in remembrance, and by remembering him may learn to love him, by loving may pity him who suffered near these places; through pity, may acquire a longing for him, by longing for him may be absolved from their sins; by absolution from sin may obtain his grace, and by his grace may be made partakers of the kingdom of heaven, being thought worthy of it by him who with the Father and the Holy Spirit lives and reigns for ever and ever. Amen.

Here begins the little book written by Theoderich about the holy places.

*

Guide to the Holy Land by Theoderich of Würzburg

1172 CE

Translated by Aubrey Stewart

Part I

1. The Ruin of the Land and the Changing of Its Names

It is evident to all who read the pages of the Old and New Testament that the land of Canaan was, by divine ordinance, given as a possession to the twelve tribes of the people of Israel. This land, divided into the three provinces of Judaea, Samaria, and Galilee, was in antiquity enriched by many cities, towns, and castles. The names and situations of all these cities were in former days well known to everyone; but the moderns, being strangers in the land, and not its original inhabitants, know only the names of a few places that we shall describe in their proper place. For since our dearest Lord Jesus Christ required vengeance for his blood — which was shed on the cross by the cruel hands of the impious Jews — the Roman princes, Vespasian and Titus, entered Judaea with an army, leveled the Temple and city to the ground, destroyed all the cities and villages throughout Judaea, and drove the murderers themselves out of their own country and forced them to depart and live among foreigners. In consequence of this all works and constructions of that people, and of the entire province, have been destroyed, so that although some traces of certain places still remain, nearly all their names have been altered.

2. Judaea

First, then, we must speak of Judaea, which is known to have been the chief province of the Jewish kingdom, which we have been able to examine with our own eyes and ears. There, as an eye in the head, is placed the Holy City of Jerusalem, from which, through our mediator with God, our Lord Jesus Christ, grace and salvation and life have flowed to all nations. Judaea is bounded on the west by the Great Sea. On the south it is separated by the desert from the mountains of Arabia and Egypt. On the east it is limited by the River Jordan, and on the north it is skirted by Samaria and Idumaea.

Now Judaea is for the most part mountainous, and round about the Holy City rises into very lofty ranges, sloping on all sides down to its aforesaid boundaries, just as, on the other hand, one ascends to it from them. These mountains are in some places rough with masses of the hardest rock, in other places they are adorned with stone excellently suited to be cut into ashlar, and in others they are beautified by white, red, and variegated marble. But wherever any patches of earth are found among these masses of rock the land is seen to be fit for the production of every kind of fruit. We have seen the hills and mountains covered with such vineyards and plantations of olive trees and fig trees, and the valleys abounding with corn and garden produce.

3. Jerusalem, the Valleys of Josaphat and Gehinnom, Mount of Rejoicing (Mons Gaudii), Tomb of Josaphat, Position of the Holy City, Its Fortifications, Gates, Streets, Houses, Cisterns, Wood

Now, on the very topmost peak of these mountains, as is affirmed by both Josephus and Jerome, is placed the city of Jerusalem, which is held to be holier and more notable than all the other cities and places throughout the world, not because it is holy in itself, or by itself, but because it has been glorified by the presence of God himself, and of our Lord Jesus Christ and his holy mother, and by the dwelling there, the doctrine, the preaching, and the martyrdom of patriarchs, prophets, Apostles, and other holy people. Although it has mountain ridges higher than itself all around it, it is itself hilly, being built on a mountain. Hence it follows that it attracts the eyes of viewers away from all the mountains by which it is surrounded.

Now, between the Hill of Moriah, on which stands the Temple of the Lord, and the Mount of Olives, which raises its head higher than any of the other mountains, lies the Cedron Brook and the Valley of Josaphat. This valley starts from the Mount of Rejoicing (Mons Gaudii), from which one enters the city on the northern side, passes by the Church of St. Mary, which is so called after her, passes the Tomb of Josaphat, king of Judaea, from whose death it itself has received this name, and passes close to the bathing Pool of Siloe, where another valley meets it. This valley bends its course from the right-hand corner of the city past the new cisterns between Mount Sion and the Field of Acheldemach, thus embracing two sides of the city with a very deep ravine. The Tomb of Josaphat stands in the midst of this valley, built of squared stone in the form of a pyramid. Round about it there are a great number of dwellings of servants of God, or hermits, all of which are placed under the care of the abbot of St. Mary's.

Now, the longest part of the city reaches from north to south, and the width of it is from west to east, and it is most strongly fortified by walls and bastions on the top of the mountain above the aforesaid valleys. There is also a barrier, or fosse, placed outside the wall and furnished with battlements and loopholes, which they call the Barbican. The city has seven gates, of which they firmly lock six every night until after sunrise; the seventh is closed by a wall and is only opened on Palm Sunday and on the day of the Exaltation of the Cross.

Since it has an oblong form, the city has five angles, one of which is transverse. Almost all its streets are paved with great stones below, and above many of them are covered with a stone vault, pierced with many windows for the transmission of light. The houses, which are lofty piles of carefully wrought stonework, are not finished with high-pitched roofs after our style but are level and flat. The people catch the rainwater that falls on them and store it up in cisterns for their own use — they use no other water, because they have none. Wood, suitable for building or for fires, is expensive there, because Mount Libanus — the only mountain that abounds in cedar, cypress, and pine wood — is a long way off from them, and they cannot approach it for fear of the attacks of the infidels.

4. The Tower of David, Mounts Sion and Moriah, the Field of Aceldama, Mount Gion, the House of Pilate, Antonia

The Tower of David is the property of the king of Jerusalem and is incomparably strong, being built of squared stones of immense size. It stands near the western gate, from which the road leads toward Bethlehem, together with the newly built solar chamber and palace that adjoins it, and it is strongly fortified with ditches and barbicans. It is situated on Mount Sion, of which we read in the Book of Kings (2 Sam. 5:7), "Now David took Sion." It is also situated over against the Temple of the Lord in the part of the city that extends sideways, with Mount Sion on the south and the Mount of Olives on the east. Mount Sion reaches from the tower as far as the Church of St. Mary outside the Walls and from the church nearly as far as the Palace of Solomon and as far as the way that leads from the Beautiful Gate to the tower, being wider but lower than the Mount of Olives. Although Mount Moriah, which overhangs the Valley of Josaphat and on which stands the Temple of the Lord and the Palace of Solomon, may be thought to be a great hill, Mount Sion surpasses it by as much as the latter seems to surpass the Valley of Josaphat.

In the Field of Acheldemach, which is only separated from it by the above-mentioned valley, is the pilgrims' burying ground, in which stands the Church of St. Mary, the Virgin Mother of God, in which also on the holy day of Palm Sunday we buried one of our brethren, named Adolf, a native of Cologne. This field is overhung by Mount Gion, on which Solomon was crowned, as may be read in the Book of Kings.

Of the other buildings, whether public or private, we have scarcely been able to find any traces, or at least very few, with the exception of the House of Pilate, near the Church of St. Anne, the mother of our Lady, which stands near the Sheep Pool. Of all the work that Josephus tells us was built by Herod and is now utterly ruined, nothing remains save one side, which is still standing, of the palace that was called Antonia, with a gate placed outside, near the court of the Temple.

5. The Church of the Holy Sepulcher: The Chapel

It only remains, then, that we should tell of the holy places, on account of which the city itself is called holy. We have thought, therefore, that it would be right to begin with the Holy of Holies; that is, with the sepulcher of our Lord. The Church of the Holy Sepulcher, of marvelous skill, is known to have been founded by the Empress Helena. Its outer wall being carried, as it were, round the circumference of a circle, makes the church itself round. The place of our Lord's sepulcher occupies the central point in the church, and its form is that of a chapel built above the sepulcher itself and beautifully ornamented with a casing of marble. It is not in the form of a complete circle, but two low walls proceed from the circumference toward the east and meet a third wall. These walls contain three doors, three feet wide and seven feet high, one of which opens on the north, another on the east, and another on the south side. The entrance is by the northern door and the exit by the southern door. The eastern door is set apart for the use of the guardians of the sepulcher.

Between these three small doors and the fourth door — by which one goes into the sepulcher itself — is an altar which, though small, is of great sanctity. On it our Lord's body is said to have been laid by Joseph and Nicodemus before it was placed in the sepulcher. Above the actual mouth of the sepulcher, which stands behind the altar, these same men are shown in a picture of mosaic work placing our Lord's body in the tomb, with our Lady, his mother, standing by, and the three Marys, whom we know well from the Gospel, with pots of perfume, and with the angel also sitting above the sepulcher and rolling away the stone, saying, "Behold the place where they laid him" (Mark 16:6). Between the opening and the sepulcher itself a line is drawn in a semicircular form, which contains these verses:

> *The place and guardian testify Christ's resurrection,*
> *Also the linen clothes, the angel, and Redemption.*

All these things are portrayed in the most precious mosaic work, with which the whole of this little chapel is adorned.

Each of the doors has very strict porters, who will not allow fewer than six, or more than twelve, people to enter at one time; for, indeed, the place is so narrow that it will not hold any more. After they have worshipped they are obliged to go out by another door. No one can enter the mouth of the sepulcher itself except by crawling upon one's knees, and having crossed it, one finds that most-

GUIDE TO THE HOLY LAND BY THEODERICH OF WÜRZBURG

wished-for treasure — I mean the sepulcher in which our most gracious Lord Jesus Christ lay for three days — which is wondrously adorned with white marble, gold and precious stones. In the side it has three holes, through which the pilgrims give their long-wished-for kisses to the very stone on which their Lord lay, which measures two-and-one-half feet in width, and the length of a man's arm from the elbow and one foot also. The floor between the sepulcher itself and the wall is large enough to allow five people to pray on their knees with their heads turned toward the sepulcher.

Round about this building outside are arranged ten pillars, which, with the arches that they support, make a circular enclosure, beneath which is a base, having this text of Scripture carved on it in letters of gold:

> *Christ, having risen from the dead, dies no more.*
> *Death has no more dominion over Him*
> *For in that he lives,*
> *He lives in God. (Rom. 6:9–10.)*

At his head, which was turned toward the west, there is an altar surrounded by partition walls, doors, and locks of iron, with lattice work of cypress wood decorated with various paintings, and with a roof of the same kind and similarly decorated, resting on the walls. The roof of the work itself is formed of slabs of gilt copper, with a round opening in the middle, round which stand small pillars in a circle, carrying small arches above them, which support a cup-shaped roof. Above the roof itself is a gilded cross, and above the cross is a dove, likewise gilded. Between every two columns throughout the circle, from each arch hangs a lamp. In the same manner two lamps hang between each of the lower columns all around the circle. Round the lower arches, on every arch, verses are written, some of which we were not able to read because of the fading of the colors. We were only able to read six plainly, which were written on three of the arches:

Within this tomb was laid
He who the world hath made:
You who His tomb do see
Haste you to be
A temple meet for me.

Lamb of God blest!
Patriarchs old,
Longed, ere their rest,
Him to behold.

Brought forth at Ephrata,
Suffered at Golgotha.
He from his rocky bed,
Adam our father led,
  Bore him on high;
Conquered the devil's arts,
And said to sinking hearts,
  "Rise, it is I!"

Around the iron enclosure that, as we have said before, is placed at the head of the sepulcher, above which is the lattice work, there runs a scroll containing these verses:

'Twas here the victory o'er Death was won
And life for us begun;
To God the pleasing sacrifice was given,
The victim fell;
Our sins are all forgiven;
There is joy in heaven,
And grief in hell;
Ends the Old Testament,
God has a New one sent:
We learn from this, O Christ, who here has bled,
That holy is the ground whereon we tread.

6. The Church or Rotunda Itself

The pavement of this church is most beautifully laid with Parian and various colored marble. The church itself is supported below by eight square pillars, which are called piers, and sixteen monolithic columns. Above, since it is vaulted both above and below like the church at Aix-la-Chapelle, it is supported in the same fashion on eight piers and sixteen pillars. The lower string course, which runs around the whole church, is covered with inscriptions in Greek letters.

The surface of the wall that lies between the middle and the upper string courses glows with mosaic work of incomparable beauty. There, in front of the choir, that is, above the arch of the sanctuary, may be seen the boy Jesus wrought in the same mosaic, but of ancient craft, depicted in glowing colors as far as the navel, with a most beautiful face; on his left hand his mother, and on his right the Archangel Gabriel pronouncing the well-known salutation, "Hail Mary, full of grace; the Lord is with thee, blessed among women, and blessed the fruit of thy womb." This salutation is written both in Latin and in Greek around the Lord Christ himself.

Further on, on the right side, the twelve Apostles are depicted in a row in the same mosaic, each of them holding in his hands praises of Christ in words alluding to the holy mysteries. In the midst of them, in a recess slightly sunken into the wall, sits in royal splendor, wearing the trabea, the Emperor Constantine, because he, together with his mother Helena, was the founder of the church. Also beyond the Apostles, the blessed Michael the Archangel glitters in wondrous array. On the left follows a row of thirteen prophets, all of whom have their faces turned toward the beautiful boy, and reverently address him, holding in their hands the prophesies with which he inspired them of old. In the midst of them, opposite her son, sits the blessed Empress Helena, magnificently arrayed. On the wall itself rests a leaden roof supported by rafters of cypress wood, having a large round opening in the middle, through which the light comes from above and lights the whole church, for it has no other window at all.

7. The Choir of the Canons

There adjoins this church a sanctuary, or Holy of Holies, of marvelous skill, which was subsequently built by the Franks, who also most sweetly sing praises there both by day and by night; that is to say, at the canonical hours, according to the cycle of the Virgin Mary. They hold prebends, and half the offerings of the Holy Sepulcher is appropriated to them for income, while the other half is appropriated for the use of the patriarch. The high altar is dedicated to the name and in honor of our Lord and Savior, and behind it is placed the patriarch's seat, above which hang from the arch of the sanctuary a very great and adorable picture of our Lady, a picture of St. John the Baptist, and also a third picture of the holy Gabriel, her bridesman. In the ceiling of the sanctuary itself is represented our Lord Jesus Christ holding his cross in his left hand, bearing Adam in his right, looking royally up toward heaven, with his left foot raised in a gigantic stride, his right still resting on the earth as he enters heaven, while the following stand around — that is to say, his mother, St. John the Baptist, and all the Apostles. Under his feet a scroll, reaching across the arch from one wall to the other, contains this inscription:

> *Praise Him crucified in the flesh,*
> *Glorify Him buried for us,*
> *Adore Him risen from death.*

Guide to the Holy Land by Theoderich of Würzburg

Beyond this, on a higher scroll drawn across the same arch, is the passage from Scripture, "Christ, ascending on high, he led away captives; he gave gifts to men." (Eph. 4:8.) About the middle of the choir there is a small open altar of great sanctity, on the flooring of which is marked a cross inscribed in a circle, which signifies that on this spot Joseph and Nicodemus laid our Lord's body in order to wash it after they had taken it down from the cross. Before the door of the choir is an altar of no small size, which, however, is only used by the Syrians in their services. When the daily Latin services are over, the Syrians usually sing their hymns either there outside the choir, or in one of the apses of the church; indeed, they have several small altars in the church, arranged and devoted to their own peculiar use. These are the religious sects that celebrate divine service in the church at Jerusalem: the Latins, Syrians, Armenians, Greeks, Jacobites, and Nubians. All these differ from one another both in language and in their manner of conducting divine service. The Jacobites use trumpets on their feast days, after the fashion of the Jews.

8. The Holy Fire

It is customary in the Church of the Holy Sepulcher, both in the church itself and in all the other churches in the city, at daybreak on the morning of Easter Eve, to put out the earthly lights, and to await the coming of light from heaven for the reception of which light one of the silver lamps, seven of which hang there, is prepared. Then all the clergy and people stand waiting with great and anxious expectation, until God shall send his hand down from on high. Among other prayers, they often shout loudly and with tears, "God help us!" and "Holy Sepulcher!" Meanwhile, the patriarch or some of the other bishops who have assembled to receive the holy fire, and also the rest of the clergy, bearing a cross in which a large piece of our Lord's cross is inserted, and with other relics of the saints, frequently visit the Holy Sepulcher to pray there; watching also whether God has sent his gracious light into the vessel prepared to receive it. The fire has the habit of appearing at certain hours and in certain places; for sometimes it appears about the first hour, sometimes about the third, the sixth, or the ninth, or even so late as the time of compline. Moreover, it comes sometimes to the sepulcher itself, sometimes to the Temple of the Lord, and sometimes to the Church of St. John. However, on the day when our humble selves, with the other pilgrims, were awaiting the sacred fire, immediately after the ninth hour that sacred fire came, upon which, behold, with ringing of church bells, the service of the Mass was said throughout the whole city, the baptismal and other services having been previously celebrated. As soon as the holy fire arrives, it is customary to present it to the Temple of the Lord before anyone, except the patriarch, has lighted his candle at it.

9. The Chapels of St. Mary and of the Holy Cross, the Lord's Prison, the Altar of St. Nicholas, the Door Leading into the Cloister

Upon the west side of the church, near the door, from which one mounts more than thirty steps from the church up to the street, in front of the door itself, there is a chapel that is dedicated to Mary, and which belongs to the Armenians. Also on the left side of the church, toward the north, there is a chapel dedicated to the holy cross, in which is also a great part of the venerable wood itself, contained in a case of gold and silver; and this chapel is in the hands of the Syrians. Again, on the same side, opposite this chapel, toward the east, is a chapel of peculiar sanctity, in which there is a most holy altar dedicated to the holy cross. A large piece of the same blessed wood covered with gold, silver and jewels, is kept in a most beautiful case, so that it can be easily seen. When necessity requires it, the Christians carry this holy symbol against the pagans in battle. This chapel is also wonderfully decorated with mosaics. Heraclius, the Roman emperor, rescued this cross from Cosdre, the king of the Persians, during the war that he waged with him, and restored it to the Christians.

Near this chapel, on the eastern side of it, one enters a dark chapel by about twenty steps, in which there is a most holy altar, under the pavement of which may be seen the mark of a cross. In this place our Lord Jesus Christ is said to have been imprisoned for a long time while he was waiting for Pilate's decision on the place of his passion, until his face was veiled and the cross erected on Calvary, so that he might be hung on it. Also, behind this chapel there is an altar dedicated to St. Nicholas. Beyond this is the gate of the cloister through which one goes into the canons' cloister, which stands round about the sanctuary. After one has made the circuit of the cloisters and is reentering the church from the other side of the door, one notices a figure of Christ on the cross painted above the door of the cloisters so vividly as to strike all beholders with great remorse. Round it these verses are inscribed:

> *You that this way do go,*
> *'Twas you that caused my woe;*
> *I suffered this for you,*
> *For my sake vice eschew.*

10. The Chapel of St. Helena, the Grotto in Which the Cross Was Found

To the eastward of this one goes down thirty steps and more to the venerable Chapel of St. Helena the empress, which is situated outside of the church itself, where there is a holy altar dedicated to her. From here, again on the right hand, one descends fifteen or rather more steps into a subterranean cave, where on the right-hand corner of the cave one may see an open altar and beneath it a cross cut on the pavement, at which spot the empress is said to have discovered the cross of our Lord. There is an altar there dedicated to St. James. This chapel has no other window than the great opening in its roof.

11. The Chapel of the Flagellation, the Tomb of Duke Godfrey and of the Kings of Jerusalem, the Chapel under the Campanile, the Chapel of John the Baptist, and Its Vicinity

In another part of the church — that is to say, on the right hand, at the back of the choir — there is a fair altar, in which stands part of the column around which our Lord was tied and scourged. Beyond this, on the south, before the door of the church, may be seen five tombs, of which the one nearest to the door, which is of white marble and costly skill, is that of the brother of the king of Jerusalem, named Baldwin; and the second one is that of King Baldwin [I], the brother of Duke Godfrey, on which is the following inscription:

> *Here Baldwin lies, a second Judas Maccabee,*
> *His country's hope, the Church's pride and strength was he;*
> *Cedar and Egypt, Dan and Damascus insolent,*
> *Dreaded his might, and gifts and tribute humbly sent.*
> *Ah, well-a-day! he lies 'neath this poor monument.*

The third tomb, beyond this, is that of his brother, Duke Godfrey himself, who by his sword and his wisdom recovered the city of Jerusalem, which had been invaded by the Saracens and Turks, and restored it to the Christians, replaced on the throne the patriarch who had been driven out by the infidels, established a body of clergy in the church and settled endowments upon them, that they might be strong to fight in God's cause. The fourth tomb is that of the father of the reigning king, Amalric; the fifth is that of the father of the abbess of St. Lazarus.

Also on the south there is a door, through which one enters the chapel under the campanile; and from it one passes into another chapel of great sanctity, dedicated to John the Baptist, in which there is also a font. From there one goes again into a third chapel. From the first chapel one ascends to the street by forty steps or more.

12. Mount Calvary, the Outside Vestibule before Golgotha, the Chapel of the Crucifixion, the Chapel of Golgotha, the Door of the Church

It remains now to speak of Mount Calvary, which shines in the church as does the eye in the head; from which by the death and blood-shedding of the Son of God, light and eternal life shall be poured forth for us. Before the entrance or door to the church, which is covered with solid bronze and is of a double form, one mounts by about fifteen steps to a small chamber, which is railed in and decorated with paintings. Here, at the top of the stairs, stand guardians watching the gate, who only allow as many pilgrims as they choose to enter, lest by excessive pressure, as often happens, there is crushing or danger to life. From that vestibule one ascends by three steps, through another door, into a chapel preeminent in sanctity and holiness beyond all other places under the sun.

This chapel is formed by four strong arches. Its pavement is beautifully composed of various kinds of marble, and its vault or ceiling is most nobly decorated with the prophets — that is to say, David, Solomon, Isaiah, and some others — bearing in their hands texts referring to Christ's passion, wrought so beautifully on it in mosaic that no work under heaven could be compared with it, if only it could be seen clearly; for this place is somewhat darkened by the buildings around it. The place in which the cross stood on which the Savior suffered death is on the eastern side, raised on a high step covered on the left side with the finest Parian marble, and it displays a round hole almost wide enough to take in a person's head, in which it is known that the cross itself was fixed. Into this hole pilgrims, out of the love and respect that they bear to him who was crucified, plunge their head and face.

On the right hand Mount Calvary itself, rising up higher, displays a long, wide, and very deep rift in the pavement, where the rock was rent asunder when Christ died. Yawning above and in front with a frightful cleft, it proves that the blood that flowed from Christ's side as he hung upon the cross found its way quite down to the earth. On the top of this rock it is customary for pilgrims to place the crosses that they have carried with them from their own countries; and we saw a great number of them there, all of which the guardians of Calvary burn in the fire on Easter Eve. In that chapel there is an altar of much sanctity, and on Good Friday the whole service for the day is celebrated at it by the patriarch and all the clergy. On the wall on the left side of the altar there is a most beautiful painting of our Lord upon the cross, with Longinus standing on his right hand piercing his side with his spear; and on his left Stephaton offering him vinegar with the sponge and reed; with his mother also standing on his left hand, and St. John on his right; while two great scrolls, covered throughout with Greek inscriptions, are carried all around this work.

On the right hand also of the same altar a picture shows Nicodemus and Joseph taking down the dead Christ from the cross; where there is also the inscription, "The Descent of our Lord Jesus Christ from the Cross." From here one descends fifteen steps into the church and comes to that chapel that is called Golgotha, of great sanctity, but very dark. At the back of it is a deep recess, which enables the beholders to see the end of the cleft in the rock that came down from Calvary. In that place it is said that the blood of Christ stood after it had run down there through the cleft. Moreover above the arch that forms the boundary of Golgotha, or in other words, on the west side of Calvary, there is a picture painted on the wall, in which these verses may be seen in golden letters:

> This place was hallowed by Christ's blood before,
> Our consecration cannot make it more;
> Howbeit, the buildings round this stone, in date
> Were on July the fifteenth consecrate
> By Fulcher patriarch in solemn state.

Outside the gate of the church, in the space between the two doors stands the Lord Christ in a saintly garment, as though just risen from the dead; while Mary Magdalen lies prostrate at his feet, but not touching them. The Lord holds out toward her a scroll containing these verses:

> Woman, wherefore weep'st thou,
>   kneeling unto him thou seekest dead?
> Touch me not, behold me living,
>   worthy to be worshipped.

13. The Chapel of the Three Marys, the Chapel of the Armenians, Another Little Chapel, the Street and Market, the Church and Hospital of St. John the Baptist, the Church of St. Mary the Great, the Church of St. Mary the Latin

As one goes out of the church toward the south, one finds a sort of square courtyard paved with squared stone, on the left side of which, near Golgotha, on the outside, there is a chapel dedicated to the three Marys, which belongs to the Latins. Further on toward the south there is another chapel, which is in the hands of the Armenians. Further on there is another little chapel. As one comes out of this open space, on the left there is a vaulted street full of goods for sale. Opposite the church is the marketplace. Here, in front of the church, stand six columns, with arches above them; and here, on the south side of the church, stands the Church and Hospital of St. John the Baptist.

As for this, no one can credibly tell another how beautiful its buildings are, how abundantly it is supplied with rooms and beds and other material for the use of poor and sick people, how rich it is in the means of refreshing the poor, and how devotedly it labors to maintain the needy, unless one has the opportunity of seeing it with one's own eyes. Indeed we passed through this palace and were unable by any means to discover the number of sick people lying there; but we saw that the beds numbered more than one thousand. It is not every one of the most powerful kings and despots who could maintain as many people as that house does every day; and no wonder, for, in addition to its possessions in other countries (whose sum total is not easily to be arrived at), the Hospitallers and the Templars have conquered almost all the cities and villages that once belonged to Judaea and that were destroyed by Vespasian and Titus, together with all their lands and vineyards. For they have troops stationed throughout the entire country, and castles well fortified against the infidels.

Next to this to the east as one stands there, comes the Church of St. Mary, in which nuns, under the rule of an abbess, celebrate divine service daily. This place is said to have been dedicated to Mary because while our Savior was being maltreated on the way to his passion, she is said to have been shut up by his command in a chamber that then stood on that spot.

There closely follows another church on the east of this, which is also dedicated to our Lady, because while our Lord was enduring such suffering for our salvation, she fainted from excess of sorrow and was carried by men's hands there into a subterranean grotto, where in the indulgence of her grief she tore her hair from her head. This hair is preserved to this day in a glass vessel in that church. There is also in this church the head of St. Philip the Apostle, lavishly adorned with gold; and the arm of St. Simeon the Apostle, and the arm of St. Cyprian the bishop. In this church monks serve God under a rule and under the orders of an abbot.

14. The Temple of the Lord: The Courtyard, the Stairs, the Subterranean Grotto, the Great Pool, the Houses, the Gardens, the School of St. Mary, the Great Stone, the Cloister and Conventual Buildings of the Clergy, and Other Pools

By a street that bends a little toward the south through the Beautiful Gate of the Temple one comes to the Temple of the Lord, crossing about the middle of the city; where one mounts from the lower court to the upper one by twenty-two steps, and from the upper court one enters the Temple. In front of these same steps in the lower court there are twenty-five steps or more leading down into a great pool, from which it is said there is a subterranean connection with the Church of the Holy Sepulcher, through which the holy fire that is miraculously lighted in that church on Easter Eve is said to be brought underground to the Temple of the Lord. In this pool victims that were to be offered in the Temple of the Lord were washed according to the precepts of the law. Now, the outer court is twice as large, or more, than the inner court, which, like the outer one, is paved with broad and large stones. Two sides of the outer court exist to this day; the other two have been taken for the use of the canons, and the Templars, who have built houses and planted gardens on them.

On the western side one ascends to the upper court by two ranges of steps, and in like manner on the southern side. Over the steps, before which we said that the pool is situated, there stand four columns with arches above them, and there, too, is the sepulcher of some rich man, surrounded by an iron grille, and beautifully carved in alabaster. On the right, also, above the steps on the south side, there stand in like manner four columns and on the left three. On the eastern side also there are fifteen double steps, by which one mounts to the Temple through the Golden Gate, according to the number of which the Psalmist composed fifteen psalms, and above these also stand columns. Besides this, on the south side above the two angles of the inner court, stand two small dwellings, of which the one toward the west is said to have been the school of the Blessed Virgin. Now, between the Temple and the two sides of the outer court — that is the eastern and southern sides — there stands a great stone like an altar, which, according to some traditions, is the mouth of some pools of water that exist there; but, according to the belief of others, points out the place where Zacharias, the son of Barachias, was slain. On the northern side are the cloister and conventual buildings of the clergy. Round about the Temple itself there are great pools of water under the pavement. Between the Golden Gate and the fifteen steps there stands an ancient and ruined cistern in which in old times victims were washed before they were offered.

15. The Description of the Temple: The Place Where Christ Was Presented and Where Jacob Saw the Ladder

The Temple itself is evidently of an octagonal shape in its lower part. Its lower part is ornamented as far as the middle with most glorious marbles, and from the middle up to the topmost border, on which the roof rests, is most beautifully adorned with mosaic work. Now, this border, which reaches round the entire circuit of the Temple, contains the following inscription, which, starting from the front, or west door, must read according to the way of the sun as follows: On the front, "Peace be unto this house for ever, from the Father Eternal." On the second side, "The Temple of the Lord is holy; God cares for it; God hallows it." On the third side, "This is the house of the Lord, firmly built." On the fourth side, "In this house of the Lord all men shall tell of his glory." On the fifth, "Blessed be the glory of the Lord out of his holy place." On the sixth, "Blessed be they who dwell in thy house, O Lord." On the seventh, "Of a truth the Lord is in his holy place, and I knew it not." On the eighth, "The house of the Lord is well built upon a firm rock. "Besides this, on the eastern side opposite the Church of St. James, there is a column represented in the wall in mosaic work, above which is the inscription, "The Roman Column."

The upper wall forms a narrower circle, resting on arches within the building and supports a leaden roof, which has on its summit a great ball with a gilded cross above it. Four doors lead into and out of the building, each door looking to one of the four quarters of the world. The church rests upon eight square piers and sixteen columns, and its walls and ceilings are magnificently adorned with mosaics. The circuit of the choir contains four main pillars or piers and eight columns, which support the inner wall, with its own lofty vaulted roof. Above the arches of the choir a scroll extends all round the building bearing this text: "'My house shall be called the house of prayer,' says the Lord. 'In it whoever asks, receives, and whoever seeks finds, and to anyone who knocks it shall be opened. Ask, and you shall receive; seek, and you shall find.'" In the upper circular scroll, similarly placed around the building, is the text:

"Have thou respect unto the prayer of thy servant and to his supplication, O Lord, my God, that thine eyes may be open and thine ears turned toward his house night and day. Look down, O Lord, from thy sanctuary and from the highest heaven, thy dwelling place." (1 Kings 8:28–29.)

At the entrance to the choir there is an altar dedicated to St. Nicholas, set off in an iron enclosure, which has on its upper part a border containing this inscription in front: "In the year 1101, in the fourth indiction, Epact II," and on the left side, "From the taking of Antioch 63 years, from the taking of Jerusalem 53." On the right side, "From the taking of Tripoli 52 years, from the taking of Berytus 51 years, from the taking of Ascalon 11 years."

There is a place toward the east side of the choir that is surrounded by an iron enclosure with doors, which is worthy of the greatest reverence, seeing it was there that our Lord Jesus Christ was presented by his parents when he was brought to the Temple with an offering on the fortieth day after his birth. At the entrance of the Temple the aged Simeon took him in his arms and carried him to the place of presentation, in front of which these verses are inscribed:

The Virgin's child, the King of kings, was offered here;
This place we therefore deck with presents and revere.

Near this place, at scarcely a cubit's distance, is the stone that the patriarch Jacob placed under his head, on which he slept when he saw the ladder reaching up to heaven, by which the angels were ascending and descending, and said, "Truly the Lord is in this place and I did not know it." (Gen. 28:16.) In front of this place are the following verses:

Jacob, with his body resting, but with mind awake,
Here saw the ladder, and his altar here did make.

16. The Chapel of St. James outside the Temple, the Place Where Our Lord Was Questioned about the Middle of the World, Where Ezekiel Saw the Waters, the Crypt under the Choir, the Windows, the High Altar, the History of the Temple

From here, through the eastern gate, one enters the Chapel of St. James the Apostle, the brother of our Lord, who was murdered by the impious Jews by being cast down from the pinnacle of the Temple, and his skull broken with a fuller's club, and was first buried in the Valley of Josaphat near the Temple, but was afterwards translated here by the faithful with all honor, as became him, and placed in a sepulcher, above which is written the following epitaph:

> Say, stone and grave, what king's bones here find room?
> Saint James the Just: he lies within this tomb.

The chapel itself is round, being wide below and narrow above, supported by eight columns, and excellently adorned with paintings. As we return from it by the same door, on the left hand, behind the jamb of the door, there is a place five feet in length and breadth on which our Lord stood when he was asked where he was in Jerusalem, which they assert is situated in the middle of the world, and he answered, "This place is called Jerusalem." Behind the same door, opposite the just-mentioned place, that is, on the northern side, there is another place that contains the waters that the prophet Ezekiel saw flowing down from under the Temple on the right side (Ezek. 47:1–2).

As we return into the great church, on the south side near the choir, there is a door through which, down about forty-five steps, one enters the crypt, to which the Scribes and Pharisees brought the woman taken in adultery to the Lord Jesus and accused her, whose sins the holy master forgave and acquitted her. In memory of this indulgences are granted to pilgrims at this place. The church itself has thirty-six windows in its lower story and fourteen in its upper story, which added together make fifty, and is dedicated to our Lady Mary, to whom also the high altar is consecrated. This church is said to have been built by the Empress St. Helena and her son the Emperor Constantine.

Let us consider how many times and by whom the Temple has been built or destroyed. As we read in the Book of Kings, King Solomon first built the Temple by divine command at a great expense — not in a round form as we see it today, but oblong (1 Kings 6:1–10). This temple lasted until the time of Sedechia, king of Judah, who was taken by Nebuchadnezzar, king of Babylon, and led away captive into Babylonia, and with him Judah and Benjamin were also made captive and led away into the country of the Assyrians. Shortly afterwards his steward, Nabuzardan, came to Jerusalem with an army and burned both the Temple and the city; and this was the first destruction of the Temple. After seventy years of captivity the children of Israel returned to the land of Judah, led by Zorobabel and Esdras, by the favor and permission of Cyrus, the king of the Persians, and they rebuilt the same Temple in the same place and adorned it to the best of their ability. In rebuilding the Temple and the city they worked, it is said, holding a stone in one hand and a sword in the other, because of the continual assaults of the Gentiles who lived round about them. So, then, this was the second building of the Temple.

Afterwards the city, as may be read in the Book of Maccabees, though not entirely destroyed by Antiochus, king of Syria, was for the most part laid in ruins, the ornaments of the Temple utterly destroyed, the sacrifices forbidden, the walls broken down, and the Temple, as well as the city, made into a virtual wilderness. After this, Judas Maccabeus and his brethren, by God's help, put Antiochus to flight, drove his generals out of Judaea, and rebuilt and restored the Temple, replaced the altar and instituted the sacrifices and offerings by regular priests as of old. This was the third building of the Temple, and it remained until the time of Herod, who, Josephus tells us, although the Jews deny it, razed this Temple to the ground and built another greater one of more elaborate skill.

This was the fourth building of the Temple, which endured until the days of Titus and Vespasian, who took the whole country by storm and overthrew both the city and the Temple to their very foundations. This was the fourth destruction of the Temple. After this, as has been said a little way before, the Temple that we now see was built by the Empress Helena and her son the Emperor Constantine in honor of our Lord Jesus Christ and his holy mother. This, then, was the fifth restoration of the Temple.

17. The Palace of Solomon, the House and the Stable of the Templars and Their Gardens, Their Stores of Wood and Water, Their Granaries and Refectories, Their New and Old Hall, and Their New Church

Next comes, on the south the Palace of Solomon, which is oblong and supported by columns within like a church. At the end it is round like a sanctuary and covered by a great round dome, so that, as I have said, it resembles a church. This building, with all its appurtenances, has passed into the hands of the Knights Templars. They dwell in it and in the other buildings connected with it and have many magazines of arms, clothing and food in it, and are ever on the watch to guard and protect the country. They have below them stables for horses built by King Solomon himself in the days of old, and adjoining the palace, a wondrous and intricate building resting on piers and containing an endless complication of arches and vaults. This stable, we declare, according to our reckoning, could take in ten thousand horses with their grooms. No man could send an arrow from one end of their building to the other, either lengthways or crossways, at one shot with a Balearic bow. Above it abounds with rooms, solar chambers, and buildings suitable for all manner of uses. Those who walk upon the roof of it find an abundance of gardens, courtyards and antechambers, vestibules and rain-water cisterns; while down below it contains a wonderful number of baths, storehouses, granaries, and magazines for the storage of wood and other necessary provisions.

On another side of the palace, that is to say, on the western side, the Templars have erected a new building. I could give the measurements of the height, length and breadth of its cellars, refectories, staircases and roof, rising with a high pitch, unlike the flat roofs of that country, but even if I did so, my hearers would hardly be able to believe me. They have built a new cloister there in addition to the old one that they had in another part of the building. Moreover, they are laying the foundations of a new church of wonderful size and skill in this place, by the side of the great court. It is not easy for anyone to gain an idea of the power and wealth of the Templars — for they and the Hospitallers have taken possession of almost all the cities and villages with which Judaea was once enriched, which were destroyed by the Romans, and have built castles everywhere and filled them with garrisons, besides the very many and, indeed, numberless estates that they are well known to possess in other lands.

18. The Ancient Walls round the Temple, the Ruins of Antonia, Moriah, the Church of the Bath or of the Manger of Our Lord, the House of Simeon the Just

Now, the city wall on the southern and eastern sides surrounds all their dwellings, but on the west and the north a wall built by Solomon encloses not only their houses, but also the outer court and the Temple itself. On the north side of the court one wall and one gate remain entire among the ruins of Antonia that Herod built. The hill itself on which the Temple stands was in ancient times called Moriah, and upon it David saw the angel of the Lord smiting the people with an unsheathed sword, when he said to the Lord, "I am he that have sinned: I have done wickedly. These that are the sheep, what have they done? Let thy hand, I beseech thee, be turned against me, and against my father's house." (2 Sam. 24:17.) On this hill was the threshing floor of Araunah the Jebusite, which David bought from him to build a house for the Lord. Here by a postern there is a narrow way between the eastern wall of the city and the garden of the Templars, whereby one comes to the most holy church, which is called the Church of the Bath or of the Manger of the Lord our Savior. In it the cradle of the Lord Christ is worshipped. This cradle stands in a place of honor at the east end on a high wall in front of a window. On the south side one sees a great basin made of stone lying on the ground, in which it is known that he was bathed as a child; and on the north side is the bed of our Lady, on which she lay while she suckled her child at her breast. One descends into this church by about fifty steps, and it once was the house of the just Simeon, who rests there in peace.

✷

Part II

19. The Bathing Pool of Siloe

As one goes southward from this church or from the angle of the city itself, down the sloping side of the hill along the outwork that the Templars have built to protect their houses and cloister, where also in ancient times the city itself stood, a little path leads to the bathing Pool of Siloe, which we are told is so-called because the water of that fountain comes there by an underground course from Mount Silo. This appears to me to be doubtful, because our mount, on which the city stands, and several other mountains, lie between them, and no valley leads directly from the mountain to the pool, nor is it possible that there can be an underground passage through such great mountains because of the distance; for Mount Silo is two miles from the city. Therefore, without pronouncing any decision upon this point, let us tell our hearers what we know to be true. We declare it to be the truth that the water bubbles up out of the earth like a fountain and that after filling the pool and running down to another pool close by, it disappears.

One descends into the pool by thirteen steps, and round about it are piers bearing arches, under which a paved walk has been constructed all round it, made of large stones, upon which those who stand can drink the waters as they run down. The second pool is square and surrounded by a simple wall. This bathing pool was once inside the city, but it is now far outside it, for the city has lost almost twice as much in this direction as it has gained in the parts near the Holy Sepulcher.

20. Bethany, Bethphage, the Golden Gate with Its Chapel

Now, we ought to arrange the course of our account according to the passion of Christ, who by his grace permits us to partake of his sufferings that we may be able thereby to partake of his kingdom hereafter. A mile from Jerusalem is Bethany, where stood the house of Simon the leper and of Lazarus and his sisters Mary and Martha, where our Lord was frequently received as a guest. Bethany stands near the Valley of Olives, in which the mount ends toward the east. So on Palm Sunday our dearest Lord Jesus Christ set out from Bethany, came to Bethphage, which is half-way between Bethany and the Mount of Olives — and where now a fair chapel has been built in his honor — and sent two of his disciples to fetch the ass and her colt. He stood upon a great stone that may be seen in the chapel and sitting on the ass went over the Mount of Olives to Jerusalem and was met by a great crowd as he descended the side of the mountain.

He went on, beyond the Valley of Josaphat and the Cedron Brook, until he arrived at the Golden Gate, which is twofold. As he approached it one of the doors opened by itself, for the bolt fell out and violently drawing out its ring made the other door fly open with a loud noise. Therefore a chapel has been consecrated in honor of it, in which this ring, which is covered with gilding, is regarded with great reverence. The gate itself is never opened except on Palm Sunday and on the day of the Exaltation of the Cross, because the Emperor Heraclius passed through it with a large piece of the wood of the cross that he had brought from Persia. Our Lord entered the Temple that same day and remained there teaching every day until the fourth day of the week.

21. Peter's Prison

With him, therefore, I wish to ascend on to Mount Sion and behold what he did after this; but, first, I wish to be imprisoned with Peter, that with him I may be taught by Christ not to deny him but to pray. On the way by which people go from the Temple to Mount Sion they pass a fair chapel. Here at a great depth beneath the earth, seeing that one descends twenty steps and more in order to enter it, is that prison in which Herod the younger bound St. Peter, and from which the angel of the Lord led him. At the entrance of the chapel these verses are inscribed:

> Arise, put on thy cloak, Peter, thy chains are broke;
> Arise and leave this place, set free by heaven's grace.
>
> O now I know indeed from prison I am freed;
> Christ's love to me be praised, that me from bonds has saved.

22. Mount Sion, Church of St. Mary, the Place Where She Died, the Room of the Last Supper, Where the Holy Ghost Came Down, Where Christ Washed the Apostles' Feet, Where Thomas Felt the Lord's Wounds, the Tomb of St. Stephen

Mount Sion, which stands to the south and is for the most part outside the city walls, contains the church dedicated to our Lady Mary. This is well fortified with walls, towers and battlements against the assaults of the infidels, and here canons regular serve God under an abbot. When you enter it you will find in the middle apse, on the left-hand side, the holy place at which our Lord Jesus Christ received the soul of his beloved mother, our Blessed Lady Mary, and raised it to heaven.

This work is square below and round above, supporting a dome. By about thirty steps on the right hand one mounts into the upper chamber, which is situated in the extremity of the apse. Here may be seen the table at which our Lord supped with his disciples, and after the departure of the traitor gave to those disciples his mystical body and blood. In the same upper chamber, at a distance of more than thirty feet to the south of that place, there stands an altar in the place where the Holy Ghost descended upon the Apostles. From here one descends by as many steps as one ascended and sees in the chapel beneath the upper chamber the stone basin, built into the wall, in which the Savior washed the feet of the Apostles. Here, close by on the right hand, there stands an altar in the place where Thomas felt the Lord's side after his resurrection, which for this reason is called the Altar of the Finger.

From this place one passes through a kind of anteroom, a round sanctuary of the church, and finds on its left-hand side a holy altar, beneath which, without doubt, the body of St. Stephen, the protomartyr, was buried by John, bishop of Jerusalem. His body, we read in history, was afterwards translated by the Emperor Theodosius from Constantinople to Rome, having been first translated from Jerusalem to Constantinople by the Empress Helena. Before the choir a column of precious marble stands near the wall, and simple-minded people like to walk around it.

23. The Cedron Brook, Gethsemane, Church of St. Mary, the Chapel of the Sepulcher, the Little Chapel on the Stairs, the Legend about a Jew Who Wished To Drag Away the Body of the Blessed Mary

From here after his supper the Lord went out across the Cedron Brook, where there was a garden. The Cedron Brook passes through the middle of the Valley of Josaphat. In the place where that garden was the Church of St. Mary, with its conventual buildings, has been founded, in which her own body was buried. Through a porch one descends by more than forty steps into a crypt, in which her holy sepulcher stands, covered with most costly decorations of marble and mosaic work. At the entrance to this crypt these two verses are written:

You heirs of life, come praise our Queen, to whom
Our life we owe, who has revoked our doom.

This sepulcher has twenty columns around it carrying arches, a border and a roof above it. On the border itself are inscribed these verses:

From hence, from Jos'phat's vale, a path leads to the sky!
The Virgin here, God's trusting handmaid, once did lie;
Spotless, from hence she rose, to her heaven's gate did ope,
Poor sinners' Light and Way, their Mother and their Hope.

The roof has a round dome above it, supported by six pairs of columns, with a ball and cross above it, and between each pair of these little columns all around the dome there hangs a lamp. One enters the sepulcher from the western side and leaves it on the northern side. Her Assumption is excellently painted on the ceiling above, which contains this sentence under a straight line: "Mary has been taken up into heaven; the angels rejoice and bless our Lady, singing her praises." Around the sanctuary of the church itself also runs a scroll, containing this inscription: "The Holy Mother of God has been exalted to the Kingdom of Heaven, above the choir of angels." From here one ascends into the church by as many steps as one descended by into the crypt.

The church itself and all the conventual building connected with it are strongly fortified with high walls, strong towers, and battlements against the treacherous attacks of the infidels, and it has many cisterns around it. As one goes out of the crypt one sees a very small chapel placed on the steps themselves. In the church also the Syrians have an altar of their own. Also on the ceiling above the steps by which one descends into the crypt the Assumption of our

Lady is shown in a painting, in which her beloved son, our Lord Jesus Christ, is present with a multitude of angels. Having received her soul, he bears it away into heaven, while the Apostles stand by in deep sorrow and devotedly minister to her. When her body is placed upon its most holy bier, a Jew is trying to pull away the covering that veils it, and an angel is cutting off both his hands with a sword. His hands are falling on the ground, and the stumps remain on his body. There is a tradition associated with this that when our Lady's soul had departed from her body on Mount Sion, as has been told in former chapters, the holy Apostles reverently placed her most blessed body upon a bier and were carrying it along the road leading toward the east, outside the city wall, to bury it in the Valley of Josaphat. Now the Jews, among whom the burning hatred and envy with which they had so long persecuted her son was not yet extinct, met it with the intention of offering some insult to it. One of them, bolder and unluckier than the rest, came up to the litter on which her holy body lay and endeavored with wicked audacity to tear away the veil that covered it. But the merits of the Blessed Virgin Mary and the vengeance of heaven severely punished his rashness, for both his hands and arms withered, which struck terror into the rest and made them flee swiftly away.

24. The Church of Gethsemane, the Church of the Prayers (of Our Savior), the High Place Where the Patriarch Blesses the Palm Branches, the Way by Which Our Lord Was Led Captive

As you journey from there southward toward the Mount of Olives, you meet with a church of no small size called Gethsemane, which our Savior entered when he came out of the garden with his disciples and said to them "Sit here while I go forth and pray" [Mark 14:32]. So as soon as you enter it you find a holy altar, and on the left hand you enter into a subterranean grotto and find four places marked, in each of which three of the Apostles lay and fell asleep. There is also on the left a great rock at the angle of the entrance to the grotto, upon which Christ pressed his fingers, leaving six holes imprinted on it. A little higher up toward the Mount of Olives, he offered up three prayers in a place where now a new church is being built. The place of one of these prayers is in the left-hand apse, that of another in the midst of the choir, and that of the third in the right-hand apse. In the space intervening between Gethsemane and the places of the prayers, on the side of the Mount of Olives where the crowds met our Lord with palm-branches, there is a high place built up of stones, where on Palm Sunday the palm branches are blessed by the patriarch. It was near these places that, while Jesus was trembling and falling, Judas came with lanterns and torches and arms, and the officers of the Jews arrested him, led him away, and brought him to the hall of the chief priest or of Caiaphas. After they had mocked him there all night, they brought him in the morning before Pilate, his judge.

25. The Pavement on Mount Sion, the Chapel of Our Lord with the Column of the Scourging, the Church of Galilee, the Grotto into Which Peter Fled, the Via Dolorosa

After he had asked him many questions, Pilate caused him to be led to the judgment hall, and he sat down, by way of a judgment-seat, in the place that is called the Pavement, which is situated in front of the Church of St. Mary, on Mount Sion, in a high place near the city wall. Here is a holy chapel dedicated to our Lord Jesus Christ, in which stands a great column round which the Lord was bound by Pilate and ordered to be scourged after he had been condemned by him to be crucified. There pilgrims are scourged in imitation of him. In front of the church, on a stone cut in the likeness of a cross, these words are inscribed: "This place is called the Pavement, and here the Lord was judged."

Beyond this, toward the east on the right hand, one descends from another part of the street down fifty steps to the church called Galilee, where two links of the chain, with which St. Peter was bound, are kept. Further on, on the left-hand side of the altar, one descends by about sixty steps into a very dark subterranean grotto, into which St. Peter fled after his denial of Christ and hid himself in the corner of it. There he is depicted sitting, resting his head upon his hands, while he weeps over his holy master's sufferings and his own denial of him, while the servant-maid threateningly presses on him, and the cock stands and crows before his feet. This church is in the hands of the Armenians.

From here our Lord was led around the city wall, where then there were gardens and now are houses, and was crucified. For as the Apostle says, "Our Lord suffered outside the gate."

Now according to the best of our ability, we have told what we learned with our own eyes about Christ and his holy places. We shall now tell what is known about his friends and about other places. After this we shall tell of some things that we have seen ourselves and some that others told us of.

26. The Palace of Pilate, the Church of St. Anne, the Pool of the Sheep-Gate, the Church and Dwellings of the Lepers, the Great Cistern of the Hospitallers, the Church of St. Stephen, the Hospice at the Gate of St. Lazarus, the Church of St. Chariton

By the side of the street that leads to the eastern gate near the Golden Gate, beyond the house or Palace of Pilate, which we have already said adjoins the same street, stands the Church of St. Anne, the mother of our Lady Mary, to whose tomb one descends into a subterranean grotto by about twenty steps. There nuns serve God under the rule of an abbess. Whoever goes on to its northern side will find the Sheep Pool, which lies in a deep valley near a rocky hill, crowned by some ancient building. This pool, as we are told in the Gospel, has five porticos, in the farthest of which stands the altar.

Whoever makes the circuit of the city walls, beginning the journey at the Tower of David, will find at the western angle of the city the church and dwellings of the lepers, which are handsome and kept in good order. Passing by the great cistern of the Hospitallers, before you reach the northern gate, you find upon a hill the Church of St. Stephen the protomartyr who, when he was cast out of the gate and stoned by the Jews, saw the heavens opened in that place. In the midst of the city there is a place raised on steps enclosed by an iron railing, in the midst of which is a holy altar of a hollow form, which stands at the place where he was stoned, and where the heavens opened above him. This church is subject to the Abbot of the Church of St. Mary the Latin. At the gate itself stands a venerable hospice, which is called a xenodochium in Greek. When you have gone some distance along this road, taking the road to the left, toward the east, you will find a church belonging to the Armenians, in which a saint named Chariton reposes, whose bones are covered with flesh, as if he were alive.

27. The Mount of Olives, the Church of Our Savior (or of the Ascension), the Little Church of St. Pelagia, the Pater Noster Church

After this, as the time and hour of his Ascension was drawing near, our Lord climbed the Mount of Olives, stood

Guide to the Holy Land by Theoderich of Würzburg

there upon a great stone and, in the sight of his Apostles and graciously bestowing on them his blessing, ascended into heaven. Now the Mount of Olives, as we have already said, is the highest of all the mountains that surround the city. It abounds with fruits of all kinds, and contains on its topmost point a church of the highest sanctity dedicated to our Savior.

One ascends into the church by twenty great steps; in the midst of the church there stands a round structure, magnificently decorated with Parian marble and blue marble, with a lofty apex in the midst of which a holy altar is placed. Beneath this altar appears the stone on which the Lord is said to have stood when he ascended into heaven. In the church divine service is performed by canons. It is strongly fortified against the infidels with towers both great and small, with walls and battlements and night patrols.

As one comes out of the church one comes upon a little church on its western side, which is dark, being in a subterranean grotto. When one has descended twenty-five steps into this, one beholds, in a large stone coffin, the body of St. Pelagia, who ended her life immured there in the service of God. Also on the west side, beside the road that leads to Bethany, on the side of the Mount of Olives, there is a church of great sanctity on the place where the Savior sat when he was asked by his disciples how they ought to pray, saying, "Our father, who art in heaven." This he wrote for them with his own hand. The writing is under the altar itself, so that pilgrims may kiss it. From the middle of the church a way also leads down about thirty steps into a subterranean grotto, in which the Lord is said to have often sat and taught his disciples.

*

Part III

28. Bethany, the Church of St. Lazarus, the Church of Mary and Martha, the Red Cistern with Its Castle, the Garden of Abraham, the Towers and House There

So having finished Jerusalem, which in my story has the same importance as the head has to the body, I must now put in the other places and, as it were, the limbs of this body.

Next comes Bethany, which also is fortified not less by the nature of the ground than by the strength of the works there. Here is a holy double church, one part of which is glorified by the body of St. Lazarus, whom our Lord raised from the dead on the fourth day and who ruled the church at Jerusalem for fifteen years, the other by the remains of his sisters, Mary and Martha. Nuns serve God there under an abbess. Here our Lord and Savior was frequently entertained as a guest.

To the eastward, beyond Bethany, at a distance of four miles from Jerusalem, there stands on a mountain a Red Cistern, with a chapel attached to it. Into this cistern Joseph is said to have been thrown by his brothers. Here the Templars have built a strong castle.[1] More than three

---

1. Tobler has an interesting note on this passage. He is unable with certainty to identify this site with that of the Templars' Bourg Maledoin, which may either have been here or on the summit of Quarantana. He conjectures that at the end of III.28 a considerable lacuna occurs in the text. The castle mentioned in III.39 may be the small predecessor of Chateau Pelerin or perhaps Merle. See Hazard, 156-59; Prawer, 206. Which castle Theoderich means in III.44 is unclear. This is probably not the castle at Paneas taken by Nur ed-Din in 1164. See Prawer, 284, n. 5. That mentioned in III.48 was probably the Tower of Sephorie. See Prawer, 288.

miles further on is the Garden of Abraham, in a beautiful plain near the Jordan, half a mile from it. Its twofold extent includes a great plain watered by a beautiful brook.

The width of the plain extends as far as the Jordan, and its length reaches down as far as the Dead Sea; it has soil fit for growing all manner of fruit, and it abounds in wood, which, however, is prickly like thistles. We saw the garden itself, full of trees bearing innumerable apples but of a small size; and we also saw ripe barley there on the Monday after Palm Sunday.

Many towers and large houses are possessed there by the power of the Templars, whose practice, as also that of the Hospitallers, is to escort pilgrims who are going to the Jordan and to watch that they are not injured by the Saracens either in going or returning, or while passing the night there.

29. The Jordan, the Mount Quarantana, the Fountain of Elisha

A mile distant from here is the Jordan, which, running in a winding and twisting stream along the mountains of Arabia, pours itself into the Dead Sea and thereafter appears no more. Between the Red Cistern and the aforesaid valley lies a frightful wilderness, into which our Lord Jesus was brought that he might be tempted by the devil. At the end of this wilderness is a terrible mountain, very lofty, and so precipitous as to be almost inaccessible, which, while it rears its huge peak above, yawns with a deep and gloomy valley below. This place the laity call Quarantana, and we may call Quadragena, because it was here that our Lord sat fasting for forty days and forty nights. The road to the place where our Lord sat goes along the middle of the mountainside, not straight, but made crooked by the irregularities of the ground, and, being everywhere slippery, in some places it forces pilgrims to crawl on their hands. At the top is a gate, and, when you have passed through it and proceeded a little way farther you will find a chapel built onto a grotto, made by human labor, and dedicated to our Lady. From here you ascend by a toilsome path that leads upward without any steps; passing over the huge and rugged clefts of the mountain, you enter another gate and by a path that bends back again twice, you gradually arrive at a third gate. Passing through this you will see a little altar dedicated to the holy cross, and, on the right hand of the little chapel that contains it, the sepulcher of a saint named Piligrinus, whose hand, still covered with flesh, is shown there.

Now ascending by about sixteen steps to the top, you will find on the east side a holy altar, and on the west the holy place itself where our Lord sat, and, as we have already said, fasted forty days and nights, and where, after his fast, angels ministered to him. This place is situated in the middle of the mountain, for its peak reaches upwards as far as its depth opens downwards.

On its summit may be seen a huge rock, on which the devil is said to have sat while he tempted him. From this mountain a view extends to a great distance beyond Jordan into Arabia, and even the frontier of Egypt beyond the Dead Sea may be seen. The crest of Mount Quarantana and its subterranean caves are full of victuals and arms belonging to the Templars, who can have no stronger fortress or one better suited for the annoyance of the infidels.

As one ascends or descends this mountain, that is to say, at its foot, a great fountain bubbles forth, which supplies the Garden of Abraham and the whole plain around it with water. There on the plain that is watered by the brook running from this fountain, pilgrims, as we have already said, pass the night, so that they may go on to Quarantana to pray and may wash themselves in the waters of the Jordan. They are protected on three sides by the garden itself from the ambushes of the infidels; on the fourth side they are guarded by patrols of the Hospitallers and Templars.

30. The Place on the Banks of the Jordan Where Our Lord Was Baptized, the Church and Convent, the Castle of the Templars, Jericho, the Mountains of Gilboa

When our humble selves also had visited this place in order to pray there, desiring to wash in the waters of Jordan with the rest, we descended the mountain after sunset, just as darkness was coming on. Looking out from its heights over the flat plain below us, we saw, according to our reckoning, more than sixty thousand people standing there, almost all of them carrying candles in their hands — all of whom could be seen by the infidels from the mountains of Arabia beyond Jordan. Indeed, there was a still larger number of pilgrims in Jerusalem who had recently visited this place.

In the very place where our Lord was baptized by John there is a great stone on which our Savior is said to have stood while he was being baptized, and thus the water of the Jordan came to him, but he did not enter it. On the very bank of the Jordan a church is built, in which six monks who inhabited it were beheaded by Sanginus, the father of Nur ed-Din. There is here a strong castle of the Templars.

As you return by the direct path from the Jordan to Jerusalem, on the flat plain before you enter the mountain district, you come upon Jericho, past which flows a brook that runs down from the mountains of Jerusalem, and which is now reduced to a small town. It is, however, situated on fertile soil, where all fruits soon ripen. Many roses grow there that expand in a lavish abundance of petals. Thus the comparison, "Like a rose planted in Jericho," befits our Lady. It is also remarkable for large and excellent grapes. This place is under the jurisdiction of the Church of St. Lazarus in Bethany, but much of the land lies uncultivated on account of the inroads of the Saracens. To the north of this road, on the right hand, by the side of the aforesaid plain, the Mountains of Gilboa can be clearly seen.

31. The Desert Elim, the Valley of Moses, the Mountains of Sinai, Hor, Abarim, and the Mount Royal, the Place Where the Children of Israel Passed over the Jordan

The desert through which the Lord once led the children of Israel, after they had come up from the Red Sea, lies between Egypt and Arabia. It was there that he fed them, as we read in the Bible with bread from heaven, and brought forth water out of the rock for them. But the desert in which the children of Israel found twelve wells of water and three-score and ten palm trees is on the borders of Arabia and is called Elim. In Arabia, also, there is a valley, that is called the Valley of Moses, because he twice struck the rock with his staff there and brought forth water from the rock for the people, from which fountain the whole land is now watered. In the same district is Mount Sinai, on which Moses fasted forty days and nights and also received the law written by the finger of God upon the stone tables. Mount Hor, upon which Aaron was buried, is in Arabia, as likewise is Mount Abarim, upon which the Lord buried Moses, whose tomb, however, is not to be found. There is also in Arabia a mountain that is called Mount Royal, which Baldwin [I], king of Jerusalem, conquered in war and placed under the dominion of the Christians.

These are the boundaries and provinces through which the children of Israel passed when they came up out of Egypt and had passed over the Red Sea, slaying Sihon, king of the Emoreans, and Och, king of Basan, which countries lie between Idumaea and Arabia. They crossed the Jordan at the very place where Christ was baptized and, having taken Jericho on the plain, gained possession of the Promised Land, as we are told. At the time of the passage of the children of Israel, Arabia was so utter a wilderness that it had not even any distinguishing name.

32. The Valley of Ennon near Jerusalem, the New Cistern, the Chapel of St. Mary Where She Used to Rest, Chabratha — the Tomb of Rachel

Whoever passes out of the western gate of the city near the Tower of David and follows a path toward the south will pass through the Valley of Ennon, which skirts two sides of the city near the new cistern. At the distance of more than half a mile one will arrive at a chapel of special sanctity, dedicated to our Blessed Lady Mary, where she would often rest when she journeyed from Bethlehem to Jerusalem. At its door there stands a cistern, at which passers-by refresh themselves. Beyond this is a field in which lie numberless heaps of stones, which the simple pilgrims delight in collecting there, because they say that on the Day of Judgment they will take their seats upon them. Close by is the place called Chabratha, where Rachel, the wife of Jacob, died after she had given birth to Benjamin. After she had been buried there Jacob piled up twelve stones over her grave, and now a pyramid stands there to which her name is attached.

33. Bethlehem, the Church of St. Mary, the Chapel of the Nativity, the Manger, the Tomb of Joseph of Arimathea and St. Jerome, the Place Where "Glory to God in the Highest" Was Sung

Next comes the famous city of Bethlehem, in which according to the predictions of the prophets, our dearest Lord Jesus Christ was born man, where there is a holy church honored by the distinction of being a bishop's cathedral church. The high altar is dedicated to our Blessed Lady Mary. At the extremity of the right-hand apse, by the side of the door, one descends by twenty-five steps into a subterranean grotto, where there is a holy altar of hollow form with a cross marked on the ground. This altar consists of four small columns, which support a large piece of marble. Upon this place are written the following two verses:

> *Of angels virtues beyond compare*
> *A virgin here the very God did bear.*

On the right hand, or toward the west, in this same cave one descends four steps and so comes to the manger, in which once not only lay hay for cattle, but where food for angels was found. The manger itself has been encased in white marble, with three round holes on the upper part, through which pilgrims offer to the manger their long-wished-for kisses. This crypt is, moreover, beautifully decorated with mosaic work.

Above the cave stands a holy chapel vaulted in a double form, in which, on the south side is a holy altar, and on the west the tomb of Joseph of Arimathea is shown in the wall. Not far from the manger of the Lord is the tomb of St. Jerome. His body is said to have been translated from here to Constantinople by Theodosius the Younger. On the roof of the church itself a star of well-gilded copper glitters on the end of a lance, in allusion to the three Magi, who, as we read in the Gospel, came there by the leading of a star and, finding the child Jesus there with Mary his mother, adored him. A mile from Bethlehem the angel appeared to the shepherds, and the glory of the Lord shone around them. Here also appeared a multitude of the heavenly host, singing "Glory to God in the highest."

34. Hebron, the Double Cave, the Red Earth, Mambre, the Oak

Further on, toward the south, near the Dead Sea, is Hebron, where Adam is said to have dwelt and been buried after he was driven out of Paradise. This city was a city of priests in the tribe of Judah. It was also a dwelling place of giants and was in olden days called Cariatharbe, or the "city of four," because four venerable patriarchs are buried there in a double cave — that is to say, Adam, the first man created; Abraham, Isaac, and Jacob, the three patriarchs; and their four wives, Eve, Sara, Rebecca and Lea. This city was before this named Arbe, and in its territory — that is, at its extremity — was a double cave looking toward Mambre, which Abraham bought for a price from Ephron, the son of Seor the Hittite. In the country near the city is found the red earth that is dug up by the inhabitants and eaten and exported to Egypt. Adam is said to have been made of this earth. Now, however much of this earth may be dug out in extent or depth, it is said to be restored the next year to as much as it was before by divine power.

Near this city is the mountain of Mambre, at whose foot stands the oak that the moderns call *dirps* beneath which Abraham beheld three angels and adored one and hospitably entertained them. This oak lasted until the time of the Emperor Theodosius, and from its trunk or root another has grown, which, although partly withered, still exists and is so wholesome that as long as a horseman holds a piece of it in his hands his horse will not founder.

Hebron was the first place reached by Caleb and Joshua and their ten companions, who were sent by Moses from Cadesbarne to spy out the Promised Land. This city was afterwards the cradle of the kingdom of David, who by divine command reigned there for seven years.

35. The Sepulcher of Lot, Lake Asphaltites, Segor, the Statue of Salt, Carnaim

Two miles from Hebron was the sepulcher of Lot, Abraham's nephew. Ten miles from Hebron, toward the east, is Lake Asphaltites, which is also called the Dead Sea, because it receives into itself nothing living, or the "Sea of the Devil," because at his instigation the four cities of Sodom, Gomorra, Seboim, and Adima went on in their wickedness and were burned with fire of brimstone from heaven and were sunk in this lake, which rose in the place of the aforesaid cities. The water of this pool is shocking from its hideous color, and its stench drives away those who approach it. Once a year, on the anniversary of the destruction of those cities, stones and wood and things of other kinds are seen to float on the surface of the lake, in testimony of their ruin.

Near the lake is the city of Segor, which is also called Bala and Cara, which was saved from destruction by the prayers of Lot and remains to this day. As Lot went out of it his wife looked back and was turned into a statue of salt, which endures to this day and which, as it grows smaller when the moon is waning, so also increases in size when she waxes and has its face turned behind its back. This lake also produces bitumen, which is called Jews' pitch and is of great use to sailors. Round about its banks is likewise found alum, which the Saracens call *katranum*. Above the lake, as one goes down to Arabia, is the city of Carnaim, on the mountain of the Moabites, upon which Balac, the son of Boer, the king of the Moabites, placed Balaam, the seer, to curse the children of Israel. This mountain, on account of its precipice, is called "Cut off." This lake divides Judaea from Arabia.

36. Gaza, Ascalon, Joppa, Arimathea, the Field of Abacuc

Ten miles westward from Hebron, on the shore of the Mediterranean Sea, stands Gaza, which is now called Gazara, where Samson did many great deeds and carried away its gates by night. Eight miles from Gaza, on the shore of the Mediterranean Sea, is Ascalon, a very strongly fortified city. These cities used to stand in Palestine, or, rather, in the country of the Philistines. On the shore of the same Mediterranean Sea is Joppa, where the Apostle Peter raised Tabitha from the dead and which the moderns call Jafis. Near it is Arimathea, from which came Joseph, the noble counselor who buried Christ. There also, that is in the land of Judah, is the field where Abacuc the prophet was carried off by an angel when he had kneaded bread in a trough and was going into the field to take it to the reapers, and was carried away to Babylon, that he might take food to Daniel in the den of the lions.

37. The Charnel-House of the Lion near Jerusalem

As you go out of the Holy City, toward the west by the gate near the Tower of David, on the right hand there is a path that leads to a chapel, in which one descends by about one hundred steps into a very deep subterranean cave and finds the bodies of numberless pilgrims, which are said to have been brought there in the following manner. All the pilgrims who came one year to pray as usual found the city full of Saracens. Being unable therefore to enter it, they besieged those who were in the city. But, as they had neither food nor arms sufficient for accomplishing of so arduous a feat, they began to be in great straits for want of provisions. While they were thus in want, the Saracens, seeing that they were unable to resist, suddenly sallied forth from the city and put them all to the sword. Now, as a stench arose from the corpses of so many people, they determined to burn them all; but that same night a lion appeared, sent from God, who cast all the bodies into that cave, which has a narrow mouth. Every particle of them may be carried across the sea; indeed, when it is put on board, the ships are said to go home of their own accord.

38. The Church of the Holy Cross, the Place in the Wood or of St. John, the Mountains of Modin or Belmont, Emmaus or Fontenoid, the Mountains of Sophim, Ramatha, Bethoron, Silo or the Mountain of the Holy Samuel

Next, beyond a certain mountain, follows a most fruitful and beautiful valley, in which stands a noble church dedicated to our Lord Jesus and to his beloved mother. There under an open altar people worship the holy place in which stood the trunk of the tree from which was cut the cross on which the Savior hung for our salvation. This church belongs to the Syrians and is strongly fortified with towers, walls and battlements against the treacherous attacks of the infidels. It is, moreover, adorned with houses, dining rooms, chambers and dwellings of all kinds suitable for all kinds of uses, raised high aloft in stonework. This tree is said to have been cut down by King Solomon, who marked it with the figure of the cross and put it away in a fitting place to await the coming of the Savior, because he foresaw in the spirit that salvation would be brought to the world through Christ's death.

From there one passes on to St. John's, or to the place that is called "In the Wood," where his father Zacharias and his mother Elizabeth lived, and where St. John himself was born, where also Mary, after she had received the salutation of the angel at Nazareth, came and saluted St. Elizabeth. Near this place are the Mountains of Modin, upon which Mathathias sat with his sons when Antiochus took the city and the children of Israel by storm. These mountains are called by the moderns Belmont.

Near these mountains is the castle of Emmaus, which the moderns called Fontenoid, where the Lord appeared to two of his disciples on the very day of his resurrection. Not far from here are the Mountains of Ephraim, which are called Sophim; and soon comes Ramatha [Ramathaim], a great city, which is now called Rames, of which Helchana, the father of the prophet Samuel, and Anna, his mother, were natives. Near Sophim is Bethoron, which now is called Beter. On the right hand, or western side of that district, two miles from Jerusalem, one ascends Mount Silo, from which springs of sweet water flow into the valleys beneath it. There the Ark of the Covenant of the Lord remained from the entry in the children of Israel into the Promised Land until the time of Heli the priest. In his time the ark was forced by the sins of the Hebrews to be captured by the Philistines and kept by them until, struck by a scourge from heaven, they placed the same ark on a wagon and unwillingly brought it back to Bethsames seven months after it had been captured. Here, as the anger of the Lord raged fiercely against both the priests and the people because they had kept the ark, the men of Cariathiarim, or Gabaa, came and took it away from Bethsames and kept it in their own country. Afterwards King David and all Israel brought it away with singing and hymns of praises and deposited it in the City of David on Mount Sion. After this, when King Solomon had built the Temple of the Lord, as aforesaid, he placed the ark in the Temple on Mount Moriah, where the threshing floor of Areuna the Jebusite had been. In Silo, also, the prophet

Samuel was buried. Thus changing its former name, the place was called St. Samuel's, and there dwells a convent of professed monks called gray monks.

39. Lydda, Cacho, Caesarea of Palestine, Mount Caipha (Carmel) and the Town

Six miles to the west of Silo, on the plain, is Lydda, the burial place, according to tradition, of St. George the Martyr. Therefore the place has lost its ancient name and is called St. George's by the moderns. From here one goes down by the way that leads toward Achon, or Ptolemais, through a pleasant and beautiful plain that extends between the mountains and the flat country by the seashore, on which are many cities and towns, both new and old. Among these are Caphar Gamala, Caphar Semala, a fortress that the moderns call Cacho, which is situated in a very fertile valley, the fortified town, which is now called Caesarea of Palestine and was once called the Tower of Strato, and the Mountain of Caipha, near which stands a half-ruined town of the same name.

Here it is said that the thirty pieces of silver were made that were given to the traitor Judas as the price of the blood of Christ. On the top of the mountain there is a castle of the Templars, which enables mariners to recognize the mainland from a distance.

40. The New Castle of Accaron, the Grove of Palms, Ptolemais

Further on by the seashore, opposite Accaron, a great castle of that name stands in a rich country and is called the New Castle. Near it is a very large grove of palm trees, and three miles further on is Ptolemais itself, a great, rich, and populous city. However, the harbor or roadstead of Ptolemais is difficult and dangerous to access when the wind blows from the south and the shores tremble under the continual shocks that they receive from the waves and are there heaped into great masses. For, since the fury of the sea is not broken by the intervention of any mountain, the terrible waves boil over more than a stone's throw onto the land. In this city the Templars have built a large house of admirable skill by the seashore, and the Hospitallers likewise have founded a stately house there.

Wherever the ships of pilgrims may have landed them, they are all obliged to repair to the harbor of this city to take them home again on their return from Jerusalem. Indeed, in the year when we were there — on the Wednesday in Easter week — we counted eighty ships in the port besides the ship called a "buss," on board of which we sailed there and returned. Along the road that leads from Jerusalem through the aforementioned places to Ptolemais one meets with many deserted cities and castles, which were destroyed by Vespasian and Titus; but one also sees very strongly fortified castles, which belong to the Templars and Hospitallers.

41. The Little Church at the Spot from Which Pilgrims First See Jerusalem, the Village of Mahomerie and the Church of St. Mary, Another Village, Sichem or Neapolis, the Saracens

Two miles from the Holy City, on the northern side, there is a little church at the place where pilgrims, filled with great joy at their first sight of the city, lay down their crosses and take off their shoes and humbly strive to seek him who deigned, for their sakes, to come there poor and humble. Three miles from here is a large village called Mahomerie by the moderns, where close by a church dedicated to Mary stands a great cross of hewn stone, raised on seven steps. These steps are climbed by pilgrims, who from here, and not without groans, see the Tower of David standing, as stated above, on Mount Sion at a distance of more than four miles. The old name of this village has escaped my memory.

Eight miles from here another great village stands on a lofty mountain height, from which, by a precipitous path, one descends through a beautiful and boundless plain and over some other mountains to a very strongly fortified city, which in ancient days was called Sichem, or Sichar, but now is called Neapolis, or the New City. As we passed along this road we were met by a multitude of Saracens, who were proceeding with bullocks and asses to plough up a great and beautiful plain, and who, by the hideous yells that they thundered out, as they usually do whenever they set about any work, struck no small terror into us. Indeed, numbers of infidels dwell there throughout the country, as well in the cities and castles as in the villages, and they till the earth under the safe conduct of the king of Jerusalem or that of the Templars or Hospitallers.

42. Sichem Again, the Well and Church of Jacob, Cain and Abel, the Terebinth of Rachel, Bethel or Luza, Mounts Gerizim and Ebal

The aforementioned city of Neapolis is situated in Samaria and abounds in springs and rivers, vineyards, olive groves, and trees of all kinds, while its soil is fertile and excellently cultivated. When our Lord Jesus came here, weary with his journey, he sat down beside the spring where he talked with the woman of Samaria. Now, the well upon which our Lord sat is half a mile from the city and stands in front of the altar in a church, which has been built over it, in which God is served by nuns. This well is known as Jacob's Well and stands on the land that he gave to his son Joseph. This city was once destroyed by the sons of Jacob, who slew Sichem, its prince, the son of Hamor the Hivite, because he had ravished Dinah, their sister. This city stands between Dan and Bethel, and in it Jeroboam, king of Israel, made two golden calves, of which he set up one in Dan and the other in Bethel. Near Sichem are two mountains; one, on which Cain is said to have offered sacrifice to God of the fruits of the earth, dry and desolate; the other, on which Abel likewise offered sacrifice to God of the fatlings of his flock, rich in trees and plentiful in fruits of all kinds. To Sichem were brought the bones of Joseph from Egypt, and near it is the terebinth beneath which his mother Rachel hid the idols that she had stolen from Laban, her father.

A mile to the east is Bethel, which before was called Luza, where Isaac's sacrifice by his father Abraham took place, and where also Jacob, sleeping with his head laid upon a stone, beheld the ladder reaching up to heaven and the angels of God ascending and descending by it, and the Lord himself standing above the same. Close by one sees Mount Gerizim over against Mount Hebal, from which Moses ordained that the people should be blessed or cursed as they deserved.

43. Samaria or Sebaste, the Crypt of Helisaeus and Abdia, the Sepulchers of the Seventy Prophets

Six miles from here is Samaria, also called Sebaste, which the moderns call St. John's and which stands on a strong though not high mount. From it the province of Samaria itself has received its name, and its great ruins give it the appearance of a city. It is rich in its soil and plenteous in vineyards and all fruits. In this place the disciples of St. John the Baptist buried the body of their master, after his head had been cut off by Herod the Younger in the castle of Machaerunta, as a present for a dancing girl. It is said to have been afterwards burned by Julian the Apostate. His head, however, was first carried to Alexandria, was translated from there to an island called Rhodes, and was afterwards removed by the Emperor Theodosius to Constantinople. Moreover, a piece of his arm is preserved there and is held most sacred. He was buried in the crypt between the prophets Helisaeus and Abdia, in the cave in which that prophet once fed seventy prophets, who are also buried there. One goes into it down thirty-five steps.

44. Ginaea, Jezrahel, the Mountains of Gilboa, Scythopolis, the Castle of Sapham, Mount Hermon, Another Castle

Ten miles from here is the town of Genin, at which place Samaria begins. Five miles from Genin is Jezrahel, which is now called *Ad Cursum Gallinarum*. Here dwelt Naboth, who was stoned for the sake of his vineyard by that impious woman Jezabel, whom afterwards Jehu caused to be trampled by his horses' feet there. Near Jezrahel is the field of Mageddo, where Ozias, king of Judah, was conquered and slain by the king of Samaria. Many ruins of this city are still to be seen, as also a pyramid called by the name of Jezabel. A mile from Jezrahel to the east are seen the mountains of Gilboa. Two miles from it stands the city that once was called Bethsan, or "The House of God," and which is now called Scythopolis, on whose wall we read that the heads of Saul and of his sons were hung when the strangers (Philistines) had slain them in war. This city marks the eastern border of Galilee, whose capital it is.

In its neighborhood, on a lofty mountain, the Hospitallers have built a very strong and spacious castle, so that they may protect the land on this side of the Jordan against the treacherous attacks of Noradin, the despot of Aleppo. There is also close by, on the west, a castle of the Templars named Sapham, strongly fortified to repel the inroads of the Turks. Beyond this, toward the Mediterranean, is Mount Hermon, at the foot of which, on the west side, the Templars have built a castle of no small size, in whose grounds they have made a large cistern with a wheeled machine for drawing water.

45. Tiberias, the Place Called the Table, the Sea of Galilee, the Mountain on Which Our Lord Used to Pass the Night, Paneas or Belinas, Jor and Dan, the Jordan, the Plain of Medan, the Valley in the Fields

Beyond this come the most beautiful and most fertile plains, at the end of which, toward the north, stands the city Tiberias on the Sea of Galilee, where our Lord satisfied five thousand people with five loaves and three fishes. Therefore this place [actually in Tabgha] is called the Table, and traces of the miracle may be seen there to this day. Near, also, is the place where the Lord appeared to his disciples after his resurrection and ate part of a fish and honeycomb in their presence. Here is the Sea of Galilee on which our Lord, walking, came to his disciples about the fourth watch of the night. Then, as Peter walked on the waves and was beginning to sink, he took him by the hand and said, "Thou of little faith, why didst thou doubt?" (Matt 14:31.) Here also, at another time, when his disciples were in danger, he made the sea quiet. Near the same sea, not far from Tiberias, is that mountain to which, seeing a multitude, he ascended. On it he often sat and addressed his disciples and the people, and on it he used to pass the night. Here also he deigned to heal the leper.

At the foot of Mount Libanus, which is the boundary of Galilee toward the north, is the city of Paneas, which after being rebuilt by Philip, the tetrarch of Ituraea and the region of Traconitis, was called Caesarea Philippi in memory of his own name and likewise in honor of Tiberius Caesar, under whom he governed. This city, which is called Belinas by the moderns, was rescued from the infidels in the year 1161 after the incarnation of our Lord Jesus Christ by the Christians, who have established a garrison of their own people in it. In this country two springs, that is, Jor and Dan, both rise, which flow separately as far as the Mountain of Gibel and from there form the Jordan.

The Jordan, as has been said in former chapters, flows from the Gibel Mountains to Lake Asphaltites through the valley that is called "The Great Valley" or "The Valley of the Meadows," which is bounded on both sides by a continuous chain of mountains from Libanus to the desert of Pharan. Its course divides Galilee from Idumaea and the land of Bosra, which is the second capital of the Idumaeans, next to Damascus. Dan from its source flows underground as far as the plain named Medan, where it displays its channel quite openly. An innumerable multitude of people assemble on this plain every year at the beginning of the summer, bringing with them all manner of things for sale, and with them come a vast number of Parthians and Arabs to protect the people and their flocks, which remain in those parts throughout the summer. After leaving this plain, Dan passes through Sueta, in which the monument of the blessed Job still exists and is held sacred by the inhabitants. From there it flows toward Galilee of the Gentiles to the city of Cedar, passes by the plain of thorns, where the medicinal places are, and joins the Jor. The Jordan, however, flows out of the lake far away from Paneas and, after passing between Bethsaida and Capharnaum through the Sea of Galilee, makes a fresh start.

46. Bethsaida, Cedar, Chorazain, Capharnaum, Bethulia, the Lake of Gennesareth, Magdalum, Cinnereth (Tiberias), Mount Tabor, Nain, Endor

This is Bethsaida to which Peter and Andrew, John and James, the son of Alphaeus belonged. Four miles from Bethsaida is Chorazain, in which it is believed that Antichrist will be born, because the Lord rebuked them, saying, "Woe to thee, Chorazain! Woe to thee, Bethsaida!" Five miles from Chorazain is Cedar, a fine city, of which the prophet says in the Psalm, "I dwell amid the tents of Cedar." (Ps. 120:5.) Capharnaum, also on the right-hand side of the same sea, is the city of the centurion whose child our Lord raised from death. Four miles from Tiberias is the city of Bethsaida, from which Judith came who slew Holofernes. Four miles from Tiberias, toward the south, is Dothaim, where Joseph found his brethren. On the left-hand side of the same sea, in the hollow of a mountain, the little plain of Gennesareth juts out. Since it is surrounded by hills on all sides and feels no wind that blows, it is said to make a wind for itself by the emission of its own breath. Two miles from Gennesareth is the town Magdalum, from which came the Magdalen. This province is called Galilee of the Gentiles and belongs to the tribes of Zebulon and Nephthalim.

In the upper parts of this Galilee are the twenty cities that King Solomon is said in the Book of Kings (1 Kings 9:11) to have given Hiram, king of Tyre. Two miles from Magdalum is Cinereth, which is also called Tiberias, of which we have already spoken. Five miles to the west of Tiberias is Mount Tabor of great height, on which our Lord Jesus Christ was transfigured in the presence of his disciples. On this mountain a glorious church has been built and dedicated to the Savior, in which monks serve God under an abbot. It is said that the service of the Mass was celebrated for the first time in this church. On the skirts of this mountain Melchisedech, the priest of the most high God and king of Salem, met Abraham as he was returning from the slaughter of Abimelech and offered him bread and wine [Gen. 14:18-24].

Two miles from Tabor is the city of Nain, at whose gate our Lord raised up the widow's son from death and restored him to her. Above Nain is Mount Endor, at whose foot, on the banks of the Cadumin Brook, which is the Cison Brook, Barach, the son of Abinoem, acting on the advice of Deborah the prophetess, triumphed over Jabin, king of the Idumaeans, and Sisara, the captain of his host, pursued Zeb and Zebee and Salmanna, the kings of the Ismahelites, Agarenes, Amalechites and Ammonites, across the Jordan, and on his return from pursuing them found Sisara himself slain by Jahel, the wife of Heber the Cinaeite, with a nail driven through his temple into the ground [Judges 4, 5; Ps. 83:12].

47. Nazareth, the Church of St. Mary, the Grotto of the Annunciation, the Tomb of Joseph, the Birthplace of the Blessed Mary, the Miracle Wrought at the Fountain of Gabriel, the Place of the Casting Down

Four miles from Tabor toward the west, on the road that leads to Achon, stands the most glorious city of Nazareth, in which there is a venerable church, which enjoys the honor of being the cathedral church [of the Annunciation] of a bishop, and which is dedicated to our Blessed Lady Mary. In the left-hand apse of this church one descends by about fourteen steps into a subterranean grotto, in which at the east end there is a small cross marked on the ground beneath an open altar, which marks the place at which the angel Gabriel delivered the message of Christ to our Lady.

On the left hand of this altar, that is, to the north, her husband St. Joseph, who brought up the Savior, lies buried. Over him is placed an altar. On the right hand, that is, on the south side, there is a place with a small cross marked on the ground and arched above, in which the Blessed Mother of God came forth from her mother's womb at her birth. All men tell of a great and wondrous miracle about this city that, whenever the infidels attempt to attack it, they are stricken with blindness or some such plague from heaven and are forced to desist.

A fountain in this city flows forth through a sprout fashioned in marble like the mouth of a lion, from which the child Jesus often used to draw water and take it to his mother. This fountain is said to derive its origin from the following events. Once when the boy Jesus came to draw water from the cistern his pitcher was broken by his comrades in their play, and he drew the water and carried it to his mother in the lap of his tunic. She refused to drink it, since he did not seem to have brought it in a sufficiently clean manner. As if in a rage, he flung it out of his lap on to the ground and from the place where it fell the fountain that still flows is said to have burst forth. A mile to the south of Nazareth is the place called the "Place of the Casting Down," because the Jews wished to cast Christ down when he passed through the midst of them and went his way.

48. Sepphoris, Cana of Galilee, the Castle of the Templars, Ptolemais, the Road That Leads from There to Jerusalem by the Mountains, and the Road That Leads to Jerusalem by the Seaside

Two miles from Nazareth is Sepphoris, a fortified city on the road to Achon. From here came the blessed Anne, the mother of the mother of Christ. Four miles from Nazareth, two miles from Sepphoris toward the east, is Cana of Galilee, from which came Nathanael and Philip, and where our Lord turned water into wine. Also three miles from Sepphoris on the road to Achon is a very strong castle of the Templars, and a little more than three miles further is Achon, or Ptolemais, itself. Now, this road that leads from Achon through Nazareth, Samaria and Neapolis to Jerusalem is called the Upper Road; and the one that leads from Achon through Caesarea and Lydda to Jerusalem is called the Seaside Road.

49. Damascus, Hus, Sueta, Theman, Naaman, Arphat, Amat, Sepharnaim, the Jabok Brook, Mount Seir, the Place Where Saul Was Converted into Paul, the Rivers Pharphar and Abana, the Plain Archas, Antioch

Arabia joins Idumaea in the district of Bosra. Idumaea is a province of Syria. Damascus is the chief city of the Idumaeans and is the city that Eliazar, the servant of Abraham, built in the field in which Cain slew his brother Abel. In Damascus once lived Esau and Seir and Edom [Gen. 25–32], after whom all that land is called Idumaea. A part of it is called Hus, from which came the blessed Job; and a part also is called Sueta, from which was Baldach the Suite. In this same province is the city of Theman, from which came Elephat [Eliphaz] the Themanite. There also is the city of Naaman, from which came Zophar the Naamathite. Arphat and Amat and Sepharnaim are cities of Damascus.

In the country of the Idumaeans, two miles from the Jordan, runs the Jabok Brook. After he had forded it on his return from Mesopotamia, Jacob wrestled with an angel who changed his name from Jacob to Israel. In Idumaea is Mount Seir, upon which stands Damascus. Two miles from Damascus is the place where Christ overthrew Saul and raised up Paul, making a friend out of an enemy and a teacher of the truth out of a persecutor of it. At the foot of the mountains of Libanus rise Pharphar and Abana, the rivers of Damascus, of which one, namely Abana, runs through the plain of Archas and empties into the Mediterranean Sea. Into those parts St. Eustachius retired after the loss of his wife and sons. Pharphar runs through Syria to Antioch, flows beneath its walls, and ten miles away from the city pours into the Mediterranean Sea at the port of Solim, which is called the Port of St. Simeon. In this city St. Peter first obtained the pontifical dignity, and it is still the seat of a patriarch.

50. Phoenicia, the Metropolis, Mamistra, Antiochia, Tripolis or Tursolt, Gibeleth, Berytus, the Wonderful Image There

Libanus divides Phoenicia from Idumaea. The city of Tyre is the chief city of the province of Phoenicia, whose inhabitants, the Syrians say, refused to receive Christ when he walked by the seashore, but he himself said that he was only sent to the lost sheep of the house of Israel. The following are the great walled cities by the sea that, being in Syria, the province of Palestine and Judaea, are subject to the dominion of the Christians: Mamistra and Antioch, and Tripolis, which is called Tursolt by the moderns, and the city that contains the very strong castle that is called Gibeleth, are cities of the province of Coele Syria.

Next, to the south, on the seashore, comes Berytus, called by the moderns Baruth, a rich and strong city, large and populous, in which the Jews, the enemies of the cross of Christ, once crucified an image of him thinking to offer an insult to him. After they had done all the shameful deeds that they had learned that their fathers did to Christ on the cross, they even pierced the side of the image with a spear, and when blood and water flowed forth, even as it did from Christ when he hung on the cross, adding sin to sin they caught it in vessels and dared to tempt God. But almighty God turned their evil into good; for since they would have had even more cause to hate him if the effects of divine virtue had not resulted from it, they anointed the limbs of the disabled with the same blood, and seeing that those who were anointed with this sacred fluid immediately recovered their health, they bent their necks to the profession of the Christian faith. This figure is to this day preserved as a sacred relic in the church of that city, which is eminent as being the cathedral church of a pope.

51. Sidon, Sarepta, Tyre, the Castle Scandalium, the Castle of Imbertus, Ptolemais and the Other Cities by the Seaside

Sixteen miles from Berytus is Sidon, a noble city, from which came Dido, who founded Carthage in Africa. Six miles from Sidon is Sarphan, which is also called Sarepta of the Sidonians, in which the widow fed Helias the prophet, and in which also by means of the same prophet, God raised the widow's son, that is the prophet Jonah, from the dead.

Eight miles from Sarphan is Tyre, which the moderns call Sur, which stands by the seashore and surpasses all the other cities in the strength of its towers and walls. The city is quadrangular in shape and presents the appearance of an island. Nearly three of its sides are surrounded by the sea; the fourth is very strongly fortified with ditches, barbicans, towers, walls, battlements, and loopholes. It has only two entrances, which are guarded by quadruple gates with towers on either side. It is remarkable, like Achon, for having a double harbor. In the inner harbor are moored the ships of the city and in the outer one those of foreigners. Between the two harbors two towers, built of great masses of stone, project into the sea. Between them, as a gate, stretches a huge chain made of iron. This gate, when closed, renders entrance or exit impossible but permits them when open. This city is honored by being the seat of a bishop.

Four miles from here is a castle named Scandalium, through which waters that rise above it run in their downward course to the sea at that place. Three miles from there is a large village, which is called by the moderns the Castle of Imbertus. Four miles further comes Accaron or Ptolemais, and three miles further Old and New Caipha. Sixteen miles further is Caesarea of Palestine, which, with the harbor that adjoins it, was splendidly built by King Herod. Also fourteen miles further is Joppa or Jafis, with a harbor that is dangerous to shipping in southerly gales. Beyond these, in order, are Gaza or Gazara and the very strong fortress of Ascalon, all of which have been described already. All these cities are on the seacoast, and all of them are large and enclosed by walls.

This account of the holy places, wherein our Lord Jesus Christ appeared in bodily presence, having taken on himself the form of a servant for our sake, we have put together partly from what we have ourselves seen, and partly from what we have heard from the truthful reports of others, in the hope that the minds of those who read or hear it may be roused to love him through their knowledge of the places that are described here.

※

The Itinerary of Benjamin of Tudela

Introduction

Every student must have felt, with myself, the entire want of a work on the geography of the Middle Ages. While on one hand Herodotus, Strabo, and the other ancient geographers have found editors and annotators without number, and on the other, not only individuals but societies have labored to make us acquainted with the present state of the world, comparatively nothing has been done to throw light on that portion of geography which comprises the ages called the dark. Thus, the curious in geography have abundant means of becoming acquainted with the political state of our planet in the times of Alexander and of Augustus, of Charles V and Victoria, but are at an utter loss for a work which treats the same subject at the period of the Crusades. Although these remarkable wars have found able historians — geography, the sister science, or rather the handmaiden of history, has been neglected to an astonishing degree. To remedy this neglect and furnish materials for a geography of the Middle Ages, is the aim of the present work, and the *Itinerary of Rabbi Benjamin of Tudela* has been selected for that purpose; not only because it contains more facts and fewer fables than any other contemporary production which has come down to us, but also because it describes a very large portion of the earth known in the twelfth century.

I am fully aware that what I now offer to the public are but scanty contributions towards the science, the study of which I aim to promote, but I hope to continue these labors to make this work a book of reference to the student of Middle Ages and comparative geography. The materials will be furnished by comparing unedited contemporary authors, both European and Oriental, as well as by unremitting attention to those accounts which may be published by travelers of all nations. I hope that the distribution of copies of this work, which has been kindly promised by the London and Paris Royal Geographical Societies, will tend to promote my humble endeavors: a few more travelers like Major Rawlinson and a great portion of my aim will be accomplished.

I consider it necessary to state, that the striking similarity of this *Itinerary* to that of Marco Polo, has induced me to avail myself as much as possible of the plan and the researches of Mr. Marsden, the able editor of the former; and I shall feel proud if I succeed in establishing the title of a good imitator.

The author, Rabbi Benjamin Ben Jonah of Tudela, a Jewish merchant, began his travels about 1160 and his itinerary comprises a great portion of the then known world.[1]

---

1. There is a considerable difference of opinion as to the exact dates at which Benjamin began and completed his journey. In my opinion, the period can be placed within a very narrow compass. Early in his journey he visited Rome, where he found Rabbi Jechiel to be the steward of the household of Pope Alexander. This can be no other than Pope Alexander III (1159-1181), who played so important a part in the struggle between King Henry II and Thomas à Becket. The German Emperor, Frederick Barbarossa, supported the anti-Pope Victor IV, and in consequence Alexander had to leave Rome soon after his election in 1159 and before his consecration. He did not return to settle down permanently in Rome until November 23, 1165, but was forced to leave again in 1167. Consequently Benjamin must have been in Rome between the end of 1165 and 1167. Benjamin terminated his travels by passing from Egypt to Sicily and Italy, then crossing the Alps and visiting Germany. In Cairo he found that the Fatimite khalif was the acknowledged ruler. The khalif here referred to must have been El-Adid, who died on Monday, September 13, 1171 — being the last of the Fatimite line. A short time before his death, Saladin had become the virtual ruler of Egypt, and had ordered the Khotba to be read in the name of the Abbaside Khalif el-Mostadi of Baghdad. It is clear, therefore, that Benjamin's absence from Europe must be placed between the years 1166 and

Introduction to Benjamin of Tudela

The only authority, which we can quote respecting the name of this traveler, is the preface to this *Itinerary*, the authenticity of which, though evidently by a later hand, we have no reason to doubt.

That Benjamin was a Jew, is too evident to require any further proof, and if we examine his work with any degree of attention, and compare it with similar productions, we shall be forced to admit, that he could only have been a merchant, who would be induced to notice, with so much accuracy, the state of trade in the towns and countries he visited. A glance at the article "commerce" of our index will be found strongly to corroborate the assertion that commerce was the vocation of our traveler.

The double object of his travels thus becomes evident: like many other Muhammedan and Christian pilgrims of the Middle Ages, Rabbi Benjamin visited Jerusalem the city, and Baghdad, the seat of the last princes of his nation, and availed himself of this pilgrimage to collect such information as might be agreeable and useful to his brethren. He was aware of their attachment to those sites and monuments, which attest their former grandeur and to which they still look up with sweet melancholy. He felt the existence of that magic, invisible tie, which even in our days of indifferentism, roused the sympathy of all European Israelites in favor of the oppressed at Damascus, but he also knew, that commerce was almost their only means of support and its success the surest way to gain influence with the princes whose yoke oppressed the

---

1171. Benjamin on his return journey passed through Sicily when the island was no longer governed by a viceroy. King William II (the Good) attained his majority in 1169, and Benjamin's visit took place subsequently. It will be found in the course of the narrative that not a single statement by Benjamin is inconsistent with this determination of date.

Jews of his own, and alas! of many succeeding ages. These considerations gave the book its present form; the accounts of the state of the Jews in the countries he saw or heard of, are ever varied by excellent notices and businesslike remarks upon the trade carried on in the cities he describes, and the *Itinerary* claims, in as high a degree, the attention of the historian, as it does that of the theologian.

His visit to Rome must have taken place subsequent to 1159; that he was at Constantinople probably in December 1161; and that his account of Egypt, which almost concludes the work, must have been written prior to 1171. If we add to these dates, which have been obtained by an examination of the text, that of his return, as given in the preface, we shall find that the narrative refers to a period of about fourteen years, viz. from 1159 or 60, to 1173.

One very peculiar feature of this work, by which its contents are divided into "what he saw" and "what he heard," as the preface has it, requires particular notice.[2]

In many towns on the route from Saragossa to Baghdad, Rabbi Benjamin mentions the names of the principal Jews, Elders, and Wardens of the congregations he met with. That a great number of the persons enumerated by Rabbi Benjamin really were his contemporaries, and the particulars he incidentally mentions of them, are corroborated by other authorities. We therefore do not hesitate to assert, that Rabbi Benjamin visited all those towns of which

2. It is doubtful whether Benjamin personally visited all the places mentioned in his *Itinerary*. His visit took place not long after the second great Crusade, when Palestine under the kings of Jerusalem was disturbed by internal dissensions and the onslaughts of the Saracens under Nur ed-Din of Damascus, and his generals. Benjamin could at best visit the places of note only when the opportunity offered.

Introduction to Benjamin of Tudela

he names the Elders and principals, and that the first portion of his narrative comprises an account of "what he saw."

But with the very first stage beyond Baghdad, all such notices cease, and except those of two princes and of two rabbis, we look in vain for any other names. So very remarkable a difference between this and the preceding part of the work, leads us to assert, that Rabbi Benjamin's travels did not extend beyond Baghdad, and that he there wrote down the second portion of our work, consisting of "what he heard." Baghdad, at this time, the seat of the Prince of the captivity, must have attracted numerous Jewish pilgrims from all regions, and beyond doubt was the fittest place for gathering those notices of the Jews, and of trade in different parts of the world, the collecting of which was the aim of Rabbi Benjamin's labors.

The languages in which Rabbi Benjamin's *Itinerary* is composed, is that which has been called Rabbinic Hebrew, an idiom in which a great many of the words of scriptural origin have entirely changed their primitive import, and which has been enriched by many other terms of comparatively modern date.

The style of our narrative proves that its author was without any pretensions to learning; it is the account of a very plain Jewish merchant, who probably preferred the idiom in which he wrote, because he understood still less of any other. The most learned of his translators have been puzzled by the language and the style.

The history of this *Itinerary* is remarkable in many respects. It appears early to have gained much credit among Jews and Christians, and the multiplied editions of it prove that it has always been in request among the learned. Its general veracity was acknowledged by the numerous quotations from, and references to, its contents, and until within a comparatively recent period, nobody doubted the authenticity of the travels. But these favorable views underwent a change in the seventeenth and eighteenth centuries: Theologians saw in Rabbi Benjamin's reports nothing but an attempt to aggrandize the real number, and to represent under bland colors, the state of the Jews in remote countries. Although eminent historians admitted, and quoted Rabbi Benjamin's authority, they attempted to prove that these travels had never been performed, but were the compilations of an ignorant Jew, who had perhaps never left Tudela.

We might claim in refutation of the ill-supported doubts of these authors, the high and undeniable authority of Rapaport, Zunz, and Tafel, and the labors of Mr. Lebrecht, who not only consider the work authentic, but have in their notes vindicated Rabbi Benjamin against his accusers. Yet, it may with truth be insisted, that the least equivocal proofs of its being an honest, however incomplete, account of what he actually saw or learned on the spot, are to be drawn from the relation itself. There numerous instances will present themselves of minute peculiarities and of incidental notices, geographical, historical, and biographical, reported by him and confirmed by the testimony of other ancient and modern authors and travelers, which he could neither have invented nor borrowed from others. Certainly it is the evidence of these coincidences, rather than any force of argument, that is likely to produce conviction in the minds of those, who are unwilling to be thought credulous. This vindication, generally, is not founded upon arguments, but upon an impartial examination of the particular details, which having been compared with and brought to the test of modern and contemporary observation, will be found remarkably correct.[3]

3. Most of the places mentioned by Benjamin are more or less identified in the very important work published by the Palestine Exploration Fund, *The Survey of Western Palestine.* Our author's

Introduction to Benjamin of Tudela

The information contained in this work, and upon the merits of which it claims the attention of the learned, may be comprised under the following heads:

a. Rabbi Benjamin's narrative contains the fullest account extant of the state and number of the Jews in the twelfth century.
b. It furnishes the best materials for the history of the commerce of Europe, Asia, and Africa at the time of the Crusades.
c. Our author is the first European, who notices with accuracy the sect of the Assassins in Syria and Persia, the trade with India (of the produce of which the Island of Kish was the principal emporium), and who distinctly mentions China and describes the dangers attendant upon a navigation of the ocean, which intervenes between that country and Ceylon.
d. The whole work abounds in interesting, correct, and authentic information on the state of the three quarters of the globe known at his time and in consideration of these advantages, stands without a rival in the literary history of the Middle Ages. None of the productions of this period are as free from fables and superstitions as the *Itinerary of Rabbi Benjamin of Tudela*.

An attentive study of the narrative in its present state, however, has forced upon us the conviction that what we possess, is but an abridgment of the original journal, which in this respect, and in many others, shared the fate of Pethachia's and Marco Polo's works.

---

statements are carefully examined, and Colonel Conder, after expatiating upon the extraordinary mistakes made by writers in the time of the Crusaders, some of whom actually confounded the Sea of Galilee with the Mediterranean, says: "The mediaeval Jewish pilgrims appear as a rule to have had a much more accurate knowledge both of the country and of the Bible. Their assertions are borne out by existing remains, and are of the greatest value."

It will further be observed that the descriptions of ten cities, and the two episodes contained in the work (a. Rome, Constantinople, Nâblus, Jerusalem, Damascus, Baghdad, Thema, Chulam, Cairo, and Alexandria; and b. The history of El-Roy and the expedition against the Ghuz) take up, in extent, more than one half of the whole, whereas about two hundred cities, some of which must have been of tantamount interest in many points of view, are noticed so briefly, that all the information concerning them is disposed of in a very narrow space; nor is it likely, that Rabbi Benjamin should have passed over in silence the commercial relations of Germany, where he mentions the city of Ratisbon and other towns, which at his time absorbed most of the trade of that country.

But these omissions are not the only disadvantage which we have to deplore, another formidable inconvenience arose from the ignorance of those transcribers, from whose copies the first editions were printed. By their misconceptions our author is often obscured, whilst their inaccuracies of orthography render it, in many instances, a matter of the utmost difficulty to recognize the proper names of persons and places. The letters of the idiom in which Rabbi Benjamin wrote, are not fit to express with accuracy, French, Italian, Greek, and Arabic appellations; and as the text was written, of course, without the Hebrew vowel points, mistakes were not easily avoided.

Well aware of all these disadvantages, we have spared no labor nor expense in our attempts to discover a complete, ancient, and genuine manuscript. But neither in Europe nor in Egypt, have we been able to discover this desideratum. Our labor in this respect has been confined, necessarily, to comparing the two first, original editions, the second of which had not been consulted by any former editor or translator. We have also added the vowel points, by which the work becomes by far more intelligible to the general reader, and we hope not to be taxed with presumption if we assert, that our text, faulty as it must necessarily be, is still superior to any hitherto published.

— A. Asher
Berlin, December 1840
— Notes by Marcus Nathan Adler, 1907

Excerpt from the Itinerary of Benjamin of Tudela

From Beirut to Banyas

1173 CE

Translated by Marcus Nathan Adler

Prologue

This is the book of travels, which was compiled by J Rabbi Benjamin, the son of Jonah, of the land of Navarre — his repose be in Paradise. The said Rabbi Benjamin set forth from Tudela, his native city, and passed through many remote countries, as is related in his book. In every place which he entered, he made a record of all that he saw, or was told of by trustworthy persons — matters not previously heard of in the land of Sepharad [Spain]. Also he mentions some of the sages and illustrious men residing in each place. He brought this book with him on his return to the country of Castile, in the year 4933 (C.E. 1173). The said Rabbi Benjamin is a wise and understanding man, learned in the Law and the Halacha, and wherever we have tested his statements we have found them accurate, true to fact and consistent; for he is a trustworthy man.

I. Beirut

From there it is two days' journey to Beirut, or Beeroth, where there are about fifty Jews, at their head being Rabbi Solomon, Rabbi Obadiah, and Rabbi Joseph.

II. Sidon

Thence it is one day's journey to Saida, which is Sidon, a large city, with about twenty Jews. Ten miles therefrom a people dwell who are at war with the men of Sidon; they are called Druzes, and are pagans of a lawless character. They inhabit the mountains and the clefts of the rocks; they have no king or ruler, but dwell independent in these high places, and their border extends to Mount Hermon, which is a three days' journey. They are steeped in vice, brothers marrying their sisters, and fathers their daughters. They have one feast-day in the year, when they all collect, both men and women, to eat and drink together, and they then interchange their wives. They say that at the time when the soul leaves the body it passes, in the case of a good man, into the body of a newborn child; and in the case of a bad man, into the body of a dog or an ass. Such are their foolish beliefs. There are no resident Jews among them, but a certain number of Jewish handicraftsmen and dyers come among them for the sake of trade, and then return, the people being favorable to the Jews. They roam over the mountains and hills, and no man can do battle with them.

III. Tyre

From Sidon it is half a day's journey to Sarepta (Sarfend), which belongs to Sidon. Thence it is a half day to New Tyre (Sur), which is a very fine city, with a harbor in its midst. At night-time those that levy dues throw iron chains from tower to tower, so that no man can go forth by boat or in any other way to rob the ships by night. There is no harbor like this in the whole world. Tyre is a beautiful city. It contains about 500 Jews, some of them scholars of the Talmud, at their head being Rabbi Ephraim of Tyre, the Dayan, Rabbi Meir from Carcassonne, and Rabbi Abraham, head of the congregation. The Jews own seagoing vessels, and there are glass-makers amongst them who make that fine Tyrian glassware, which is prized in all countries. In the vicinity is found sugar of a high class, for men plant it here, and people come from all lands to buy it. A man can ascend the walls of New Tyre and see ancient Tyre, which the sea has now covered, lying at a stone's throw from the new city. And should one care to go forth by boat, one can see the castles, market places, streets, and palaces, in the bed of the sea. New Tyre is a busy place of commerce, to which merchants flock from all quarters.

IV. Acre

One day's journey brings one to Acre, the Acco of old, which is on the borders of Asher; it is the commencement of the land of Israel. Situated by the Great Sea, it possesses a large harbor for all the pilgrims who come to Jerusalem by ship. A stream runs in front of it, called the Brook of Kedumim. About 200 Jews live there, at their head being Rabbi Zadok, Rabbi Japheth, and Rabbi Jonah.

V. Haifâ

From there it is three parasangs to Haifâ, which is Hahepher on the seaboard, and on the other side is Mount Carmel, at the foot of which there are many Jewish graves. On the mountain is the cave of Elijah, where the Christians have erected a structure called St. Elias. On the top of the mountain can be recognized the overthrown altar which Elijah repaired in the days of Ahab. The site of the altar is circular, about four cubits remain thereof, and at the foot of the mountain the Brook Kishon flows. From here it is four parasangs to Capernaum, which is the village of Nahum, identical with Maon, the home of Nabal the Carmelite.

VI. Caesarea

Six parasangs from here is Caesarea, the Gath of the Philistines, and here there are about 200 Jews and 200 Cuthim — these are the Jews of Shomron, who are called Samaritans. The city is fair and beautiful, and lies by the sea. It was built by Caesar, and called after him Caesarea.

VII. Kako/Ludd/Sebastiya

Thence it is half a day's journey to Kako, the Keilah of Scripture. There are no Jews here. Thence it is half a day's journey to St. George, which is Ludd, where there lives one Jew, who is a dyer. Thence it is a day's journey to Sebastiya, which is the city of Shomron, and here the ruins of the palace of Ahab, the son of Omri, may be seen. It was formerly a well-fortified city by the mountain-side, with streams of water. It is still a land of brooks, gardens, orchards, vineyards, and olive groves, but no Jews dwell here.

VIII. Nâblus

Thence it is two parasangs to Nâblus, which is Shechem on Mount Ephraim, where there are no Jews; the place is situated in the valley between Mount Gerizim and Mount Ebal, and contains about 1,000 Cuthim, who observe the written law of Moses alone, and are called Samaritans. They have priests of the seed (of Aaron), and they call them Aaronim, who do not intermarry with Cuthim, but wed only amongst themselves. These priests offer sacrifices, and bring burnt offerings in their place of assembly on Mount Gerizim, as it is written in their law — "And thou shalt set the blessing on Mount Gerizim." They say that this is the proper site of the Temple. On Passover and the other festivals they offer up burnt offerings on the altar which they have built on Mount Gerizim, as it is written in their law — "Ye shall set up the stones upon Mount Gerizim, of the stones which Joshua and the children of Israel set up at the Jordan." They say that they are descended from the tribe of Ephraim. And in the midst of them is the grave of Joseph, the son of Jacob our father, as it is written — "and the bones of Joseph buried they in Shechem." Their alphabet lacks three letters, namely *He*, *Heth*, and *Ain*. The letter *He* is taken from Abraham our father, because they have no dignity, the letter *Heth* from Isaac, because they have no kindliness, and the letter *Ain* from Jacob, because they have no humility. In place of these letters they make use of the *Aleph*, by which we can tell that they are not of the seed of Israel, although they know the law of Moses with the exception of these three letters. They guard themselves from the defilement of the dead, of the bones of the slain, and of graves; and they remove the garments which they have worn before they go to the place of worship, and they bathe and put on fresh clothes. This is their constant practice. On Mount Gerizim are fountains and gardens and plantations, but Mount Ebal is rocky and barren; and between them in the valley lies the city of Shechem.

From the latter place it is a distance of four parasangs to Mount Gilboa, which the Christians call Mont Gilboa; it lies in a very parched district. And from there it is five parasangs to a village where there are no Jews. Thence it is two parasangs to the valley of Ajalon, which the Christians call Val-de-Luna. At a distance of one parasang is Mahomerie-le-Grand, which is Gibeon the Great; it contains no Jews.

IX. Jerusalem

From there it is three parasangs to Jerusalem, which is a small city, fortified by three walls. It is full of people whom the Muhammedans call Jacobites, Syrians, Greeks,

Georgians, and Franks, and of people of all tongues. It contains a dyeing-house, for which the Jews pay a small rent annually to the king, on condition that besides the Jews no other dyers be allowed in Jerusalem. There are about 200 Jews who dwell under the Tower of David in one corner of the city. The lower portion of the wall of the Tower of David, to the extent of about ten cubits, is part of the ancient foundation set up by our ancestors, the remaining portion having been built by the Muhammedans. There is no structure in the whole city stronger than the Tower of David. The city also contains two buildings, from one of which—the hospital—there issue forth four hundred knights [Crusaders]; and therein all the sick who come thither are lodged and cared for in life and in death. The other building is called the Temple of Solomon; it is the palace built by Solomon, the king of Israel. Three hundred knights are quartered there, and issue therefrom every day for military exercise, besides those who come from the land of the Franks and the other parts of Christendom, having taken upon themselves to serve there a year or two until their vow is fulfilled. In Jerusalem is the great church called the Sepulcher, and here is the burial place of Jesus, unto which the Christians make pilgrimages.

Jerusalem has four gates: the Gate of Abraham; the Gate of David; the Gate of Zion; and the Gate of Gushpat, which is the Gate of Jehoshaphat, facing our ancient Temple, now called *Templum Domini*. Upon the site of the sanctuary Omar ben al Khattab erected an edifice with a very large and magnificent cupola, into which the Gentiles do not bring any image or effigy, but they merely come there to pray. In front of this place is the western wall, which is one of the walls of the Holy of Holies. This is called the Gate of Mercy, and thither come all the Jews to pray before the wall of the court of the Temple. In Jerusalem, attached to the palace which belonged to Solomon, are the stables built by him, forming a very substantial structure, composed of large stones, and the like of it is not to be seen anywhere in the world. There is also visible up to this day the pool used by the priests before offering their sacrifices, and the Jews coming thither write their names upon the wall. The Gate of Jehoshaphat leads to the Valley of Jehoshaphat, which is the gathering place of nations. Here is the pillar called Absalom's Hand, and the sepulcher of King Uzziah.

In the neighborhood is also a great spring, called the Waters of Siloam [Pool of Siloe], connected with the Brook of Kedron. Over the spring is a large structure dating from the time of our ancestors, but little water is found, and the people of Jerusalem for the most part drink the rain water, which they collect in cisterns in their houses. From the Valley of Jehoshaphat one ascends the Mount of Olives; it is the valley which separates Jerusalem from the Mount of Olives. From the Mount of Olives one sees the Sea of Sodom, and at a distance of two parasangs from the Sea of Sodom is the Pillar of Salt into which Lot's wife was turned; the sheep lick it continually, but afterwards it regains its original shape. The whole land of the plain and the valley of Shittim as far as Mount Nebo are visible from here.

In front of Jerusalem is Mount Zion, on which there is no building, except a place of worship belonging to the Christians. Facing Jerusalem for a distance of three miles are the cemeteries belonging to the Israelites, who in the days of old buried their dead in caves, and upon each sepulcher is a dated inscription, but the Christians destroyed the sepulchers, employing the stones thereof in building their houses. These sepulchers reach as far as Zelzah in the territory of Benjamin. Around Jerusalem are high mountains.

On Mount Zion are the sepulchers of the House of David, and the sepulchers of the kings that ruled after him.

The Holy Land

The exact place cannot be identified, inasmuch as fifteen years ago a wall of the church of Mount Zion fell in. The patriarch commanded the overseer to take the stones of the old walls and restore therewith the church. He did so, and hired workmen at fixed wages; and there were twenty men who brought the stones from the base of the wall of Zion. Among these men there were two who were sworn friends. On a certain day the one entertained the other; after their meal they returned to their work, when the overseer said to them, "Why have you tarried today?" They answered, "Why need you complain? When our fellow workmen go to their meal we will do our work." When the dinnertime arrived, and the other workmen had gone to their meal, they examined the stones, and raised a certain stone which formed the entrance to a cave. Thereupon one said to the other, "Let us go in and see if any money is to be found there." They entered the cave, and reached a large chamber resting upon pillars of marble overlaid with silver and gold. In front was a table of gold and a scepter and crown. This was the sepulcher of King David. On the left thereof in like fashion was the sepulcher of King Solomon; then followed the sepulcher of all the kings of Judah that were buried there. Closed coffers were also there, the contents of which no man knows. The two men essayed to enter the chamber, when a fierce wind came forth from the entrance of the cave and smote them, and they fell to the ground like dead men, and there they lay until evening. And there came forth a wind like a man's voice, crying out: "Arise and go forth from this place!" So the men rushed forth in terror, and they came unto the patriarch, and related these things to him. Thereupon the patriarch sent for Rabbi Abraham el Constantini, the pious recluse, who was one of the mourners of Jerusalem, and to him he related all these things according to the report of the two men who had come forth. Then Rabbi Abraham replied, "These are the sepulchers of the House of David; they belong to the kings of Judah, and on the morrow let us enter, I and you, and these men, and find out what is there." And on the morrow they sent for the two men, and found each of them lying on his bed in terror, and the men said: "We will not enter there, for the Lord doth not desire to show it to any man." Then the patriarch gave orders that the place should be closed up and hidden from the sight of man unto this day. These things were told me by the said Rabbi Abraham.

X. Bethlehem

From Jerusalem it is two parasangs to Bethlehem, called by the Christians Beth-Leon, and close thereto, at a distance of about half a mile, at the parting of the way, is the pillar of Rachel's grave, which is made up of eleven stones, corresponding with the number of the sons of Jacob. Upon it is a cupola resting on four columns, and all the Jews that pass by carve their names upon the stones of the pillar. At Bethlehem there are two Jewish dyers. It is a land of brooks of water, and contains wells and fountains.

XI. Hebron

At a distance of six parasangs is St. Abram de Bron, which is Hebron; the old city stood on the mountain, but is now in ruins; and in the valley by the field of Machpelah lies the present city. Here there is the great church called St. Abram, and this was a Jewish place of worship at the time of the Muhammedan rule, but the Gentiles have erected there six tombs, respectively called those of Abraham and Sarah, Isaac and Rebecca, Jacob and Leah. The custodians tell the pilgrims that these are the tombs of the Patriarchs, for which information the pilgrims give them money. If a Jew comes, however, and gives a special reward, the custodian of the cave opens unto him a gate of iron, which was constructed by our forefathers, and then he is able to descend below by means of steps, holding a lighted candle in his hand. He then reaches a cave, in which nothing is to be found, and a cave beyond, which is likewise empty, but when he reaches the third cave behold there are six sepulchers, those of Abraham, Isaac and Jacob, respectively facing those of Sarah, Rebecca and Leah. And upon the graves are inscriptions cut in stone. Upon the grave of Abraham is engraved "This is the grave of Abraham"; upon that of Isaac, "This is the grave of Isaac, the son of Abraham our Father"; upon that of Jacob, "This is the grave of Jacob, the son of Isaac, the son of Abraham our Father"; and upon the others, "This is the grave of Sarah," "This is the grave of Rebecca," and "This is the grave of Leah." A lamp burns day and night upon the graves in the cave. One finds there many casks filled with the bones of Israelites, as the members of the house of Israel were wont to bring the bones of their fathers thither and to deposit them there to this day.

Beyond the field of Machpelah is the house of Abraham; there is a well in front of the house, but out of reverence for the Patriarch Abraham no one is allowed to build in the neighborhood.

XII. Shiloh/Beit Nûba

From Hebron it is five parasangs to Beit Jibrin, which is Mareshah, where there are but three Jews. Three parasangs further one reaches St. Samuel of Shiloh. This is the Shiloh which is two parasangs from Jerusalem. When the Christians captured Ramlah, the Ramah of old, from the Muhammedans, they found there the grave of Samuel the Ramathite, close to a Jewish synagogue. The Christians took the remains, conveyed them unto Shiloh, and erected over them a large church, and called it St. Samuel of Shiloh to this day.

From there it is three parasangs to Mahomerie-le-Petit, which is Gibeah of Saul, where there are no Jews, and this is Gibeah of Benjamin. Thence three parasangs to Beit Nûba, which is Nob, the city of priests. In the middle of the way are the two Crags of Jonathan, the name of the one being Bozez, and the name of the other Seneh. Two Jewish dyers dwell there.

XIII. Ramleh

Thence it is three parasangs to Rams, or Ramleh, where there are remains of the walls from the days of our ancestors, for thus it was found written upon the stones. About 300 Jews dwell there. It was formerly a very great city; at a distance of two miles there is a large Jewish cemetery.

XIV. Jaffa

Thence it is five parasangs to Yâfah or Jaffa, which is on the seaboard, and one Jewish dyer lives here. From here it is five parasangs to Ibelin or Jabneh, the seat of the Academy, but there are no Jews there at this day. Thus far extends the territory of Ephraim.

XV. Ashdod/Ascalon

From there it is five parasangs to Palmid, which is Ashdod of the Philistines, now in ruins; no Jews dwell there. Thence it is two parasangs to Ashkelonah or New Ascalon, which Ezra the priest built by the sea. It was originally called Bene Berak. The place is four parasangs distant from the ancient ruined city of Ascalon. New Ascalon is a large and fair place, and merchants come thither from all quarters, for it is situated on the frontier of Egypt. About 200 Rabbanite Jews dwell here, at their head being Rabbi

Zemach, Rabbi Aaron, and Rabbi Solomon; also about forty Karaites, and about 300 Cuthim. In the midst of the city there is a well, which they call Bir Abraham; this the patriarch dug in the days of the Philistines.

XVI. Jezreel/Sepphoris

From there it is a journey of a day to St. George of Ludd — thence it is a day and a half to Zerin or Jezreel, where there is a large spring. One Jewish dyer lives here. Three parasangs further is Saffuriya or Sepphoris. Here are the graves of Rabbenu Hakkadosh (Rabbi Judah the Prince), of Rabban Gamaliel, and of Rabbi Chiya, who came up from Babylon, also of Jonah the son of Amittai; they are all buried in the mountain. Many other Jewish graves are here.

XVII. Tiberias/Sea of Kinnereth

Thence it is five parasangs to Tiberias, which is situated upon the Jordan, which is here called the Sea of Kinnereth. The Jordan at this place flows through a valley between two mountains, and fills the lake, which is called the Lake of Kinnereth; this is a large and broad piece of water, like the sea. The Jordan flows between two mountains, and over the plain which is the place that is called Ashdoth Hapisgah, and thence continues its course till it falls into the Sea of Sodom, which is the Salt Sea. In Tiberias there are about fifty Jews, at their head being Rabbi Abraham the Astronomer, Rabbi Muchtar, and Rabbi Isaac. There are hot waters here, which bubble up from the ground, and are called the Hot Waters of Tiberias. Nearby is the synagogue of Caleb ben Jephunneh, and Jewish sepulchers. Rabbi Johanan ben Zakkai and Rabbi Jehudah Halevi are buried here. All these places are situated in Lower Galilee.

XVIII. Tymin/Meron/Almah/Kades

From here it is two days to Tymin or Timnathah, where Simon the Just and many Israelites are buried, and thence three parasangs to Medon or Meron. In the neighborhood there is a cave in which are the sepulchers of Hillel and Shammai. Here also are twenty sepulchers of disciples, including the sepulchers of Rabbi Benjamin ben Japheth, and of Rabbi Jehudah ben Bethera. From Meron it is two parasangs to Almah, where there are about fifty Jews. There is a large Jewish cemetery here, with the sepulchers of Rabbi Eleazar ben Arak, of Rabbi Eleazar ben Azariah, of Chuni Hamaagal, of Raban Simeon ben Gamaliel, and of Rabbi Jose Hagelili.

From here it is half a day's journey to Kades, or Kedesh Naphtali, upon the Jordan. Here is the sepulcher of Barak, the son of Abinoam. No Jews dwell here.

XIX. Banyas

Thence it is a day's journey to Banyas, which is Dan, where there is a cavern, from which the Jordan issues and flows for a distance of three miles, when the Arnon, which comes from the borders of Moab, joins it. In front of the cavern may be discerned the site of the altar associated with the graven image of Micah, which the children of Dan worshipped in ancient days. This is also the site of the altar of Jeroboam, where the golden calf was set up. Thus far reaches the boundary of the land of Israel towards the uttermost sea.

*

Gazetteer

A'bilîn (N 13). Lies south of Dâmûn. Guérin considers A'bilîn to represent the ancient Zabulon, destroyed by Cestius. The Muslim prophet Hûd is the biblical Eber. He was sent to convert the ancient 'Adites, who, refusing to listen to him, were destroyed by a burning wind (Koran 7.63).

Accaron, see Achon.

Achon (J IV; N 12–15; T III.39, 40, 48 and 51; B IV). Accaron or Acre, also Akka, 'Akkah, Achon, Accho, Acco, Ptolemais, and St.-Jean d'Acre. Port city on Mediterranean 11mi NNE of Haifâ. See Hazard, 4–11, 113–15, 160–61. On the approach from Acre, (Ptolemais III.40) see Prawer, 204.

Achon: Crusader sea wall, c.1920–33. Source: Library of Congress.

Achon, New Castle of (T III.40). New Castle of Accaron. Tobler thinks this can hardly be identified with Wilken's "Chateauneuf" (i, suppl., pp. 35–38).

Achon, Ox Spring (N 12). 'Ain al Bakar, this "Ox Spring" was a place held sacred by Jews, Muslims, and Christians alike, and

THE HOLY LAND

Achon: St. Jean d'Acre April 24th 1839 by David Roberts. Source: Library of Congress.

Achon: The Crusader Castle, c.1920–33. Source: Library of Congress.

Ajalon: Valley of Ajalon and Beth Horon, c.1900–20. Source: Library of Congress.

was a place of visitation. The Muslims had built a mosque here, dedicated to 'Ali, the Prophet's son-in-law, the eastern part of which the Crusaders made into a church.

Ad Dârdûm (M VIII). Deiran, anciently Daroma.

Adomim (J XIV). Adummim, now Tal'at ed Dumm, on the road from Jerusalem to Jericho.

Ajalon (J VI, B VIII). Aijalon, Yalo, 12 mi NW of Jerusalem.

Al Firmâ, see Pelusium.

Al Kusaifah (M VII). Tell Kuseifeh, lying to the east of Beersheba, 45 mi SW of Jerusalem.

Al Madînah (M II et passim, N 35). Medînah, burial place of the Prophet Muhammad in central western Saudi Arabia.

Al Madînah: Courtyard (southeast corner) of the holy mosque with the Garden of Fâtima. Source: Library of Congress.

Al Masjid al Yakîn (M VII, N 2). Later known as Khurbat Yakîn and Makâm Nabi Yakîn.

Aleppo (N 2, T III.44). Halab, Haleb, city and province in NW Syria. Attacked by Crusaders in 1118 and 1124; fell to Saladin in 1183. Tyrant was Nur ed-Din; See Runciman, 2:239–44, 278–87, 333–42 et passim.

Aleppo: View of from the castle, c.1900–20. Source: Library of Congress.

Ammân (M XVII). The Biblical Rabbath Ammon, the capital of Og, king of the Ammonites. In Greek times it was called Philadelphia, after Ptolemy Philadelphus of Egypt, its second founder. The Castle of Goliath is the citadel on the hill to the north of the town.

Ammân. Solomon's Circus (M XVII). The theater, originally capable of seating 6,000 spectators.

Ammân: View from acropolis hill, showing Roman theater [Solomon's Circus], c.1920–33. Source: Library of Congress.

Amos, Rock of (P VII). An allusion to Tekoa, Kh. Tekûa, the birthplace of Amos, and to the prophet's shepherd origin.

'Annabah (M I). The village of 'Annabah lies west of Ramleh, which has a gate named for the 'Annabah Mosque. In Jerome's *Onomasticon* it is mentioned under the name of Anab, which was also called Betho Annaba.

Antipatris (J V). Ras al-Ayn, Tel Afek, between Caesarea Maritima and Lydda, two miles inland.

Ar Rakîm (M XVIII). Often identified with Petra or Wâdî Musa, near Mount Hor, on the hypothesis that the name represents the Arekem of Josephus (*Antiq.* 4. 4, 7, and 4. 7, 1). This identification, however, was very justly shown to be impossible. Mukaddasî here confirms this by placing Ar Rakîm three miles from 'Ammân. Further Ibn al Athîr (*Chronicle* 11), states that Ar Rakîm lies two days' march north of Karak, on the road between Damascus and that fortress.

Archas (T III.49). In the time of the Crusades Arcas was a mountain fortress, 5,000 paces from the sea and as many from Tripoli, about 40 mi N of Beirut. Its ruins are mentioned by Rey 5. 69. It is the modern Erek.

Arimathea (J V, T III.36). Probably Rantieh, on the plain north of Lydda.

'Arkah (N 6). The city of the Arkites (Gen. 10:17), and the Arcados of the Crusaders.

Arphat (T III.49). See John of Würzburg, chap. 24, p. 64.

Arsûf (M XIII). Arsuf was in Greek times called Apollonia. By Crusaders it was supposed to represent the ancient Antipatris.

Ascalon (M XI; N 45; T I.15, III.36 and 51, B XV). Askelon, 'Askalân, important Crusader port on Mediterranean 15 mi NE of Gaza. Destroyed in 1270; now an archaeological site. See *Encyclopedia of Archeological Excavations* 1:121–30; Avi-Yonah, 265–66.

View of Ascalon.

Azerbaijân (N 13). The northwestern province of Persia, corresponding to the ancient Media.

Bait Jibrîl (M VIII). Bait Jibrîm, meaning the House of Gabriel, as in fact the place was called by William of Tyre. In Greek times it was named Eleutheropolis, and it is the Beth Gubrin of the Talmud. The Franks sometimes called this town Gibelin.

Banyas, see Paneas.

Beirut (J IV; T I.15, III.50 and 51; B I). Baruth, Berytus, Beeroth, in West Lebanon on the Mediterranean. See Prawer, 292, 397, 410–11, 451–52. In Theoderich's discussion of their sacrilege, Stewart reads *temptare* instead of *temperare*, in the phrase "to tempt God." Regarding the miraculous conversion of its inhabitants, Theoderich may have heard such a legend on the site. The city still had a significant Jewish population, while it also had a house of lepers, both of which may have given rise to this story. See Prawer, 242, 276. Regarding the image of Christ, see Hazard, 13. Regarding the image of cathedra, church, St. Peter was first enthroned at Antioch. See John of Würzburg, chap. 24, p. 63 and chap. 25, p. 65.

Beit Nûba (B XII). Near Ramleh, it has been "identified without proof with Nob**e**. Richard Coeur-de-Lion encamped here some twenty-five years after Benjamin's visit. He, with the army of the

The Holy Land

Crusaders, passed through Ibelin on his way to Askelon" (Itinerary of Benjamin of Tudela, 88).

Bethel (J XV, P VIII, T III.42). Beitîn or Baytin, about 11 mi N of Jerusalem, now an archaeological site.

Bethel, c.1900–20. Source: Library of Congress.

*Bethlehem by David Roberts, April 6th 1839.
Source: Library of Congress.*

Bethlehem (J VIII, P IV, M VI, N 41, T III.33, B X). Village of Christ. City and shrine 5 mi S of Jerusalem. Murphy-O'Connor, 165–71. For Bethlehem's place in the medieval itinerary, see Hazard, 58–59. For the Inn of Mary of the Virgin (J VIII, P IV), compare the curious description of the "holy inn of the Virgin," the grotto, the stable and the manger, in J VI–VIII. The Bordeaux Pilgrim (333 CE) simply mentions a basilica built by order of Constantine at Bethehem where "Christ was born."

Bethlehem. Grotto of our Savior (J VIII, P VII). The Grotto of the Nativity.

Bethlehem. Inn of Mary (J VIII, P IV).

Bethlehem. Manger (J VIII, P IV, T III.33). In the Church of the Nativity. See *Encyclopedia of Archeological Excavations* 1:204; Murphy-O'Connor, 165–71, esp. fig. 55 n. 9.

Bethlehem, the Manger, c.1890–c.1900. Source: Library of Congress.

Bethlehem. Nativity, Church or Basilica of the (M VI, T III.33). Traditional site of birth of Jesus. For a plan of this remarkable church and description, see Freeman-Grenville, 77–85, Murphy-O'Connor, 167–71. See also Stanley, chaps. 14, 32, p. 439. For Theoderich's twenty-five steps down to the grotto, Phocas (chap.

22, p. 32), says "sixteen." For a description and analysis of mosaic work in the crypt, see Hazard, 119–23; for the frescoes, see pp. 254–58. The tombs of Joseph and Jerome, as well as Eusebius, Paula, and Eustochium, are in the caves beneath the church. See Murphy-O'Connor, 171.

Bethlehem: Shrine of the Nativity Bethlehem, April 6th 1839 by David Roberts. Source: Library of Congress.

Bethlehem: Tomb of David by P. Bergheim, between 1860 and 1880. Source: Library of Congress.

Bethlehem. Tomb of David (P VII, B IX). According to the Bordeaux Pilgrim (p. 27), the Tomb of David was not far from the basilica; according to Antoninus Martyr (p. 23), it was half a mile from the town.

Bethoron (J VI). Beit Ur, Beitûr el Foka and Beitûr el Tahta, 11.5 mi NW of Jerusalem

Bethphage (J XIII, T II.20). From "Bethphace," signifying in Syriac the "house of the jaw," the jaw in the sacrifices being the portion of the priests. In the vicinity of the Mount of Olives; exact location of biblical site is uncertain. It is probably the chapel found in 1877, between the Mount of Olives and Bethany. See Murphy-O'Connor, 114–15. On the frescoes in the chapel, which is now the starting point of the Palm Sunday procession, see Hazard, 123, n. 9, 261–62. John of Würzburg says (chap. 6, p. 24): "Between this Bethany and the top of the Mount of Olives, about half-way was Bethphage, a village of priests, traces of which still remain in two stone towers, one of which is a church."

Bethphage, between 1898 and 1914. Source: Library of Congress.

Bethsaida (T III.46). In Galilee, near or on Sea of Galilee, about 2.5 mi W of Capernaum, but exact site is uncertain; see Rogerson, 128 (map), 140–41.

Bethsames (T III.38). Beth-shemesh, Ir-shemesh, Har-heres; in the Shephelah, about 13.5 mi WNW of Bethlehem. See 1 Sam. 6; Rogerson 84–85 (map), 86–88.

Bethsaida, approximately 1900 to 1920. Source: Library of Congress.

Bethsames (Beth Shemesh), May 1931. Source: Library of Congress.

Bethsan (T III.44). Beisan or Bet Shean; city in Harod Valley near Jordan River. See Murphy-O'Connor, 171–75; Prawer, 17, 64, 146, 162, 164, 166, 363; Avi-Yonah, 267–68. Site of Hospitallers' Castle mentioned in T III.44. See Prawer, 286.

Bethsan, between 1900 and 1920. Source: Library of Congress.

Bethsur (J X). Beit Sûr, Bethsura or Beth-zur, between Bethlehem and Hebron.

Bîla'ah (N 19, M I). Kariat-al-'Anab. There is some doubt as to the reading of this word, but very probably it is the same name for both the gate and the church at Ramleh. We have possibly reference here to the ancient, biblical town of "Baalah which is Kirjath-jearim" (The Village of Grapes) (Joshua 15.9; also 9.17.17, and 15.60), identified with the modern Karyet al 'Inab or Abû Ghosh, 12 km west of Jerusalem.

Bîr Ayyûb (M III). Bir Eyûb, Job's Well; Christians since the sixteenth century have been in the habit of calling this the Well of Nehemiah. May be En Rogel — the Fuller's Spring — mentioned by Joshua (15. 7) as on the boundary line between the tribes of Judah and Benjamin; unless this last be the Virgin's Fount.

Birwah (N 13). With Tell Birwah lies about three miles to the east of Acre (Achon).

Cadesbarne (T III.34). Kadesh-barnea, on the western edge of the high Negev, SW of Dead Sea, and near the border between the Negev and Sinai; Rogerson, 114–15 (map), 123–24.

Ain Gedeirat, possibly Cadesbarne, between 1920 and 1933. Source: Library of Congress.

Caesarea of Palestine (J V, M XIV, N 15 and 16, T III.39 and 51, B VI). Caesarea Palaestina, Kaisâriyyah, Qisarya; ancient city and port on Mediterranean 20 mi S of Haifâ. See Murphy-O'Connor, 179–81.

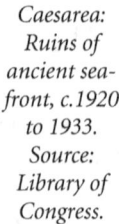

Caesarea: Ruins of ancient seafront, c.1920 to 1933. Source: Library of Congress.

Caesarea. Tower of Strato (J V, T III.39). The ancient anchorage. See Murphy-O'Connor, 179.

Cana, between 1989 and 1946. Source: Library of Congress.

Cana (J XVII, P VIII, N 14, T III.48). Chana, Cana of Galilee. Village about 4 mi NE of Nazareth. Also Kafar Kannah (Kafr Kanna). There is some uncertainty about the location of Cana of Galilee (John 2:1–2), and rival sites were identified by ecclesiastical tradition. The ruins of a church in the neighborhood of Kafar Kannah probably formed part of the monastery (*Sûmi'ah*), referred to by Nâsir-i-Khusrau. See John of Würzburg, chap. 1, p. 4, n. 7; Rogerson, 128–29 (map), 141.

The Holy Land

Capernaum (J XVII, P VIII, T III.45 and 46, B V). Kefar Nahum, Capharnaum on the north shore of the Sea of Galilee.

Capernaum: Ruins of the synagogue. (Tel Hum), between 1898 and 1943. Source: Library of Congress.

Caphar Barucha (J XII). Now Bani Nâîm, 5 mi east of Hebron; sometimes called Kefr Bâreka or Kafr al-Barik.

Cappadocia (P II). Roman province in Eastern Asia Minor between Pontus and Cilicia on the Mediterranean coast.

Cariathiarim (T III.38). Abû Ghosh, Kirjath-jearim, Karyet al 'Inab, ancient Baalah; 8 mi WNW of Jerusalem. See 2 Sam. 6. See Rogerson, 162–63 (map).

Cariathsepher (J X). Kirjath Sepher, Tell Beit Mirsim or Debir, now Edh Dhâherîyeh, south-

Cariathiarim: Crusader church, north aisle, Oct. 10, 1941. Source: Library of Congress.

Gazetteer

west of Hebron. The allusion is to the system of irrigation by small canals from the springs.

Castle of Imbertus (T III.51). Casale Lamberti on Marino Sanudo's map. See Nebenzahl, 44.

Caves of the Prophets (J XVI, P VII). According to Jerome, Abdias, or Obadiah, hid the prophets in two caves. The prophet Obadiah, according to a Jewish tradition, was the same as Obadiah the 'governor' of Ahab's house; the hill shown to St. Paula appears to have been near Samaria.

Cariathiarim: Excavations at Tell Beit Mirsim (Kirjath-Sepher) 1926. Source: Library of Congress.

Charnel House of the Lion (T III.37). For the miraculous powers of relics, in general, see Brooke and Brooke, 14–30.

Chorraei (J XVIII). Apparently Horraei; identified as possibly Eleutheropolis (Bait Jibrîl), about 13 mi WNW of Hebron.

Coele Syria (J IV, P II). The valley between Lebanon and Anti-Lebanon.

Constantia (J I). The ruins of Salamis are about 3 mi N of the modern Famagusta on Cyprus.

Dâjûn (M I). The modern Bait Dîjân, the Beth Dagon of Judah, approximately 10 km SE of Haifâ. Rogerson 79 (map).

Dead Sea (M VII; N 14; T III.28, 29, 34 and 35, B IX and XVII). Sea of Sodom, Lake of Sughar, Lake of Asphaltites, Salt Sea. A salt lake bordered by Jordan to the east and Israel and the West Bank to the west See Murphy-O'Connor, 197–201; Rogerson 192–95. For medieval knowledge and legend on the sea, see Wright, 208–9.

Dead Sea: looking towards Moab by David Roberts, April 4th 1839. Source: Library of Congress.

Desert of Paul and Anthony. (J I) The desert of the Wâdî Arraba, on the west shore of the Red Sea, south of Suez.

Diaspolis see Lydda.

Dor (J V). Now Tantûra, Tantoura, lies on the sea coast a few mi north of Caesarea of Palestine.

Elim (T III.31). Exod. 15:27.

Emmaus (J V, T III.38). Location is uncertain. Wrongly identified with the Emmaus of the New Testament; identified with Nicopolis (Imwas or Amwas), 19.3 mi from Jerusalem; Abû Ghosh, 6.8 mi; El Qubeibah, 7.2 mi; Motza, 3.7 mi; see Rogerson, 162–63 (map), 188–89; Murphy-O'Connor, 132–34; Hazard, 112.

Endor, see Kedumim and Mount Endor.

Escol (J X). Perhaps Halhul, approximately 3 mi north of Hebron.

Fountain of Elisha (T III.29). "No one," says Mr. Grove, "who has visited the site of Jericho, can forget how prominent a feature in the scene are the two perennial springs, which, rising at the base of the steep hills of Quarantana behind the town, send their streams across the plain towards the Jordan." See "Elisha" in Harper's Bible Dictionary, 159–60; Hazard, 59; Rogerson 194. 2 Kings 2:15–19.

Fountain of Elisha, approximately 1900 to 1920.
Source: Library of Congress.

Fountain of Gabriel (T III.47). Stewart has given the probable meaning of the corrupt *cupellum, hoc est leonis de marmore*, etc.

Fountain of Samson (J XVIII). The spring appears to have been shown near Chorraei, Beit Jibrin, perhaps the 'Ain Umm Judei'a. Compare Ant. Mart. (32).

Fountain of the Eunuch (P VII). The fountain is placed by the Bordeaux Pilgrim (p. 2) at Bethsura (Beth-zur or Beit Sûr) between Bethlehem and Hebron; Rogerson 95 (map).

259

Fountain of the Law (J XIV). 'Ain es Sultan north of Jericho.

Gabaa (J VI and XV, T III.38, B XII). Gibeah-Phinehas, 'Awertah; Gibeah of Benjamin, north of Jerusalem.

Gabaon (J VI). El Jib, Gibeon, 6 mi NW of Jerusalem.

Galgala (J XIV). Birket Jiljulieh. Theodorus (chap. 16.) makes Galgala 1 mi from Jericho; Antoninus (chap. 13.) not far from Jericho; compare also Bordeaux Pilgrim, and Willibald (chap. 17).

Sea of Galilee see, **Kinnereth, Sea of**.

Garden of Abraham (T III.28 and 29). The text of the description here seems to be corrupt. "Apples" here is a vague term for fruit of all kinds.

Genin (T III.44). The Arabic Dschenin; Ginae, Beth-haggan, En-gannim, west of Jordan River, about 18 mi N of Neapolis. See John of Würzburg, chap. 1, p. 6, n. 8.

Gessen (J XVIII). Goshen, located in the eastern Nile Delta of Egypt and also known as "Gesem" or "Kesem".

Gethaei (J XVIII). Probably Gath, Tell es-Safi and Blanche Garde(?).

Gibeleth (N 8, T III.50). Gebal, Giblet, Jubail, Jubayl, Jebeil, or ancient Byblos (Greek). Town on the Mediterranean, 17 mi NNE of Beirut. See Prawer, 406, 486. On the castle, see Hazard, 144–45, 338.

Gibeleth, approximately 1900 to 1920. Source: Library of Congress.

GAZETTEER

Great Sea (T I.2, B IV). The Mediterranean.

Hadhîrah (N 13). Hazûr, Hazîreh, which, meaning merely an "enclosure" (the Biblical "Hazeroth"), is applicable to many sites. There are several places in these regions north and west of Irbid that have at the present day the name of Hadhîrah.

Haifâ (N 15, T III.39 and 51, B V). Caipha. Port on Mediterranean at foot of Mount Carmel. Developed by Crusaders and destroyed by Saladin in 1191. See Murphy-O'Connor, 298–99; Rogerson, 72–76.

Haifâ: View from top of Carmel approximately 1920 to 1933. Source: Library of Congress.

Hebron (J XI, M VII, N 41, T III.34, B XI). Habrâ, Cariatharbe or Kariath-arba or Kirjath-arba or Matlûn; 21 mi SSW of Bethlehem; west of Dead Sea. In the early Arab annals is divided into four quarters or villages— Habrûn, Marthûn, Bait 'Ainûn, and Bait Ibrâhîm. *Mathlûn* is doubtless a corruption of the second of these names. See Hazard, 99; Rogerson, 98–100; Murphy-O'Connor, 229–33. For the legend of Adam's life and death here, see Hazard, 56. Matlûn Hebron. See also Yakut's *Geographical Dictionary,* text, 2:195.

261

*Hebron, between 1950 and 1977. Matson Photo Service.
Source: Library of Congress.*

Hebron. Bedstead of Abraham (M VII). Later known as Cain's Grave. The mosque in which it was found was said by Ulaimi to have been built in AH 352, CE 963.

Hebron. Cave of the Patriarchs (J XI, P VII, M VII, N 41 and 42, T III.34, B XI). (See plan.) Tombs of Abraham, Isaac and Jacob; Cave of Machpelah; Sanctuary (of Abraham); Ibrahimi Mosque, or Mash-had. The exact orientation of the quadrangle is fifty degrees true bearing and consequently the great Mihrâb of the Kiblah point lies almost exactly southeast. The exact dimensions externally of the Haram Walls, as measured by T.R.H. Prince Albert Victor and Prince George of Wales during their visit (1882), are one hundred and ninety-seven feet by one hundred and eleven feet. Our pilgrim's measurement is considerably under the real size. The average outside height of the ancient (or Herodian?) walls is forty feet, or twenty cubits, as in the text.

Hebron. Sanctuary (of Abraham), see **Hebron.** Cave of the Patriarchs.

Hebron. Tombs of Abraham, Isaac and Jacob, see **Hebron.** Cave of the Patriarchs.

Hermoniim (J XVII, P VIII). Probably Jebel Duhy, "Little Hermon."

Gazetteer

Idumaea (J XVIII; T I.2, III.31, 45 and 49). Edom, ancient country south of the Dead Sea. Includes Mount Seir and Hor. According to Jerome, Idumaea extended as far westward as Eleutheropolis. See Rogerson, 202–3 (map).

Irbil (N 13). Now generally called Irbid, the site of the ancient Arbela.

Istakhr (M II). Istakhr is the ancient Persepolis, the capital of Fârs.

Jabal Nusrah (M VII). The reading is uncertain. Besides Mukaddasî, other authorities make no mention of this name of the district, and it does not occur in the accounts of modern travellers. The name may signify "the well-watered hills."

Idumaea: Sunrise over Mountains of Edom from Dead Sea, approx. 1900 to 1920. Source: Library of Congress.

Jacob's Well (J XVI, T III.42). On eastern edge of Neapolis, ancient Sichem, 30 mi N of Jerusalem. Rogerson, 159; Murphy-O'Connor, 244; Hazard, 74, 111–12.

Jaffa (J V, M XII, T III.36, B XIV). Joppa, Yâfah, an ancient port city, the oldest part of modern Tel Aviv.

Jaffa by David Roberts, March 26th 1839. Source: Library of Congress.

263

Jerusalem (J II, P II, M II, N 12, T I.3, B IX). (See plan.) Hierosolyma, Al-Quds, Yerushalayim, Aelia Capitolina, site of the City of David, whose son, Solomon, built the first temple there. City is 35 mi E of Mediterranean and about 13 mi W of the north end of the Dead Sea. On the important surrounding pilgrim sites see Hazard, 55–56; Prawer, 204–13. See the Bordeaux Pilgrim, Appendix 3. Paula and Eustochium's comparison of Jerusalem (P V) with the Babylon of Jeremiah 51.6 and Revelations 18.2 contrasts it strongly with Bethlehem, and the quiet, secluded life of those who resided there. It shows how bitter the antagonism must have been between Jerome and the monastic party, and the bishop of Jerusalem and his clergy. Îliyâ is the Arabic form of the first part of Aelia Capitolina, the name given to the Holy City by the Emperor Hadrian. The word Al Balât may be translated the "Imperial residence" or "Court." See Quatremère, *Hist. des Sultans Mam.*, 2.1: 278. It is a corruption of the Latin "Palatium." In his introductory chapter Mukaddasî notes that in Jerusalem "one can find neither defect nor deficiency. Wine is not publicly consumed, and there is no drunkenness. The city is devoid of houses of ill-fame, whether public or private. The people too are noted for piety and sincerity. At one time, when it became known that the governor drank wine, they built up round his house a wall, and thus prevented from getting to him those who were invited to his banquets."

Jerusalem. Aksâ Mosque (M II, N 25, 28, 29, 34). (see plan 1 & 2).The Further Mosque, Masjid al Aksâ, on Temple Mount, Jerusalem. When referred to as "mosque" (Masjid) it includes not only the main edifice and its courts, but also the whole of the area (here the Temple Area or Noble Sanctuary) that is round the mosque and all the buildings thereunto appertaining. When the "covered part" is discussed (Al Mughattâ) it refers normally to the main building only.

Mosque el-Aksâ, approximately 1934 to 1939. Source: Library of Congress.

Jerusalem. Antonia Palace (T I.4 and 18). Or Fortress. In Muslim Quarter NW of Temple Mount, inside the current St. Stephen's (Lions') Gate; beneath the site of the Flagellation Monsatery. See Hazard, 91–92; *Encyclopedia of Archeological Excavations* 2:607; Murphy-O'Connor, 30 (map), 32.

Jerusalem. As Sâhirah (M V). The Plain; possibly that from which the Bâb as Sâhirah, Gate of the Plain, (Gate of Jeremiah's Grotto) in the north wall, takes its name.

Jerusalem. Barbican (T I.3). This is probably on the north wall outside the medieval St. Stephen's Gate or Damascus Gate. See *Encyclopedia of Archeological Excavations* 2:624.

Jerusalem. Bethany (T II.20 and III.28). On the east slope of the Mount of Olives. Murphy-O'Connor, 115–18; Hazard, 98, 261–62; Prawer, 172, 210. See John of Würzburg, chap. 6, p. 22. Theoderich does not mention any church or convent at Bethany, but Stewart mentions that there was a convent at Bethany dedicated to St. Lazarus, of which Judith, one of King Fulke's daughters, was abbess. Fulke's tomb — he is the father of Amalric — is mentioned in T I.11. There was a Church of St. Mary Magdalen in Bethany, which once had been the house of Simon the Leper. See Tobler's note.

Bethany by David Roberts, April 1st 1839. Source: Library of Congress.

Jerusalem. Bethany. Tomb of Lazarus (J XIII, P VII). The tomb of Lazarus was shown to the Bordeaux Pilgrim (p. 25); the tomb and house of Mary and Martha were shown to St. Paula.

Jerusalem. Birkat 'Iyâd (M II). The Tank of 'Iyâd, within the city but difficult to identify. Named after 'Iyâd ibn Ghanm, a companion of the Prophet, who accompanied the Khalif Omar to the capitulation of Jerusalem. He died in AH 20 (CE 641), and, according to Mujîr ad Dîn, he built a bath in the Holy City, but he acknowledges his ignorance of its situation. Either this or the Birkat Sulaimân may be the pool called Birkat Hammâm al Butrak, the Pool of the Patriarch's Bath, not far from the Jaffa Gate, and very generally identified with the Pool Amygdalon of Josephus.

Tomb of Lazarus, between 1898 and 1914. Source: Library of Congress.

Jerusalem. Birkat Bani Israîl (M II). The well-known Jerusalem Pool situated near the north wall of the Temple area. Mukaddasî wrote at the close of the tenth century ad and it may be worth noting that this corrects the notion it was constructed after the eleventh century — a notion based on the premise that no account of Jerusalem until that time mentioned the Birket Israîl.

Jerusalem. Birkat Sulaimân (M II). The Tank of Sulaiman within the city but difficult to identify. Le Strange was unable to discover whether it is called after King Solomon, or after some distinguished Muslim of the name of Sulaimân. Either this or the Birkat 'Iyâd may be the pool called Birkat Hammâm al Butrak, the Pool of the Patriarch's Bath, not far from the Jaffa Gate, and very generally identified with the Pool Amygdalon of Josephus.

Gazetteer

Jerusalem. Blessed Virgin, School of the (T I.14). See *Encyclopedia of Archeological Excavations* 2:624.

Jerusalem. Calvary, see Jerusalem. Holy Sepulcher Church, Chapel of the Crucifixion.

Jerusalem. City of David (M II, T III.38). Al Kal'ah. The citadel, the oldest part of Jerusalem, on the Ophel Ridge running south from Temple Mount near the Jaffa Gate. In the Middle Ages it was known as the City of David, and included the site of the Towers Hippicus and Phasaelus of Josephus, and probably part of the ground occupied by Herod's Palace.

Jerusalem. Column of the Flagellation (J VII, T I.11). See *Ant. Mart. Itin.* chap. 22, where the column of flagellation is said to have been in the church, formerly the house of St. James. Sion (in J) appears to be the western hill, or the modern Sion. This column is mentioned by Saewulf (p. 11), ad 1102, before the Crusaders' church was built. See Willis, Church of the Holy Sepulchre (London: J. Parker, 1849), 92, note. It is shown at the present day in the Chapel of the Apparition, in which services are held according to the Latin rite. See Fabri 8:349. This chapel is in the southeast corner of the Church of the Holy Sepulcher to the right of the entrance. Murphy-O'Connor, 48.

Jerusalem. Covered Street (T I.13). The Valuted Street; ran north-south in Christian Quarter in center of the Old City of Jerusalem behind the churches of St. Mary the Great and St. Mary the Latin. See "The City of Jerusalem" in The City of Jerusalem, chap. 16, p. 18.

Jerusalem. Dome of the Ascension (M II, N 36). Kubbat al Mi'râj to the northwest of the Dome of the Rock. The Ascension has reference to the Prophet's ascent into heaven, during his celebrated Night Journey, as opposed to the Dome of the Ascension on the Mount of Olives, also known as the Church of Our Savior and associated with the Ascension of Jesus. Le Strange in his notes conflates this structure with the Dome of the Prophet.

The Holy Land

*Jerusalem: Dome of the Ascension, between 1898 and 1946.
Source: Library of Congress.*

Jerusalem. Dome of the Chain (M II, N 35). Kubbat-as-Silsilah, facing the eastern door of the Dome of the Rock.

Jerusalem. Dome of the Prophet (M II, N 36). Kubbat an Nabî, Kubbat ar Rasûl, one of the small shrines to the northwest of

Dome of the Chain: Interior, 1940–46. Source: Library of Congress.

the Dome of the Rock and distinct from the Kubbet el Arwâh. Also referred to as the Dome of the Prophet David.

Jerusalem. Dome of the Rock, see Jerusalem. Temple of the Lord.

Jerusalem. Field of Acheldemach (T I.3 and 4). Aceldama, Haceldama; a Christian "Potter's Field" of Matt 27:7, south of Mount Sion. See Murphy-O'Connor, 95; Fabri, 7:536; Peters, 613.

Jerusalem. Galilee, Church of (T II.25). In Jerusalem, it was also called "Gallicantus," or "In Gallicantu," though this name properly belonged to the Grotto of the Cock-crowing within the church. Abbot Daniel (chap. 42, p. 37) says that thirty-two steps led down to this grotto. See John of Würzburg, chap. 9, p. 29. This church is possibly to be identified with the Ramban Synagogue, east of the south end of Temple Mount. See Murphy-O'Connor, 72. See also Hazard, 95, 272 and 294.

Jerusalem. Gates (M II). To account for the difficulties experienced in identifying the gates mentioned by Mukaddasî, it will be enough to recall what changes the Holy City has undergone since ad 1000. Besides the alterations effected by the

The Holy Land

Crusaders, and those dating from the period when, after the expulsion of the Christians, the city had come into the hands of Saladin (CE 1187): the walls themselves were in CE 1219 systematically destroyed, together with all the fortifications (except the City of David), when by treaty the Holy City was ceded to the Emperor Frederick II. The present walls were built (doubtless following the old lines), for the most part as late as the time of Sultan Soleiman the Magnificent, in CE 1542. Following in the track of Mukaddasî, subsequent geographers down to Yakût (in the thirteenth century, CE), and the author of the *Jihân Numâ* (in the 17th century), servilely reproduce our author's enumeration; but, bearing in mind the constant borrowings of Arab writers, it need not be concluded that the eight gates were in their times still open, or were known, under the same names. There is, besides, direct evidence to the contrary.

Jerusalem. Gate Al Asbât (M II, N 26 and 33). Bâb Al Asbât, Gate of the Tribes, at the eastern angle of the north wall of the Temple area on Temple Mount.

Jerusalem. Gate Dâûd (M II). Bâb Dâûd, Gate of David, the Bâb as Silsilah, Gate of the Chain, in the western wall of the Temple area on Temple Mount.

Jerusalem. Gate of Al Walîd (M II). Unable exactly to identify, but it must have opened in the western wall of the haram area on Temple Mount.

Jerusalem. Gate of David's Oratory (M II). Bâb Mihrâb Dâûd, the Jaffa, Haifâ or Hebron Gate (Bâb

Gate Dâûd: David's Gate, date unknown. Source: Library of Congress.

al Khalîl), which, even as late as Mujîr ad Dîn's times, was known under the more ancient name.

Gate of David's Oratory: Jaffa Gate by P. Bergheim, between 1860 and 1880. Source: Library of Congress.

Jerusalem. Gate of Damascus (M II, T II.26). Gate of the Columns, Bâb al 'Amûd, Northern Gate. It was this gate that in

Gate of Damascus.

the times of the Crusaders went under the name of St. Stephen's Gate.

Jerusalem. Gate of Ibrahîm (M II). Gate of Abraham; the northernmost in the west wall in the Temple area on Temple Mount. Known as the Bâb al Ghawânimah (of the Ghânim tribe).

Jerusalem. Gate of Jeremiah's Grotto (M II). Bâb Jubb Armiyâ. Le Strange identifies this as a closed one in the northern wall known as the Bâb as Sâhirah (the Gate of the Plain). In ancient times it was called Herod's Gate.

Jerusalem. Gate of Jericho (M II). Bâb Arîhâ. Le Strange concluded without hesitation that it was called St. Stephen's by the Franks, and known to the Arabs as the Gate of Our Lady Mary. Mujîr ad Dîn, however (p. 262), says: "The gate known anciently as the Gate of Jericho has now altogether disappeared, leaving no trace thereof. It apparently stood in the vicinity of the buildings that stand over against the Mount of Olives." If the Jericho Gate of Mukaddasî is not the modern St. Stephen's Gate, Mukaddasî's Gate of the Desert of the Wanderings might then be identified with this St. Stephen's Gate.

Jerusalem. Gate of Mercy (M II, N 26 and 33). Bâb Ar Rahmah; the long since closed Golden Gate in the eastern wall of the Temple area on Temple Mount. The double gates were those of Mercy (Rahmah) and Repentance (Taubah).

Jerusalem. Gate of Pardon (M II). Gate of Indulgence, Gate of Remission, Bâb Hittah. This gate is in the northern wall of the haram area on Temple Mount.

Jerusalem. Gate of Siloe (M II). Bâb Silwân. It must have opened to the southeast, and Le Strange took it to be that known as the Mogrebin or Dung Gate (Gate of the Desert of the Wanderings).

Jerusalem. Gate of Sion (M II). Bâb Sihyûn. Mujîr ad Dîn states, "is now called the Gate of the Jews' Quarter." It opens between the Haifâ Gate (Gate of David's Oratory) and that near the Mogrebin

Mosque (Gate of the Desert of the Wanderings) and is the one later called Bâb an Nabî Dâûd (of the Prophet David).

Jerusalem. Gate of St. Lazarus (T II.26). For the road past this gate, see John of Würzburg, chap. 16, p. 48.

Jerusalem. Gate of the Birkat Bani Israîl (M II). This must have opened near the pool of the Temple area on Temple Mount, which the present Bâb Hittah overlooks. The gate next to this last, on the west, is the present Bâb al 'Atm (of the Darkness), more anciently called either Dawâdâriyyah (of the Privy Seal), or the Gate of the Glory of the Prophets; and it was perhaps, before this again, known as the Gate of the Pool of the Bani Israel.

Jerusalem. Gate of the Desert of the Wanderings M II). Bâb at Tîh, Gate of the Mogrebin Mosque, Dung Gate. Le Strange suggests its being the gate known in Mujîr ad Dîn's time as the Postern Gate (Bâb Sirr, a small gate adjacent to the Armenian Convent) opening westward, in the wall to the south of the Haifâ Gate (Gate of David's Oratory).

Jerusalem. Gate of the Palace (M II). Gate of the Court, Gate al Balât, Bâb al Balât. Tobler imagines this to represent the long walled-up Golden Gate in the eastern wall of the Haram area. But this, by Arab writers, is never considered as a gate of the city; and further, the so-called Golden Gate is mentioned by Mukaddasî in its proper place among the gates of the Haram area. Le Strange has made the suggestion that the Bâb al Balât may be the same as the Bâb ar Rahbah (of the Public Square), of Mujîr ad Dîn, which is described by him as opening in the western city wall, not far from the Jaffa Gate. But Le Strange found none there.

Jerusalem. Gate of Umm Khâlid (M II). Gate of the Mother of Khâlid; unable exactly to identify, but it must have opened in the western wall of the Haram area on Temple Mount.

Jerusalem. Gates of the Haram Area (M II, N 25 and 26). See plan. Unidentified and unmentioned in the text are Bâb as Sarai (of the Palace); Bâb an Nâthir (of the Inspector), more anciently

The Holy Land

Golden Gate by David Roberts, published 1842.
Source: Library of Congress.

called of Mikaîl (the Angel Michael); Bâb al Hadîd (of Iron); Bâb al Kattanîn (of the Cotton Bazaar); Bâb al Mutawaddâ or Matarah (of the Place of Ablutions or of Rain); and between these five must lie the choice for the three mentioned gates of the haram area that Le Strange was unable to identify: the Hâshimite Gates, the Gate of Al Walîd, and the Gate of Umm Khâlid.

Jerusalem. Gates of the Mihrâb Maryam (M II). Gates of Mary's Oratory; perhaps the small gate, near Mary's Oratory, in the eastern wall of the Temple area on Temple Mount, called by Mujîr ad Dîn, Bâb al Janâiz (of the Funerals), and in his time closed.

Jerusalem. Gates of the Prophet (M II). According to Mujîr ad Dîn, the Gate of the Maghribîn was also known as the Gate of the Prophet. It lies southernmost of those in the western wall of the haram area, i.e., near the southwest corner on Temple Mount.

Jerusalem. Golden Gate (N 26; T II.14, 20 and 26). Seventh gate of Jerusalem, the eastern gate of the Temple Mount, which is enclosed by a wall and opened only on Palm Sunday and the Feast of the Exaltation of the Cross. Murphy-O'Connor, 83–84; Hazard, 83, n. 6; *Encyclopedia of Archeological Excavations* 2:623.

Jerusalem. Hâshimite Gate (M II, N 7). Unable exactly to identify, but it must have opened in the western wall of the haram area on Temple Mount.

Jerusalem. Gethsemane (T III.23). The village of Gethsemane is mentioned by Abbot Daniel (chap. 20, pp. 22–23), and John of Würzburg (chap. 18, p. 53). No trace of it remained in Stewart's day. The site of the Garden of Gethsemane at the foot of the Mount of Olives presently includes the Church of All Nations. See Murphy-O'Connor, 107–10; Rogerson, 188, 190–91. See also Hazard, 55, for its place in the pilgrim's itinerary; for general descriptions, see 96–97; *Encyclopedia of Archeological Excavations* 2:626–27.

Gethsemane and Mount of Olives, 1933 or 1934.
Source: Library of Congress.

Jerusalem. Gethsemane, Church of (T III.24). The site of the church in the Garden of Gethsamene at the foot of the Mount of Olives is now occupied by the Church of All Nations. Theoderich's account (T III.24) of the church reads as though there were two churches. John of Würzburg (chap. 8, p. 27) speaks only of the Chapel of Agony and the "new church enclosing the place where Our Lord prayed in whose flooring stand out three unwrought stones," etc. See Hazard, 97. Regarding the "six" holes imprinted in the rock at the entrance to the grotto, John of Würzburg (chap. 8, p. 27) says "five."

Jerusalem. Gethsemane, Church of St. Mary (M IV, T II.23). Church of the Tomb of the Virgin Mary, outside the modern Gate of St. Stephen, on the opposite slope of the Kedron Valley, north of the Garden of Gethsemane. A Benedictine abbey and rule with "Cluniac influence." See Hazard, 96–97, 110, 114; Murphy-O'Connor, 108–9. On its crypt, see Hazard, 97, who gives 48 steps down, rather than Theoderich's "more than forty"; on the mosaic work in crypt, see Hazard, 97; for the inscription (T II.23) these and the following verses are quoted by John of Würzburg (chap. 18, p. 52). The sepulcher has a border: Limbus — a word is used very loosely by Theoderich. Here it seems to mean a "tambour" extending around the church above the arches and carrying the upper range of columns with the dome.

Gethsemane, Church of St. Mary, Tomb of the Virgin, by P. Bergheim, between 1860 and 1880. Source: Library of Congress.

Jerusalem. Hinnom, Valley of (T I.3 and III.32). Valley of Gehinnom or Valley of Ennon, Gehenna. Borders the Old City of Jerusalem on the west and south below Mount Sion; included in the Wâdî Jahannam.

Jerusalem. Holy Sepulcher Church (J VI, P VII, T I.5). (See plan.) In center of Old City, in Christian Quarter. See Hazard,

Jerusalem: Holy Sepulcher Church, Crusader's Façade, photo between 1898 and 1946. Source: Library of Congress.

74–84; *Encyclopedia of Archeological Excavations* 2:626; Prawer, 422, 424–28, 431–37, 452–54; Peters, 311–14. The present church differs significantly. For a description of the site following the fire of 1808 and the earthquake of 1927, see Murphy-O'Connor, 43–51. Regarding entrances, compare the account given in Abbot Daniel, chap. 10, pp. 12–13. On the standard pilgrim's itinerary, see Hazard, 58, 75–76. On mosaic work (T I.5, T I.6), see Hazard, 117–18. According to the Bordeaux Pilgrim (p. 24), it was a vault, a stone's throw from Golgotha. In Nâsir, it is called Baiʿat-al-Kumâmah, literally, the Church of the Dunghill, for the word *Kumâmah* is a designed corruption on the part of the Muslims of *Kayâmah,* the Arabic name of the church, meaning Anastasis, or Resurrection. The church was laid in ruins in the year 1009 CE by the mad Khalif Hâkim's orders and was not rebuilt until 1037, under Al Mustansir, who granted this privilege to the Emperor Michael IV, the Paphlagonian, on consideration of his setting free five thousand Muslim captives.

Jerusalem. Holy Sepulcher Church, Altar of St. Nicholas (T I.9). Apparently on the site of the modern Chapel of St. Longinus in the NE corner of the church. See Tobler.

Jerusalem. Holy Sepulcher Church, Canons' Choir (T I.7). Holy of Holies; or Chorus dominorum, evidently the translation of the German *Domherrenchor.* "King Godfrey also instituted canons with prebends and gave them habitations round about the church." William of Tyre 9.9: "In Ecclesia Dominici Sepulchri sunt Canonici Sancti Augustini, qui habent Priorem, sed soli Patriarchae obedientiam promissunt." See Brocardi *Descriptio Terrae Sanctae,* CE 1230; Prawer, 426–28; Hazard, 76–78. For its ceiling, celatura, see Hazard, 117–18. Stewart found under the word "ceeling with syllure" in the *Promptorium Parvulorum,* ed. Albert Way, 1865, the following note: "The Catholicon explains celo to signify sculpere, pingere, and celamen or celatura sculpted or painted decoration. Lydgate, in the *Troye Boke,* uses the word *celature* to describe vaulted work of an elaborate character. It appears doubtful whether the verb "to cele," and the word "ceiling," which is still in familiar use, are derivable from *coelo,* or may not be traced more directly to *coelum* and the French *ciel,* signifying not only vaulting or ceiling, but also the canopy or baldaquin over an altar; the hangings or estate over a throne that are sometimes called daïs, from the throne being placed in that part of an apartment to which that name properly belonged; and lastly, the canopy of a bed, "celler for a bedde," *ciel de lit.* The altar, described in T I.7 as the "spot Joseph and Nicodemus laid our Lord's body...to wash it," is that of the compas or center of the earth. See John of Würzburg, chap. 11, p. 34, and note. Possibly Theoderich confused his cicerone's account of this altar with that of the altar in the Angel Chapel. What is now shown as the Stone of Unction and mentioned by Fabri (8:373–74) and other writers, stands in another part of the church. Innominatus 7 (p. 70), says, "To the eastward of the sepulcher, in the midst of the choir, is the middle of the world, where the Lord was laid when Nicodemus took him down from the cross." For medieval Christians the actual omphalos, or center of the world, was marked by a cross in the pavement of the Canons' Choir, described as an altar. See Peters, 274, photo. On Jerusalem as the navel, or center, of the earth, see T I.16, Prawer, 428; Wright, 259–60; Marcea Eliade, *The Sacred and the Profane* (New York: Harper & Row, 1961), 42–45. In his note on the representation of Christ in the ceiling of the Canons' Choir (described in T I.7), Tobler remarks that there is in the Bavarian National Museum at Munich an ivory carving of the fourth century, on which Christ is represented in precisely this attitude. Regarding the inscription on the scroll under Christ's feet, compare Fabri, 8:425. See T I.11, regarding the clergy who sang the offices.

Jerusalem. Holy Sepulcher Church, Canons' Cloister (T I.9). On the east side of the church. See Murphy-O'Connor, 51; Hazard, 79–80. On crucifix painted above its door (T I.9), see Hazard, 118.

Jerusalem. Holy Sepulcher Church, Chapel of Holy Sepulcher (T I.5). On inscription at base of enclosing arcade, described in T I.5, John of Würzburg (chap. 12, pp. 37–38) says "silver." See the Preface to the First Edition of Theoderich for discusion of visits by him and John. For a description of the interior (T I.5), see Abbot Daniel, Appendix 2, pp. 91–92. The gilding (T I.5) is probably the work of the Emperor Manuel Comnenus. See John of Würzburg, chap. 12, p. 36; and Phocas, chap. 14, pp. 19. See also Hazard, 78. The present tomb has been "indulgently described as a 'hideous kiosk,'" see Murphy-O'Connor, 49. Instead of sixteen monolithic columns (T I.6), there are actually 18 pillars. The plan may have involved alternating piers and columns. See Hazard, 76–77; Prawer, 427. The apostles in the mosaic (T I.6) are depicted on the south side. The ancient Christian practice of separating men and women in church is carried out in this mosaic.

Jerusalem: Holy Sepulcher Church, Holy Sepulcher Chapel, between 1989 and 1914. Source: Library of Congress.

Jerusalem. Holy Sepulcher Church, Chapel of St. Helena (T I.10). See Hazard, 77, 80.

Jerusalem: Holy Sepulcher Church, Chapel of St. Helena, published February 8, 1944. Source: Library of Congress.

Jerusalem. Holy Sepulcher Church, Chapel of St. Mary of Egypt (T I.9). On the south side of the church, see Hazard, 79.

Jerusalem. Holy Sepulcher Church, Chapel of the Apparition. Present site of the Column of the Flagellation (T I.11). Services in this chapel are held according to the Latin rite. See Fabri, 8:349. This chapel is in the southeast corner of the church to the right of the entrance. Murphy-O'Connor, 48.

Jerusalem. Holy Sepulcher Church, Chapel of the Crucifixion (T I.12). Calvary Chapel, in the southeast section of Church of the Holy Sepulcher, behind the Greek chapel. The verses in gold, mentioned by Theoderich, with the exception of the last one, are quoted by John of Würzburg (chap. 13, p. 39). For a description of the chapel, see Hazard, 79, 81, 118, 318, pl. xxx; see also Avi-Yonah, 128, 176, 274; Murphy-O'Conner, 47–48.

The Holy Land

Jerusalem: Chapel of Calvary in Church of the Holy Sepulcher, March 1942. Top, Greek, Left, Latin. Source: Library of Congress.

Jerusalem. Holy Sepulcher Church, Chapel of the Holy Cross (T I.9). See Hazard, 79. In the description of the pavement in the adjoining chapel (T I.9), the statement "under the pavement of which" probably means "in the pavement under which," etc.

Jerusalem. Holy Sepulcher Church, Chapel of the Invention of the Cross (T I.10). At the eastern end of the Church of the Holy Sepulcher. John of Würzburg (chap. 13, pp. 38–39) alludes to this and the Chapel of St. Helena. Theoderich, Tobler tells us, is the first writer who distinctly describes the Chapel of the Invention of the Cross. See Murphy-O'Connor, 51; Hazard, 77, plan; Avi-Yonah, 128.

GAZETTEER

Jerusalem: Chapel of the Invention of the Cross in the Church of the Holy Sepulcher, between 1898 and 1914. Source: Library of Congress.

Jerusalem. Holy Sepulcher Church, Chapel of the Three Marys (T I.13). Tobler tells us that the Chapel of St. John the Baptist and of Mary Magdalen were in the west side of the forecourt of the church. We must look for the Chapel of the Three Marys, that of the Armenians and the "other little chapel upon the east side." See Hazard, 77 (plan).

Jerusalem. Holy Sepulcher Church, Facade (T I.9). See Hazard, 78–79; Prawer, 431–37.

Jerusalem, Holy Sepulcher Church, Prison of Christ(T I.9). The prison is in the northeast corner of the Church of the Holy Sepulcher. See Hazard, 79.

Jerusalem. Holy Sepulcher Church, Tombs (T I.11). Stewart discusses these in his Preface to Theoderich. These tombs of the kings of Jerusalem were under the Greek chapel just north of the Latin chapel. The Tomb of Godfrey and the Tomb of Baldwin II were removed by the Greeks in 1809. See also Hazard, 90. The tomb of Amalric's father, the fourth tomb, is

283

the Tomb of King Fulke, the father of Baldwin III and Amalric. The fifth tomb is the Tomb of Baldwin II (T I.11) whose daughter Judith was abbess of the Convent of St. Lazarus of Bethany. His eldest daughter, Queen Milicent, married Fulke of Anjou, who was the ancestor of the English Plantagenet kings.

Jerusalem. Last Supper, Table of the (T II.22). Traditional site is in the Church of the Coenaculum on Mount Sion. See Murphy-O'Connor, 93–94.

Jerusalem. Market (T I.13). Its columns, with the arches above them, probably resembled the existing arcade at the entrance to the Haram area. On this and Jerusalem's other markets, see Prawer, 409–10; *Encyclopedia of Archeological Excavations* 2:624.

Jerusalem. Mosque of 'Omar (M II, V and IX; N 29; B IX). Several locations are mentioned, including a small mosque near the Aksâ Mosque on Temple Mount, perhaps only a sanctuary or prayer niche; a mosque near the Church of the Holy Sepulcher; one reportedly on the Mount of Olives, one in Bethlehem. and one in Gaza At one time, the name of "Omar" was identified with the building on the site of the Aksâ Mosque.

Jerusalem. Mount Gion (T I.4). Gihon on the Ophel Ridge. See Murphy-O'Connor, 96, 100; 1 Kings 1:33–34.

Jerusalem. Mount Moriah (T I.4 and 18 and III.38). Moria, or Temple Mount (see plan), site of the Dome of the Rock, Temple of the Lord. See *Encyclopedia of Archeological Excavations* 2:580.

Jerusalem. Mount of Olives (J XIII, P VII, M V, T II.27, B IX). Jabal Zaitâ, across the Kedron Valley, site of the shrines of the Paternoster and Credo and the Church of the Our Savior; traditional site of the Ascension of Jesus. The Plain, As Sâhirah, of the Resurrection, is the level space on the norther side of the Mount of Olives. The Bordeaux Pilgrim (24, 25) connects the Transfiguration with the Mount of Olives and does not allude to the Ascension. See Hazard, 97; Murphy-O'Connor, 104–18.

Jerusalem: Mount of Olives and Gethsemane, general view, between c.1890 and c.1900. Source: Library of Congress.

Jerusalem. Mount Sion (J VII, T II.22). SW corner outside Old City, site of St. Peter in Gallicantu, David's Tomb, and the Coenaculum. See Murphy-O'Connor, 92–95; *Encyclopedia of Archeological Excavations* 2:580–96; Hazard, 57.

Jerusalem. Mount Sion, Church of St. Mary (T I.3 and 4 and II.22 and 25). The Church and Benedictine Abbey of the Dormition of Mary, Church of St. Mary outside the Walls, the Nea Church. Built by Crusaders, and demolished by Arabs in 1219. See Murphy-O'Connor, 93; *Encyclopedia of Archeological Excavations* 2:617, 626–27; Prawer, 171, 178. *"In ecclesia Montis Sion est Abbas et Canonici regulares."* Brocardi *Descriptio Terrae Sanctae,* CE 1230. He was a mitred abbot. See Hazard, 95. For the upper chamber, compare the descriptions given by John of Würzburg (chap. 7, p. 25); the City of Jerusalem (chap. 1, p. 2); the Abbot Daniel (chap. 41, pp. 36–37); and Phocas (chap. 14, p. 18). For the Table of the Last Supper, see Murphy-O'Connor, 93–94; Hazard, 67. For its sanctuary, see Hazard, 95, 262–63. On column before the choir, see Murphy-O'Connor, 71.

Jerusalem. New Cistern (T III.32). The Birket es-Sultan, once the Serpent's Pool at Mount Sion, SW of Old City. See Tobler's note.

Jerusalem. Our Savior, Church of (T II.27). Also Church of the Ascension, now Dome of the Ascension on the Mount of Olives; traditional site of the Ascension of Jesus. *"In ecclesia Montis Oliveti est Abbas et monachi nigri,"* (Brocardi *Descriptio Terrae Sanctae*, CE 1230). He, as well as the Abbot of Mount Sion of the Temple, was a mitred abbot. For a description of the church, see Hazard, 97–98. For the stone which Christ ascended from. See Hazard, 97. Not to be confused with the Dome of the Ascension on Temple Mount, associated with the ascent of the Prophet.

Jerusalem: Church of the Ascension on the Mount of Olives by Francis Frith, 1862? Source: Library of Congress.

Jerusalem. Pavement (T II.25). Tobler's admirable note makes it abundantly clear that in the time of Theoderich, in the last days of the Frankish kingdom of Jerusalem, the house of Pilate, the Praetorium, and the prison had been confused with one another. Here Theoderich follows the western of the routes introduced by the Latins, as opposed to the one to the north of the Temple or the eastern route, where the Via Dolorosa now begins. See Murphy-O'Connor, 33–34; Hazard, 95.

Jerusalem. Pilate's House (T I.4 and III.26). This house in Jerusalem stood to the west across the Sheep Pool from St. Anne's on Jehoshafat Street north of Temple Mount. See *Encyclopedia of Archeological Excavations* 2:624.

Jerusalem. Pool of Siloe (M III, T I.3 and II.19, B IX). 'Ain Sulwân, Pool or Waters or Spring of Siloam, in City of David, on the Ophel ridge. See Murphy-O'Connor, 101–2. Not properly speaking a spring, but a tank fed by the aqueduct from the Virgin's Fount (called also 'Ain Umm ad Daraj, the Fountain of the Steps), and having an intermittent supply consequent on the intermittent flow of the upper spring. It was on the wall of the tunnel connecting the Pool of Siloe with the Virgin's Fount that, in 1880, the now celebrated Siloe Inscription was accidentally discovered by a party of Jewish schoolboys.

Fountain of Siloam in the Valley of Jehosophat by David Roberts, published 1842 Source: Library of Congress.

Jerusalem. Pools (M II, T I.14). The ancient tanks or pools within the city were, according to Le Strange, difficult to identity. He suggests that those mentioned by Mukaddasî — Birkat Bani

Israîl, the Birkat Sulaimân, and the Birkat 'Iyâd — might be identified with one of the following: (1) A double cistern 70 feet long in the Muristan and most probably the one mentioned by Mujîr ad Dîn as that in the Street Marzubân, belonging to and near the bath of 'Alâ ad Dîn al Basîr; (2) A pool discovered by Clermont Ganneau, not far from the Birkat Israîl and identified by him as the Pool of Strouthion, which supplied with water the Antonia Palace, erected on the north of the Temple area (Josephus, Wars, 5.2, 4); or (3) the well-known Pool Al Burâk. Mukaddasî's three pools are, as usual, inserted without comment in the works of later Arab geographers.

Jerusalem. Sheep Pool (T I.4 and II.26). The Pool of Bethesda, ancient reservoir in Jerusalem, north of Temple Mount, between Lions' Gate and Herod's Gate (Gate of Jeremiah's Grotto). See Hazard, 94.

Jerusalem. Solomon's Palace (T I.4 and 17, B IX). The south end of Temple Mount in, on the site of Aksâ Mosque. See Prawer, 39, 97, 171, 176, 178; Peters, 320–24; *Encyclopedia of Archeological Excavations* 2:623–34. Jacques de Vitry writes, "There was also another immense temple besides the Dome of the Rock, located to the southeast of it, and from this [so-called] Temple of Solomon, not from the Temple of the Lord, the Templars took their name" (*History of Jerusalem*, bk. 1). Concerning the description in T I.17, see the translation of Procopius, *De aedificiis*, in the Palestine Pilgrim's Text Society series, bk. 5, chap. 6, and Appendix 1; also John of Würzburg, chap. 5, pp. 20–21.

Jerusalem. Solomon's Temple, see Jerusalem. Temple of the Lord.

Jerusalem. St. Anne, Church of (T II.26). In Muslim quarter, north of Temple Mount. Built in 1140; crypt is traditionally thought to be the home and birthplace of Mary. Still intact. See Murphy-O'Connor, 29–31; Hazard, 73, 93–94, 271–72.

*Church of St. Anne, approximately 1900 to 1920.
Source: Library of Congress.*

Jerusalem. St. James, Church of (T I.15 and 16). Chapel of St. James the Apostle, St. James the Less. The little mosque now called the Kubbet es-Silsile, or Kubbat as-Silsilah, or Dome of the Chain (see Edrisi 5), was called the Chapel of St. James (Jacob) "the Less" by the Crusaders. See *Encyclopedia of Archeological Excavations* 2:623–24; Hazard, 86; Murphy-O'Connor, 80.

Jerusalem. St. Mary the Latin, Church of and Church of St. Mary the Great (T I.13). At the Muristan in the Christian Quarter. The former is east of the latter. See Hazard, 84–85; *Encyclopedia of Archeological Excavations* 2:626; Prawer, 170, 178, 209. For the position of both of these convents see Williams' *Memoir on Jerusalem* (London: J.W. Parker), 17, 18; and Tobler's elaborate note on this passage. See also his note on Innominatus 1, chap. 2, p. 2. The site is now occupied by the late 19th century Church of the Redeemer. On St. Mary the Great, see *Encyclopedia of Archeological Excavations* 2:624, 627; Prawer, 170–71; Hazard, 84, 270–71.

Jerusalem. St. Mary, Church of (T I.4). Fabri, who was in Jerusalem in CE 1483, says that there was once a church in the Field of Acheldemach, or Haceldama, south of Mount Sion, which was built by the Empress Helena and dedicated to All Saints. Fabri, *Wanderings,* 8:534–35. See Prawer, 209.

Jerusalem. St. Peter's Prison (T II.21). Probably St. Peter in Chains, possibly the site of the Ramban Synagogue, in the Jewish Quarter. John of Würzburg (chap. 16, pp. 46–47) describes this chapel and tells us that he celebrated mass there on St. Peter's Day (August 1). He quotes the verses without any variation. See Murphy-O'Connor, 66 (fig. 20, T), 72.

Jerusalem: Stone of Unction, between 1934 and 1939. Source: Library of Congress.

Jerusalem. St. Stephen, Church of (T II.26). Northwest of Jerusalem outside the medieval St. Stephen's Gate or the Damascus Gate. See Abbot Daniel, Appendix 1, pp. 83–90. For the frescoes there, see Hazard, 262–63.

Jerusalem. Stone of Unction (T I.5). The stone on which the body of Christ was placed by St. Joseph of Arimathea and Nicodemus. What is now shown as the Stone of Unction is opposite the door of the Church of the Holy Sepulcher. The first one appeared in the twelfth century. The present one dates from 1810. See Murphy-O'Connor, 49.

Jerusalem. Templars, Church of the (T I.17). See John of Würzburg, chap. 5, p. 21, n. 2. This church was destroyed by Saladin.

Jerusalem. Templars, Stable of the (T I.17). John of Würzburg (chap. 5, p. 21) declares that these stables could hold more than two thousand horses or fifteen hundred camels. See *Notes to the Ordnance Survey of Jerusalem*; *Encyclopedia of Archeological Excavations* 2:623–24.

Jerusalem. Temple of the Lord (M II; N 35, 37 and 38; T I.8, 14 and 15 and III.38; B IX). Dome of the Rock (see plan), Solomon's Temple (see plan) on Temple Mount. The street referred to at the opening of the passage in Theoderich is probably Temple Street. The Temple itself is the Dome of the Rock, on the site of the Temple of Solomon. See Prawer, 94, 171, 209, 418–19; Hazard, 86–90, 272–73; *Encyclopedia of Archeological Excavations* 2:590, 604–6, 623–24, 626; Peters, 316–20; Murphy-O'Connor, 73–86. On the steps leading to the great pool: *In Templo Domini Abbas*

Jerusalem: The Dome of the Rock, south façade, showing the ablution basin through the cypress trees, between 1898 and 1946.
Source: Library of Congress.

Jerusalem: The Dome of the Rock, north façade from arched street, between 1898 and 1946. Source: Library of Congress.

est et Canonici regulares. Et est sciendum, quod aliud est Templum Domini, aliud Templum militiae, illi clerici sunt, isti milites. Brocardi Descriptio Terrae Sanctae, CE 1230. See the *Encyclopedia of Archeological Excavations* 2:623–24. Theoderich's description of the outer and inner courts (T I.13) agrees materially, although not in detail, with that given by John of Würzburg, chap. 4, pp. 12–20. On its mosaic work, see Murphy-O'Connor, 78–79. The door-jamb described in I.16 is probably the "pierced-rock" that marked the site of Solomon's Temple and the Rock of Muhammad's Ascension. The Dome of the Rock had four gates: Mukaddasî gives the orientation of two of the gates. Mujîr ad Dîn states that the Eastern Gate, facing the Dome of the Chain, was that called the Gate of the Angel of Death Isrâfîl subsequently called the Gate of the Chain; and the northern gate is called Bâb al Jannah, Gate of Paradise. Nâsir gives a thorough description of the building.

Jerusalem. Temple Mount see Jerusalem. Mount Moriah.

Jerusalem. Temple Street. Possibly the street referred to at the beginning of T I.14 leading from the Vegetable Market and the Covered Street past the Latin Money Exchange. See *Encyclopedia of Archeological Excavations* 2:624.

Jerusalem. Tomb of Absalom (N 22, B IX). Also Absolom or Absalom's Hand. In the Kedron Valley off the SE corner of

Temple Mount, just below the SE angle of the Haram Area. In memory of Absalom's disobedience to his father, it was customary with the Jews to pelt this monument with stones. The adjoining tomb is traditionally known as that of Zechariah, (2 Ch. 24.20). It also went by the name of Tantûrak Fira'ûn or Pharaoh's Cap. Nâsir refers to it as the Pharaoh's House.

Jerusalem: Tomb of Absalom, photo by P. Bergheim, between 1860 and 1980. Source: Library of Congress.

Jerusalem. Tomb of Helena (J VI). Helena of Adiabene. Identified with the "tombs of the kings" on the north side of Jerusalem.

Jerusalem. Tomb of Josaphat (T I.3). Probably the Tomb of Absolom.

Jerusalem. Tomb of King Uzziah (B IX). Otherwise Azariah, was buried on Mount Sion, close to the other kings of Judah (2 K. 15.7) See Murphy-O'Connor, 103; *Encyclopedia of Archeological Excavations* 2:601, 629–30.

Jerusalem. Tomb of the Virgin, see **Jerusalem. Gethsemane, Church of St. Mary.**

The Holy Land

Jerusalem. Tower of David (J VII; T I.4, II.26, III. 32, 37 and 41; B IX). On Mount Sion; the Phasael Tower, originally dating from Herod's reign. See Murphy-O'Connor, 24, 92, 93 (map); *Encyclopedia of Archeological Excavations* 2:599, 604–26; Hazard, 33; Prawer, 323–24, 435.

Jerusalem: Tower of David with Citadel in background between 1898 and 1946 (above); Via Dolorosa, between 1898 and 1914 (below left). Source: Library of Congress.

Jerusalem. Via Dolorosa (T II.25). Follows the Way of the Cross from the Chapel of the Flagellation in the Muslim Quarter, north of Temple Mount, to the Church of the Holy Sepulcher. The chief authorities will be found in the *Harper's Bible Dictionary*, article on "Jerusalem," 314–21. See also Murphy-O'Connor, 33–34.

Jerusalem. Wâdî Jahannam (N 22, M IV). Jahannum, Valley of Kedron and Jehoshaphat. It is worthy of remark that the Valley of Hinnom (Gehenna, Jahannam) is the name of the deep gorge to the west and southwest of the city. Mukaddasî's and Nâsir's Valley of Jahannum, however, would be the valleys of Jehoshaphat and the Kedron together, the modern Wâdî Sitteh Maryam.

Jezrahel (T III.44, B XVI). Jezreel, Zerin, about 18 mi SW of south end of Sea of Galilee. See Prawer, 46, 55; Rogerson, 146–47 (map).

Jerusalem: Valleys of Jehoshaphat and Hinnom with Kedron Brook, between c.1900 and 1920. Source: Library of Congress.

Jordan River (J XIV; P VII; T I.2, III. 28–31, 44–46 and 49; B VIII, XIX). Flows south from the basin of Lake Hulah in Upper

Jordan River, between 1920 and 1933. Source: Library of Congress.

Galilee for 200 mi, through the Sea of Galilee and ending in the Dead Sea. The theory that it is formed by the Jor and Dan (T III.45) was first proposed by Eusebius or Jerome. See Nebenzahl, 12, 18–19, 38–42, 106–7; Rogerson, 128–29 (map). The spot alluded to by Paula (P VII) is near the Kusr el Yehûd; it is mentioned by the Bordeaux Pilgrim, and the site is discussed in "Antoninus Martyr," App. 1: "The Holy Places on and near the Jordan." It is connected by Jerome with the place at which the Israelites crossed Jordan, and at which Elijah and Elisha passed over. See note to Antoninus, chap. ix.

Jubail, see Gibeleth.

Kafar Kannah, see Cana.

Kafar Sâbâ see Kafar Sallâm.

Kafar Sallâm (N 17). This town, confused in Nasir with the extant Kafar Sâbâ, had entirely disappeared by the late nineteenth-century maps, but its site is probably that of *Râs al 'Ain,* the Antipatris of Acts 23:31 and Josephus. Mukaddasi mentions both towns separately and gives their respective distances from Ramlah as in each case one day's march.

Kâ-in (M II). Kâ-în is in the Kohistân, between Ispahân and Nishâpûr.

Kako (B VII). Kâkôn (Qaqun), Benjamin identified it as ancient Keilah in 1160, but Qila, 7 mi (11 km) NW of Hebron, and Khuweilfeh, between Beit Jibrin (Eleutheropolis) and Beersheba are also possibilities.

Kalamûn (N 8). The village of Kalamûn represents the Calamos of Pliny and the Calamon which, according to Polybius, was destroyed by Antiochus.

Kariat-al-'Anab, see Bîla'ah.

Kunaisah (N 15). The Little Church, or Tell Kanisâh, a few miles north of Atlit. The Crusaders considered this to be the site of Capernaum.

Kedumim, Brook of (J XVII, P VIII, T III.46, B IV). Brook of Endor, Cison, Kishon or Qison River, 45 mi long; rises near Mount Gilboa and flows NW into Mediterranean just north of Haifâ. It is about 5 mi S of Acre (Achon), nearest to the town of Belus, noted for its fine sand suitable for glassmaking. It is not unlikely that Rabbi Benjamin alludes to the celebrated ox-spring of which Arab writers have much to say. Mukkadasî writes in 985: "Outside the eastern city gate is a spring. This they call 'Ain al Bakar, relating how it was Adam — peace be upon him! — who discovered this spring, and gave his oxen water therefrom, whence its name."

Brook of Kedumin (Kishon River), between 1900 and 1920. Source: Library of Congress.

Kinnasrîn (N 1). The ancient Chalcis.

Kinnereth, Sea of (P VIII, B XVII). Sea of Galilee, also Sea of Gennesareth or Chinnereth or Lake Tiberias.

Sea of Kinnereth, c.1925 to 1946. Source: Library of Congress.

Lachis (J XVIII). Lachish; either Tell el Hesy or Umm Lakis, on the road from Eleutheropolis (Bayt Jabrin) to Gaza.

Lilybaeum (P I). Now Marsala, in Sicily. Cicero, when one of the two quaestors of Sicily, resided at Lilybaeum. The coins of the town are exclusively Greek, a proof of the extent to which Greek civilization prevailed in that part of the island.

Lod or **Ludd** see Lydda.

Lydda (J V, T III.39 and 48, M I, B VII). Ludd, Lod, ancient Diaspolis, also St. George; 23 mi NW of Jerusalem in the . See Hazard, 6; Rogerson, 78–79 (map).

Christian Church of St George at Lud ancient Lydda by David Roberts, March 29 1839. Source: Library of Congress.

Mahomerie (T III.41). 7 mi N of Jerusalem. Probably the town of Al-Qubeiba. Burckhard, quoted by Tobler on the subject of the mosque at Hebron, says: *Sed de ecclesia cathedrali fecerunt Saraceni Marmariam.* (Sonst Mahomeria, Moschee), etc. Tobler's Theoderich, 213. See John of Würzburg, chap. 4, p. 14, n. 3; Prawer, 84; Rogerson, 162–64 (map).

Majuma, see Mîmâs.

Makkah (M II et passim). Mecca.

*Mecca: Bird's-eye view of uncrowded Kaaba, c.1910.
Source: Library of Congress.*

Mambre (J XI, T III. 34). Mamre; Terebinthus; about 12 mi SW of Bethlehem. See Genesis 18:1; Murphy-O'Connor, 277; Rogerson, 94–95 (map). See also Oak of Abraham.

*Mambre Excavations, between 1950 and 1977.
Source: Library of Congress.*

Manbij (N 1). Ancient Hierapolis.

Maresa (J XVIII, B XII). Mareshah, now Tel Maresha, near Bayt Jibrin. Now part of the Israeli national park of Beit Guvrin.

Medan (T III.45). The theory concerning the Dan under the Plain of Medan possibly derives from the swampy nature of the region prior to the twentieth century. See Rogerson, 128–34.

Megiddo (J IV). St. Paula appears to have travelled from Ptolemais (Achon) viâ Legio (Lejjûn) to Caesarea, and thus to have passed over the plain of Esdraelon.

Methone (J III). Modon, to the west of Cape Gallo, on the south coast of the Peloponnesus.

Mîmâs (J XIX, M X). Or Maimas, is the Majuma of Gaza mentioned by Antoninus Martyr (33). The name may be of Egyptian origin, and comes from the two words meaning "maritime town." Both Ascalon and Gaza had ports called Maiuma, and Jamnia likewise, according to Pliny.

Miyâfârikîn (N 1). The chief city of the province of Diyâr Bakr, in Upper Mesopotamia.

Mount Ebal & Mount Gerizim, with Nâblus in foreground, between 1898 and 1946. Source: Library of Congress.

GAZETTEER

Mount Ebal (M XV, T III.42, B VIII). Mount Hebal, Mountain of Cursing, north of Neapolis; Rogerson, 148–49 (map). See also Mount Gezirim.

Mount Endor (T III.46). See Stanley, 337. Unidentified, but see also Mount Tabor.

Mount Gerizim (J XVI, M XV, B VIII). Mountain of Blessing, south of Neapolis. See also Mount Ebal.

Mount Gilboa (T III.30 and 44, B VIII). West of the Jordan and south of the Plain of Esdraelon, near the source of the Kedumim or Kishon.

Mount of Rejoicing (T I.3, III.38 and 41). Mons Gaudii, Montjoye, Ramathaim. First view of Jerusalem was from this mountain, so it was known to the Crusaders as "Montjoye." The position of Ramathaim is uncertain; but the place long pointed out as Samuel's Tomb is the height most conspicuous of all in the neighborhood of Jerusalem immediately above the town of Gibeon (See B VIII). Called at times Neby Samwil, the Prophet Samuel. See "Samuel," in *Harper's Bible Dictionary*, 641; Prawer, 16, 208. Prawer (291) notes that on the southern route from the coast one approached the city from Qastel (Belvoir) and Suba (Belmont).

Mount Royal (T III.31). Montréal. Built by Baldwin I in 1115, about 18 mi from Petra. See Hazard, 149; Prawer, 50, 131, 14, n. 22, 282.

Mount Tabor (J XVII, P VIII, T III.46). Itabyrium. (The name occurs in the same form in the Septuagint and Josephus). Traditional site of the Transfiguration of Jesus (Mark 9:2–8); 6 mi SE of Nazareth. See John of Würzburg, chap. 1, pp. 4–6; the description of Mount Tabor from Greek sources in Phocas (pp. 13, 14); and Abbot Daniel (chap. 86, pp. 66–67). See also Rogerson, 128–29 (map), 140–41. The abbey referred to is a fortified Benedictine house on the site of a former Greek one. See Prawer, 173, 288. The Basilica of the Transfiguration was consecrated in 1924, modeled after Syrian architecture of the

Roman period it is the work of Antonio Barluzzi, architect of the Church of All Nations in Gethsemane.

Mount Tabor from the Plain of Esdraelon by David Roberts, April 19th 1839. Source: Library of Congress.

Multiplication of the Loaves and Fishes, Place of the (J XVII, P VIII, T III.45). In Heptapegon or Tabgha, on NW shore of Sea of Galilee. After an archaeological excavation in 1892, a modern church was constructed on the site of the original Byzantine church, which was destroyed in 614. Site of miracle recounted in Matt. 14:13–21; Mark 6:30–40; John 6:1–14. See Murphy-O'Connor, 233–37; Rogerson, 129 (map), 141.

Nâblus (J XVI, M XV, T III.41, 42 and 48, B VIII). Nâbulus, Neapolis, 30 mi N of Jerualem between Mount Ebal on the north and Mt. Gerizim on the south. See Murphy-O'Connor, 307–9; Hazard, 6, 111, 376; Prawer, 288–90; Rogerson, 148 (map), 158–59. On pilgrims' safe conduct through area (T III.41), see Prawer, 360; on fertility of area (T III.42), see Prawer, 362–65. Benjamin of Tudela (B VIII) conflates Sichem and Neapolis, the latter was built on the site of the former ancient city.

Nâblus, between 1898 and 1946. Source: Library of Congress.

Nain (J XVII, P VIII, T III.46). Naim. In Galilee 5 mi SSE of Nazareth. See Rogerson, 129 (map), 140–41.

Nazareth (J XVII, P VIII, T III.47). Biblical home of Joseph, Mary, and Jesus; approximately 19 mi ESE of Haifâ. The proper

Nazareth by David Roberts, April 28th 1839. Source: Library of Congress.

Hebrew name of Nazareth was Nétzer, a "shoot" or "sprout." The comparison of Nazareth with a flower (P VIII) is not uncommon in the works of later pilgrims. Quaresmius compares it to a rose.

Nazareth. Basilica of the Annunciation (T III.47). Church of St. Mary. See Murphy-O'Connor, 311. The twelfth-century Crusader church has been replaced by a twentieth-century church. Much of the work must have been in progress when Theoderich visited the town. For a description of the medieval buildings, see Hazard, 102–5, 275–76, 279–80; Prawer, 437–38.

Neapolis see Nâblus (Nâbulus).

Nitria (J XVIII). The celebrated monasteries in the valley in which the Natron Lakes are situated, to the west of the Nile, and northwest of Cairo.

Nobe (J V). Beit Nûba; the Biblical Nob must, however, have been in the mountains near Jerusalem.

Oak of Abraham (J XI, T III.34). Also Râmet el Khulîl (Khalil), Mambre, or Mamre, between Halhul and Hebron. See Gen. 18:1. See also Mambre.

Paneas (T III.45, B XIX). Caesarea Philippi, Baniyas, Banyas,

Paneas, the ancient Caesarea Philippi by Francis Frith, 1862?
Source: Library of Congress.

Gazetteer

Banyas, the ancient Paneas; on Mount Hermon, approximately 25 mi N of the Sea of Galilee; and the same distance inland from Tyre. See Prawer, 132, 166. Theoderich probably never visited this region. The city was actually given to the Crusaders in 1129, changed hands several times, and finally was lost to Nur ed-Din in 1164. See Prawer, 132, 265–66, 284; Runciman 2:179–80, 370–71; Rogerson, 202 (map).

Pelusium (J XVIII, M II). Also Al Firmâ, Sena, Per-Amun, Tell el-Farama, about 17 mi (30 km) SE of Port Said in Lower Egypt.

Pharan (T III.45). The Wilderness of Paran, a desert region in NE Sinai Peninsula. See Rogerson, 114–15 (map), 123.

Pontia (J III). Now Ponza, WNW of Ischia.

Pontus (P II). Roman province in eastern Asia Minor on the Black Sea coast.

Primacy of Peter, Church of the (T III.45). In Heptapegon or Tabgha, on NW shore of Sea of Galilee. See Murphy-O'Connor, 233–37; Rogerson, 129 (map).

Quarantana (T III.29). The Mount of Quarantine, above Jericho. See Hazard, 59, 379. It was for the purpose of defending the pilgrims down these passes that, in 1118, the nine knights

View from Quarantana of the Jordan Valley, approximately 1900 to 1920. Source: Library of Congress.

The Holy Land

banded together who formed the nucleus of the Order of the Templars. See Stanley, chap. 7, p. 314. For bibliography on the Templars, see Prawer, 550–51; and Seward.

Ramleh (M I, B XIII). Ar-Ramleh, Ramla, Er Ramle, named from the "sandy" nature of the soil where the town stands. It "did not exist in Bible times. It was founded in 716, after the Muslim Conquest, by the Omeyyad Khalif Sulaimân, the son of 'Abd al Malik (AH 96–99, CE 715–718), and was made the capital of the province of Palestine (Filastîn) and as such was often referred to under the name of its province. The same is the usage with regard to Shâm (Damascus or Syria), Misr (Cairo or Egypt), and other places. It prospered to such an extent that it became as large as Jerusalem. It was a good deal damaged by an earthquake in 1033. Ramleh had a large Muslim population, and the Jews there remained comparatively unmolested by the Crusaders. This latter fact accounts for the somewhat large number of Jews residing there" (*Itinerary of Benjamin of Tudela*, 88). See Murphy-O'Connor, 325–27; Freeman-Grenville, 131–32; including descriptions of the White Mosque and the Great Mosque. In his introductory chapter Mukaddasî writes: "If Ar-Ramlah had only running-water the town would be without compare the finest in

Ramleh, between c.1890 and c.1900. Source: Library of Congress.

Islâm; for it is pleasant and pretty, standing between Jerusalem and the frontier towns, between the Ghaur of the Jordan and the sea. Its climate is mild, its fruits are luscious, its people generous — being, however, also rather foolish: it is an emporium for Egyptian goods, and an excellent commercial station for the two seas." Al 'Askar is mentioned by Mukaddasî in his introductory chapter as the name of one of the quarters of Ar-Ramlah.

Red Cistern (T III.28). John of Würzburg (chap. 2, p. 7) places this cistern on the plain of Dothaim, between Genon and Sebaste, or Samaria.

Rhodos (J III, T III.43). Rhodes, island in SE Aegean Sea near Turkey.

Sâhirah, see Jerusalem. Mount of Olives.

Saida (B II). Sidon, on Mediterranean 25 mi N of Tyre and 25 mi S our Beirut.

Samaria (J XVI; P VII; T I.1 and 2, III.43, 44 and 48; B VII). Sebaste, Sebastiya, Shomron. The ruins of this ancient city are in the Samarian mountains about 6 mi NW of Neapolis. See Prawer, 134, 211. For a description, see Murphy-O'Connor, 327–31, especially 330–31 for the sites associated with John the Baptist, including the place where his head was discovered and his reputed tomb. On fertility of area (T III.43), see Prawer, 361–63. As burial site of John the Baptist (T III.43), see John of Würzburg, chap. 2, p. 7. On the tombs, cf. Theodorus (27); Ant. Mart. (8); and Willibald (27).

Samaria: Church of St. John, interior, approximately 1900–1920. Source: Library of Congress.

Sarepta (J IV, T III.51, B III). Sarphan, Zarephath, As-Sarafand, Sarfend, Sarafand, Surafend, a Phoenician city on the Mediterranean, 33 mi S of Beirut, between Sidon and Tyre. 2 Kings 14:25. The legend that the son of the widow of Zarephah was the prophet Jonah is mentioned by Jerome. See note to *Ant. Mart. Itin.* (2).

*Sarepta by David Roberts, April 27th 1839.
Source: Library of Congress.*

Scandalium (T III.51). Scandelion, Escandelion, or Iskanderune; on Mediterranean between Tyre and Acre (Achon). See Prawer, 131–32.

Seleucia see **Solim**.

Sepphoris (T III.48, B XVI). Diocaesarea, Suffuriya, Tzipori, Zippori, a village and archaeological site about 3.7 mi NNW of Nazareth. See Rogerson, 129 (map), 137, 141; Petersen, 335.

Sepulcher of Michaea (J XVIII). Probably Tell Sandahannah, near Beit Jibrin, where there are the ruins of a church and rock hewn caverns and tombs.

Sermon of the Mount, Church of the (T III.45). In Heptapegon or Tabgha, on NW shore of Sea of Galilee. Site of sermon in Matt. 5:1. See Murphy-O'Connor, 233–37; Rogerson 129 (map), 141.

Sepphoris: Roman remains, approximately 1920 to 1933. Source: Library of Congress.

Sichem (J XVI, M XV, T III.41 and 42, B VIII). Shechem, 1 mi SE of Neapolis, the site of its rebuilding. The two mountains shutting in Shechem are to the south, Mount Gerizim and Mount Ebal, to the north. See Rogerson, 148–49 (map), 151–53, 158; Prawer, 211.

Silo (J XVI, P VIII, T II.19 and III.38, B XII). Shiloh, Seilûn; ruins of ancient village are 15 mi W of the Jordan River on the east slope of Mount Ephraim. See *Encyclopedia of Archeological Excavations* 4:1098–1100; Rogerson, 148–49 (map), 152–53. "Silo, at the time of the Crusaders, was considered to occupy the site of Mizpeh, the highest mountain near Jerusalem, where the national assemblies were held at the time of the Judges. The present mosque is dilapidated, but the substructure, which dates from the Frank period, is beautifully jointed. The apse is raised. The reputed tomb of Samuel is on the western side of the church. It is still called Nebi Samwil, venerated alike by Jew and Moslem," (*Itinerary of Benjamin of Tudela*, 87.) See also Mount of Rejoicing.

Sior (J XVIII). Or Sichor, apparently the Nile.

Sochot (J XVIII). Shuweikeh, about 20 mi from Jerusalem on the road to Gaza.

Solim (J IV, T III.49). This must be Seleucia (ad Mare), now Samandag, in southern Turkey, the harbor of Antioch, north of the mouth of the Orontes. See Hazard, 194. Tobler suggests that the name may be a contracted form of Suleimán, the prince of Iconium, CE 1084, who was lord of Antioch. It is mentioned in John of Würzburg (chap. 25, p. 65 and n. 5), as likewise are most of the places mentioned in the last chapters of Theoderich.

Solomon's Pools (M II, N 30). Mukaddasî mentions these as two pools "at a certain valley, about a stage from the city." They are two hours from Jerusalem on the road to Hebron. The conduit, bringing the water from these to the Holy City, was constructed by Pontius Pilate (Josephus, *Antiq.* xviii. 3, 2).

Tanis (J XVIII). A city in the north-eastern Nile delta, Egypt on the silted-up Tanitic branch..

Tarpeian Rock (P IV). The *rupes Tarpeia* on the southeast side of the Capitoline Hill at Rome.

Thamnathsare (J XV). Timnath-serah or Timnath-heres, probably Kefl Hareth, a town in the mountainous region of Ephraim, north of Mount Gaash and 9 mi. southwest of Nâblus, the location of the tomb of Neby Lush'a(Josh. 24:30).

Thecua (J XIII). Tekoa or Khurbet Tekûa, now Tuqu'. A town 7.5 mi southeast of Bethlehem.

Thorns, Plain of (T III.45). See John of Würzburg, chap. 20, p. 56 and chap 25, pp. 65–66; and Stanley, chap. 11.

Tiberias (J XVI, N 14, T III.45 and 46, B XVII). Tabariyyah, Kinneret. A city on the west bank of the Sea of Galilee.

Tomb of Rachel (J VIII, T III.32, B X).

Tower Ader (J IX). Beit Sahûr, near Bethlehem; the tower is mentioned by Arculf; also referred to (P VII) as the folds of the shepherds.

GAZETTEER

Tiberias: view, between 1934 and 1939. Source: Library of Congress.

Two Holy Cities (M II). Makkah (Mecca) and Al Madînah (Medînah).

Tyre (J IV, N 11, T III.50 and 51, B III). The second city of the kingdom of Jerusalem, south of Sidon on Mediterranean. See Prawer, 82, 86–89, 101; Hazard, 10, 13–15. On its fortifications, see Prawer, 292–93, 319–22; Hazard, 160. On its archbishopric,

Tomb of Rachel, on the road near Bethlehem, between 1898 and 1946. Source: Library of Congress.

see Prawer, 163–66; Hazard, 100, 105–6. "Tyre was noted for its glassware and sugar factories up to 1291, when it was abandoned by the Crusaders and destroyed by the Moslems," *(Itinerary of Benjamin of Tudela)*.

Valley of Achor (J XV). Wady Qelt. A valley or stream flowing across the Judaean Desert from near Jerusalem almost to Jericho.

Valley of Moses (T III.31). Wâdî Mousa; the miracle referred to in Num. 20:1–13 occurred at Cadesbarne.

Wâdî Tamasih (N 15). This is the valley of the Crocodile River (Pliny), known also as the Nahr Zarkâ or Blue River.

*Ancient Tyre from the Isthmus by David Roberts, April 27th 1839.
Source: Library of Congress.*

Bibliography

Reference Works

Ancient Maps of the Holy Land. Jerusalem: University Booksellers, 1958.

Avi-Yonah, Michael. *The Holy Land.* New York: Holt, Rinehart and Winston, 1972.

Deschamps, P. "La toponomastique en terre sainte au temps des croisades." *Mémoires et documents publiés par la Société de l'Ecole des Chartes,* 22.1 (1955): 352–56.

Encyclopedia of Archeological Excavations in the Holy Land. M. Avi-Yonah and E. Stern, ed. 4 vols. London: Oxford University Press; Englewood Cliffs, NJ: Prentice-Hall, 1975–78.

Freeman-Genville, G.S.P. *The Holy Land: A Pilgrim's Guide to Israel, Jordan and the Sinai.* New York: Continuum, 1996.

Harper's Bible Dictionary. Madeleine S. Miller and J. Lane Miller, ed. New York: Harper & Row, 1973.

Kroyanker, David. *Jerusalem Architecture.* New York: Rizzoli, 1994.

Murphy-O'Connor, Jerome. *The Holy Land: An Archeological Guide from Earliest Times to 1700.* New York: Oxford University Press, 1986; fifth edition, 2008.

Nebenzahl, Kenneth. *Maps of the Holy Land.* New York: Abbeville Press, 1986.

Petersen, Andrew. *A Gazetteer of Buildings in Muslim Palestine.* Part 1 Part 1. Oxford: Published for the Council for British Research in the Levant by Oxford University Press, 2001.

Prawer, Joshua and M. Benvenisti. *Crusader Palestine, Atlas of Israel,* sheet. Jerusalem, 1972.

Rogerson, John. *Atlas of the Bible.* New York: Facts on File, 1986.

Primary Sources

Anonymous Pilgrims, XIth and XIIth Centuries. Aubrey Stewart, trans. London: Palestine Pilgrims' Text Society, 1894; reprint ed., New York: AMS, 1971.

Antoninus Martyr. *Of the Holy Places Visited by Antoninus Martyr.* Aubrey Stewart, trans. C.W. Wilson, annotations. London: Palestine Pilgrims' Text Society, 1896.

Arculfus, bishop. *The Pilgrimage of Arculfus in the Holy Land (c. AD 670).* James Rose McPherson, ed. and trans. London: Palestine Pilgrims' Text Society, 1889.

Benjamin of Tudela. *The Itinerary of Benjamin of Tudela: Travels in the Middle Ages.* Malibu, CA: Joseph Simon/Pangloss Press, 1987.

Bernard the Wise. *The Itinerary of Bernard the Wise (AD 870); How the City of Jerusalem is Situated.* J.H. Bernard, trans. London: Palestine Pilgrims' Text Society, 1893.

Bordeaux Pilgrim. *Itinerary from Bordeaux to Jerusalem (333 AD).* Aubrey Stewart, trans. London: Palestine Pilgrims' Text Society, 1887; reprint ed., New York: AMS, 1971.

Breydenbach, Bernhard von, and Isolde Mozer. *Bernhard von Breydenbach: Peregrinatio in terram sanctam. Eine Pilgerreise ins Heilige Land. Frühneuhochdeutscher Text und Übersetzung.* Berlin: De Gruyter, 2010.

Burhard of Mount Sion. *Description of the Holy Land.* Aubrey Stewart, trans. London: Palestine Pilgrims' Text Society, 1896; reprint ed., New York: AMS, 1971.

Casola, Pietro. *Canon Pietro Casola's Pilgrimage to Jerusalem in the Year 1494.* Margaret Newett, trans. Manchester: University Press, 1907.

City of Jerusalem and Ernouls' Account of Palestine, The. C.R. Conder, trans. London: Palestine Pilgrims' Text Society, 1896; reprint ed., New York: AMS, 1971.

Cline, Eric H. *Jerusalem Besieged: From Ancient Canaan to Modern Israel.* Ann Arbor: University of Michigan Press, 2004.

Descriptiones Terrae Sanctae ex Saeculis VIII, IX, XII, XV. Leipzig: J.C. Hinricks, 1874.

Epitome of S. Eucherius about Certain Holy Places (c.AD 440) and Breviary or Short Description of Jerusalem (c.AD 530). Aubrey Stewart, trans. London: Palestine Pilgrims' Text Society, 1890.

Fabri, Felix. *Wanderings in the Holy Land.* Aubrey Stewart, trans. London: Palestine Pilgrims' Text Society, 1892–93; reprint ed., New York: AMS, 1971.

Fetellus. James Rose Macpherson, trans. London: Palestine Pilgrims' Text Society, 1892; reprint ed., New York: AMS, 1971.

Friar Felix at Large: A Fifteenth Century Pilgrimage to the Holy Land. New Haven: Yale University Press, 1950.

Gilo, of Paris. *De via Hierosolymitana. The Historia vie Hierosolimitane of Gilo of Paris, and a second, anonymous author.* C.W. Grocock and J.E. Siberry, ed. and trans. Oxford: Clarendon Press New York: Oxford University Press, 1997.

Guidebook to Palestine (Circa AD 1350). John H. Bernard, ed. London: Palestine Pilgrims' Text Society, 1894.

Itinera Hierosolymitana crucesignatorum (saec. xii-xiii). Sabino de Sandoli, OFM, ed. Jerusalem: Franciscan Printing Press, 1980.

Itinera Hierosolymitana et descriptiones Terrae Sanctae bellis sacris anteriora et latina lingua exarata. Vol 1. Titus Tobler and A. Molinier, ed. Vol. 2. A. Molinier and Charles Kohler, ed. Geneva: J.D. Fick, 1879-85.

John of Würzburg. *Description of the Holy Land.* Aubrey Stewart, trans. London: Palestine Pilgrims' Text Society, 1896; reprint ed., New York: AMS, 1971.

Mukaddasi. *Description of Syria, Including Palestine: By Mukaddasi (Circ.985 A.D.).* Translated from the Arabic and Annotated by Guy Le Strange. London: Palestine Pilgrims' Text Society, 1892.

Nâsir ibn Khusrau, 'Alawî, and Guy Le Strange. *Diary of a Journey Through Syria and Palestine.* London: Palestine Pilgrims' Text Society, 1897.

Peregrinationes tres: Saewulf, John of Würzburg, Theodericus. R.B.C. Huygens, ed. Corpus Christianorum, Continuatio Mediaevalis 139. Turnhout: Brepols, 1994.

The Pilgrimage of Etheria (Peregrinatio Aetheriae). M.L. McClure and C.L. Feltoe, ed. London: SPCK, New York: Macmillan, 1919.

The Pilgrimage of S. Silvia of Aquitania to the Holy Places (c.385 AD). J.H. Bernard, ed. and trans. Appendix by C.W. Wilson. London: Palestine Pilgrims' Text Society, 1891.

Phocas, John. *The Pilgrimage of Johannes Phocas.* London: Palestine Pilgrims' Text Society, 1896; reprint ed., New York: AMS, 1971.

Poggibonsi, Niccolo. *Fra Niccolo of Poggibonsi, A Voyage Beyond the Seas (1346-1350).* T. Bellorini and E. Hoade, trans. Jerusalem: Franciscan Printing Press, 1945.

Poloner, John. *Description of the Holy Land.* Aubrey Stewart, trans. London: Palestine Pilgrims' Text Society, 1894; reprint ed., New York: AMS, 1971.

Saewulf. Canon Brounlow, trans. London: Palestine Pilgrims' Text Society, 1892; reprint ed., New York: AMS, 1971.

Sanudo, Marino. *Secrets for True Crusaders.* Aubrey Stewart, trans. London: Palestine Pilgrims' Text Society, 1896; reprint ed., New York: AMS, 1971.

Theoderich. *Description of the Holy Places.* Aubrey Stewart, trans. London: Palestine Pilgrims' Text Society, 1897; reprint ed., New York: AMS, 1971; second ed., Ronald G. Musto, ed, New York: Italica Press, 1986.

Theoderici libellus de locis sanctis. Titus Tobler, ed. St. Gall-Paris: 1865.

Theodericus. *Libellus de locis sanctis.* M.L. and W. Bulst, ed. Heidelberg: Editiones Heidelbergensis, 1976.

Theodosius. *Description of Jerusalem. (AD 530).* J.H. Bernard, trans. London: Palestine Pilgrims' Text Society, 1893.

Visit to the Holy Places of Egypt, Sinai, Palestine and Syria in 1384 by Frescobaldi, Gucci and Sigoli. T. Bellorini and E. Hoade, ed. Jerusalem: Franciscan Printing Press, 1948.

Von Suchem, Ludolf. *Description of the Holy Land and the Way Thither.* Aubrey Stewart, trans. London: Palestine Pilgrims' Text Society, 1895; reprint ed., New York: AMS, 1971.

William of Tyre. *A History of Deeds Done beyond the Sea.* E.A. Babcock and A.C. Krey, trans. 2 vols. New York: Columbia University Press, 1943.

Secondary Works

Armstrong, Karen. *Jerusalem: One City, Three Faiths.* New York: Knopf, 1996.

Berriot-Salvadore, Evelyne, ed. *Le mythe de Jerusalem: Du Moyen Age à la Renaissance.* Saint-Etienne: Publications de l'Universite de Saint-Etienne, 1995.

Boehm, Barbara Drake and Melanie Holcomb, eds., *Jerusalem,*

1000–1400: Every People under Heaven. New York: Metropolitan Museum of Art, 2016.

Brefeld, Josephie. *A Guidebook for the Jerusalem Pilgrimage in the Late Middle Ages: a Case for Computer-Aided Textual Criticism.* Hilversum: Verloren, 1994.

Brooke, Rosalind, and Christopher Brooke. *Popular Religion in the Middle Ages: Western Europe 1000–1300.* New York: Thames & Hudson, 1984.

Caüasnon, C. *The Church of the Holy Sepulchre.* London: British Academy, 1974.

Coleman, Simon, and John Elsner. *Pilgrimage: Past and Present in the World Religions.* Cambridge: Harvard University Press, 1995.

Davidson, Linda Kay, and Maryjane Dunn-Wood. *Pilgrimage in the Middle Ages: A Research Guide.* New York: Garland, 1993.

Dolbeau, François. "Théodericus, De locis sanctis. Un second manuscrit, provenant de Sainte-Barbe de Cologne." *Analecta Bollandiana* 103.1–2 (1985): 113–14.

Elad, Amikam. *Medieval Jerusalem and Islamic Worship: Holy Places, Ceremonies, Pilgrimage.* Leiden and New York: E.J. Brill, 1995.

Forum Internationale Photographie, Alfried Wieczorek, Michael Tellenbach, and Claude W. Sui. *To the Holy Lands: Pilgrimage Centres from Mecca and Medina to Jerusalem: Photographs of the 19th Century from the Collections of the Reiss-Engelhorn Museums, Mannheim.* Munich: Prestel, 2008.

Gertwagen, Ruth, and Elizabeth Jeffreys, ed. *Shipping, Trade and Crusade in the Medieval Mediterranean: Studies in Honour of John Pryor.* Farnham, Surrey: Ashgate, 2012.

Harvey, P.D.A. *The Hereford World Map: Introduction.* Hereford: Hereford Cathedral, 2010.

Hazard, Harry W., ed. *The Art and Architecture of the Crusader States.* Vol. 4 in *A History of the Crusades.* Kenneth M. Setton, ed. 6 vols. Madison, WI: University of Wisconsin, 1977.

Howard, Donald R. *Writers and Pilgrims: Medieval Pilgrimage Narratives and Their Posterity.* Berkeley: University of California Press, 1980.

Kline, Naomi Reed. *Maps of Medieval Thought: The Hereford Paradigm.* Woodbridge: Boydell & Brewer, 2001.

Kuhnel, Bianca. *Crusader Art of the Twelfth Century: A Geographical, an Historical, or an Art Historical Notion?* Berlin: Mann, 1994.

Labarge, Margaret Wade. *Medieval Travellers: The Rich and the Restless.* London: Hamish Hamilton, 1982.

Le Beau, Bryan F., and Menachem Mor, ed. *Pilgrims & Travelers to the Holy Land.* Omaha, NE: Creighton University Press, 1996.

Lipton, Sara. *Dark Mirror: The Medieval Origins of Anti-Jewish Iconography.* New York: Metropolitan Books/Henry Holt and Company, 2014.

Mitchell, Rosamund Joscelyne. *The Spring Voyage: The Jerusalem Pilgrimage in 1458.* London: J. Murray, 1964.

Novikoff, Alex J. *The Twelfth Century Renaissance: A Reader.* Toronto: University of Toronto Press, 2016.

Oursel, Raymond. *Pelerins du Moyen Age: Les hommes, les chemins, les sanctuaires.* Paris: Fayard, 1978.

Peters, F.E. *Jerusalem.* Princeton: Princeton University Press, 1985.

—. *The Hajj: The Muslim Pilgrimage to Mecca and the Holy Places.* Princeton, NJ: Princeton University Press, 1994.

Prawer, Joshua. *The Crusaders' Kingdom.* New York: Praeger, 1972.

Prescott, Hilda Frances Margaret. *Jerusalem Journey: Pilgrimage to the Holy Land in the Fifteenth Century.* London: Eyre & Spottiswoods, 1954.

Pringle, Denys. *The Churches of the Crusader Kingdom of Jerusalem.* Cambridge and New York: Cambridge University Press, 1993.

—. *Pilgrimage to Jerusalem and the Holy Land, 1187–1291.* Ashgate, 2012.

Riain, Diarmuid Ó. "An Irish Jerusalem in Franconia: The Abbey of the Holy Cross and Holy Sepulchre at Eichstätt," *Proceedings of the Royal Irish Academy. Section C: Archaeology, Celtic Studies, History, Linguistics, Literature* 112C (2012): 219–70.

Riley-Smith, Jonathan Simon Christopher. *The Crusades, Christianity, and Islâm.* New York: Columbia University Press, 2008.

Rosovsky, Nitza. *City of the Great King: Jerusalem from David to the Present.* Cambridge: Harvard University Press, 1996.

Ross, Elizabeth. *Picturing Experience in the Early Printed Book: Breydenbach's Peregrinatio from Venice to Jerusalem.* University

Park: The Pennsylvania State University Press, 2014.

Rubenstein, Jay. *Armies of Heaven: The First Crusade and the Quest for Apocalypse*. New York: Basic Books, 2011.

Runciman, Steven. *A History of the Crusades*. 3 vols. New York: Harper & Row, 1964.

Sand, Shlomo. *The Invention of the Land of Israel*. London: Verso, 2012.

Sebag Montefiore, Simon. *Jerusalem: The Biography*. New York: Alfred A. Knopf, 2011.

Seward, Desmond. *The Monks of War*. Frogmore, UK: Paladin, 1974.

Setton, Kenneth M., ed. *A History of the Crusades*. 6 vols. Madison, WI: University of Wisconsin Press, 1955–83.

Shatzmiller, Maya, ed. *Crusaders and Muslims in Twelfth-Century*. Leiden and New York: Brill, 1993.

Stanley, Arthur P. *Sinai and Palestine*. New York: A.C. Armstrong, 1883. https://archive.org/details/sinaiandpalesti02stangoog

Sumption, Jonathan. *Pilgrimage: An Image of Medieval Religion*. London: Faber & Faber, 1975.

Tolan, John V. *Saracens: Islâm in the Medieval European Imagination*. New York: Columbia University Press, 2002.

—. *Sons of Ishmael: Muslims through European Eyes in the Middle Ages*. Gainesville: University Press of Florida, 2008.

Vauchez, André. *The Spirituality of the Medieval West: From the Eighth to the Twelfth Century*. Kalamazoo, MI: Cistercian Publications, 1993.

Wilkinson, John, with Joyce Hill and W.F. Ryan, eds. *Jerusalem Pilgrimage, 1099–1185*. London: Hakluyt Society, 1988.

Wright, John Kirtland. *The Geographical Lore in the Time of the Crusades*. New York: American Geographical Society of New York, 1925; new ed., with intro. by Clarence J. Clacker, New York: Dover, 1965.

Maps and Views of the Holy Land

*Detail of Map of the Holy Land, c.1140.
From* The Classical Atlas of Ancient Geography *by Alexander G. Findlay, 1849.*

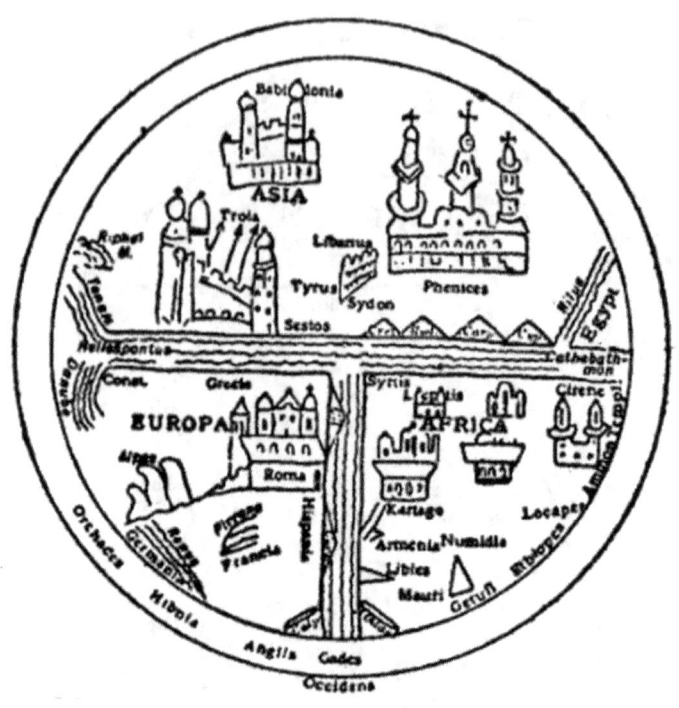

Sallust-Type Map, c.1200. Emery Walker reconstruction, c.1911.

It is called a "Sallust-type" because variations of this map appeared in medieval manuscripts of Sallust's De bello Jugurthino. Based on ancient and medieval "T-O" types, this map divides the circle of the world into three parts. The map is "oriented," that is, East appears at the top, above the largest division of Asia. Europe is at the left, and Africa at the right. The continents are divided by the "T" of oceans. The arms are the Hellespont and the Nile, the stem the Mediterranean. At the center, where the continents and seas meet, is the Holy Land, with Jerusalem, the large three-towered city with crosses, the center of the world. Tyre and Sidon are below the squiggle of "Libanus" to the left of the city. Rome is four-towered city in the left division; the Alps are the three peaks to its left (north). The Rhine flows at the bottom left. Anglia is in the Ocean on the bottom rim. Africa is less certain to the medieval European. Egypt and the Nile are the extreme right stem. Syria is in the upper left corner, Cirene on the upper right. Carthage, Armenia, Libya and Numidia all to the right center of the T-stem. Ethiopia is toward the bottom right rim.

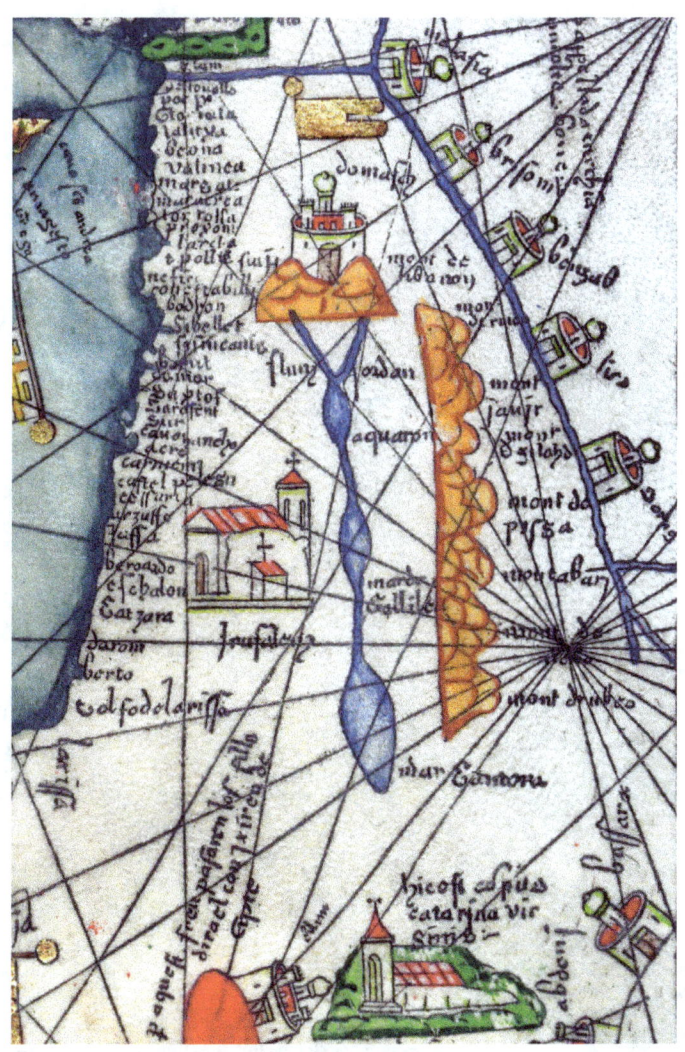

View of the Holy Land by Abraham and Jehuda Cresques, 1375. From The Catalan Atlas.

View of the Holy Land (left panel) by Bernhard von Breydenbach, 1486. From Peregrinatio in Terram Sanctam. *Mainz. The Jewish National and University Library & The Hebrew University of Jerusalem.*

View of the Holy Land (center panel) by Bernhard von Breydenbach, 1486. From Peregrinatio in Terram Sanctam. Mainz. *The Jewish National and University Library & The Hebrew University of Jerusalem.*

View of the Holy Land (right panel) by Bernhard von Breydenbach, 1486. From Peregrinatio in Terram Sanctam. Mainz. *The Jewish National and University Library & The Hebrew University of Jerusalem.*

World Map with Jerusalem at the Center, 1581.
Stylized in the shape of a clover-leaf (the classical three continents of Europe, Asia, Africa), from Heinrich Bünting, *Die eigentliche und warhafftige gestalt der Erden u[nd] des Meers, Magdeburg, 1581.*

Hannouer meines lieben Vaterlandes Wapen. V

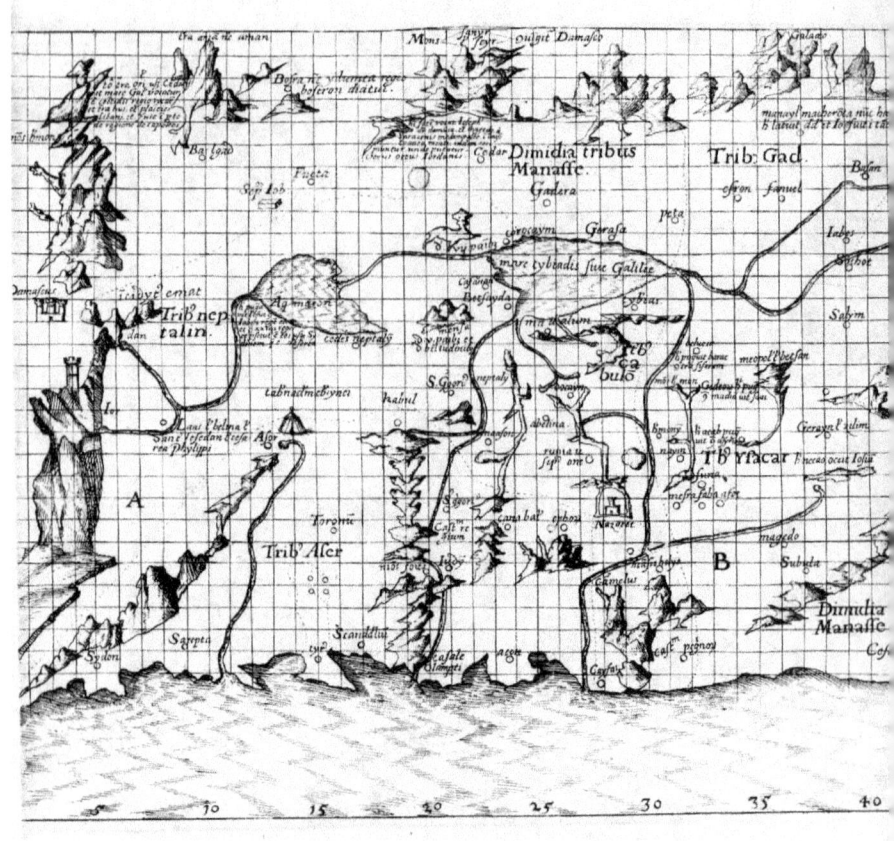

Map of the Holy Land by Marino Sanudo, 1611.
From Liber secretorum fidelium crucis, Hanau: *Christian Wechelius, 1611. Map no. II.*

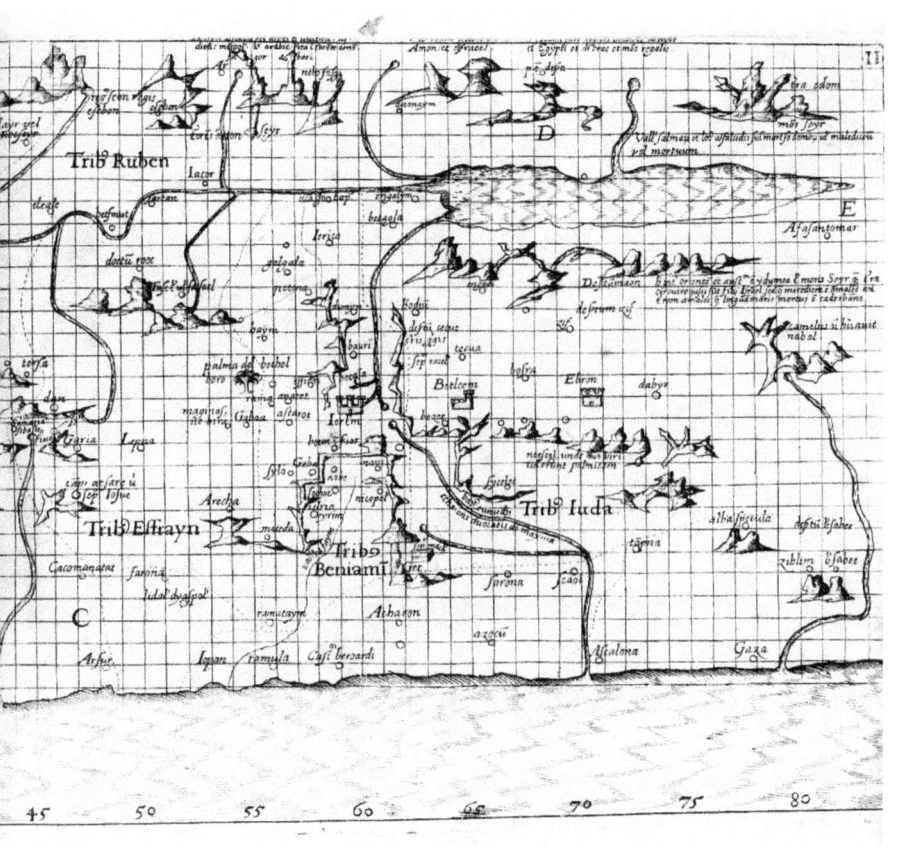

Maps and Views of Jerusalem

Madaba Map of Jerusalem, c.570.
Byzantine floor mosaic from St. George Church, Madaba, Jordan.

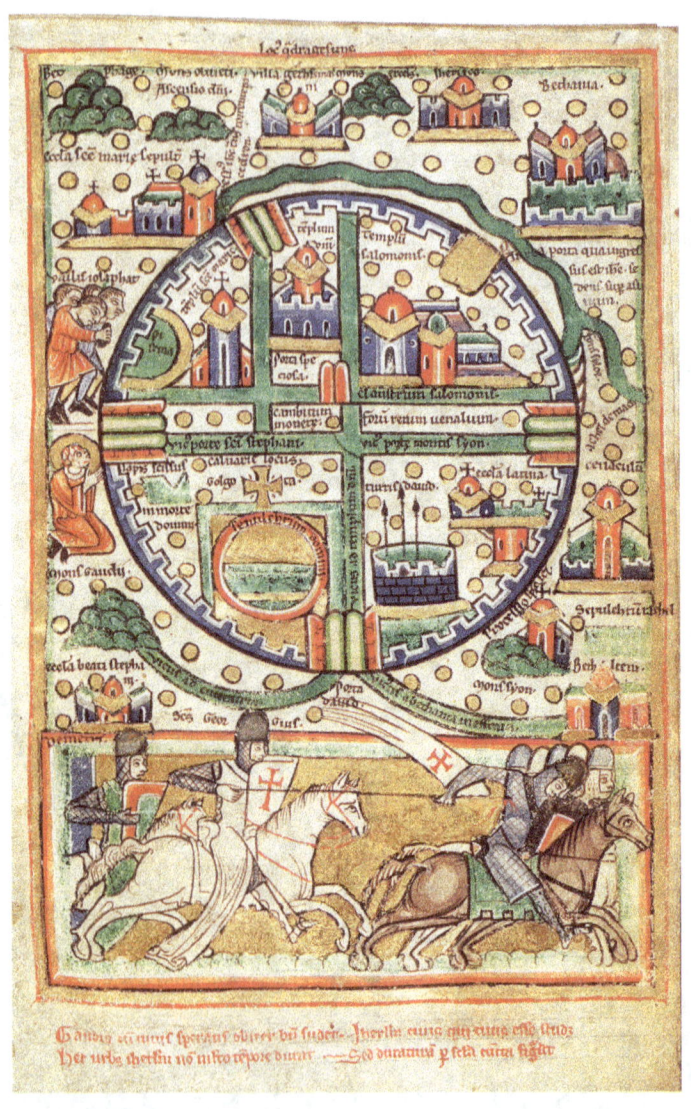

Plan of Jerusalem, c.1200. From Psalter-fragment (The Hague, KB, 76 F5), Courtesy of the Medieval Illuminated Manuscripts Project. Koninklijke Bibliotheek © National Library of the Netherlands.

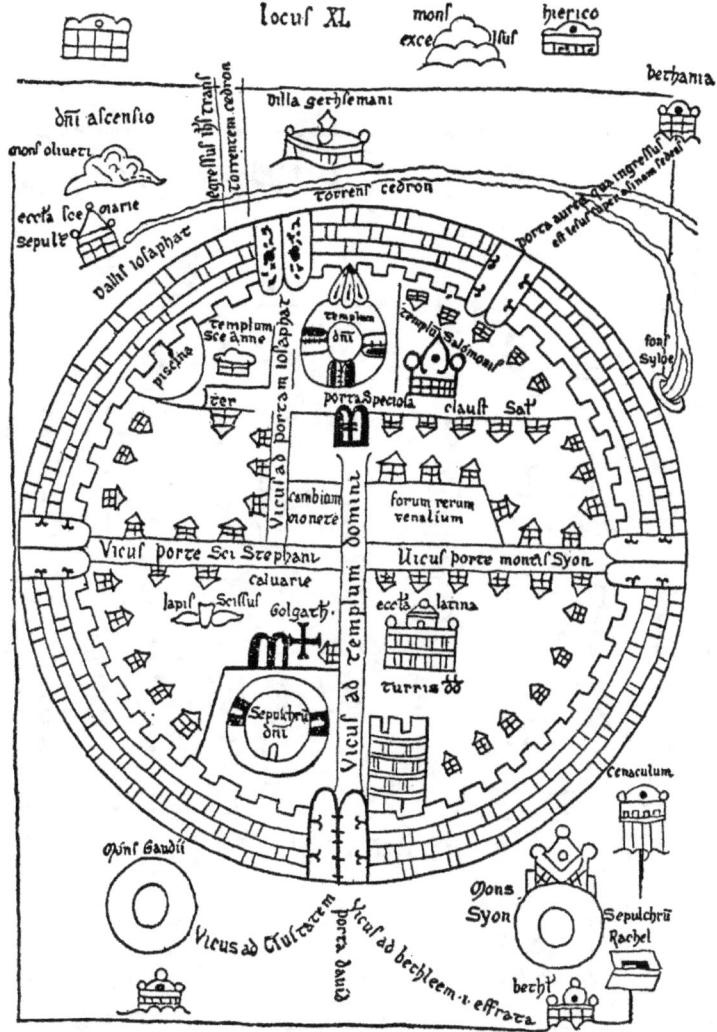

Plan of Jerusalem, c.1200.

The holy city shown as the circle, the ideal form. The map is "oriented," the East is at the top. Above the walls are the Valley of Josaphat and the Cedron Brook. Within the walls the circle is divided into four by the crossing of the Temple Street (bottom to top) and of St. Stephen's and Mount Sion Streets (left to right). The Temple of the Lord is the circle at the top; the Holy Sepulcher that in the bottom left. Outside the walls below are the circles of Mons Gaudii on the left and Mount Sion on the right. Other landmarks include the Temple of Solomon (top right), St. Anne's (top left), the Covered Market (center, right), and the Tower of David (bottom, center).

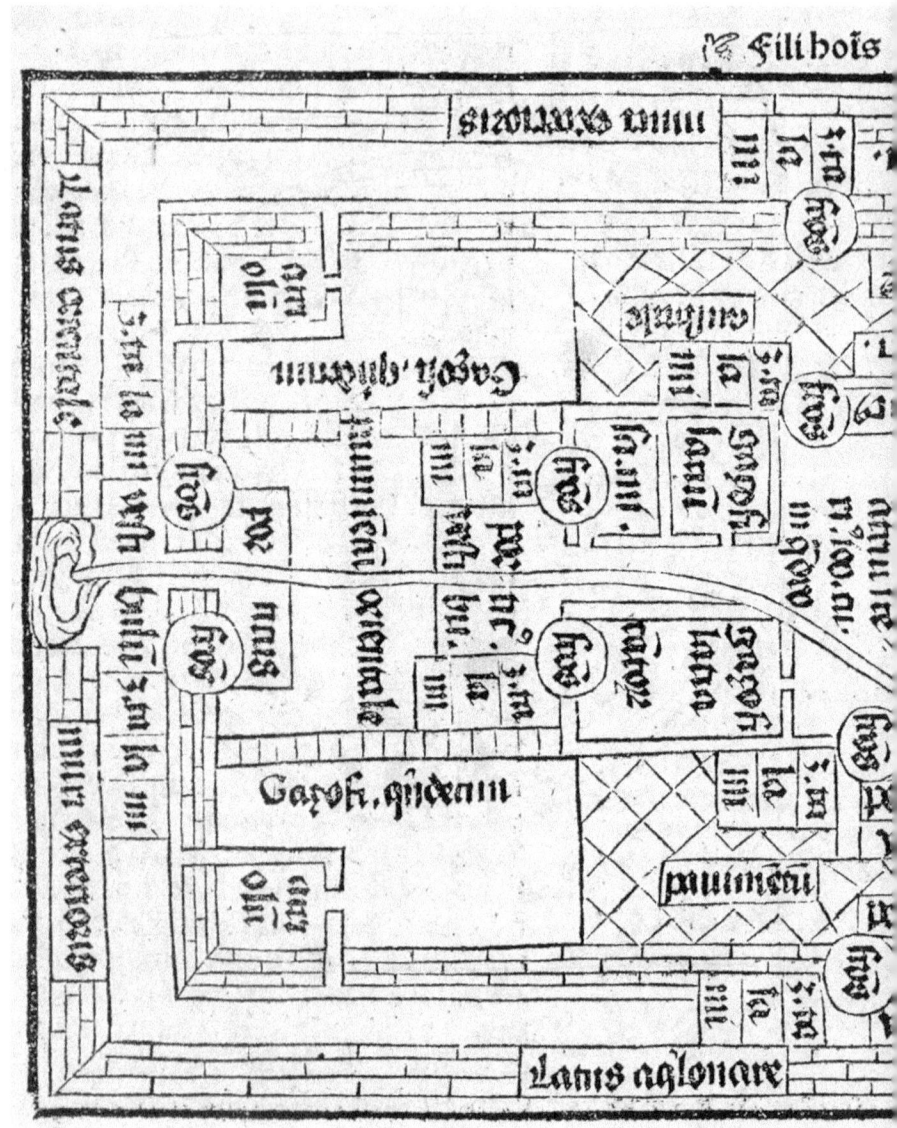

Map of Jerusalem by Nicolas of Lyra, c.1270-1349. From Prima-sexta pars Biblia...expositio Lyre. Basel, Johannes Petri and Johannes Froben, 1498. Vol. IV, Ezechielis Cap. XLVII. The Jewish National and University Library & The Hebrew University of Jerusalem.

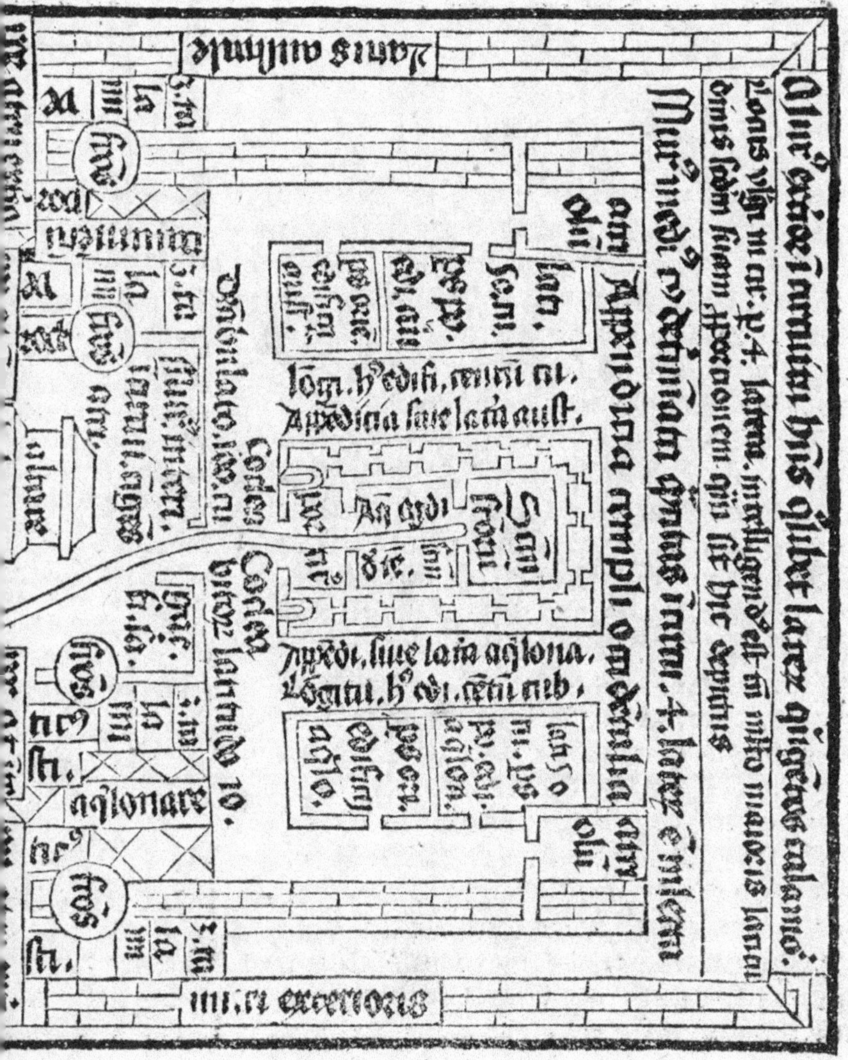

Et dixit.

[A woodcut diagram of a temple plan with Latin inscriptions, including labels such as "Ianis austialis", "Marmoz", "Apriodua templi", "Sanstron", "Cortes", "iiii.m excemonis", and various measurements.]

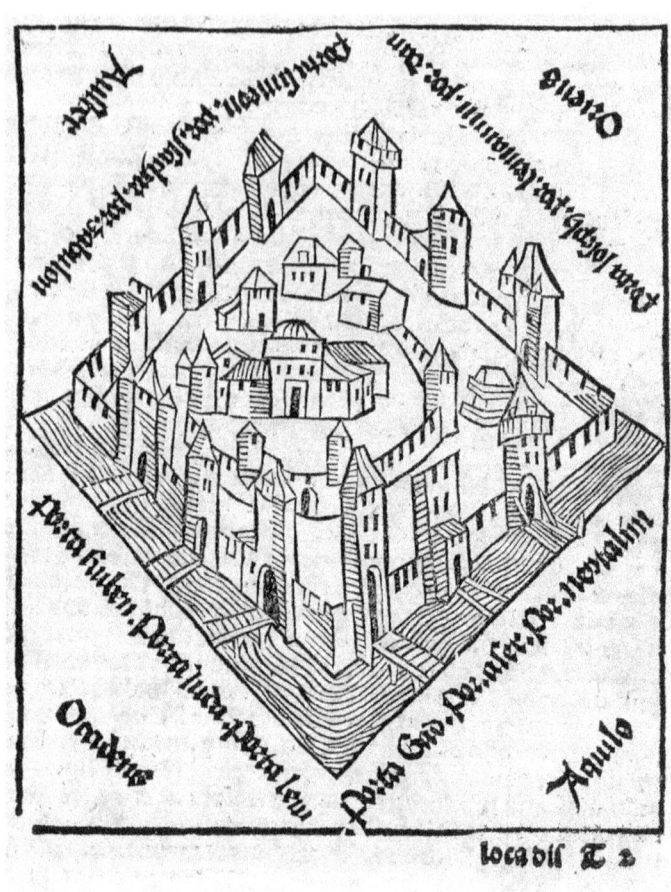

View of Jerusalem by Nicolas, of Lyra, c.1270-1349.
From Prima-sexta pars Biblia...expositio *Lyre*. Basel, Johannes Petri and Johannes Froben, 1498. Vol. IV, Ezechielis Cap. XLVII. The Jewish National and University Library & The Hebrew University of Jerusalem.

View of Jerusalem, c.1455.
From Burchard du Mont-Sion's Descriptio Terrae Sanctae *in Jean Mielot's 1455 translation for Philip the Good. Badische Landesbibliothek Karlsruhe, Cod. St. Peter, pap. 32.*

View of Jerusalem by Conrad Grünenberg, 1487.
From: Description of Travel from Konstanz to Jerusalem.
Bodenseegebiet, 1487. Badische Landesbibliothek Karlsruhe, Cod. St. Peter, pap. 32.

View of Jerusalem by Hartmann Schedel, 1493.
From **Nuremberg Chronicle.** *Nuremberg, 1493, page. xvii.*

Destruction of Jerusalem by Hartmann Schedel, 1493.
From Nuremberg Chronicle. *Nuremberg, 1493, 63v–64r.*

Imaginary View of Jerusalem by Sebastian Brant, 1515. Woodcut from Wolfgang Aytinger, Tractatus super Methodius. *Basel, Michael Furter, 1515. The Jewish National and University Library & The Hebrew University of Jerusalem.*

*View of Jerusalem by Sebastian Muenster, 1550.
Woodcut from* Cosmography. *Basel, Henricus Petri, 1550, p.1014.
The Jewish National and University Library & The Hebrew University
of Jerusalem.*

View of Jerusalem by Sebastian Muenster, 1550.
Woodcut from Cosmography. *Basel, Henricus Petri, 1550, p.1015-1018.*
The Jewish National and University Library & The Hebrew University of Jerusalem.

*View of Jerusalem by Noe Bianchi, ante 1569.
Printed, Bassano, 1675.
The Jewish National and University Library & The Hebrew University
of Jerusalem.*

*Map of Jerusalem by Benedictus Arias Montanus, 1572.
From* Biblia polyglotta, *Antwerp, Christopher Platin, 1572.
The Jewish National and University Library &
The Hebrew University of Jerusalem.*

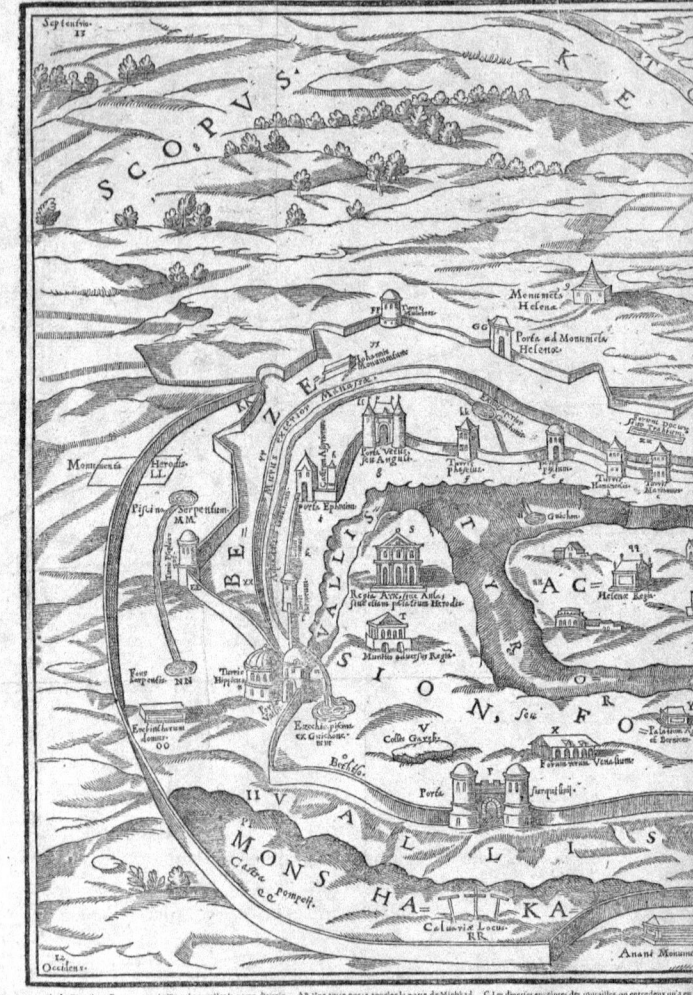

Woodcut Map of Jerusalem, c.1580.
The Jewish National and University Library & The Hebrew University of Jerusalem.

EMPS DE DAVID, ET A CONTINVE DEPVIS IVSQVES A CE QV'ELLE FVST RASEE PAR LES RO-
stinee par Tite fils de Vespasian Empereur Romain. Or afin que ceste figure peust seruir à plusieurs nations, on l'a dressee
auquel le tout doit estre rapporté c'est le troisiesme chapitre de Nehemie.

D La premiere tour de Iehan. E La seconde tour de Iehan. F La troisiesme tour de Iehan. G La quatriesme tour de Iehan. H La porte aux chevaux. I La grand' tour qui
Dauid. Q Les degrez de la cité de Dauid. R Ceste partie de la ville appelée Sion, ou la plus haute place, ou mesme le plus haut marché. S La forteresse, ou hostel du Roy, ou
appellé Gethlia. a La porte du bestail. b La tour de Meach. c La tour de Mistianeel. d La tour de Hananeel. e La porte des poissons. F La tour Phaseleu. g La porte vieille
appellé Gethlia. p La porte du fient. q La porte de la fontaine. r Le iardin du Roy. ſ La piscine de Siloë. t La piscine faite, ou refaite. u La porte de l'enseignure.
des Tyrepoons. ff La fontaine de Silod. gg L'endroit par lequel l'eau de la fontaine Silod s'esconduit dedans la piscine qu'on pourroit appeler le conduit bas des eaux d
Ceste porte de la ville appelée Acca ou Daux tours, qui s'estoyent du costé du Temple. pp La vallée qui fut en fin remplie & applanie. qq L'hostel Royal d'He-
se monument de Iehan. zz Le marché appellé Drocan, ou bientost marché aux poulets. AA Le marché où se vendoyt Paluin, la laine, & tout ce de quoy on se vestoit.
u. FF Les tours des femmes. GG La porte tendante aux monuments d'Helene. HH Les cauernes, ou croses Royales. II La vallée de Hinnom, autrement la vallée des
des Trebinthes, où le tiro des poix chiches. PP La montagne de Mesoldeno. QQ Le lieu où se campa Pompée. RR Le lieu de Caluaire. SS Le Monument
* Assauoir ment la vallée de Iosaphat. 2 La vallée de Cedron. 3 Le torrent de Cedron. 4 La montagne des Oliuiers. 5 Le lieu appellé Bethphagé. 6 Le lieu appellé Bethá-

Map of Jerusalem by Electus Zwinner, 1661. From Blumen Buch des Heiligen Lands Palestinae. *Muenchen, Wilhelm Schell, 1661. Fol.70. The Jewish National and University Library & The Hebrew University of Jerusalem.*

Plans of Important Buildings

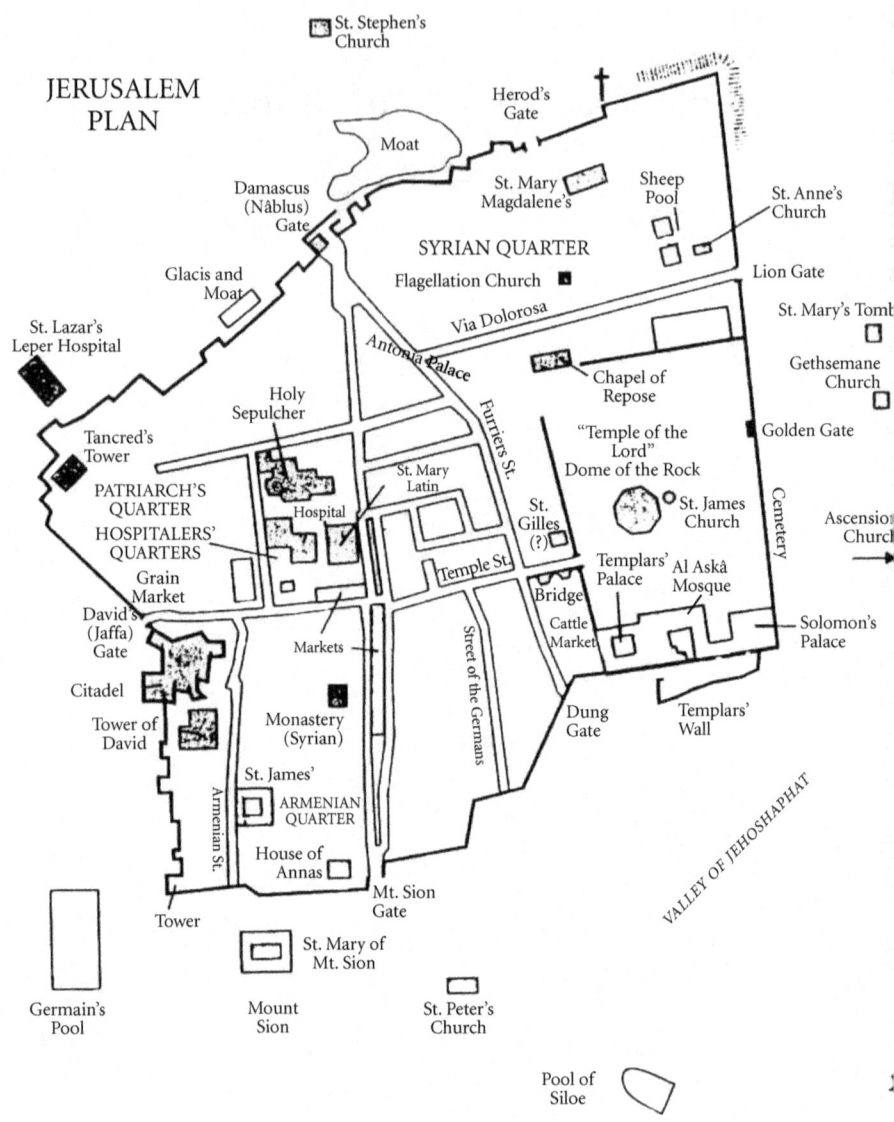

Plan of Jerusalem.

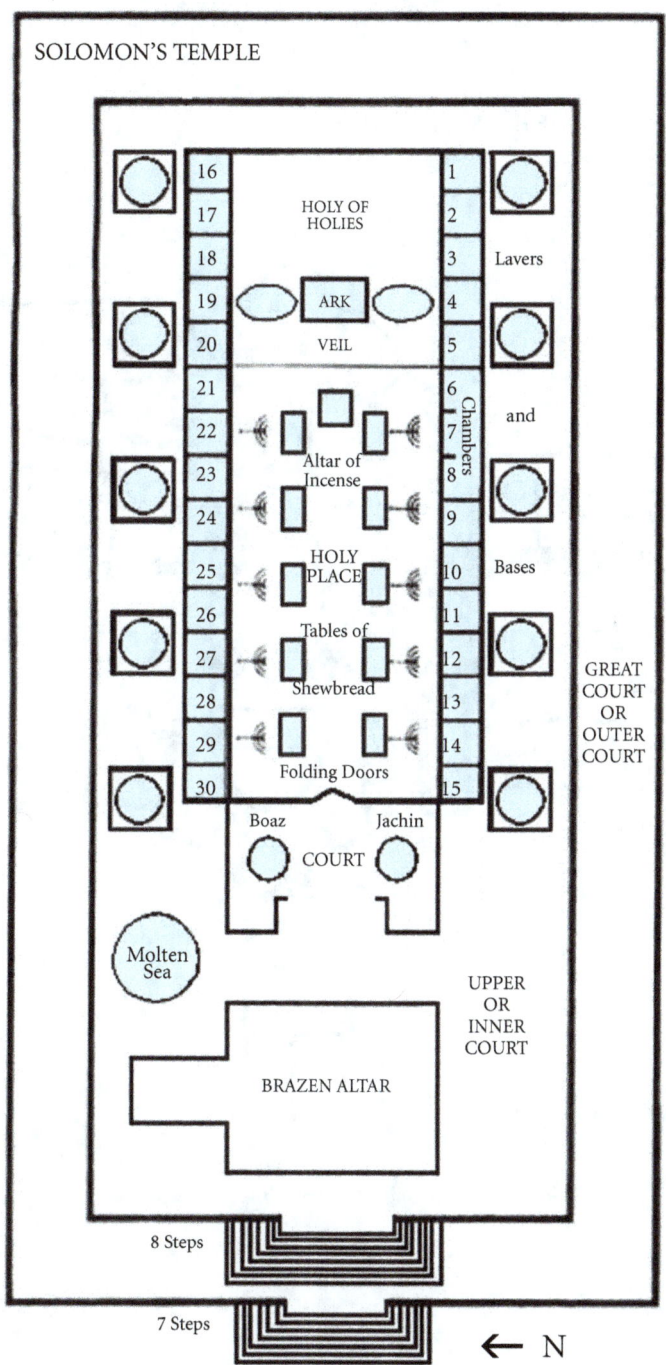

Plan of Solomon's Temple.

CHURCH OF THE HOLY SEPULCHER

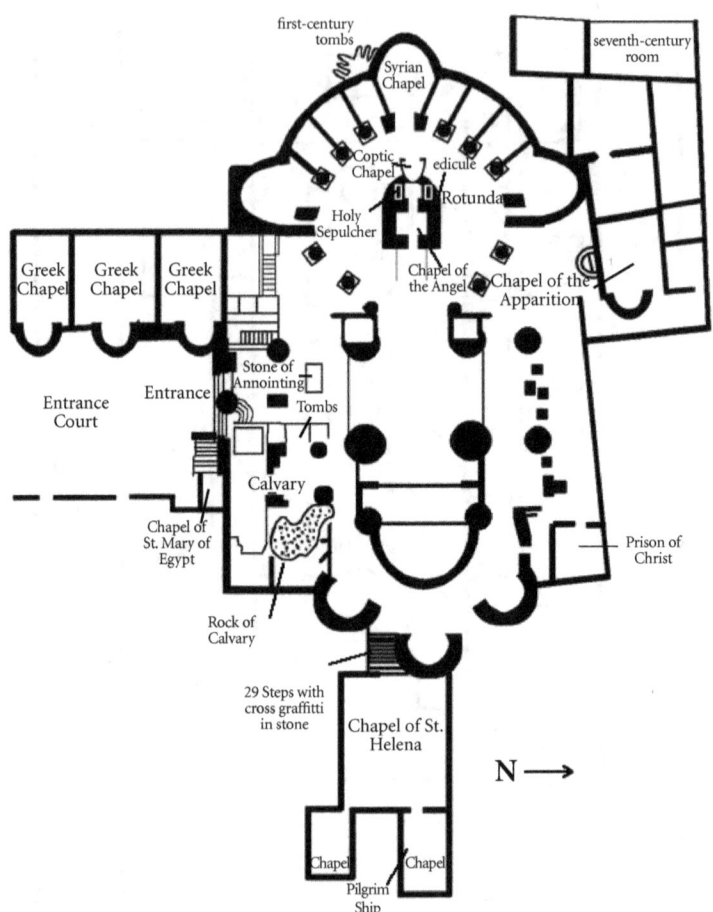

Interactive Plan of the Church of the Holy Sepulcher.

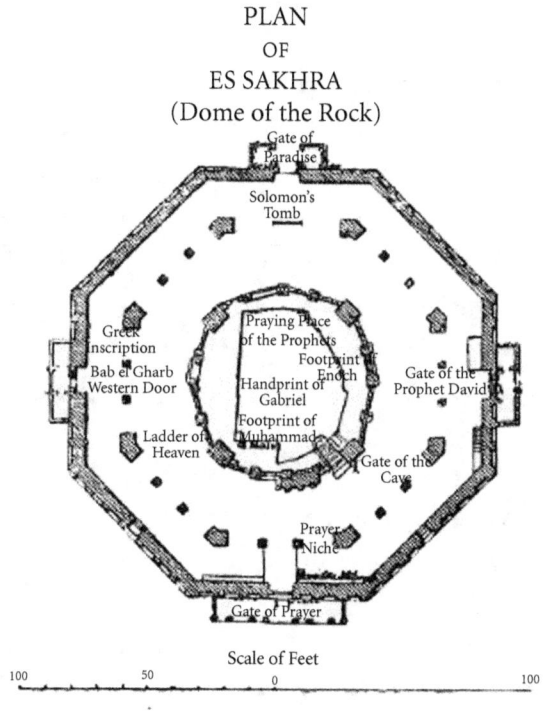

Plan of the Dome of the Rock.

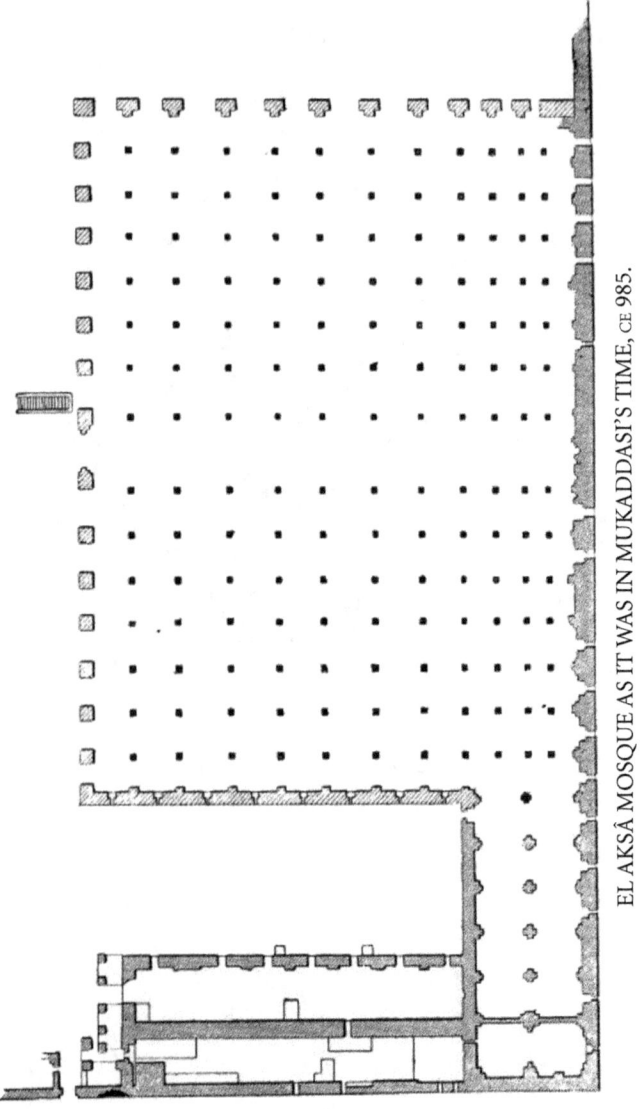

Plan of El Aksâ Mosque, c.985.

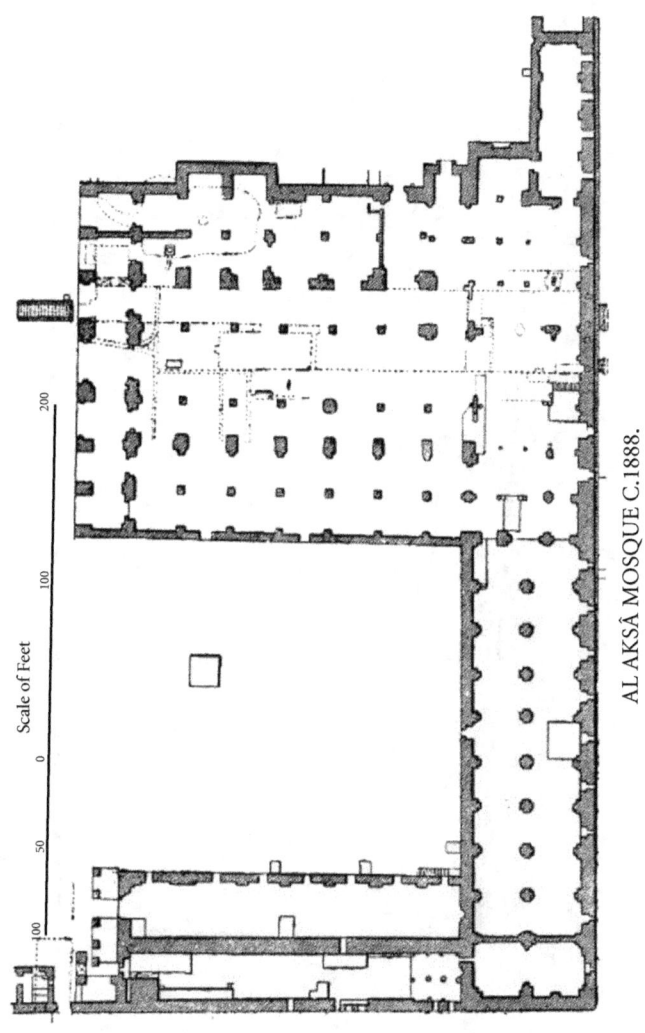

Plan of El Aksâ Mosque, 1888.

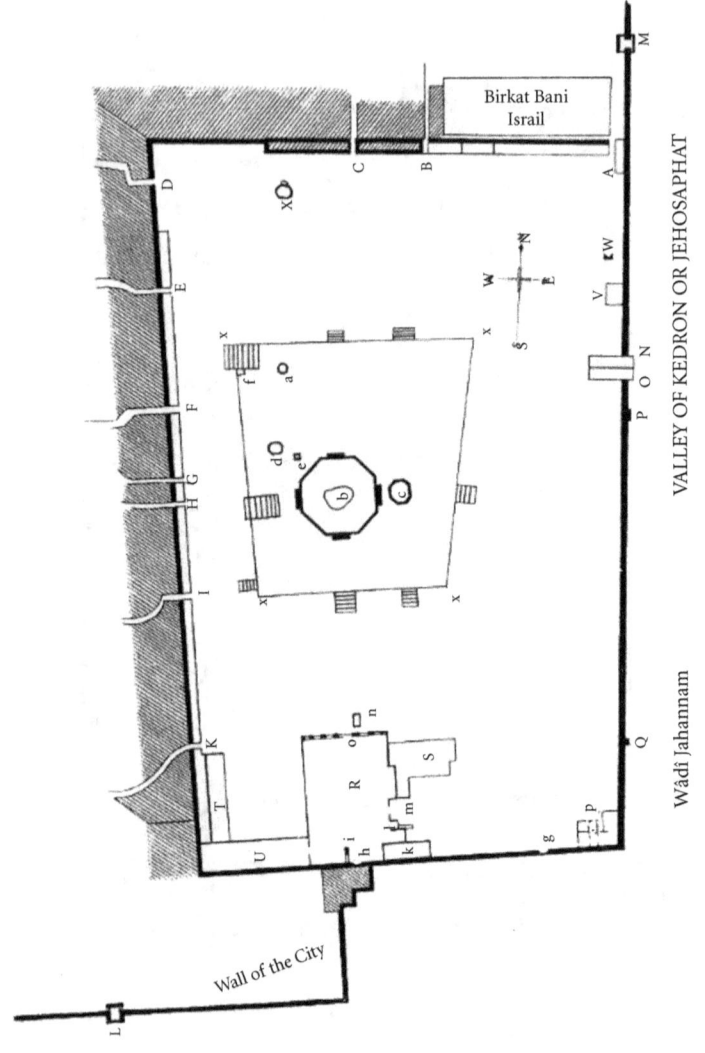

HARAM ASH SHARĪF AT JERUSALEM WITH THE EXISTING BUILDINGS
From the Pal. Expl. Fund Survey

REFERENCES TO THE PLAN[1]

A. Bâb al Asbât (Gate of the Tribes)
B. Bâb Hittah (of Remission)
C. Bâb Sharaf al Anbiyâ (of the Glory of the Prophets) or Ad Dawâdariyyah (of the Secretariat), or Al 'Atm (of Darkness)
D. Bâb al Ghawânimah
E. Bâb an Nâhir (of the Inspector), later of 'Alâ ad Dîn al Busîrî
F. Bâb al Hadîd (of Iron)
G. Bâb al Kattânîn (of the Cotton Merchants)
H. Bâb al Mutawaddâ (of the Place for Ablution)
I. Bâb as Silsilah (of the Chain), or As Sakînah (of the Shechinah)
K. Bâb al Maghâribah, or An Nabî (of the Mogrebins, or of the Prophet)
L. City Gate, called Bâb al Maghâribah; and by the Franks the Dung Gate
M. City Gate, Bâb Sitti Maryam; and by the Franks the Gate of St. Stephen
N. Bâb at Taubah (of Repentance) ⎱ Golden Gate
O. Bâb ar Rahmah (of Mercy) ⎰
P. Bâb al Burâk or Al Janâiz (of the Funerals)
Q. Pillar in the Wall, marking the place of the Bridge As Sirat
R. Jâmi' al Aksâ
S. Madrasah al Farsiyyah
T. Jâmi' al Maghâribah
U. Aksâ al Kadîmah (ancient Aksâ)
V. Kursî Sulaimân (Solomon's Throne)
W. Makâm Iliyâs or Khidr (Station of Elias or St. George)
X. Kursî 'Isâ (Throne of Jesus)
x, x, x, x. Platform of the Rock
a. Kubbat al Alwâh (Dome of the Tablets)
b. The Rock
c. Kubbat as Silsilah (Dome of the Chain)
d. Kubbat al Mirâj (Dome of the Ascension)
e. Kubbat Jibrail (Gabriel)
f. Kubbat al Khidr (St. George)
g. Mihrâb Daûd (David's Prayer-niche),
h. Great Mihrâb of the Aksâ Mosque
i. Mimbar (Pulpit),
k. Jâmi' 'Omar
1. Mihrâb Zakariyyah (Prayer-niche of Zachariah)
m. Eastern Door of Mosque
n. Well of the Leaves,
o. Great Gate of the Mosque
p. Mahd 'Isâ (Cradle of Jesus)

1. This represents the Haram Area as it existed in 1888 and is reduced from the Plan of the Ordnance Survey (Pal. Expl. Fund), with additions from the work of M. de Vogûé

CAVE OF THE PATRIARCHS AT HEBRON.

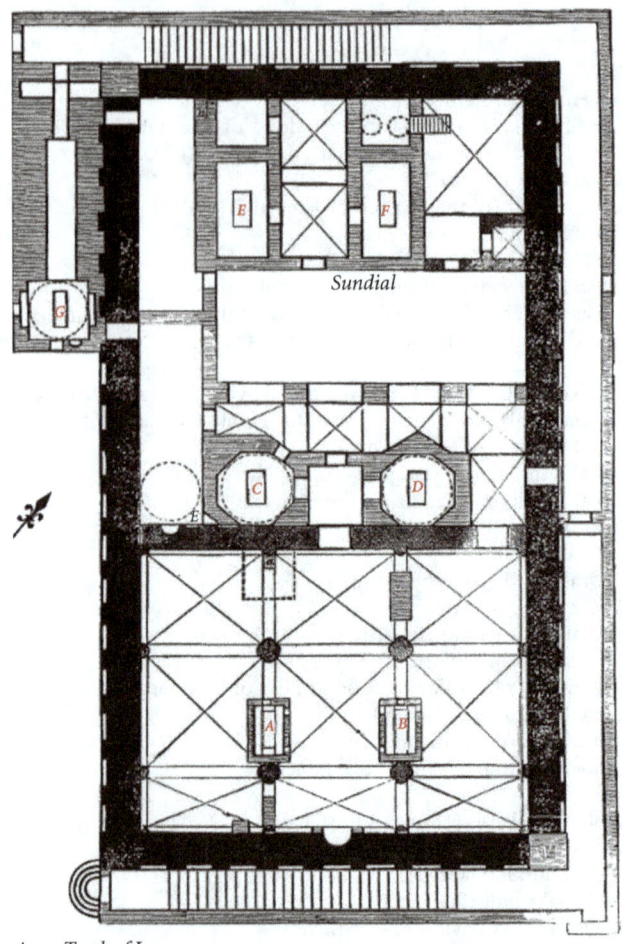

- A Tomb of Isaac
- B Tomb of Rebecca
- C Tomb of Abraham
- D Tomb of Sarah
- E Tomb of Jacob
- F Tomb of Leah
- G Tomb of Joseph

Plan of the Cave of the Patriarchs.

Index

A

Aaron 194, 230
Aaronim 230
Aaron, rabbi 238
Abacuc, prophet 199
Abana River 212
'Abbâs, house of 30, 32
Abbasides 32, 42, 56, 218
'Abd Allah 27, 43, 53
'Abd Allah ibn Tâhir 43
'Abd al Malik, khalif 38, 42, 46, 306
Abdia 25, 205, 206
Abdias 18, 257
Abel 204, 205, 212
A'bilîn 76, 241
Abimelech 209
Abinoem 210
Abiram 17
Abraham el Constantini, rabbi 234, 235
Abraham, patriarch: alphabet 231; Bedstead of 49; Bethel 205; Hebron 47–48, 112–13, 119, 197–98, 235–36; Rock (Jerusalem) 104; father of Isaac 111; Mount Tabor 209; oak of 4, 15; tomb of 25
Abraham, rabbi 228
Abraham the Astronomer, rabbi 238
Absalom 293
Abu 'l 'Ala 66
Abu 'l 'Alâ Ma'arrî 65
Abu 'Abd Allah Muhammad. *See* Mukaddasî.
Abu 'Akil 73
Abu Bakr 'Abd al Karîm At Tâi' Billah 30
Abu Bakr as Sabahî 49
Abu Bakr Hamadânî 114
Abu Bakr ibn Sa'îd 53
Abu Bakr, the architect 27, 28
Abû Ghosh. *See* Bîla'ah (Baalah).
Abu Hurairah 79, 80
Abu-l Fadl Muhammad ibn Mansûr 53
Abu'l Kâsim, kâdi 39
Abu Mansûr Nizâr Al 'Aziz Billah 30
Abu Mu'in Nasir 55
Abu-t Tayib ash Shawâ 27
Abu Yahya ibn Bahrâm, chief kâdi 39
Academy, of Ibelin 237
Accaron. *See* Achon.
Achaia 146
Achon (Acco, Acre) 241–42; biblical 9; Castle of 202, 241; Christian port 129, 134, 146, 149, 210–15; Jewish 229; Muslim 27, 73–75, 80–81; population 147. *See also* Ptolemais.
Achor, valley of 17
Adam 15, 74, 160, 162, 197, 261, 297
Adama and Seboim 15
Ad Dârdûm (Deiran, Daroma) 49, 243
Adima 198
'Adites 241
Adolf of Cologne 127, 157
Adomim (Adummim) 4, 16, 243
Adriatic Sea 9, 144
'Adud ad Daulah 32
Aelius. *See* Hadrian, emperor.
Aeneas 10
Afghanistan 32
Africa 214, 324, 33; North 32
Agarenes 210

agriculture & food xii, 13, 15, 143, 145, 177, 196; almonds 40, 65; apples 48, 191, 260; bakeries 48, 98; bananas 40, 52, 68; barley 65, 113, 134, 149, 191; biscotum 146; bread 10, 12, 18, 19, 26, 37, 51, 65, 84, 113, 146, 194, 199, 207, 209; cheese 49, 146; citron 68, 81; corn (wheat) 11, 84, 154; cotton 124, 274, 371; dates 30, 32, 40, 52, 63, 68, 70, 95, 131, 132, 149, 169, 218, 219, 220, 270, 291, 309; figs 37, 40, 65, 81, 82, 84, 110, 154, 249, 290; fish 78, 207; flour 113; flowers 52, 108; fruit 37, 40, 48, 50, 51, 52, 68, 69, 72, 154, 161, 189, 191, 193, 205, 260, 307; gardens 46, 68, 72, 79, 80, 81, 86, 110, 171, 178, 187, 230, 231; grain 64; granaries 177, 178; grapes 14, 39, 48, 65, 194; herbs 74; honey 40, 49; honeycomb 207; irrigation 37, 49, 84, 257; jasmine 78; juice 68; lemons 68; lentils 48, 113; meat 69, 146; milk 40, 49, 51, 53; mills 51, 52, 113; mulberry 76; narcissus flowers 67; nuts 40; olive oil 46, 48, 49, 84; olives 46, 48, 49, 51, 65, 81, 84, 110, 113, 149, 154, 204, 230; olive trees 51, 154; oranges 40, 68, 81; orchards 48, 72, 110, 149, 230; palm 37, 47, 52, 70, 80, 81, 149, 186, 194, 202; pistachios 65; plantations 154, 231; ploughmen 2; produce 12, 49, 84, 154, 223; raisins 49, 113; red earth 197; red juniper 116; roses 17, 42, 70, 106, 149, 184, 194, 304; rue 83; soil 37, 68, 79, 83, 84, 149, 191, 193, 204, 205, 306; spices 144; sugar 40, 49, 68, 72, 144, 229, 312; sugar-cane 68; sumach 110; sycamore 16, 50; thistles 191; trees 37, 48, 49, 51, 65, 68, 70, 72, 79, 80, 81, 84, 109, 114, 191, 194, 202, 204, 205; vegetables 146; vineyards 15, 46, 48, 154, 170, 204, 205, 230; wheat 65, 113; wine 15, 26, 55, 146, 209, 211, 264; work routines 149
Ahab 229, 230, 257
Aidhab 58
'Ain al Bakar (the Ox Spring) 74, 241, 297
'Ain es Sultan. *See* Fountain of the Law.
'Ain Sulwân. *See* Pool of Siloe (Siloam, 'Ain Sulwân).
'Ain Umm Judei'a. *See* Fountain of Samson.
Aix-la-Chapelle 127, 161
Ajalon (Aijalon) 10, 231, 243
'Akik 79
'Akkah, founder of Acre 75
Al 'Âdil, the Shâr 48
Al 'Ajûz 119
Al Akhmâs (the Quintans) 46
Alaric 6
Al Baki' 79
Al Balât. *See* Jerusalem.
Albania 144
Al Bashârî. *See* Mukaddasî.
Aleppo 2, 64, 67, 206, 244; gates 64
Alexander III, pope 218
Alexandria 5, 19, 205, 224
Al Fadl ibn Hammâd 53
Al Firmâ 39, 243, 305
Al Fusûl wa-l Ghâyat (The Divisions and Conclusions) 66
Al Hajjâj 39
Ali ar Rizâ, imâm 55
'Ali, khalif 31, 243
Al Jâr 57
Al Kâim, khalif 32
Al Kusaifah 49, 243
Allah 27, 40, 45, 48, 49, 52, 53, 54, 79, 80, 84, 86, 88, 93, 95, 96, 106, 110, 112, 113, 115
Al Madînah. *See* Medînah.
Almah 239; Jews 239
Al Mahdi, khalif 42
Al Malik an Nâsir Hasan 120
Al Mamûn, khalif 96

INDEX

Al Masjid Al Yakîn mosque 49, 244
Al Muktadir Billah, khalif; mother of 44
Al Muktadir, khalif 44, 119
Al Mustansir, khalif 57, 278
Alphaeus 208
Alps 144, 147, 218, 324
Al Yakîn 49
Amalechites 210
Amalric, king 131, 132, 167, 265, 283, 284
Amat 212
Amaury 131
Ambrose of Milan 1
Amid 57
Amittai 238
'Ammân 37, 244, 245, 246; Circus of Solomon 52; Tomb of Uriah 52
Ammonites 16, 210, 244
Amos 16, 25, 246
Ana 32
Anacletus II, pope 140
Andalusia 31, 70
Andrew, St., apostle 208
Andromeda 10
Anglia 324
animals & husbandry 74; asses 9, 12, 61, 115, 181, 204, 228; bullocks 204; cocks 187; colts 16, 181; flocks 14, 22, 52, 205, 208; horses 60, 177, 178, 197, 206, 291; lions 11, 18, 199, 200, 211; mules 113; oxen 12, 74, 113, 297; sheep 13, 14, 179, 213, 233
'Annabah 38, 246
Anna, mother of Samuel 201
Anne, St. 211
Anthony, St., of Egypt 2, 7
Antichrist 208
Antioch 1, 3, 7, 9, 64, 68, 144, 174, 212, 213, 247, 310
Antiochia 213
Antiochus, king 176, 201, 296
Antipatris 3, 10, 246, 296
antiquity 67, 68, 140, 141, 153

Antoninus Martyr 150, 251, 296, 300, 314
Apollonia. See Arsûf.
Apostles 16, 17, 155, 161, 162, 182, 183, 185, 186, 189
Apostle, the. See Paul, St., apostle.
Arabia 33, 58, 148, 154, 191, 192, 193, 194, 195, 198, 199, 212
Arabs 68, 69, 114, 129, 208, 272, 285
'Arafât. See religious practice & life.
Ar'ar 114
Araunah the Jebusite 179
Arbe. See Hebron.
Arbela. See Irbil (Irbid).
Archas 212, 246
archeology 135, 149
Arculfus 150
Areuna the Jebusite 201
Ariel 11
Arîhâ. See Jericho.
Arimathea 3, 10, 196, 199, 246
Aristotle 140
'Arkah (Arcados) 67, 246
Arkites 246
Ark of the Covenant 201
Ark of the Shechînah 101
Armenia & Armenians 22, 57, 164, 169, 187, 188, 283, 324
arms 56, 71, 174, 177, 185, 186, 192, 199; arrows 178; Balearic bow 178; garrisons 178; swords 166, 176, 179, 185, 200
Arnold of Brescia 140
Arnon 114, 239
Arphat 212, 246
Ar Rakîm (Arekem) 52, 246
Ar-Ramlah 37, 38, 50, 307. See also Ramleh (Rams).
Arsenius 20
Arsûf 37, 51, 246
architecture: ancient 71; arches 44, 71, 73, 89, 90, 94, 96, 103, 107, 108, 132, 138, 159, 160, 167, 170, 172, 173, 177, 180, 184, 276, 284; ashlar 154; capitals 32, 37, 39, 49, 52, 57, 71, 72, 89,

375

94, 103, 107, 206, 208, 244, 306; cenotaphs 111, 112; cloisters 90, 123, 165; colonnades 42, 43, 44, 45, 78, 89, 90, 91, 94, 96; columns 38, 43, 44, 46, 71, 72, 73, 78, 82, 90, 92, 93, 94, 95, 96, 103, 105, 106, 108, 138, 159, 161, 170, 172, 173, 175, 177, 184, 196, 235, 276, 280, 284; cornices 107, 108; crypts 175, 183, 184, 196, 206, 250, 276, 288; daryûzah 90, 123; domes 43, 47, 69, 85, 89, 90, 91, 95, 102, 104, 105, 106, 112, 133, 177, 182, 184, 276; marble 82, 89, 115, 138, 172; (Parian) marble 168, 189; mihrâbs (prayer niches) 38, 41, 42, 43, 45, 78, 91, 93, 94, 95, 100, 106, 109, 111, 122, 125, 262, 270, 274, 284, 371, 384, 385, 386, 393; oratories 87, 89, 91, 93; pavements 161, 165, 166, 167, 168, 172, 279, 282; piers 102, 103, 104, 105, 106, 107, 138, 161, 173, 177, 180, 280; pillars 20, 43, 89, 90, 102, 103, 104, 107, 159, 161, 173, 234, 235, 280; precious stones 159; riwâk 89; spolia 72; sutûn 102, 107; ustuwânah 102; volutes 103

arts, brocade 111, 112, 115; Damascene brass-work 89, 91; enamels 88, 95, 107; fresco 250, 251, 290; gilding 132, 133, 181, 280; gold work 44, 54, 61, 73, 89, 95, 107, 108, 111, 115, 132, 143, 159, 164, 165, 171, 234, 281; images 213; inscriptions 65, 79, 82, 87, 88, 91, 95, 96, 104, 108, 132, 159, 160, 161, 162, 163, 165, 166, 168, 169, 173, 174, 182, 184, 187, 233, 236, 276, 279; jaspar 142; jewels 143, 144, 165; marble 38, 43, 44, 46, 49, 50, 69, 71, 73, 78, 79, 81, 89, 92, 94, 95, 96, 101, 102, 103, 104, 105, 106, 107, 108, 154, 158, 159, 161, 166, 167, 183, 184, 196, 211, 234; mosaics 43, 44, 52, 158, 161, 165, 167, 173, 184, 196, 250, 276, 278, 280, 292, 339; music 24, 25, 149, 163, 201; niello work 96; ornament 82; painting 115, 116, 129, 158, 159, 162, 165, 167, 168, 169, 175, 184, 185, 278, 279; pearls 143; poetry 59, 66, 140; portraits 116; sculpture 82, 115; silver work 133, 163, 164; utensils 104, 113; woodwork 104

Ascalon ('Askalân, Askelon, 'Askalân, Ashdod) 37, 50, 116, 148, 174, 199, 215, 246, 247, 300; Jewish 237
Ashdoth Hapisgah 238
Asher 229
Ashkelonah 237
Ash-Shâfi'î 50
'Âsi. *See* Orontes River.
Asia 332; central 32, 151; western 68
Asia Minor 64, 144, 256, 305
Asiût 58
Assassins 223
Assyrians 176
Athanasius 6
Athens 21, 22
Atlit 296
At Tâi', khalif 30, 32
Augusta. *See* Sebaste (Sebastiya).
Augustus, emperor 10, 18, 217
'Awertah. *See* Gabaa.
Azerbaijân 57, 75, 247

B

Babylon & Babylonia 24, 142, 176, 199, 238, 264
Baghdâd 30, 32, 56, 96, 218, 219, 220, 221, 224
Bait al Lahm (Bait Lahm). *See* Bethlehem.
Bait-al-Makdis. *See* Jerusalem.
Bait al Mukaddas. *See* Jerusalem.
Bait Jibrîl 37, 49, 247, 257
Bala 15, 198

Balaam 198
Balac, the son of Boer 198
Baldach the Suite 212
Baldwin I, king of Jerusalem 131, 166, 194, 301
Baldwin II, king of Jerusalem 131, 283, 284
Baldwin III, king of Jerusalem 131, 132, 284
Bâli'ah, Christian church 38
Balkâ 52
Balkans 144
Balkh 55, 58, 59, 64, 83
Bani Marwân 56
Bani Nâîm. *See* Caphar Barucha.
Banyas 148, 227, 239, 247, 304, 305
Barach 19, 210
Barachias 172
Barak, the son of Abinoam 239
Bari 144
Barkûk, sultan 120
Barluzzi, Antonio 302
Basrah 58, 68
Bavaria 146
bedawîn 52, 114
Beersheba 243, 296
Beirut (Bairût, Baruth, Berytus, Beeroth) 3, 9, 71, 72, 139, 149, 174, 213, 214, 227, 246, 247, 260, 307, 308
Beit Jibrin 236, 259, 296, 308
Beit Nûba (Nobe) 3, 10, 147, 236, 237, 247, 304
Belinas. *See* Paneas.
Belmont 129, 200, 201, 301. *See also* Place in the Wood or of St. John.
Belus 297
Belvoir 301
Bene Berak. *See* Ashkelonah.
Benedict the Pole 151
Benjamin ben Japheth, rabbi 239
Benjamin of Tudela xii, 150, 217, 223, 227, 247, 302, 306, 309, 312
Benjamin, patriarch 12, 176, 195
Benjamin, tribe of 10, 18, 233, 253
Benoni. *See* Benjamin, patriarch.

Bernard of Clairvaux 140
Bernard the Wise 150
Bethany 4, 135, 148, 181, 189, 194, 251, 265, 284; Church of Mary and Martha 190; Church of St. Lazarus 190; Garden of Abraham 190, 191, 192; house of Mary and Martha 266; Red Cistern 190, 191, 307; St. Lazarus 131; tomb of Lazarus 266
Bethel (Beitîn, Baytin) 4, 5, 17, 26, 204, 205, 248
Beth Gubrin. *See* Bait Jibrîl.
Bethlehem 249–51; Christian 148; Church of the Nativity 4–5, 12, 47, 196, 249; Inn of Mary 249; Jews 235; late Roman 2, 20, 23; Mary 195; Muslim 110; Nativity 197; tomb of David 251; tomb of Rachel 235
Betho Annaba. *See* 'Annabah.
Bethoron (Beter) 10, 200, 201, 251
Bethorons 3
Bethphage 16, 135, 148, 181, 251
Bethsaida 208, 209, 252
Bethsames 201, 252
Bethsan 206, 253
Bethsur (Beit Sûr) 4, 14, 253, 259
Bible, Hebrew (Old Testament) 14, 15, 141, 153, 160, 223; Septuagint 10, 301; study of 140; Genesis 194; Gen. 11:13 74; Gen. 11:16 74; Gen. 14:18–24 209; Gen. 18 15, 304; Gen. 25–32 212; Gen. 28:16 174; Gen. 35:18 12; Gen. 49:10 13; Exod. 15:27 258; Num. 20:1-13 312; Josh. 9:22-27 10; Josh. 15:7 253; Josh. 15:9 253; Josh. 15:15 15; Josh. 15:16–19 15; Josh. 15:60 253; Judg. 1:10 15; Judg. 4, 5 210; Kings 157; 1 Kings 6:1–10 176; 1 Kings 8:28–29 174; 1 Kings 9:11 209; 2 Kings 5:7 156; 2 Kings 24:17 179; 2 Kings 24:20 293; Psalms 5, 24, 172; Ps. 42:6 26; Ps. 83:9,

10 26; Ps. 83:12 210; Ps. 87:1,
2 11; Ps. 120:5 209; Ps. 132:3–5
13; Ps. 132:6, 7 13; Ps. 132:14,
17 14; Cant. 3:4 26; Is. 1:3 12;
Is. 15:5 15; Is. 19:18 19; Is. 24:1
11; Is. 28:16 17; Is. 32:20 12; Is.
63:3 14; Jer. 51:6 24, 264; Ezek.
10:18, 19 16; Ezek. 47:1–2 175;
Joel 2:28 12; Mich. 5:2 13; Zach.
3:9 17 Maccabees 176; Talmud
228; Torah 41
Bible, Christian (New Testament):
New Testament 139, 141, 153,
258; Gospels 14, 16, 21, 116,
140, 141, 158, 188, 197; Matt.
5:1 308; Matt. 14:31 207; Matt.
15:24 13; Matt. 24:28 22; Mark
9:2–8 301; Mark 14:32 185;
Mark 16:6 158; Luke 2:14 14;
John 2:1–2 255; Acts 21; Acts
13:46 13; Acts 20:16 21; Acts
21:5 9; Acts 21:13 21; Acts 23:31
296; Eph. 4:8 163; Phil. 3:5 10;
Apocalypse (Revelations) 24,
142, 143; Apoc. 18:2 24, 264;
Apoc. 18:4 24
Bîla'ah (Baalah) 38, 253, 296
Bir Abraham 238
Bîr Ayyûb (Bir Eyûb) 46, 133, 253
Birket es-Sultan 133, 286
Birwah 76, 254
Bitlis 57
Biyâr 27
Bordeaux Pilgrim 6, 150, 249, 251,
259, 260, 264, 266, 278, 284, 296
Bosra 208, 212
Brindisi 144
British Museum 59, 60, 66
Brook Kishon 229
Brook of Kedumim 229, 297
Burâk, Muhammad's horse 106, 109
Busrah 39
Buyides 32, 56
Byblos. *See* Gibeleth (Gebal,
Giblet).
Byzantium 69, 70, 115, 144, 302,
339

C

Cacho 202. *See also* Caphar
Semala.
Cadesbarne 198, 254, 312
Cadumin Brook 210
Caesar, builds Caesarea 230
Caesarea (Anatolia) 144
Caesarea of Palestine (Caesarea
Palaestina) 2, 3, 10, 37, 51, 81,
147, 207, 212, 215, 230, 246, 254,
258, 304; Tower of Strato 202,
255
Caiaphas 186
Cain 204, 205, 212
Caipha 37, 50, 202, 215, 261. *See
also* Haifâ.
Cairo 31, 39, 56, 57, 111, 119, 218,
224, 304, 306
Caleb 15, 49, 198
Caleb ben Jephunneh 238
Cana (Chana, Kafar Kannah) 4, 19,
26, 80, 211, 255, 296
Canute 30
Cape Gallo 300
Capernaum (Capharnaum) 4, 19,
26, 208, 209, 229, 252, 256, 296
Caphar Barucha 4, 15, 256
Caphar Gamala 202
Caphar Semala 202
Cappadocia 22, 256
Cara 198
Cariatharbe (Kariath-arba,
Kirjath-arba) 15, 197, 261. *See
also* Hebron.
Cariathiarim 201, 256, 257. *See
also* Gabaa.
Cariathsepher 15, 256
Carnaim 198
Carthage 214, 324
Casale Lamberti. *See* Castle of
Imbertus.
Castile 227
Castle of Goliath 52, 245
Castle of Imbertus 214, 215, 257
Castle of Sapham 206
Castle Scandalium 214
Caves of the Prophets 257

Cedar 208, 209
Cedron brook 133, 155, 181, 183, 341
Cestius 241
Ceylon 223
Chalcis. *See* Kinnasrîn.
Chariton, St. 187, 188
Charles V, emperor 217
Charnel House of the Lion 257
Chateau Merle 190
Chateau Pelerin 147, 190
China 105, 151, 223
Chiya, rabbi 238
Chorazain 208, 209
Chorraei 19, 257, 259
Chulam 224
Cicero 21, 298
Cilicia 256
Cilician Gates 144
Cinnereth 208. *See also* Tiberias.
Cirene 324
Cities of Lot 49. *See also* Dead Sea.
City of the Giants. *See* Jericho.
clash of civilizations xi
Cleophas, house of 10
climate 29, 39, 40, 68, 307
Cochin China 105
Coele Syria 3, 9, 22, 213, 257
Cologne 127, 137, 138, 157
commerce & industry 37, 49, 137, 223; Africa 223; alum 198; ambergris 105; Asia 223; asphalt 78, 79; bazaars 64, 65, 69, 72, 73, 84, 85, 88, 116; bitumen 73, 198; camphor 105; carpets & rugs 65, 73, 92, 94, 104, 106, 111, 113; cedar 38, 44, 156, 166; Chinese porcelain 81; clothing 177; copper 159, 196; curtains 116; customs 64, 69; cypress 38, 156, 159, 162, 291; dyers 228, 230, 232, 235, 237, 238; emeralds 107; emporia 49, 50, 146, 223, 307; fondachi 146; glass 116, 171, 229, 297; handicrafts 228; hangings 73, 279; harbors 3, 7, 10, 50, 51, 74, 149, 202, 203, 214, 215, 228, 229, 310; indigo 52; iron 159; ivory 144, 279; Jews' pitch 198; katranum 198; lamps 73, 77, 90, 93, 95, 104, 112, 159, 163; lanterns 73, 90, 95, 112, 186; lead 97; marble quarries 49; markets 39, 40, 50, 284; Mekkah sand 80, 81, 82; merchandise 64, 70; merchants 50, 64, 229, 237; oak 4, 15, 197; oil of Sandaracha 116; paper 69, 88, 152; perfume 68, 114, 158; pine wood 57, 156; prayermats 79; reeds 79; rugs, zîlû (prayer) 109; sâj-wood 105; shipbuilding 80; shipping 229; silks 144; silkworms 50; tapers 105, 106; teak 105; traders 64; Tyrian glassware 229; varnish 116; wares 50; wax 104, 105; wax tapers 104; wood 191
Constantia 7, 257
Constantine I, emperor 161, 176, 177, 249
Constantinople 64, 144, 183, 196, 206, 220, 224
Cordova 31
Cornelius, house of 10
Cosdre, Persian emperor 165
Council of Clermont 30
Crags of Jonathan 237
Crete 146
Crocodile River 312
crusades & crusaders: architecture 243, 267, 270, 285; campaigns 244, 248; decline 144, 145, 151, 312; first 30, 143; garrisons 232; geographical knowledge 139; guidebooks 150; Hattîn 77; Muslim recapture of Jerusalem 95; period 130, 217, 223, 309; place names 92, 124, 246, 289, 296, 301; ports 246, 261; religious tolerance 306; routes 144; second 220; state 137; states 143, 144, 305; studies xi, 137, 143
Cuthim 230, 238

Cyclades 9
Cyprian, St. 171
Cyprus 1, 2, 3, 7, 9, 146, 257
Cyrus 176
Cythera 9

D

Dâjûn (Bait Dîjân, Beth Dagon) 38, 257
Damascus 3, 42, 64, 67, 73, 166, 208, 212, 219, 220, 224, 246, 265, 290, 306, 364; mosque 34
Damasus, pope 1, 2
Damghân 56
Dâmûn 76, 241
Dan 77, 148, 166, 205, 207, 208, 239, 296, 300
Danegelt 30
Danes 30
Daniel, abbot 150
Daniel, prophet 199
Danube River 144
David, king 11, 13, 24, 91, 92, 105, 167, 179, 198, 201; Temple 42; tomb 25
Dead Sea 49, 78, 148, 150, 191, 192, 197, 198, 254, 257, 258, 261, 263, 264, 296
Deborah, prophetess 210
De Goeje, *Bibliotheca Geographorum Arabicorum* 34
Dehli 59
desert 2, 4, 7, 15, 19, 26, 49, 50, 52, 56, 58, 81, 83, 154, 208, 305; Elim 150, 194; Paul and Anthony 258
Dhâhir li Izâzi Din Allah, khalif 64
Dhu'l Kifl 76
Diaspolis. *See* Lydda; *See* Ludd (Lod).
dîbâ. *See* arts: brocade.
Dido 214
Dinah 204
Diospolis 10
Diyâr Bakr 57, 64, 300
Diyâr Modhar 57
Dolbeau, François 137
Domitian, emperor 8

Dor 10, 258
Dorcas 10
Dositheus 18
Dothaim 209, 307
Druzes 30, 228
Dschenin. *See* Genin
Dyrrhachium 144

E

Eber 241
Edessa 144
Edom 212, 263
Egypt 58, 116; ancient 244; Cairo 306; Christian 22; commerce & industry 48, 61, 64, 68, 105, 197; crusader 166; Exodus 14, 19, 195; Fatamite 27, 30, 31, 33, 56, 57, 69, 88, 95, 104, 108, 111, 113, 115; Flight into 12; frontier 50, 154, 192, 194, 224, 237; Joseph (patriarch) 205; Mamlûk 120, 218, 220; maps 324; Nile Delta 260, 305, 310
Eichstätt 138
El-Adid, khalif 218
Elburz 56
Eleazar ben Arak, rabbi 239
Eleazar ben Azariah, rabbi 239
Eleazar, son of Aron 17
Elephat (Eliphaz) the Themanite 212
Eleutheropolis 4, 247, 257, 263, 296, 298. *See also* Bait Jibrîl.
Eliazar 212
Elijah (Elias), prophet 17, 18, 26, 45, 206, 214, 229, 296, 371
Elim 150, 194, 258
Elisha 25, 259, 296; fountain of 4
Elizabeth, St. 200, 201
El Jîb. *See* Gabaon.
el-Mostadi, khalif 218
El-Roy 224
Emaded-Din Zenghi 130
Emmaus 3, 10, 148, 200, 201, 258
Emoreans 195
Endor 26, 208, 209, 258, 297; Brook of 26, 297

Engaddi 4, 15
England 30, 34
English Channel 30
En Roge. *See* Fuller's Spring.
Ephraim; territory of 237, 310; tribe of 231
Ephraim of Tyre, rabbi 228
Ephratah 12, 13
Ephron 197
Epiphanius, bishop of Salamis 1, 7, 9
Erasmus of Rotterdam 2
Erek. *See* Archas.
Errajân 58
Esau 76, 212
Escol 4, 14, 258
Esdraelon 3, 300, 302
Esdras 76, 176
Ethelred the Unready, king 30
Ethiopia 22, 324
Ethiopian eunuch 14
Euphrates River 57, 63
Europe; agriculture 68; architecture 138; central 144; commerce 223; in cartography 324, 332; paper 69; travel 146
Eusebius 250, 296
Eusebius, tomb 250
Eustachius, St. 212
Eustochium xi, 1, 2, 5, 6, 8, 21, 264; tomb 250
Eve 129, 163, 168, 171, 197
Ezekiel, prophet 175
Ezra (Esdras) 76, 237

F
Falaj 58
Famagusta 257
Fârs 30, 58, 263
Fâtimah 31
Fatimites 30, 31, 32, 56, 57, 61, 64, 69, 88, 95, 104, 108, 113, 115, 218
Field of Abacuc 199
Filastîn. *See* Palestine; *See* Ramlah (Ramah).
Flavia Domitilla 8

Flood, biblical 17
Fontenoid 129, 200, 201. *See also* Emmaus.
food. *See* agriculture & food.
Fountain of Elisha 191, 258, 259
Fountain of Gabriel 210, 259
Fountain of the Eunuch 259
Fountain of the Law 260
France 30
Franciscans 140, 151
Franks 70, 162, 232, 247, 272, 371
Frederick I Barbarossa, emperor 218
Frederick II, emperor 270
Fretillus, Eugesippus 127
Fulcher, patriarch 130, 169
Fulke, king 132, 265, 284
Fuller's Spring 253

G
Gabaa 3, 10, 17, 201, 260. *See also* Gibeah of Benjamin.
Gabaon (Gibeon) 10, 260
Gabaonites 10
Gabriel, archangel 45, 106, 161, 162, 210, 247, 367
Gad 77
Galgala 4, 17, 260
Galilee: biblical 19, 26, 211, 238, 255; Christian 128, 147, 148, 153, 206–9; mountains of 75
Gamaliel, rabban 238
Garden of Abraham 260
Gath 230, 260
Gaul 22
Gaza (Gazara) 4, 5, 14, 37, 50, 144, 148, 199, 215, 246, 284, 298, 300, 310
Genin (Ginae) 206, 260
Gennesareth 26, 129, 208, 209, 297
Genoa 144, 146, 147
Genon 307
Gentiles 13, 14, 16, 24, 176, 208, 209, 232, 235
geography xi, 28, 135, 139, 140, 150, 217; omphalos 279
George, Prince of Wales 262

381

George, St. 45, 67, 202, 230, 238, 339, 371
Georgians 232
Germanus 133
Germany 144, 218, 224
Gessen (Goshen) 5, 19, 260
Gethaei 19, 260
Ghaur 52, 307
Ghazzah. *See* Gaza (Gazara).
Ghurjistân 48
Ghuz 224
Ghuznî 56
Gibeah of Benjamin 3, 237, 260
Gibeah of Saul 237
Gibeah-Phinehas. *See* Gabaa.
Gibeleth (Gebal, Giblet) 213, 260, 296
Gibelin. *See* Bait Jibrîl.
Gibeon 231, 260, 301
Gibeon the Great 231. *See also* Mahomerie-le-Grand.
Gildemeister, J. 34
Ginaea 206
Godfrey of Bouillon 131, 166, 283
Gomorrah. *See* Sodom and Gomorrah.
Great Sea. *See* Mediterranean Sea
Greece 146
Greeks; Byzantine 67, 69, 70, 84, 231, 283
Greek Sea. *See* Mediterranean Sea.

H

Habrâ. *See* Hebron.
Hadhîrah 76, 261
Hadrian, emperor 11, 264
Haifâ 34, 80, 241, 254, 257, 261, 270, 273, 297, 303; Jewish 229
Hâkim, khalif 30, 31, 115, 278
Hakkadosh, rabbenu 238
Halab (Haleb). *See* Aleppo.
Halhul. *See* Escol.
Hamaagal, Chuni 239
Hamâ (Hamath) 64, 67
Hamdânîs 32
Hamor the Hivite 204
Hamzah ibn 'Abd al Mutallib 99

Harrân 57
Hâshim ibn 'Abd Manâf 50
health and comfort: baths 78, 266, 288; bîmâristâns 86; blindness 211; disability 213; drought 84; druggists 79; famine 11, 18, 25, 58; fleas 52; heat 39, 40, 52, 58; hospitals 86, 170, 232; impotence 50; leprosy 188, 247; medicinal places 208; pestilence & plague 24, 58, 211; sandfly called "dalam" 50; scorpions 41, 52, 65; serpents 18, 52; sewerage 77; snakes 52; Tariyâkiyyah 52; Theriack or Antidote 52; worms 79
heaven xi, 8, 12, 14, 17, 45, 47, 93, 99, 106, 109, 116, 137, 142, 152, 160, 162, 163, 167, 174, 182, 184, 185, 189, 194, 198, 201, 205, 267, 367
Heber the Cinaeite 210
Hebrews 15, 201
Hebron 4, 5, 15, 48, 49, 110, 113, 114, 148, 197, 198, 199, 253, 256, 257, 258, 259, 261, 270, 296, 298, 304, 310; Al Kala'ah (the Castle) 120; Bedstead of Abraham 262; Cain's Grave 262; Cave of Machpelah 262; Cave of the Patriarchs 262; Dome 120; Eunuch's Spring ('Ain at Tawâshî) 120; field of Machpelah 235, 236; mosque of Abraham 120, 262; Sanctuary of Abraham 262; tombs: of Abraham 47, 109, 112, 236, 262, 372; of Isaac 47, 235, 236, 262, 372; of Jacob 47, 112, 119, 235, 236, 262, 372; of Joseph 112, 119, 120, 196, 210, 372; of Leah 112, 235, 236, 372; of Rebecca 235, 236, 372; of Sarah 112, 235, 236, 372; of the Patriarchs 235
Helchana 201
Helena, empress 157, 161, 162, 176, 177, 183, 290; discovery of Cross 166

INDEX

Helena, queen of Adiabeni 3, 11
Helias. *See* Elijah (Elias), prophet.
Helisaeus (Helisseus). *See* Elijah (Elias), prophet.
Helisarus 17
Heli the priest 201
hell 45, 116, 160
Henry II, king 218
Heraclius, emperor 165, 181
Hermon 19, 262, 305
Hermoniim 19, 26, 262
Herodium 110
Herod, king 10, 12, 18, 71, 157, 177, 179, 182, 205, 215, 267, 272, 288, 294, 364
Herodotus 217
Hiel 17
Hierapolis. *See* Mambij.
Hijjâz 32, 56, 58, 107, 114
Hijrah 87
Hillel 239
Hims (Emessa) 64
Hinnom 129, 133, 277, 295
Hinnom brook 129, 133, 277, 295
Hiram, king 209
Hirsau 137, 138
Hishâm ibn 'Abd al Malik, kalif 38
Hishâm II 31
history xi, 1, 27, 59, 77, 137, 140, 141, 142, 143, 149, 150, 183, 217, 221, 223, 224
Holofernes 209
Holy Cities. *See* Mecca, Medînah.
Holy City. *See* Jerusalem.
Holy Spirit 4, 12, 26, 152, 182, 183
Horraei. *See* Chorraei.
Hospitallers 129, 170, 178, 187, 188, 191, 193, 203, 204, 206, 253
Hûd 76, 241
Hugh Capet 30
Hungary 30
Hus 212
Husain, imâm 31

I

Ibelin (Jabneh) 237, 248
Ibn 'Abbâs 47
Ibn Abi Maryâm 53
Ibn al Athîr 246
Ibn Haukal Istakhri 29
Ibn Khallikan 27, 79
Ibn Khurdadbih 29
Ibn Tûlûn 27
Ibrahim ibn Ahmad al Khalanjî 119
Iconium 144, 310
Idumaea & Idumaeans 19, 148, 154, 195, 208, 210, 212, 213, 263
Îliyâ. *See* Jerusalem.
India 22, 32, 55, 68, 105, 223
Innocent II, pope 140
Iraq ('Irâk) 64, 68, 96
Irbil (Irbid) 77, 263
Isaac 15, 25, 104, 111, 115, 119, 197, 205, 231
Isaac, rabbi of Tiberias 238
Isaiah, prophet 17, 167
Isfahân 58
'Ish. *See* Esau.
Ishmael 115
Isidore of Seville, *Etymologies* x
Isidorus the Confessor, bishop 20
Islâm 28, 29, 30, 31, 37, 38, 44, 47, 48, 52, 67, 101, 307
Ismahelites 210
Ismâ'îl ibn Ibrahîm ibn 'Ukbah 53
Ispahân 58, 296
Israel 13, 16, 19, 52, 78, 100, 153, 176, 194, 195, 199, 201, 205, 212, 213, 229, 231, 232, 236, 239, 258, 273
Issachar 77
Istakhr 39, 263
Istanbul Express 146
Itabyrium. *See* Mount Tabor.
Italy 146, 218
Itinera Hierosolymitana et Descriptiones Terrae Sanctae 6
Ituraea 207
Izra 114

J

Ja'afar (Jughri Beg) 55
Jabal Faradîs 110

383

Jabal Nusrah 48, 263
Jabal Zaitâ. *See* Jerusalem: Mount of Olives.
Jabin, king 210
Jabok Brook 212
Jacob, patriarch 11, 13; and alphabet 231; and angel 212; as shepherd 14, Bethel 17; image of 115; ladder of 172, 174, 205; and Rachel 195; sons 235; tomb 15, 25, 77, 112, 197; well of 18, 133, 204, 263
Jacobites 163, 231
Jaffa (Jafis, Joppa) 2, 3, 10, 38, 147, 199, 215, 237, 263, 266, 267, 270, 271, 273, 364
Jahel 210
James, St., apostle 166, 208, 267
Japheth, rabbi 229
Jebus. *See* Jerusalem.
Jechiel, rabbi 218
Jehu 206
Jehudah ben Bethera, rabbi 239
Jehudah Halevi, rabbi 238
Jephunneh (Jephone) 15
Jeremiah, prophet 24, 265, 288
Jericho: biblical 4; Christian 129, 130, 134, 193–95; fountain of Elisha 258–59; late Roman 16, 17; Muslim 52; oasis of 148
Jeroboam, king 205, 239
Jerome, St. xi, 1, 2, 4, 5, 6, 7, 150, 154, 196, 246, 257, 263, 264, 296, 308; *Onomasticon* 246; tomb 250
Jerusalem 114; Abbey of the Dormition of Mary 285; Absalom's Hand 233, 292; 'Akabat at Takiyah 124
Jerusalem, Aksâ Mosque 42, 43, 45, 86, 87, 89, 90, 91, 93, 94, 95, 96, 97, 98, 99, 101, 117, 121, 122, 264, 284, 288, 368, 369, 371; Al Khidr 45; Birkat (or Pool of) Bani Isrâîl 45; Bridge As Sirât 45; dimensions 46; Dome of Jacob 87, 90; endowment 46;

Haram Area 43, 61, 87, 88, 89, 90, 91, 92, 93, 94, 95, 96, 97, 98, 99, 100, 101, 102, 109, 118, 121, 122, 123, 273, 293, 371; Hâshimite Gates 45, 123, 125, 274; Kubbat Ya'kûb 87, 90; Mihrâb Maryam (the Oratory of Mary) 45; Mihrâb of Zakariyyâ 91; Place of the Ant 45; Place of the Fire 45; Place of the Ka'abah 40, 45; Sakhrah 87, 101; Station of Jibraîl (Gabriel 45; Station of the Prophet 45; Ya'kûb 45; Zakariyyah 45, 371
Jerusalem, Al Kal'ah 41, 267; Altar of the Finger 183; Antonia fortress 148, 156, 157, 178, 179, 265, 288, 364; approaches to 211; as Aelia Capitolina 11, 264; as capital of Judaea 154; as center of world 150; as City of David 201, 264, 267, 270, 287; as heavenly city 143; as omphalos or navel 142; As Sâhirah 47, 265, 284; Assyrian sack 176; Barbican 155, 265; Birkat Hammâm al Butrak 266; Brook of Kedron 233; Calvary 128, 148, 165, 167, 168, 169, 267, 281, 282, 366; Catholicon 131, 278; cemeteries 85; Chabratha 195
Jerusalem, chapels: of St. Helena 131, 165, 281, 282, 366; of St. James 175; of St. Mary 195, 281, 366; of the Apparition 267; of the Armenians 169; of the Flagellation (Scourging) 186, 294; of the Sepulcher 183; of the Three Marys 169, 283
Jerusalem, Charnel-House of the Lion 199; Christian 128, 131, 137, 141, 144, 146, 147, 148
Jerusalem, churches: All Nations 275, 302; Galilee 186, 187, 269; Gethsemane 275; Pater Noster 133, 188; St. Anne 157, 187, 188, 288, 289, 341; St. Chariton 187;

384

INDEX

St. James 173, 289; St. John 164, 307; St. Lazarus 167; St. Mary 155, 156, 157, 170, 182, 183, 186, 196, 203, 210, 265, 276, 285, 293, 304; St. Mary the Great 169, 267, 289, 290; St. Mary the Latin 169, 188, 267, 289; St. Pelagia 188; St. Peter in Gallicantu 285; St. Stephen 187, 188, 290; Templars 291; the Ascension 188; the Bath 178, 179; the Coenaculum 284; the Flagellation 267; the Lepers 187; the Resurrection 31, 84, 115, 116

Jerusalem, Cradle of Jesus 92, 93, 371; Cross 3, 21, 25, 156, 164, 165, 168, 275, 282, 283, 294; Dome of Jacob (Kubbat Ya'kûb) 87; Dome of the Ascension 43, 106, 267, 268, 286, 371; Dome of the Chain (Kubbet es-Silsile) 43, 105, 124, 268, 269, 289, 292, 371; Dome of the Prophet 43, 106, 267, 268, 269; Dome of the Rock 43, 44, 45, 102, 103, 104, 105, 106, 107, 117, 124, 267, 268, 269, 284, 288, 291, 292, 364, 367; environs 190; Field of Acheldemach (Haceldama) 155, 157, 269, 290; Flagellation Monastery 265; fosse 155; gardens 46

Jerusalem: gates: Bâb an Nisâ 44; As Sûr 43; 43; 41, 155, 269, 270; Bâb al Abwâb 90, 101, 123, 125; Bâb al 'Amûd 41, 271; Bâb al 'Atm 87, 88, 90, 109, 123, 125, 273; Bâb al Ghawânimah 123, 125, 272, 371; Bâb al Hadîd 124, 125, 274, 371; Bâb al Kattânîn 124, 371; Bâb al Mutawaddâ (of the Place for Ablution) 371; Bâb an Nabî 98, 100, 121, 122; Bâb an Nâdhir (Nâhir) 89, 123, 124, 125, 371; Bâb an Nahâs al A'tham (Great Brazen) 43; Bâb as Sakar 89, 123, 125; Bâb as Sakînah (of the Shechînah, or Divine Presence) 100, 124, 125; Bâb as Salâm 100, 124, 125; Bâb Sharaf al Anbiyâ 371; Beautiful 157, 171; Golden 91, 123, 125, 172, 181, 187, 272, 273, 274, 364, 371; Hâshimite 275; Kiblah [Southern] of Abraham (Ibrahîm) 45, 123, 232, 272; of Al Walîd 45, 123, 270, 274; of Burâk 124; of Damascus 3, 265, 290; of David (Bâb Dâûd, Bâb as Silsilah, Bâb Mihrâb Dâûd) 41, 45, 89, 100, 122, 123, 124, 125, 232, 270, 271, 273; of David's Oratory (Haifâ Gate) 272; of Funerals (Bâb al Janâiz) 100, 124, 371; of Gates 90, 123; of Gushpat 232; of Hell 89, 123; of Isrâfîl 43, 124; of Jehoshaphat 124, 232, 233; of Jeremiah's Grotto (Bâb Jubb Armiyâ) 41, 272; of Jericho (Bâb Arîhâ) 41, 272; of Mercy (Bâb ar Rahmah) 45, 91, 122, 232, 272, 371; of Michael 123; of Muhammad 121; of Pardon (Bâb Hittah) 45, 90, 100, 121, 122, 123, 125, 272, 273, 371; of Repentence (Bâb at Taubah) 91, 122, 371; of Siloe (Bâb Silwân) 41, 272; of Sion (Bâb Sihyûn) 41, 272; of St. Lazarus 273; of the Bath 124; of the Birkat 45, 123, 125, 273; of the Chain (Bâb as Silsilah) 89, 100, 122, 124, 270, 292, 371; of the Desert of the Wanderings (Bâb at Tîh) 41, 273; of the Mihrâb Maryam 45, 274; of the Palace (Bâb al Balât) 41, 273; of the Prophet (Bâb al Maghâribah) 45, 98, 99, 114, 121, 122, 274, 367, 371; of the Spring (Bâb al 'Ain) 100, 122, 125; of the Tribes (Bâb al Asbât) 45, 90, 123, 125, 270, 371; of Umm Khâlid 45, 124, 125, 273, 274; of Zion 232; St. Stephen's (Lions') 265

THE HOLY LAND

Jerusalem, Gethsemane 183, 185, 186, 275, 276, 285, 293, 302, 364; Golgotha 160, 167, 168, 169, 278; Great Pool 171, 172; Haram 43, 45, 61, 87, 88, 89, 90, 91, 92, 93, 94, 95, 96, 97, 98, 99, 100, 101, 102, 109, 113, 118, 119, 120, 121, 122, 123, 262, 273, 284, 293, 371; historical names 264; Holy Sepulcher 3, 4, 25, 42, 115, 116, 127, 128, 131, 132, 138, 148, 157, 162, 163, 164, 171, 180, 232, 267, 277, 278, 279, 280, 281, 282, 283, 284, 290, 294, 341, 364, 366; column of the flagellation 4; Hospice of St. Lazarus 187; Hospital of St. John the Baptist 169, 170; House and the Stable of the Templars 177; House of David 233, 235; House of Mary and Martha 16; House of Pilate 156, 157; House of Simeon the Just 178, 179; houses 156; Jâmi' al Maghâribah 371; Jewish 219, 224, 231, 232; Kedron Valley 148, 276, 284, 292; Kubbat al Alwâh (Dome of the Tablets) 371; Kubbat al Khidr (St. George) 371; Kubbat ar Rasûl (Dome of the Prophet) 106, 268; Kubbat as Silsilah 105, 371; Kubbat Jibraîl (Dome of Gabriel) 106, 371; Kubbat Sulaimân 109; Kursî Sulaimân 91, 109, 371; late ancient 2, 3, 5, 16, 21; Latin Kingdom 137, 138, 139, 147; Latin Money Exchange 292; Madrasah al Farsiyyah 371; Makâm an Nabî 107; Makâm Ghûri 107, 108; Makâm Shâmî 108; Makâm Sharkî 108; Maksûrah 89, 94, 95, 111, 112; market 170, 284; Masjid al Aksâ 42, 93, 264; Mihrâb 38, 42, 43; Mogrebin Mosque 272; Mons Gaudii (Montjoye) 129, 147, 154, 155, 301, 341; Mosque of 'Omar 47, 284; Mount Gion (Gihon) 156, 157, 284; Mount Moriah 133, 155, 156, 157, 178, 179, 201, 284, 292; Mount of Olives 16, 25, 47, 135, 148, 155, 156, 157, 181, 185, 186, 188, 189, 233, 251, 265, 267, 272, 275, 284, 285, 286, 307; Mount Sion (Zion) 4, 11, 41, 148, 155, 156, 157, 182, 185, 186, 201, 204, 233, 234, 267, 269, 277, 284, 285, 286, 290, 293, 294, 341, 364; Muristan 288, 289; Muslim 27, 31, 39, 40, 41, 56, 57, 130, 232; New Cistern 195, 286; Noble Sanctuary 87, 88, 91, 92, 95, 97, 98, 99, 100, 101, 103, 105, 107, 109, 264; Olivet 5; Ophel Ridge 267, 284; Palace of Pilate 187; Palace of Solomon 156, 157, 177; patriarchs 185, 234; Pavement 186, 187, 286; Peter's Prison 182, 290; Pharaoh's House 85, 293; Pillar in the Wall 371; Platform of the Rock 371; Pool of Siloe (Siloam, 'Ain Sulwân, Spring of Siloam, Silwân) 46, 155, 180, 233, 287; Pool of the Sheep-Gate 187; population 147; Potter's Field 127, 269; Praetorium 3, 286

Jerusalem, quarters: Christian 267, 277, 289; Jewish 272, 290; Muslim 288

Jerusalem, Ramban Synagogue 269, 290; Rock 102, 107; Roman 11; Roman Column 173; Room of the Last Supper 182; Sâhirah 47, 85, 86, 265, 284, 307; School of St. Mary 171; School of the Blessed Virgin 267; Sepulcher of Mary 46; Sheep Pool (Pool of Bethesda) 157, 188, 287, 288; Solomon's Stables 92, 232; Spring of Siloam (Silwân) 86, 100, 287; Stone of Unction 290

Jerusalem, streets: Covered Market 341; Covered (Vaulted) 267,

292; Jehoshafat 287; Marzubân 288; Mount Sion 341; paving 156; St. Stephen 341; Temple 292; the Street and Market 169; Via Dolorosa 148, 186, 286, 294, 364
Jerusalem, Synagogue 84; Templar Gardens 177; Temple 16, 93, 96, 131, 153, 155, 156, 157, 164, 171–82, 201, 230, 232, 264, 265, 266, 267, 269, 270, 272, 273, 274, 275, 284, 286, 287, 288, 291, 292, 293, 294, 341, 364, 365, 370; Temple of the Lord 131, 155, 156, 157, 164, 171, 172, 173, 201, 269, 284, 288, 291, 341, 364; Throne of Solomon 91, 109
Jerusalem, tombs: of Absalom 292; of David 6, 234, 285; of Helena 293; of Josaphat 154, 155, 293; of King Uzziah 293; of Latin kings 283; of Lazarus 16; of Rachel 195, 310, 311; of Samuel 301, 309; of the kings 3; of the Virgin 293; of Uzziah 233
Jerusalem, topography 149; Tower Hippicus 267; Tower of David 156, 188, 195, 199, 203, 232, 294, 341, 364; Tower Phasaelus 267; Tree of the Houris 109; Valley of Ennon 195, 277; Valley of Gehenna 85 (*See also* Jerusalem: Wâdî Jahannam); Valley of Hinnom 129, 133; Valley of Jehoshaphat (Josaphat) 85, 155, 157, 175, 181, 183, 185, 233, 341; Valley of Kedron 47, 85, 295; Valley of Olives 181; Vegetable Market 292; Wâdî Jahannam 46, 86, 277, 295; walls 155
Jerusalem, water: 41; baths 41; Birkat Bani Israîl 41, 266, 273, 287; Birkat Israîl 288; Birkat 'Iyâd 41, 266, 288; Birkat Sulaimân 41, 266, 288; reservoirs 42; Well of the Leaf 97
Jesus: Ascension 4, 9, 14, 16, 18, 22, 23, 25, 26, 106, 152, 162, 170, 188, 189, 190, 200, 210, 267, 268, 284, 286, 292, 364, 371; baptism 17, 148, 193; birth 196, 249; burial 232; childhood 161, 179, 211, 303; crucifixion 139, 168; death 17; infancy 12, 93; Lamb of God 14, 160; Last Supper 183; miracles 207, 211; Multiplication of the Loaves and Fishes 302; Passion 21, 185; portrayals 115; Resurrection 142; Saviour 129, 133; Transfiguration 209, 301
Jesus, son of Nave 10, 15, 17
Jethro 77
Jews: anti-Semitism 130, 139, 183, 185, 213; Beirut 227; Caesarea 230; communities in Holy Land 220, 222, 223; diaspora 153; in Gospels 175, 177, 186, 188, 211; in Jerusalem 31, 41, 232; in Koran 76; pilgrimage 84; Ramleh 237, 306; religious practice 163, 233, 241, 293; Shiloh 236–37; textual community 221
Jezabel 206
Jezrahel (Jezreel) Valley 147, 206, 238, 295
Jiddah 58
Jinns 47
Job 76, 133, 208, 212
Job's Well. *See* Bîr Ayyûb (Bir Eyûb).
Joel 12
Johanan ben Zakkai, rabbi 238
John, bishop of Jerusalem 183
John of Monte Corvino, OFM 151
John of Plano Carpini, OFM 151
John of Würzburg 127, 128, 132, 133, 150
John Phocas 132, 150
John, St., apostle & evangelist 12, 168, 208
John the Baptist 18, 25, 162, 166, 167, 170, 205, 283, 307
Jonah (Jonas) 10, 80, 214, 218, 227, 238, 308

387

Jonah, rabbi 229
Jor 207
Jordan 154, 192, 253, 258, 260, 295, 339
Jordan River 4, 5, 17, 25, 52, 129, 130, 148, 149, 191, 193, 194, 195, 206, 207, 208, 210, 212, 231, 238, 239, 259, 296, 301, 305, 307, 309
Jor, spring 148, 208, 296
Jose Hagelili, rabbi 239
Joseph, patriarch: brothers 16, 190, 209; tomb 77, 119–20, 204, 205, 231
Joseph of Arimathea 10, 158, 163, 168, 196, 199, 279, 290
Joseph, rabbi 227
Joseph, St. 12, 20, 210, 250, 303
Josephus 67, 154, 157, 177, 246, 266, 267, 288, 296, 301, 310
Joshua, son of Nun 10, 49, 78, 139, 198, 231, 253
Josiah 9
Jubail (Jebeil, Jubayl) 70, 71, 296. See also Gibeleth (Gebal, Giblet).
Judaea 10, 147, 153, 154, 155, 170, 176, 178, 199, 213
Judaean Desert 312
Judaean Hills 147, 148
Judah 12, 13, 176, 197, 199, 206, 234, 235, 257, 293
Judah the Prince, rabbi 238
Judah, tribe of 253
Judas Iscariot 186, 202
Judas Maccabeus 166, 176
Judith 131, 209, 265, 284
Judith, abbess 131
Jughri Beg 55, 58
Julian the Apostate, emperor 205
Jurisconsults 41
Jurjân 27

K

Kafar Sâbâ 81, 296
Kafar Sallâm 81, 296
Kafar Tâb 66
Kain 58
Kâ-in 39, 296

Kaisâriyyah. See Caesarea of Palestine.
Kako (Keilah) 230, 296
Kalamûn (Calamos) 70, 296
Kanîsah. See Kunaisah.
Karaites 238
Karak 246
Kariat-al-'Anab (Karyet al 'Inab) 83, 253, 296
Kasvîn 56
Kedesh (Kades) Naphtali 239
Kedumim 229, 258, 297, 301. See also Endor.
Kefar Nahum. See Capernaum (Capharnaum).
Kefr Bâreka. See Caphar Barucha.
Kenaz (Kenez) 15
Khâjih 'Abd ul Jalîl 58
Khison (Cison) Brook 19, 210, 297
Khurasân 27, 48, 55, 56, 58, 88
Khurbat Yakîn. See Al Masjid Al Yakîn mosque.
Khurramites 27
Khusrau 55
Khuweilfeh 296
Kinnasrîn 64, 297
Kirjath-jearim. See Bîla'ah.
Kish 223
Kishon 229, 297, 301
Kohistân 296
Koran 66, 101; 2.55 45, 100; 5.25 52; 7.63 241; 7.71 74; 7.83 77; 9.30 76; 17.1 93; 19.29 47; 21.71 49; 112 79
Kubbat as Sakhrah. See Jerusalem: Dome of the Rock.
Kubbat-as-Silsilah. See Jerusalem: Dome of the Chain (Kubbet es-Silsile).
Kumis 56
Kunaisah 81, 296
Kustantiniyyah. See Constantinople.

L

Laban 205
Lachis 4, 19, 298

INDEX

Lacus Germani. *See* Cairo.
Lahsa 58
Lake Asphaltites 198, 208. *See also* Dead Sea.
Lake Hulah 148, 295
Lake of Gennesareth 208
Lake of Sughar. *See* Dead Sea.
Lamartine 129
languages; Arab annals 261; Arabic 33, 34, 60, 63, 65, 70, 79, 88, 94, 119, 224, 260, 264, 278; geographers 270; Canaanitish 19; Dutch 33; English 35; French 59, 224; German 34; Greek 18, 21, 140, 161, 168, 188, 224; Hebrew 5, 79, 221; Italian 224; Latin 21, 138, 140; multiple usages 163, 232; Norman-French 129; Persian 59, 61, 94, 110; Shikastah 59; Syriac 15, 163, 251
Latrûn 82, 83
Lazarus 16, 25, 131, 167, 181, 190, 194, 265, 266, 284
Lea 197
Lebanon 144, 149, 247, 257. *See also* Libanus, Mount Libanus.
Lejjûn (Legio) 3, 300
le Strange, Guy 121
Levant 144, 146, 151, 313
Levites 16
Lewis, Hayter 117
Lexotius 8
Libanus 156, 207, 208, 212, 213, 324. *See also* Lebanon, Mount Libanus.
Libya 324
Lilybaeum 21, 298
Little Damascus. *See* Nâbulus.
Lombardy 147
London Royal Geographical Society 127, 130, 132, 218, 267, 289
Longinus 168, 278
Lot 15, 78, 150, 198, 233
Ludd (Lod) 38, 230, 238, 298
Luza. *See* Bethel (Beitîn, Baytîn).
Lycia 3, 9

Lydda 3, 10, 38, 147, 202, 212, 246, 258, 298

M
Maâb 49
Maʿarrah 65, 66
Maʾarrah an Nuʾman 65
Macarius, St. 20
Machaerunta 205
Madînat ʾAkkah. *See* Achon.
Magdalum 208, 209
Mageddo 206
Maghrib 66, 70
Magi 12, 196
Mahdi, khalif 42, 113
Mahmûd of Ghaznah, sultan 32, 55
Mahomerie 203, 298
Mahomerie-le-Grand 231
Mahomerie-le-Petit 237. *See also* Gibeah of Benjamin.
Mahrubân 58
Maimâs 37
Majuma in Gaza 5, 20, 299, 300
Makâm Nabi Yakîn. *See* Al Masjid Al Yakîn mosque.
Malea 9
Malta 146
Mambre 197, 299, 304
Mamistra 213
Mamlûks 120
Manbij 63, 300
Mandeville, John 151
Manuel Comnenus, emperor 132, 280
Maon. *See* Capernaum (Capharnaum).
Marcella xi, 5, 6, 21, 25
Marco Polo 151, 218, 223
Maresa (Mareshah) 4, 19, 300
Marsala 298
Marsden, Mr. 218
Marseille 144
Marv 55, 56, 58
Mary and Martha 16, 181, 190
Mary Magdalen 169, 209, 265, 283
Marys, three 158

389

Mary, Virgin 12, 13, 14, 20, 23, 93, 139, 157, 162, 164, 172, 174, 176, 182, 185, 188, 195, 249, 253, 276, 287; and Passion 170; Annunciation 161, 201; Assumption 184; Bethlehem 196; birth of Jesus 197; in Nazareth 303; Mother 129

Mash-hads 73, 110, 111, 262

Masjid al Aksâ. *See* Jerusalem: Aksâ Mosque.

Mas'ûd 55

Mathathias 201

Matlûn 110, 261. *See also* Hebron.

measurements, distance: farsakh 60; leagues 47, 49, 52, 57, 60, 64, 65, 67, 70, 72, 73, 77, 80, 81, 82, 83, 86, 97, 103, 109, 110; parasangs 60, 229, 230, 231, 233, 235, 236, 237, 238, 239

measurements, length: ârsh 60, 61, 64, 73, 87, 88, 104; cubits 60, 61, 64, 65, 69, 71, 73, 86, 87, 88, 94, 95, 100, 101, 102, 103, 104, 106, 107, 111, 117, 118, 174, 229, 232, 262; dhira' 60; ells 42, 44, 46, 49, 61, 71, 74, 88, 89, 90, 91, 92, 94, 95, 99, 100, 101, 102, 103, 104, 112, 113, 118; feet 60, 79, 101, 102, 104, 117, 118, 145, 158, 159, 175, 183, 262, 288; gâm 82; gez 60, 61, 71, 88, 104; inches 79; paces 82, 246; shibr 105; spans 104; yard 60; mann 61, 65, 113

measurements, time: Bahman 63; Dhlû-1 Ka'adah 114; Dhu-l Hijjah 83; Dhû l Ka'adah 95; Dhû-l Ka'adah 109; Isfandârmuz 63, 71; Muharram 82, 114; October 145; Persian months 63; Rajab 63, 64, 66, 87; Ramadan 59, 81, 82, 83; September 145; Sha'abân 67, 68, 75, 81; St. John's Day 133; St. Peter's Day 290; Yazdagird 63, 71; zodiacal sign 79

measurements, weight: ass-load 61; dhâhirî ratl 64; dirham 48, 64; gallons 81, 84; kharwar 61; manns 71, 81, 84, 104; pound 64; pound avoirdupois 61; ton 71, 104

Mecca (Mekkah): 99, 105; 'Arafât 46, 57; Haram Mosque 52, 96; Holy City 32, 56, 311; Ka'abah 40, 45, 87, 299; Night Journey 93; pilgrimage 28, 55, 58, 83, 114, 116; prayer towards 45, 95; size 41

Medan 207, 208, 300

Media 57, 247

Medînah 32, 40, 56, 58, 114, 243, 311

Mediterranean Sea: coast 206, 212, 213, 264, 297; climate & weather 145–46; geography & maps 136, 223, 324; Great Sea 261; Greek Sea 51; ports 199, 241, 246, 247, 254, 256, 260, 261, 307, 308, 311; shipping 144–45; urbanism 147

Medon (Meron) 239

Megiddo 3, 9, 300

Meir from Carcassonne, rabbi 228

Melchisedech, king & priest 209

Memoirs of the Survey of Western Palestine 35

Mesopotamia 22, 32, 33, 56, 57, 212, 300

Methone 3, 9, 300. *See* Modon.

Metropolis 213

Metropolitan Museum of Art xi, 137; *Jerusalem, 1000–1400: Every People under Heaven* xi

Micah 4, 239; tomb of 4

Michaea 19

Michael, archangel 161

Michael IV, emperor 278

Michaeus 12

Milicent, queen of Jerusalem 131, 284

Mîmâs 50, 299, 300

Mîná. *See* arts: enamels.

Minneapolis 138
Misr. *See* Cairo.
Miyâfarikîn 57
Mizpeh 309
Moab & Moabites 16, 198, 239, 258
Modon 3, 300
money 116, 235; ancient 234; deposits at mosques 75; dînâr 61, 109, 111; dirham 48, 49, 64; Greek 298; land-tax (kharâj) 69; Maghribî 61, 79, 95, 111; silver 202; taxes 41; wealth 1, 2, 23, 28, 29, 65, 66, 73, 129, 178
Morasthim 4, 19
Morea 146
Moses 18, 26, 49, 77, 87, 194, 198, 205, 230, 231
mosquea; Arsûf 51
mosques; Acre 73–75; 'Ammân 52; Ar-Ramlah 37, 38, 51; Ascalon 116; Baghdad 32; Caesarea 81; Caipha 51; Dâjûn 38; Damascus 34, 38, 44; Gaza 50; Hadhîrah 76, 77; Hebron 47, 120, 262, 298; Jerusalem 39–46, 85, 87, 89, 94, 95, 96, 109, 115, 117, 264, 284, 289; Kaisâriyyah 51; Ma'arrah an Nu'man 65; Medînah 243; Nâbulus 51; Ramlah 82; Ramleh 37; Sidon 72; Friday Mosque 72; Silo 309; Tripoli 70
Mosul 32
Mount Abarim 194
Mountain of Gibel 208
Mountain of Hattîn 77
Mountain of Temptation 129
Mountain of the Holy Samuel 200
Mountains of Ephraim 201
Mountains of Gilboa 193, 194, 206, 231, 297, 301
Mountains of Modin 200, 201
Mountains of Sophim 200
Mount Caipha 202
Mount Carmel 147, 202, 229, 261
Mount Ebal (Hebal) 51, 204, 205, 230, 231, 300, 301, 302, 309
Mount Endor 209, 258, 301
Mount Ephraim 17, 230, 309
Mount Gaash 17, 310
Mount Gerizim 18, 51, 204, 205, 230, 231, 300, 301, 302, 309
Mount Hermon 206, 228, 305
Mount Hor 194, 246, 263
Mount Libanus 156, 207. *See also* Lebanon, Libanus.
Mount Nebo 233
Mount of Rejoicing 154, 155, 301, 309
Mount of the Beatitudes 77
Mount Quarantana (Quadragena) 148, 190, 191, 192, 193, 259, 305
Mount Royal (Montréal) 194, 301
Mount Seir 212, 263
Mount Silo 180, 201
Mount Sinai 194
Mount Tabor 4, 19, 26, 129, 208, 209, 210, 301, 302
Muchtar, rabbi 238
Muhammad al Mukaddasî 28
Muhammad, the Prophet; Ascent into Heaven (Mi'râj) 99, 106, 267; burial place 243; family 92; footprint 367; Night Journey 267; Prophet 31, 40, 87
Muhammedans. *See* Muslims.
Mujîr ad Dîn 109, 121, 122, 123, 124, 125, 266, 271–74, 288, 292
Mukaddasî xi, education 28
Multân 55
Musa. *See* Moses.
Muslims 45, 67, 69, 86, 131, 149, 241, 243, 278
Mustansir billah 56

N

Naaman 212
Nabal the Carmelite 229
Nâblus (Nâbulus, Neapolis) 37, 49, 51, 148, 203–4, 211, 224, 230, 263, 300, 302–4, 309. *See also* Sichem (Shechem, Sichar).
Naboth 206

Nabuzardan 176
Nâfi' 53
Nahum. *See* Capernaum (Capharnaum).
Nain (Naim) 19, 26, 58, 208, 209, 303
Nâsir-i-Khusrau xii, 55, 57, 58, 59, 62, 63, 104, 117, 121, 255
Nathanael 211
Natron Lakes 304
natural events and prodigies: earthquakes 82, 95, 117, 278, 306; marine monsters 81
Nawwâb Ziyâ ad Dîn Khân 59
Nazareth 4, 5, 19, 26, 129, 148, 201, 211, 255, 301, 303, 308; Basilica of the Annunciation 304; Grotto of the Annunciation 210
Neapolis *See* Nâblus (Nâbulus).
Nebuchadnezzar, king 176
Negev 254
Nephthalim 209
Nicea 144
Nicholas, St. 165, 174
Nicodemus 158, 163, 168, 279, 290
Nicopolis 3, 10, 258
Nile River 4, 58, 260, 304, 309, 324; Pelusiac 4, Tanitic 310
Nishâpûr 56, 296
Nitria 2, 5, 19, 304
No 19
Nob (Nobe). *See* Beit Nûba.
Noyon 30
Nuʻman ibn Bashîr 65
Numidia 324
Nur ed-Din 148, 190, 193, 206, 220, 244, 305

O
Oak of Abraham 299, 304
Obadiah 257. *See also* Abdias.
Obadiah, rabbi 227
Ocean 324
Og (Och), king of Basan 195, 244
Omar ben al Khattab 232
Omar, khalif 31, 45, 50, 53, 86, 266
Omeyyads 31

Omri 230
Orleans 30
Orontes River 3, 67, 310
Ostia 3
Othmân ibn 'Affân, khalif 46
Othniel (Othoniel) 15
Otto, emperor 30
Outremer 143, 145
Ozias, king 206

P
Palestine: agriculture 68; biblical 199; late Roman 2, 5, 11, 25; Christian 144, 213, 220; Muslim 27, 30–31, 37, 50, 55–57, 306; water 98
Palestine Exploration Fund 1343
Palestine Pilgrims Text Society xii
Paneas 131, 190, 207, 208, 247, 304, 305
Paradise 39, 64, 116, 197, 227, 292, 367
Paris 30
Parthians 208
Patara, in Lycia 3
patriarchs, tomb of 18
Paula 1–7, 12, 19, 21, 150, 257, 264, 266, 296, 300; tomb 250
Paulinus, bishop of Antioch 1, 7, 9
Paul, St., apostle 2, 9, 10, 21, 141, 146, 187; Saul's conversion 212
Paul, St., of Egypt 7
Pelagia, St. 189
Peleg 74
Peloponnesus 300
Pelusium 5, 20, 243, 305
Perigrinatio Sanctae Paulae 6
Persepolis 263
Persian Gulf 58
Persia & Persians : 58, 247; Abbasid 27, 32, 56; agriculture & food 68, 69; ancient 176; Assassins 223; commerce & industry 80; late ancient 22, 63, 71, 165, 181; language 59, 61, 94, 110; pilgrims 75
Peter, Egyptian monk 6

Peter, St., apostle 26, 141, 182, 187, 199, 207, 208; as patriarch 213, 247
Peter the Hermit 30
Pethachia 223
Petra 246, 301. *See* Ar Rakîm (Arekem).
Pharan 208, 305
Pharisees 175
Pharphar River 212
Philadelphia. *See* 'Ammâm.
Philip, house of 10
Philip, St., apostle 25, 171, 211
Philip, tetrarch 207
Philistines 9, 199, 201, 206, 230, 237, 238
Phinees 17
Phocas 132, 249, 280, 285, 301
Phoenicia 9, 149, 213
Pilate, Pontius 156, 157, 165, 186, 286, 287, 310
Pilgrimage of St. Paula 6
Piligrinus, St. 192
Pillar of Salt 233
Pisa 144, 146, 147
Place in the Wood or of St. John 200
Plain of Esdraelon 301, 302
Plain of Medan 207, 300
Plain of Sharon 298
Plain of Thorns 310
Plains of Megiddo 3, 9
Plantagenets 284
Pliny 296, 300, 312
Polybius 296
Pontia (Ponza) 3, 8, 305
Pontus 22, 256, 305
population 50, 73, 77, 147, 247, 306
Port of St. Simeon. *See* Solim.
Praetorium 3, 11, 286
Prince, T.R.H. 262
Promised Land. *See* Holy Land.
Prophet 65, 99. *See* Muhammad, the Prophet.
Ptolemais 3, 9, 129, 202, 203, 211, 214, 215, 241, 300
Ptolemy Philadelphus 244

Q
Qila 296
Qisarya. *See* Caesarea of Palestine (Caesarea Palaestina).

R
Rabbath Ammon. *See* 'Ammâm.
Rachel 195, 205; tomb of 4, 12
Ramatha (Ramathaim, Rames) 148, 200, 201, 301
Ramlah (Ramah) 37, 38, 50, 51, 75, 81, 82, 116, 236, 296, 307
Ramleh (Rams) 37, 147, 237, 246, 247, 253, 306; Al Abyad (the White Mosque) 38; Dâjûn Gate 38; Egypt Gate 38; Gate of Bîla'ah 38; Gate of Jerusalem 38; Gate of the 'Annabah Mosque 38; Gate of the Soldier's Well (Darb Bîr al 'Askar) 38; Jaffa Gate 38, 266, 267, 271, 273; Lydda Gate 38; Mihrâb 38
Rantieh. *See* Arimathea.
Ras al-Ayn. *See* Antipatris.
Ratisbon (Regensburg) 144, 224
Rawlinson, Major 218
Ray (Rhages) 56
Rebecca 111, 197
Red Sea 57, 58, 194, 195, 258
religious practice & life; ablution 96, 97, 291; alms 2, 12, 21, 48, 66, 170; angels 11, 101, 158, 174, 179, 182, 184, 185, 192, 196, 197, 199, 201, 205, 210, 212; animal sacrifice 172; anointing 213; 'Arafât, Night of 46, 57, 114; Armenian 163; ascetics 5, 29, 65; baptism 164; bonfires 128; burnt offerings 230; candles 193; charity 5, 48, 113, 129, 140; circumcision 17, 83; cult of the saints 137, 141; Day of Judgment 40, 129, 195; defilements 231; devotions 91, 130; Druses 228; Easter 128, 129, 133, 134, 149, 163, 168, 171, 203; Exaltation of the Cross 156, 181, 275; fasting

66, 191; golden calves 205, 239; Good Friday 168; Gospel imitation 140; Greek 163; Halacha 227; hermits 155; holy fire 128, 163, 164, 171; hymns 132; images 239; imitation of Christ 142; Jacobite 163; Khotba 218; Kiblah 43, 74, 87, 90, 92, 98, 101, 102, 104, 106, 107, 111, 112, 113, 262; Latin 163, 169; mariolatry 129; martyrdom 8, 70, 73, 75, 146, 155; Mass 164, 209; monks 2, 5, 20, 22, 24, 25, 116, 130, 152, 171, 193, 202, 209; mortifications 146; Mujâwirân 96; Nubian 163; nuns 22, 25, 170, 188, 204; palms 185; Palm Sunday 127, 134, 156, 157, 181, 186, 191, 251, 274; Passover 230; penitence 16, 142, 143; pilgrimage & pilgrims: 302, 304; (Christian) 1–3, 5, 20, 30, 128, 129, 130, 133, 134, 137–50, 157, 159, 164, 167–68, 175, 186–87, 189, 191–93, 195–96, 199, 203, 232, 235, 264, 275, 278, 305; (Jewish) 219, 221–23, 229; (Muslim) 28, 48, 55–61, 67, 83, 96, 110–114, 120, 219; (taxes on) 31; popular spirituality 137, 141; prayer: (biblical) 198; (Christian) 6, 23, 116, 130, 163, 173–74, 186; (Muslim) 32, 45, 66, 75, 78, 87, 90–91, 93, 97, 101, 105; preaching 140; priests 7, 10, 16, 17, 20, 116, 130, 177, 186, 197, 201, 209, 230, 233, 237, 251; relics 3, 141, 164, 165, 171, 181, 186, 214, 257; ritual bathing 231; sacrifices 233; Syrian 163; Torah 227; worshippers 104
Rhapsodists 29
Rhetoricians 29
Rhineland 139
Rhine River 127, 138, 146, 324
Rhodes 3, 9, 205, 307
Richard Coeur-de-Lion 247
Rome: as symbol of secular rule 142; Capitoline Hill 310; destruction of Jerusalem 178; education in 21; Jewish 218, 220, 224; late ancient 1, 2, 3; law 140; martyrs 183; pilgrimage to 141; poverty in 6; Roman roads 3; sack by Alaric 6; Tarpeian Rock 23, 310
Romulus 18
Rufina 8
Rûm 110, 115. *See* Byzantium.

S

Sabine women 18
Saewulf 150, 267
Saffuriya. *See* Sepphoris.
Saida. *See* Sidon (Saidâ) & Sidonians.
Salâh-ad-Dîn (Saladin) 77, 95, 121, 137, 218, 244, 261, 270, 291
Salamis, Cyprus 7, 257
Salem 11, 209. *See* Jerusalem.
Sâlih, prophet 74
Salmanna, king 210
Salt Sea. *See* Dead Sea.
Samanides 32
Samaria & Samaritans 4, 5, 18, 38, 147, 153, 154, 204, 205, 206, 211, 230, 257, 307; caves 25
Samaritan, Good 16
Samarkand 69
Samson, fountain of 4, 19, 259
Samuel the Ramathite, prophet 201, 202 236
Sanginus 130, 193
Sara 15, 197
Saracens 31, 122, 129, 166, 191, 194, 198, 199, 200, 203, 204, 220
Saragossa 220
Sarakhs 56, 58
Sarepta (Sarfend) 9, 214, 228, 308
Sarmin 65
Sarphan 214, 308
Sarûj 57, 63
Saudi Arabia 243
Saul, king 206

Index

Scandalium (Scandelion) 214, 308
Schelah 74
science 28, 140, 217
Scribes 175
Scriptures 6, 9, 22
Scylla and Charybdis 9
Scythopolis 206
Sea of Galilee (Gennesareth, Kinnereth) 5, 260, 296, 297; late Roman 26; in Benjamin of Tudela 238; in Theoderich of Würzburg 129, 147–48, 207–8
Sea of Sodom. *See* Dead Sea.
Sea of the Devil. *See* Dead Sea.
Sebaste (Sebastiya) 18, 205, 230, 307
Seboim 15, 198
Sedechia, king 176
Segor 15, 198
Segub 17
Seir 212, 263
Seleucia 3, 9, 308, 310
Seljûk (Saljûkî) Turks 32, 55, 56
Seor the Hittite 197
Sepharad. *See* Spain.
Sepharnaim 212
Sepphoris 211, 238, 308, 309
Sepulcher of Michaea 308
Serapion 20
Seventy Prophets 78, 205
Seville 31
Shaddâd ibn Aus ibn Thâbit 47
Shahâb ad Dîn Ahmad al Yaghmûrî 120
Shammai 239
Shams ad Dîn. *See* Mukaddasî.
Sham'ûn. *See* Simeon.
Shemirân 57
Shî'ah Islam 70, 73, 80
Shiloh (Silo) 4, 5, 13, 18, 26, 148, 200, 201, 202, 236, 309
shipping 5, 7, 8, 58, 74, 116, 145, 146, 203, 229. *See also* commerce & industry; travel.
Shomron 230, 307
Shrine at Mash-had 55
Shu'aib. *See* Jethro.

Shuweikeh. *See* Sochot.
Sichem (Shechem, Sichar) 4, 18, 51, 133, 203–5, 231, 263, 302, 309. *See also* Nâblus (Nâbulus, Neapolis).
Sicily 21, 56, 68, 70, 146, 218–19, 298
Sidon (Saidâ) & Sidonians 9, 72, 214, 228, 307, 308, 311, 324; Jews 228
Sihon, king 195
Siloam (Siloe) 155, 233, 287, 364. *See also* Jerusalem: Pool of Siloe (Siloam, 'Ain Sulwân).
Silvia, St. 150
Simeon 76, 171, 174
Simeon ben Gamaliel, raban 239
Simon the Just 239
Simon the leper 181
Sinai 144, 150, 194, 254, 305
Sind 33
Sior (Sichor) River 19, 309
Sisara 19, 210
Sisera 26
slavery 54, 56, 65, 108, 113, 144
Sochot 4, 19, 310
Sodom and Gomorrah 4, 15, 150, 198
Solim 213, 308, 310
Solomon, king 209; city founder & builder 10, 78, 87, 91, 98, 99, 179; and Cross 200; coronation 157; prophet 167; Stables & Palace 177, 232, 288, 364; tomb 234, 367; Temple 119–20, 176, 201, 264, 291–92, 341, 365; throne 109
Solomon, rabbi 227, 238
Sophim 200, 201. *See also* Mountains of Ephraim.
Sophronius, patriarch 31
Spain 33, 68, 141, 227
St. Abram de Bron. *See* Hebron.
Statue of Salt 198
Stephaton 168
Stephen, king 30
Stephen, St. 182, 183
Stewart, Aubrey 7, 21, 127, 134, 135, 137

395

St. James of Compostela 141
St.-Jean d'Acre. *See* Achon.
St. John's. *See* Sebaste (Sebastiya).
Strabo 217
Strasbourg 137
Strato's Tower. *See* Caesarea of Palestine.
St. Samuel of Shiloh. *See* Shiloh (Silo).
Sueta 208, 212
Suez 258
Sûfîs 29, 90, 91, 123
Suleimân the Magnificent, sultan 41, 91, 109, 124, 266, 270, 288, 306
Suleimân, prince of Iconium 310
Sulwân. *See* Siloam (Siloe).
Sunni Islam 73
Sur. *See* Tyre.
Suyûti 88, 100
synagogues: Jerusalem 84; Shiloh 236; Tiberias 238
Syria & Syrians 82, 114, 144, 148, 212; ancient 72, 176; architecture 27; Assassins 223; Christians 164, 184, 200, 213, 231, (persecuted) 31; cities 63; climate 84; coast 67, 83; Fatamite 32, 56, 57, 108; language 33, 66, 83; maps 324; religious practice & life 96, 110, 163; trade 64, 68

T

Tabariyyah. *See* Tiberias.
Tabgha 207, 302, 305, 308
Tabitha 199
Tabrîz 57
Tabûs 58
Tal'at ed Dumm. *See* Adomim (Adummim).
Talmud 228, 247
Tamim ad Dârî 48
Tanis 5, 19, 310
Tantûra (Tantoura). *See* Dor.
Tarâbarzan 70
Tarim 57
Tarsus 144

Tehran 56
Tekoa 4, 130, 246, 310
Tel Afek. *See* Antipatris.
Tell Kuseifeh 243. *See also* Al Kusaifah.
Templars: Acre 203, 211; Chateau Pelerin 190; holdings of 129, 133, 170, 180, 191, 193, 204; Jerusalem (Armory) 90; (gardens) 179; (church of) 291; (Stables) 177–78, 291; (Temple) 171, 288; Mount Carmel 202; Mount Quarantana 192; Sapham 206; origins 305–6
Terebinth of Rachel 204
Terebinthus. *See* Mambre.
Thamnathsare 17, 310
Thamûd, tribe of 74
Thecua 4, 16, 310. *See* Tekoa.
Thema 224
Theman 212
Theoderich of Würzburg *Guide to the Holy Land* xii
Theodosius, emperor 183, 197, 206
Theodosius, pilgrim 150
Theodosius the Younger, emperor 196
Thietmar 128
Thomas à Becket 218
Thomas, St., apostle 182, 183
Tiberias 129, 148, 207, 208, 209, 310, 311; commerce 79; Friday Mosque 78; Herod's Castle 79; Hot Waters 238; Jasmine Mosque 78; Jews 238; lake of 19, 77, 78, 147, 297; sanitation 77, 78; tombs 80
Tiberius Caesar, emperor 207
Tigris River 32
Timnathah. *See* Tymin.
Tînah 116
Tinnîs 116
Titus, emperor 67, 153, 170, 177, 203
Tower Ader 14, 310
Tower of Helias 9
Tower of Sephorie 190

Index

Tower of Strato. *See* Caesarea in Palestine.
Traconitis 207
trade. *See* commerce & industry.
Transjordan 148
travel: accommodations 145; buss ship 129, 145, 203; caravans & caravanserais 57, 60, 70, 73, 114; conditions 143; fire 146; fleas 37; galleys 145; geographies 150; political 139; sacred 139; hospices 37, 145, 188; hostelries 37, 41, 69; hostile tribes 144; inns 2, 5, 20, 145; itineraries 150; land route 57, 144; lice 146; literature 137; meals 146; navigation 137, 223; *new compendium* 150; *old compendium* 150; *passagium aestivale* 133, 145; *passagium vernale* 133, 145; passengers 145; pilgrim guides 150; piracy 144; rats 146; roads xi, 37, 52, 67, 75, 144; robbery 75; sea route 144; Seaside Road 147; sea-voyage 116; shipping companies 144; ships 69, 70, 74, 80, 116, 129, 145, 146, 200, 203, 214, 228; snows 145; storms 145; tolls 144; vermin 146; water 146; winds 8, 44, 96, 98, 116, 119, 145, 146, 203, 209, 241; xenodochia 188
Tripolis (Tursolt) 213
Tripoli (Tarabulus) 64, 67, 68, 69, 70, 83, 144, 174, 246
Tudela 222, 227
Tughrul Beg 55, 56
Tûn 58
Turkey & Turks 32, 130, 144, 166, 206, 307, 310
Turkistân 33
Tursolt. *See* Tripolis (Tursolt).
Twelfth Century Renaissance 137, 140
Tymin 239
Tyre 311–12; biblical 9, 209, 213; Christian 214; harbor 149; Jewish 228–29; map 324; Muslim 72–73; population 147; Venetian fondaco 146

U

'Ubâdah ibn as Sâmit 47
Ulaimi 262
Urban II, pope 140
Urfa. *See* Edessa.
Urtâs Valley 110
'Uzair. *See* Ezra (Esdras).

V

Val-de-Luna. *See* Ajalon (Aijalon).
Valley of Achor 17, 312
Valley of Moses 194, 312
Valley of Shittim 233
Van, lake 57
Venice 144
Vespasian, emperor 153, 170, 177, 203
Via Egnatia 144
Victor, Albert 262
Victoria, queen 217
Victor IV, antipope 218
village of Christ. *See* Bethlehem.
Virgil, *Eclogues* 1.67 22

W

Wâdî Arraba 258
Wâdî-l Kurâ 114
Wâdî Môjib 114
Wâdî Musa. *See* Ar Rakîm (Arekem).
Wâdî Tamasih 81, 312
Waldensians 140
water 11, 29; aqueducts 73, 97, 287; bathing 37, 38, 41, 71, 78, 98, 178, 180, 193, 238; brooks 230, 235; channels 9, 48, 110, 208, 214; cisterns 38, 41, 42, 51, 97, 98, 133, 155, 156, 172, 178, 184, 188, 190, 195, 207, 211, 233, 288, 307; conduits 97, 98, 101; drainage 77; drinking 78, 180; fountains 4, 14, 17, 25, 69, 73, 81, 86, 180, 192, 194, 211, 231,

235, 259; Jericho 52; lakes 77; oceans x; pipes 97; pollution 50, 198; pools 42, 172, 287, 288, 310; quality 52, 77; rain 38, 42, 53, 65, 82, 84, 96, 97, 98, 101, 156, 178, 233; running 81, 114; sacred 15, 17, 26, 175; salt 78; sewers 78; springs 2, 15, 42, 51, 52, 56, 67, 70, 74, 76, 77, 78, 83, 84, 86, 103, 110, 133, 145, 201, 204, 208, 233, 238, 257, 259, 287, 297; streams 51, 52, 67, 97, 148, 191, 229, 230, 259, 312; tanks 41, 67, 69, 82, 84, 96, 97, 98, 101, 102, 110, 287; troughs 83; underground 46; 150, 180; water-tanks 67, 97; wells 38, 51, 65, 97, 194, 235
Well of Nehemiah. *See* Bîr Ayyûb (Bir Eyûb).
West Bank 258
William II (the Good), king 219
William of Rubruck, OFM 151
William of Tyre 247, 278
Wilson, C. 35, 61
Würzburg 127

Y

Yâfah. *See* Caipha.
Yakût, geographer 270
Yalo. *See* Ajalon.
Yamâmah 58
Yûnis. *See* Jonah (Jonas).
Yûsha'ibn Nûn. *See* Joshua, son of Nun.
Yûsûf. *See* Joseph.

Z

Zabulon 241. *See also* A'bilîn.
Zacchaeus, sycamore of 16
Zachariah (Zacharias) 17, 45, 91, 93, 172, 200, 371
Zadok, rabbi 229
Zamzam, holy well at Makkah 46
Zebee, king 210
Zeb, king 210
Zebulon 77, 209
Zeitschrift des Deutschen Palaestina-Vereins 34
Zelzah 233
Zemach, rabbi 238
Zerin. *See* Jezreel.
Zibâj 105
Zoar 4, 15
Zophar the Naamathite 212
Zorobabel 176

---

*This Print Edition Was Completed
On December 15, 2016 at
Italica Press, New York.
It Was Set in Minion
and Minion Pro.*

* * *
* *
*